Lecture Notes in Computer Science 14599

Founding Editors

Gerhard Goos
Juris Hartmanis

Editorial Board Members

Elisa Bertino, *Purdue University, West Lafayette, IN, USA*
Wen Gao, *Peking University, Beijing, China*
Bernhard Steffen ⓘ, *TU Dortmund University, Dortmund, Germany*
Moti Yung ⓘ, *Columbia University, New York, NY, USA*

The series Lecture Notes in Computer Science (LNCS), including its subseries Lecture Notes in Artificial Intelligence (LNAI) and Lecture Notes in Bioinformatics (LNBI), has established itself as a medium for the publication of new developments in computer science and information technology research, teaching, and education.

LNCS enjoys close cooperation with the computer science R & D community, the series counts many renowned academics among its volume editors and paper authors, and collaborates with prestigious societies. Its mission is to serve this international community by providing an invaluable service, mainly focused on the publication of conference and workshop proceedings and postproceedings. LNCS commenced publication in 1973.

Stefan Pickl · Bernhard Hämmerli ·
Päivi Mattila · Annaleena Sevillano
Editors

Critical Information Infrastructures Security

18th International Conference, CRITIS 2023
Helsinki Region, Finland, September 13–15, 2023
Revised Selected Papers

Springer

Editors
Stefan Pickl 🆔
University of the Bundeswehr Munich
Neubiberg, Germany

Bernhard Hämmerli 🆔
Lucerne University of Applied Sciences
Luzern, Switzerland

Päivi Mattila 🆔
Laurea University of Applied Sciences
Vantaa, Finland

Annaleena Sevillano 🆔
Laurea University of Applied Sciences
Vantaa, Finland

ISSN 0302-9743   ISSN 1611-3349 (electronic)
Lecture Notes in Computer Science
ISBN 978-3-031-62138-3   ISBN 978-3-031-62139-0 (eBook)
https://doi.org/10.1007/978-3-031-62139-0

This Springer imprint is published by the registered company Springer Nature Switzerland AG
The registered company address is: Gewerbestrasse 11, 6330 Cham, Switzerland

If disposing of this product, please recycle the paper.

Preface

Focus on Critical Information Infrastructures Security and Hybrid Threats

The Critical Information Infrastructures Security CRITIS conference 2023, held on September 13–15, 2023 at the Laurea University of Applied Sciences in Finland, had a special focus on hybrid threats. It was organized by the Laurea Security Research Program and its special team led by its Director Päivi Mattila in cooperation with Stefan Pickl, Bundeswehr Universität Müchen COMTESSA (Core Competence Center for Operations Research, Management Intelligence-Tenacity-Experience, Safety & Security ALLIANCE), and Bernhard Hämmerli, Cyber Security Department, Lucerne University of Applied Sciences and Acris GmbH, Switzerland. The Honorary Chair was Udo Helmbrecht.

The Laurea RDI Vice President, Mari Vuolteenaho, and Bernhard Hämmerli, Chair of the CRITIS Steering Committee, welcomed ca. 80 participants from science, industry, and government, and especially critical infrastructure practitioners. The conference addressed four scientific focus areas, namely information, infrastructures, security and hybrid threats, in an interdisciplinary manner and specifically using context-based analyses and complex optimization methods. Within the framework of the conference, these central areas were examined from various sides, both scientifically and practically, under the aspect of criticality. This proceedings documents the CRITIS 2023 focus areas and topics that were discussed during the three interesting conference days.

The conference papers were selected according to a two-round peer review process. In the first round the review was conducted as double blind and at least three peer reviewers reviewed each paper. In the second round the peer review was conducted as single blind and one or two persons reviewed each paper. Finally, we were happy to accept 13 full papers, 3 short papers, and 1 paper in progress.

In the CRITIS 2023 keynote, Bernhard Hämmerli highlighted a variety of complex challenges in cyber security. While various measures can be taken to counter these challenges, ultimate security is seen as very challenging. Presenters at the conference talked about some key challenges and how to overcome them. The editors warmly thank all CRITIS 2023 participants for their contributions in this ever-evolving technological and security landscape.

April 2024

Stefan Pickl
Jarno Limnéll
Päivi Mattila
Tiina Haapanen
Johanna Karvonen
Annaleena Sevillano
Isto Mattila
Bernhard Hämmerli
Udo Helmbrecht

Organization

General Chairs

Päivi Mattila   Laurea University of Applied Sciences, Finland
Mari Vuolteenaho   Laurea University of Applied Sciences, Finland

Honorary Chair

Udo Helmbrecht   Universität der Bundeswehr München, Germany

Program Co-chairs

Stefan Pickl   Bundeswher Universität Müchen, COMTESSA, Germany
Jarno Limnéll   Aalto University, Finland (Member of Finnish Parliament)

Steering Committee

Chairs

Bernhard M. Hämmerli   Lucerne University of Applied Sciences, Acris GmbH, Switzerland
Javier Lopez   University of Malaga, Spain
Stephen D. Wolthusen   Royal Holloway, University of London, UK and NTNU, Norway

Members

Sandro Bologna   AIIC, Italy
Gregorio D'Agostino   ENEA, Italy
Eric Luiijf   Luiijf Consultancy, The Netherlands
Roberto Setola   Università Campus Bio-Medico di Roma, Italy
Stefan Pickl   Bundeswher Universität Müchen, COMTESSA, Germany

Alain Mermoud   Cyber-Defence Campus, armasuisse S+T,
                                       Switzerland

Program Committee

Alberto Tofani   ENEA, Italy
Magnus Almgren   Chalmers University of Technology, Sweden
Cristina Alcaraz   University of Malaga, Spain
Joe Gardiner   University of Bristol, UK
Fabrizio Baiardi   University of Pisa, Italy
Sandro Bologna   AIIC, Italy
Tom Chothia   University of Birmingham, UK
Dimitris Gritzalis   Athens University of Economics & Business,
                                       Greece
Bernhard Hämmerli   Acris, Switzerland
Chris Hankin   Imperial College London, UK
Vytis Kopustinskas   European Commission, Joint Research Centre,
                                       Italy
Panayiotis Kotzanikolaou   University of Piraeus, Greece
Linas Martišauskas   Lithuanian Energy Institute, Lithuania
Simin Nadjm-Tehrani   Linköping University, Sweden
Stefan Pickl   Universität der Bundeswehr München, Germany
Peter Popov   City University, UK
Andre Samberg   i4-Flame OU, Estonia
Roberto Setola   Università Campus Biomedico, Rome, Italy
Vladimir Stankovic   City University of London, UK
Stephen Wolthusen   Norwegian University of Science and Technology,
                                       Norway
Basel Katt   Norwegian University of Science and Technology,
                                       Norway
Mikel Iturbe   Mondragon Unibertsitatea, Spain
Gregorio D'Agostino   ENEA, Italy
Alain Mermoud   Cyber-Defence Campus, armasuisse S+T,
                                       Switzerland

Contents

Short Papers

Work in Progress

Full Papers

Full Papers

Mapping and Analysis of Common Vulnerabilities in Popular Web Servers

Matyas Barocsai[1]($\boxtimes$), Johan Can[2], Martin Karresand[1]⬤,
and Simin Nadjm-Tehrani[2]⬤

[1] Department of Cyber Defence and C2 Technology, Swedish Defence Research
Agency (FOI), Stockholm, Sweden
{matyas.istvan.barocsai,martin.karresand}@foi.se
[2] Department of Computer and Information Science, Linköping University,
Linköping, Sweden
johca907@student.liu.se, simin.nadjm-tehrani@liu.se

Abstract. The digitalization of the modern society has made many
organizations susceptible to cybercrime through exploitations of software vulnerabilities. The popular web servers Apache HTTP and Nginx
make up around 65% of the market for web server software and power
the majority of all websites on the internet. Vulnerabilities that occur
in these two software programs therefore pose a significant risk to the
millions of users.

This paper maps the most common vulnerability types in these web
servers by retrieving, filtering, and analyzing information related to
around 195,000 reported vulnerabilities. The results not only show that
5 vulnerability types according to the NIST classification, namely CWE-
20, CWE-200, CWE-22, CWE-79, and CWE-787, account for almost
25% of all reported vulnerabilities in Apache HTTP and Nginx, but
also that these vulnerability types are commonly found in other web
software as well. The outcomes of this study are useful for constructing
proof-of-concept insecurity demonstrations and for applying in awareness
exercises and cybersecurity education.

Keywords: Cybersecurity · Demonstration · Vulnerability · Web
Server · NVD · CVE

1 Introduction

The prevalence of attacks on enterprise systems and their historical development
has highlighted interfaces that are hard to fix once and for all. Web interfaces
have been shown to be notoriously hard to secure, and remain a fertile ground
for attacks through exploiting both application-related features and weaknesses
in mechanisms introduced to fix security (identity and authentication management, access control, logging and monitoring, etc.) [21]. Stopping adversarial
access to systems through vulnerabilities requires hardening strategies at both

S. Pickl et al. (Eds.): CRITIS 2023, LNCS 14599, pp. 3–22, 2024.
https://doi.org/10.1007/978-3-031-62139-0_1

the client [19] and the server ends. This paper focuses on understanding which web server weaknesses persist over time.

Application developer awareness of security controls and attack surfaces is promoted as a long term approach to improve security while the attack and defence landscapes change over time [20]. The backdrop of our work is the provision of learning environments where demonstration of attacks in a realistic environment can enhance the security awareness of developers and users. In this paper we attempt to understand the landscape of web service security in order to identify which types of demonstrations can be used to show the absence of security. We begin by trying to identify the range of web server vulnerabilities seen in massively deployed frameworks. We also expose the historical development of relevant vulnerabilities and provide an overview of the trends.

Vulnerabilities in software can be reported to organizations that run vulnerability databases, which aim to evaluate and catalog vulnerabilities. There are several such databases including Common Vulnerabilities and Exposures (CVE)[1], National Vulnerability Database (NVD)[2], and VulnDB[3]. CVE is a program with the goal of identifying, cataloging and disclosing known vulnerabilities to the public, and is operated by the MITRE Corporation. NVD is a publicly available vulnerability database maintained by National Institute of Standards and Technology (NIST) under the U.S. Department of Commerce. VulnDB is maintained by a commercial enterprise.

Many studies have been conducted to analyze these databases and detect trends and patterns in reported vulnerabilities, but most focus on other software such as operating systems and programming languages, and less on web servers. However, with the increasing number of web servers and internet users, the discovery and exploitation of vulnerabilities in web servers have greater consequences than before.

While education and demonstrations of vulnerabilities can help to increase knowledge of information security, the demonstration of attacks needs performing the learning exercise in an environment that does not create harm. Cyber ranges such as Crate[4] can be used for training and testing without risking damage to real systems, but developing demonstrations and exercises for vulnerabilities can be a slow process due to the different configurations and versions of software. Thus, it is important to know where the focus of a particular exercise should be to provide high impact outcomes. The work in this paper helps to identify web server vulnerabilities that can be considered most relevant when performing such exercises currently.

The paper has the following contributions:

– A systematic investigation of known web server vulnerabilities with the aim of understanding the trends and current state.

---

[1] https://www.cve.org/.

[2] https://nvd.nist.gov/.

[3] https://vulndb.cyberriskanalytics.com/.

[4] https://www.foi.se/en/foi/research/information-security/crate---swedens-national-cyber-training-facility.html.

– Devising a set of criteria to identify and extract the most relevant vulnerabilities to focus current awareness campaigns on those.

The work includes developing tools that automatically extract web server related vulnerabilities from the NVD database between 1988 and 2022 (amounting to 1 GB of data), and then analyzing the extracted records with respect to interesting properties: the criticality of the vulnerability, the dominance of common weaknesses given their applicability within highly popular frameworks, and the most frequent frequent Common Weakness Enumerations (CWEs). We focus on two web server frameworks, Apache and Nginx, that together comprise the majority of all deployed web software today [15]. All in all, 195,777 CVE records are included in the collected data (up to and including October 2022), from which 174,448 records have a labelled criticality degree. The records are further analyzed and mapped to the categories of interest in terms of dominant weaknesses for each web engine type.

The paper is organized as follows. Section 2 covers the needed background and describes the related works. Section 3 explains the methodology for collecting and processing the vulnerability records and the results from each step of the analysis. Section 4 presents the outcomes of the analysis from Sect. 3. Section 5 discusses the outcomes presented in Sect. 4, and main takeaways of the study. Section 6 concludes the paper and presents future works.

2   Background and Related Work

The vulnerabilities in the CVE database, known as CVE records, are discovered and reported to the CVE Program by organizations, researchers or private individuals. Reported vulnerabilities are evaluated and published by partnered organizations in the CVE Program. Additionally, each vulnerability processed by the CVE Program receives an identifier, the CVE ID, which can be used to uniquely identify the vulnerability. As of April 2023 a little over 199,000 vulnerabilities have been reported to the CVE Program.

Many CVE core vulnerabilities can be similar in terms of their characteristics, causes, or their consequences when exploited. Therefore, there is value in categorizing these vulnerabilities into different types. CWE is a list of identified vulnerability types found in software or hardware. Unlike a CVE record, which refers to a specific vulnerability in a software, a CWE type represents a weakness or characteristic, potentially shared by multiple vulnerabilities, and can be used to categorize CWE vulnerabilities into larger groups. Example CWE types, encountered during our study and thereby relevant for the paper are presented in Table 1.

Common Vulnerability Scoring System (CVSS) is a system for scoring the severity of a vulnerability. The severity is reflected as a numerical value between 0 and 10 and is the result of an evaluation of the vulnerabilities' characteristics. During evaluation multiple factors are rated, each a member of one of three categories: *Base, Environmental* or *Temporal*. The CVSS scoring is often given as both CVSS v2 and v3 values. In CVSS v3 the criticality is extended to also

Table 1. CWE types relevant for the study (sorted by CWE ID)

ID	Name
CWE-16	Configuration
CWE-20	Improper Input Validation
CWE-22	Improper Limitation of a Pathname to a Restricted Directory ('Path Traversal')
CWE-78	Improper Neutralization of Special Elements used in an OS Command ('OS Command Injection')
CWE-79	Improper Neutralization of Input During Web Page Generation ('Cross-site Scripting')
CWE-89	Improper Neutralization of Special Elements used in an SQL Command ('SQL Injection')
CWE-94	Improper Control of Generation of Code ('Code Injection')
CWE-119	Improper Restriction of Operations within the Bounds of a Memory Buffer
CWE-120	Buffer Copy without Checking Size of Input ('Classic Buffer Overflow')
CWE-125	Out-of-bounds Read
CWE-190	Integer Overflow or Wraparound
CWE-200	Exposure of Sensitive Information to an Unauthorized Actor
CWE-264	Permissions, Privileges, and Access Controls
CWE-287	Improper Authentication
CWE-295	Improper Certificate Validation
CWE-310	Cryptographic Issues
CWE-319	Cleartext Transmission of Sensitive Information
CWE-399	Resource Management Errors
CWE-400	Uncontrolled Resource Consumption
CWE-416	Use After Free
CWE-444	Inconsistent Interpretation of HTTP Requests ('HTTP Request/Response Smuggling')
CWE-476	NULL Pointer Dereference
CWE-787	Out-of-bounds Write
NVD-CWE-Other	Other
NVD-CWE-noinfo	Insufficient Information

Table 2. Comparison of the levels of severity between CVSS v2 and CVSS v3

Severity	CVSS v2	CVSS v3
None		0.0
Low	0.0–3.9	0.1–3.9
Medium	4.0–6.9	4.0–6.9
High	7.0–10.0	7.0–8.9
Critical		9.0–10.0

include *None* and *Critical* and the value ranges adjusted accordingly. Table 2 shows the CVSS v2 and v3 scores as defined by their specification documents [4, 5].

The reported vulnerabilities in the NVD are synchronized with the CVE Program, meaning that newly discovered and published CVE records will be added to the NVD as well. The purpose of the NVD project is to analyze published CVE records and contribute additional detailed information to each vulnerability. The NVD extends the CVE Program by providing evaluations of the CVSS score, the CWE type as well as giving a list of known configurations of software in which the vulnerability has been found.

2.1 Vulnerabilities, Attacks and Security in Web Servers

Understanding the intricacies of web servers, such as common attacks, security and development process can greatly aid in understanding why certain vulnerabilities and CWEs occur to a greater extent.

Morton, Werner, Kintis, Snow, Antonakakis, Polychronakis, et al. [14] investigated the risks of the new asynchronous web server architecture, particularly in Nginx. Asynchronous web servers offer performance and scalability benefits by enabling memory sharing between clients, something that could potentially pose risks. The authors aimed to investigate if the risk of memory-based vulnerabilities is higher in these new architectures. They presented a method and framework to identify security-critical data by tracking clients' memory handling and examined how this can be used to analyze the exploitation of historical vulnerabilities in Nginx. The study concluded that the asynchronous architecture of Nginx poses a greater risk for memory-based attacks.

Woo, Alhazmi, and Malaiya [23] conducted a study on the potential number of undiscovered vulnerabilities in the popular web server software Apache and Microsoft Internet Information Services (IIS). They used two quantitative discovery models primarily designed for operating systems to estimate the number of undiscovered vulnerabilities, utilizing vulnerability data from NVD. The study revealed that the discovery process for vulnerabilities in web server software follows a pattern that can be modeled, which can be used to predict potential undiscovered vulnerabilities. The authors concluded that the discovery models developed for operating systems can also be applied to web server software.

Alhazmi and Malaiya [1] studied the number of undiscovered vulnerabilities in web server software and the possibility of predicting the number of vulnerabilities in future years. Like Woo, Alhazmi, and Malaiya [23], the authors examined the web server software Apache and Microsoft IIS and used vulnerability data from NVD. They also investigated the use of two models they created to predict undiscovered vulnerabilities. Based on their results, the authors argue that both models have applications in software development processes but that further research is needed to increase their accuracy.

Piantadosi, Scalabrino, and Oliveto [17] investigated the vulnerability fixing process in open-source software. The authors examined who fixes the vulnerabilities, how long it takes to fix them, and the process for fixing them. They analyzed 337 reported CVE vulnerabilities in two open-source programs, Apache HTTP Server and Apache Tomcat, and linked each vulnerability to the specific changes made in the software to fix it.

Piantadosi, Scalabrino, and Oliveto found that the programmers who fixed the vulnerabilities were typically more experienced than the average developer, and that most vulnerabilities were fixed with just one patch. However, approximately 3% of vulnerabilities were not fixed and reappeared in the future. About 80% of vulnerabilities were fixed before the CVE was announced, which is desirable. The remaining vulnerabilities varied greatly in the time taken to fix them, ranging from within 10 days to several years.

While studies such as [1, 14, 17, 23] do not provide a list of the most common vulnerabilities in web servers, their research greatly highlights that web server architecture and development process does have an impact on which vulnerabilities occur and potentially reoccur in web server software. Additionally, they demonstrate how vulnerability databases such as NVD and CVE can be utilized in the research of web servers. Notably, Woo, Alhazmi, and Malaiya [23] and Alhazmi and Malaiya [1] illustrate how information provided by the NVD can be used to map vulnerabilities to certain web server technologies. Our work, therefore builds on those insights and extends them to the full range of web server vulnerabilities.

2.2   Analysis of Vulnerability Databases

Analyzing records in vulnerability databases such as NVD and CVE can reveal trends and previously unknown relations between vulnerabilities and web servers. Studies which have explored NVD data provide a solid foundation for finding trends, and their methodology can be applied to identify the most common vulnerabilities in web servers.

Gorbenko, Romanovsky, Tarasyuk, and Biloborodov [10] investigated which operating systems have the highest number of reported vulnerabilities and the life-cycle of these vulnerabilities. The authors combined and mapped known vulnerabilities from the CVE and NVD databases between 2012 and 2016. The results show that both the number of reported vulnerabilities and security risk have increased between 2012 and 2016. Furthermore, the authors found that the average time it takes for developers to fix a vulnerability is the same regardless of how critical the vulnerability is.

Kuhn, Raunak, and Kacker [13] analyzed trends in older and current vulnerabilities by examining reported vulnerabilities in the NVD vulnerability database between 2006 and 2016. Their earliest analysis between 2006 and 2010 showed that the most common vulnerability types were XSS and SQL injection attacks (CWE-79 and CWE-89). About 15% of the reported vulnerabilities during this time were unclassified and did not belong to any vulnerability type. A later analysis between 2010 and 2017 showed that the most common vulnerability types were CWE-16: Configuration and CWE-20: Improper Input Validation. The authors attribute the decrease in SQL injection and XSS vulnerabilities partly to new tools and methods that facilitate their discovery. Furthermore, the later analysis showed that the number of unclassified vulnerabilities has decreased, which the authors believe shows how the work in cybersecurity has developed and become normalized over the years.

Fan, Li, Wang, and Nguyen [7] created a vulnerability database for large open-source software written in C/C++. They combined information from the CVE vulnerability database with related vulnerability information, and connected vulnerabilities to the specific code that was vulnerable and the code that fixed the vulnerability. The authors aimed to facilitate vulnerability analysis by providing information on the specific vulnerable code. The result was a database with 3754 vulnerabilities from 348 different GitHub projects. The authors analyzed trends in their vulnerability database and found that CWE-119: Improper Restriction of Operations within the Bounds of a Memory Buffer and CWE-20: Improper Input Validation were the most common vulnerability types among the examined software.

Anwar, Abusnaina, Chen, Li, and Mohaisen [2] investigated the quality of the evaluations performed by NVD for each reported CVE. The study examines whether NVD's evaluations are consistent and, among other things, whether correct CVSS scores and CWE types are provided by NVD. Furthermore, the authors investigate whether the publication date listed in NVD adds value and whether it correctly reflects the vulnerability's public awareness. By examining URLs listed as references in NVD for each vulnerability, the authors found that in several cases, the vulnerability's existence had been publicly disclosed several months before the publication date in NVD. The authors argue that the publication date shown in NVD only indicates when a vulnerability was published in the database and not when it was first mentioned in the public domain. Therefore, the publication date may not necessarily be valuable, and the first detection date should possibly be provided instead.

Regarding CWE types, Anwar et al. found that several vulnerabilities categorized as NVD-CWE-Other actually contained a specified CWE type in the vulnerability description. Therefore, the authors could correctly categorize an additional 1732 vulnerabilities identified as NVD-CWE-Other into their correct CWE types. Finally, the authors conclude that they have been able to assess and address several of the inconsistent attributes in NVD that they identified. They believe that it is valuable to address these inconsistencies to increase the quality of NVD, not only because the vulnerability database is widely used in cybersecurity but also because a consistent vulnerability database would provide a better overview of vulnerability trends.

Williams, Dey, Barranco, Naim, Hossain, and Akbar [22] investigated hidden trends in NVD by analyzing its content with machine learning. They aimed to examine how the most common vulnerabilities relate to the products with the most reported vulnerabilities by analyzing recurring words and phrases in vulnerability descriptions. The study identified the top 50 software products and top 50 vulnerability types between 2000 and 2017. The results show unexplored trends in NVD and clear connections between common vulnerability types and products they occur in. The authors suggest that the results, reinforced by various machine learning models, are valuable for developing secure software. Further research will be conducted on the presented analysis model, Supervised Topical Evolution Model (STEM), to predict vulnerabilities in software in the future.

None of the studies by Gorbenko et al., Kuhn et al., Fan et al., Anwar et al., Williams et al. provide an overview and analysis of the vulnerability trends in web servers and which CWEs that contribute to the most vulnerabilities in these technologies. Williams et al. for example uses machine learning to detect phrases related to CWEs. Their results estimate which of these phrases are most commonly associated with vulnerabilities, but they do not identify the specific CWE types that are most prevalent. Furthermore, Williams et al. only examine vulnerabilities reported to NVD between 2000 and 2017, which means that a great amount of vulnerabilities since 2017 remain unmapped.

Despite being unrelated to web technologies, the methodology used by Anwar, Abusnaina, Chen, Li, and Mohaisen [2], Fan, Li, Wang, and Nguyen [7], Gorbenko, Romanovsky, Tarasyuk, and Biloborodov [10], Kuhn, Raunak, and Kacker [13], and Williams, Dey, Barranco, Naim, Hossain, and Akbar [22] can be viewed as an evidence that conducting a quantitative investigation of vulnerability trends is feasible, relevant, and valuable. Furthermore, it highlights how valuable the data in the NVD is. To the best of our knowledge, no other works have devised tools to systematically extract and analyze the web server-specific vulnerabilities from the NVD/CVE databases and CWE categorizations, in order to provide insights on trends and weaknesses in this domain.

3   Systematic Analysis of Web Server Vulnerabilities

The analysis and investigation of potential trends in vulnerabilities were pursued by adopting a methodology that consisted of four stages. The four stages were as follows:

Data collection: Collect data on reported vulnerabilities
Data filtering: Convert/filter the data into a manageable format
Analysis: Analyze the data for trends and patterns and identify relationships
   between common vulnerabilities and popular web servers
Presentation: Present the results of the analysis using a suitable visualization

Each of the four stages presented challenges that had to be overcome. The subsequent subsections provide an account of these challenges and their corresponding solutions.

3.1   Vulnerability Data Collection

In this study, data was retrieved from NVD, as this database is; openly accessible to individuals, large and contains many vulnerabilities, reliable, and has frequently been used in previous research [1,2,10,13,22,23]. Furthermore, NVD can be seen as an extension of the CVE database. The two databases are fully synchronized, but NVD also provides some additional information about vulnerabilities, such as CVSS score, references, CWE type, and possible vulnerable system configurations. The data in the NVD can be accessed through their website or by downloading the vulnerability data to a local machine. The NVD offers various formats for downloading the data, such as XML and JSON. For this study, JSON was selected as it was considered to be the most manageable. A total of 21 separate JSON files were downloaded, containing unfiltered information on all reported vulnerabilities between the years 1988 and 2022, summarised in Table 3.

3.2 Vulnerability Data Filtering

In Table 3, it is clear that manual filtering of vulnerabilities would not be feasible due to the large amount of data that would need to be manually reviewed. For this reason, there was a need to automate the filtering of the data obtained from the JSON files. To this end, a tool was developed with the purpose of auto-

Table 3. Overview of downloaded JSON files

JSON file	Year	Lines	Size [MB]
1	1988–2002	622,643	21.1
2	2003	170,922	6.0
3	2004	352,021	12.6
4	2005	565,333	19.9
5	2006	862,034	30.5
6	2007	807,329	28.5
7	2008	940,392	33.3
8	2009	890,111	32.4
9	2010	946,944	34.7
10	2011	942,934	34.8
11	2012	1,096,774	40.1
12	2013	1,240,427	45.5
13	2014	1,124,411	40.8
14	2015	1,114,185	40.2
15	2016	1,433,754	51.6
16	2017	2,070,494	73.9
17	2018	2,174,419	77.1
18	2019	2,476,073	87.2
19	2020	3,247,700	112.8
20	2021	3,585,469	124.4
21	2022	1,665,930	58.7
Total	34 years	28,330,299	1,006.1

matically filtering all vulnerabilities in the downloaded JSON files and storing them in a local database. The tool was developed in the Python programming language[5], as this language has good compatibility with JSON files. Furthermore, the SQLite database[6] was chosen because it has good compatibility with Python.

The developed tool was useful and necessary because it could filter out useful fields of each vulnerability instead of having to deal with irrelevant data related to the vulnerabilities. Much of the information provided about CVE vulnerabilities from the JSON files was unnecessary and therefore needed to be filtered out. The majority of all data such as reference links, information about configurations, details about how CVSS values were calculated, the latest modification date, and who assigned the vulnerability CVE ID were not relevant to this work.

The purpose of the filtering was to find vulnerabilities based on the type of vulnerability, when it was reported, how serious it was, and its ID. Therefore, data fields that did not have information about this could be filtered out. The following fields were left after filtering the JSON files through the developed Python tool:

CVE ID: This field is used to identify the vulnerability. The CVE ID assigned to a vulnerability is unique and is therefore well suited as a key for a database entry.

CVSS v3: The newer CVSS v3 is the primary way of rating the severity level of vulnerabilities from 2016 onwards. Using this field, the severity level among the reported vulnerabilities can be analyzed.

CVSS v2: The older CVSS v2 used to rate the severity level of vulnerabilities before 2016, but it also appears frequently in newer vulnerabilities.

Publication date: This field shows on which date the vulnerability was published in the NVD. This field can be used to examine vulnerability trends over time.

CWE: This field shows the CWEs that are associated with the vulnerability and can be used to investigate how different vulnerability types have developed over time.

Description: This field provides a brief summary and explanation of the vulnerability and in which software it can be found. This field can be used to find vulnerabilities related to specific technologies, in our case web servers.

By using these limited number of database fields, the amount of information stored about each vulnerability was greatly decreased. Consequently, it became significantly easier to find desired data and investigate potential trends in the reported vulnerabilities.

3.3 Criteria for Vulnerability Selection

With the local database, which contained the filtered contents of the NVD, extraction and exploration of hidden vulnerability trends was made significantly

---

[5] https://www.python.org/.
[6] https://www.sqlite.org/index.html.

easier. The use of an SQLite database made it possible to write SQL queries in order to extract the data which was pursued.

Some vulnerability types would clearly be more prevalent than others. Nevertheless, most software systems still have a wide variety of vulnerability types reported, some which have only been reported once throughout the software's lifespan. To focus only on the most common vulnerability types, those types that were only reported once or twice were disregarded and grouped together. This way only the historically 15 most reported vulnerabilities were analyzed and investigated.

A few points of interest were pursued when extracting data for the analysis of trends in the reported vulnerabilities for the web servers Apache HTTP and Nginx. When examining the data extracted, the following points were studied:

- Has the number of reported vulnerabilities increased or decreased since the introduction of the web server?
- Which vulnerability types have been the most common?
- Is there a uniquely prominent vulnerability type, which has occurred in a far greater extent?
- Are there any specific years which are distinctive for the web servers?
- How does the most common vulnerability types compare between the two web servers?

Figure 1, shows how trends in the NVD can be explored using the SQL queries, in this case simply the number of reported vulnerabilities each year.

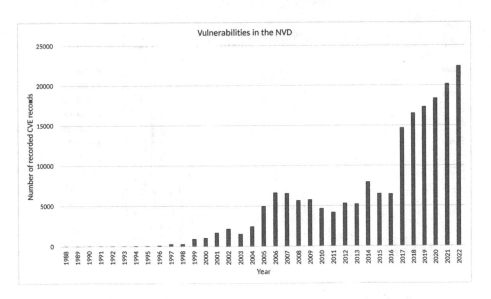

Fig. 1. Reported vulnerabilities in the NVD between the years 1988 and 2022

Even in this simple example, Fig. 1, interesting trends and characteristics can be seen. It is evident that the number of reported vulnerabilities increases each year when examining the long-term trend. There are also two significant increases in 2005 and 2017. Between these two major increases, during the years 2000–2005 and 2006–2016, the number of reported vulnerabilities remained relatively stable. Since 2017, there has been a consistent annual increase in the number of reported vulnerabilities. Apart from the two major spikes of increase, the year 2014 stands out, with a visibly higher number of reported vulnerabilities compared to the surrounding years.

4   Analysis Outcomes

By collecting, filtering, and examining the reported CVE records in the NVD, the investigation for the most common vulnerability types in Apache HTTP and Nginx could be completed. This section presents the results of this analysis.

4.1   General Overview of the Vulnerabilities in the NVD

When not considering the program or system in which a reported vulnerability occurs, the most common vulnerability type reported in the NVD can be found. Studying which vulnerability types are the most common in the entire NVD can be beneficial as it gives an insight into which types are common regardless of system. In Fig. 2, the three most commonly reported vulnerabilities each year can be seen, without regard to the system it occurred in.

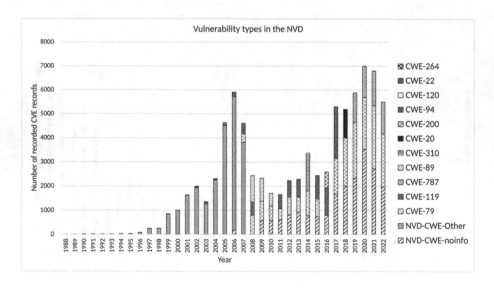

Fig. 2. The 3 most common vulnerabilities each year in NVD

In Fig. 2, it can be observed that until 2008, the vulnerability type NVD-CWE-Other dominated, followed by the dominance of the vulnerability type

NVD-CWE-noinfo. Both types are used in the publication of unclassified vulnerabilities by the NVD. Furthermore, it is evident that the vulnerability types CWE-79 and CWE-119 have been commonly occurring for an extended period between 2007 and 2017, while the type CWE-787 has had a clear presence since 2019.

Year 2014 stands out, as the vulnerability type CWE-310 suddenly becomes one of the most prevalent types, only to diminish in the year after. Similarly, the types CWE-200 and CWE-20 emerge among the most reported vulnerability types in 2016 and 2018, respectively, but diminish in later years. Table 4 presents the 5 most reported vulnerability types out of a total 195,477 reported vulnerabilities.

In Table 4, it is clear that the vulnerability types NVD-CWE-Other and NVD-CWE-noinfo constitute the largest proportion of all reported vulnerabilities in the NVD, accounting for over 20% of all reported vulnerabilities. Furthermore, when considering only properly classified vulnerabilities, it can be observed that the type CWE-79: Improper Neutralization of Input During Web Page Generation, stands out as the most prevalent vulnerability type.

Table 4. The 5 most common vulnerability types in NVD

Vulnerability type	N	% of total
NVD-CWE-Other	23,419	11.9
NVD-CWE-noinfo	20,273	10.3
CWE-79	18,979	9.7
CWE-119	7,479	3.8
CWE-787	5,319	2.7
Sum	75,469	38.4

4.2   Historical View of Web Server Vulnerabilities

The result of the investigation analyzing reported vulnerabilities related to the web servers Apache HTTP and Nginx shows that between 1997 and 2022, 300 different vulnerabilities related to Apache HTTP were reported. Furthermore, 141 vulnerabilities related to the web server software Nginx were reported between 2009 and 2022. In Fig. 3, the development of the 5 most common CWE types and their frequency for vulnerabilities related to Apache HTTP can be seen, and in Fig. 4, the corresponding information for Nginx are displayed.

In Fig. 3, it is clear that vulnerability types representing non-classifiable vulnerabilities, CWE-Other and NVD-CWE-noinfo, constitute a significantly large portion of the 5 most common vulnerability types. Furthermore, it can be seen that NVD-CWE-Other was more common between 1997 and 2007, while NVD-CWE-noinfo was more common after 2007.

Two vulnerability types representing classifiable vulnerabilities, CWE-20 and CWE-200, are commonly found between 2011 and 2017. CWE-79 is common

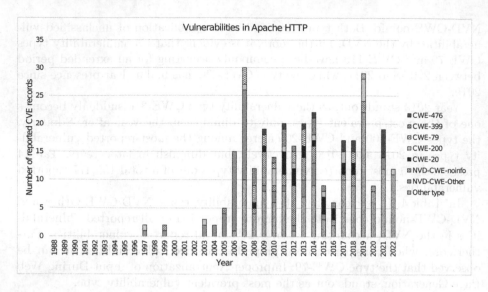

Fig. 3. The 5 most common vulnerabilities in Apache HTTP

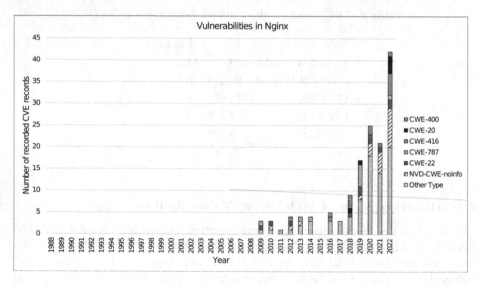

Fig. 4. The 5 most common vulnerabilities in Nginx

between 2007 and 2013 but has since then decreased in frequency. Of the total of 300 vulnerabilities related to Apache HTTP, 82 vulnerabilities are classified in one of the 5 most common CWE types. 87 vulnerabilities have not been classified and therefore belong to either CWE-Other or NVD-CWE-noinfo, and 131 vulnerabilities were classified to CWE types that are not among the 5 most common.

The number of reported vulnerabilities each year since 2006 is approximately the same, around 15–20. Distinctive years are 2007 and 2019 when more vulnerabilities were reported than the average. Furthermore, 2015, 2016, and 2020 are distinctive years when significantly fewer vulnerabilities were reported than the average during these years.

For reported vulnerabilities in Nginx, as shown in Fig. 4, it can be seen that the vulnerability type representing non-classifiable vulnerabilities, NVD-CWE-noinfo, is prevalent, especially in the last three years. Of the total of 141 vulnerabilities related to Nginx, 42 of these are classified in one of the 5 most common CWE types, while 78 vulnerabilities have been classified to CWE types that are not among the 5 most common. 21 vulnerabilities have not been classified and belong to NVD-CWE-noinfo. Between 2009 and 2017, approximately the same number of vulnerabilities were reported each year. From 2018 onwards, there is a clear increase in reported vulnerabilities each year. A distinctive year is 2022, where almost twice as many vulnerabilities were reported as the previous year.

4.3   The Most Common Vulnerabilities

The analysis of reported vulnerabilities in Apache HTTP and Nginx web servers reveals that the most common vulnerability types represent over 50% of all reported vulnerabilities, with slight variations in occurrence percentages. The analysis investigated 441 vulnerabilities in web servers and found that some vulnerability types are common in both web server software.

As shown in Table 5a, the 15 most common vulnerability types represent just over 51% of all reported vulnerabilities related to the Apache HTTP web server, and the vulnerability type CWE-20 is the most common.

Analogously, in Table 5b, it is clear that the 15 most common vulnerability types represent around 55% of all reported vulnerabilities related to the Nginx web server. Furthermore, the vulnerability type CWE-22 is the most common. The table shows that the number of the three most common vulnerability types differs very little. CWE-22 has only occurred in 1–2 more instances than CWE-787 and CWE-416. The gap between CWE-416 and CWE-20 is clearer, with a difference in percentage of more than 2% points. For the other vulnerability types in the table, there are no significant differences in either number or percentage, with most vulnerability types being equally common.

The result of the analysis, which investigated 441 vulnerabilities in web servers, 300 in Apache HTTP and 141 in Nginx, shows that some vulnerability types occur more frequently than others and that some vulnerability types are prevalent in both web server softwares. Table 6 presents the 5 most common vulnerability types in Apache HTTP and Nginx.

In Table 6, vulnerability CWE-20 is the most common vulnerability type among the web servers Apache HTTP and Nginx. This vulnerability type has occurred 7 times more than other vulnerability types. CWE-200, CWE-22, and CWE-79 are equally common, occurring on a par with CWE-787, and each account for 4.5% of the 441 reported vulnerabilities. Together, the top 5 most

Table 5. The 15 most common vulnerabilities in Apache HTTP and Nginx, excluding the categories NVD-CWE-Other and NVD-CWE-noinfo

(a) Apache HTTP				(b) Nginx		
CWE-ID	N	% of total (300)		CWE-ID	N	% of total (141)
CWE-20	21	7.0		CWE-22	11	7.8
CWE-200	17	5.7		CWE-787	10	7.1
CWE-79	17	5.7		CWE-416	9	6.4
CWE-399	14	4.7		CWE-20	6	4.3
CWE-476	13	4.3		CWE-125	6	4.3
CWE-119	10	3.3		CWE-400	6	4.3
CWE-22	9	3.0		CWE-295	5	3.5
CWE-787	9	3.0		CWE-287	4	2.8
CWE-400	8	2.7		CWE-200	3	2.1
CWE-94	7	2.3		CWE-190	3	2.1
CWE-444	6	2.0		CWE-119	3	2.1
CWE-264	6	2.0		CWE-319	3	2.1
CWE-287	5	1.7		CWE-476	3	2.1
CWE-89	5	1.7		CWE-78	3	2.1
CWE-416	5	1.7		CWE-79	3	2.1
Sum	152	50.8		Sum	78	55.2

Table 6. The 5 most common vulnerability types in both web servers Apache HTTP and Nginx

CWE-ID	N	% of total (441)	Rank (Apache HTTP)	Rank (Nginx)
CWE-20	27	6.1	1	4
CWE-200	20	4.5	2	9
CWE-22	20	4.5	7	1
CWE-79	20	4.5	3	15
CWE-787	19	4.3	8	2
Sum	106	23.9		

common vulnerability types make up 24% of all reported vulnerabilities among the web servers.

5   Why Do We Need to Act?

The above analysis brings us insights about the current state of common web server vulnerabilities. In this section we discuss why having this data can help us to focus on problems that are most relevant to fix. But before that, we need to get the attention of software developers and system owners about these issues.

5.1   Impact of Severe Vulnerabilities

The exploitation of a vulnerability can have a large impact on systems used globally. Noteworthy examples such as HeartBleed in 2014 [6], EternalBlue in 2017 [9], and ZeroLogon in 2020 [16] have all caused severe impacts on numerous systems worldwide. A more recent example is Log4Shell in 2021 [8,11], a vulnerability in the Apache Log4j logging utility, which led to significant disruptions worldwide due to the broad usage of the logging library.

While severe and impactful vulnerabilities most likely will not disappear entirely, developers can prepare by having a good understanding of what vulnerabilities they can expect. Possessing a deep understanding of all the vulnerability types found in the CWE list is an unrealistic demand. Therefore, it becomes highly valuable to identify a narrower subset of vulnerability types that occur in the systems in which they work, such as the most common or the most severe ones. Even for the narrower class of vulnerabilities the recent history tells us that systems are not patched immediately once a CWE has been associated with a component in them. Therefore, we need to keep pressing for attention towards the prevalent ones.

5.2   Demonstrations to Raise Awareness

Cybersecurity demonstrations serve not only as a means to raise awareness about cybersecurity issues but can also be valuable as an educational tool. Puys, Thevenon, and Mocanu [18] and Kalyanam and Yang [12] show that incorporating cybersecurity demonstrations into training platforms for cybersecurity education can have a significant effect on the participants' understanding of challenges within cybersecurity and secure development practices.

In order for cybersecurity demonstrations to be effective, it is necessary that they demonstrate interesting and relevant cybersecurity issues. When focusing on web servers, demonstrating the exploitation of a well-known vulnerability can provide valuable insight into the impacts and consequences of insecure systems. However, selecting an appropriate well-known vulnerability to base a demonstration on is a non-trivial task.

Simplifying this task could potentially be achieved through mapping the most common vulnerabilities in the most popular web servers. The identification of the most common vulnerability types can prove to be valuable as they signify recurring security concerns and highlight design flaws within the systems. For developers working with these web servers, understanding the impact and consequences of the most common vulnerability types can be advantageous, as well as understanding the reason for the vulnerabilities occurrence. Subsequent to our analysis, demonstrations of the most relevant ones were realised in a virtualized environment. However, the details of these implementations are beyond the scope of this paper and the interested reader is referred to the work by Barocsai and Can [3] for details.

6   Conclusions

Vulnerability databases offer immense value with their contents, but they can also potentially provide far more information, beyond their intended purpose. Through thorough analysis, one can extract valuable information about vulnerability trends and the relationship between vulnerability and software.

In this study, over 195,000 vulnerability records were collected, filtered and analyzed to investigate the prevalence of different vulnerability types in the two widely used web server softwares, Apache HTTP and Nginx. Results show that the top 15 most frequently reported CWE types account for almost half of all reported vulnerabilities. Furthermore, it can be seen that almost 25% of the reported vulnerabilities in these web servers are categorised to be of just 5 CWE types.

Cybersecurity demonstrations play a crucial role in education and raising awareness. However, they require that their contents and demonstrated vulnerabilities are both interesting and relevant. Finding suitable vulnerabilities to demonstrate is therefore a challenging and time-consuming task. This study aims to contribute to this area, by narrowing the down the selection of vulnerabilities, making it easier to find a suitable match.

Acknowledgements. The fourth author was supported by the Resilient Information and Control Systems (RICS) project financed by the Swedish Civil Contingencies Agency (MSB).

The authors have no competing interests to declare that are relevant to the content of this article.

References

1. Alhazmi, O.H., Malaiya, Y.K.: Measuring and enhancing prediction capabilities of vulnerability discovery models for apache and IIS HTTP servers. In: 2006 17th International Symposium on Software Reliability Engineering, pp. 343–352 (2006). https://doi.org/10.1109/ISSRE.2006.26
2. Anwar, A., Abusnaina, A., Chen, S., Li, F., Mohaisen, D.: Cleaning the NVD: comprehensive quality assessment, improvements, and analyses. IEEE Trans. Dependable Secure Comput. **19**(6), 4255–4269 (2022). https://doi.org/10.1109/TDSC.2021.3125270
3. Barocsai, M., Can, J.: Kartläggning, demonstration och hantering av vanliga sårbarheter i populära webbservrar. MSc thesis. Linköping University, Sweden (2023). https://www.diva-portal.org/smash/get/diva2:1743044/FULLTEXT01.pdf
4. Common Vulnerability Scoring System Version 2. https://www.first.org/cvss/v2/guide. Accessed 27 Oct 2023

5. Common Vulnerability Scoring System Version 3.1. https://www.first.org/cvss/specification-document. Accessed 27 Oct 2023
6. Durumeric, Z., Li, F., Kasten, J., Amann, J., Beekman, J., Payer, M., et al.: The matter of heartbleed. In: IMC 2014. Vancouver, BC, Canada: Association for Computing Machinery, pp. 475–488 (2014). isbn: 9781450332132. https://doi.org/10.1145/2663716.2663755
7. Fan, J., Li, Y., Wang, S., Nguyen, T.N.: AC/C++ code vulnerability dataset with code changes and CVE summaries. In: Proceedings of the 17th International Conference on Mining Software Repositories, pp. 508–512 (2020). https://doi.org/10.1145/3379597.3387501
8. Feng, S., Lubis, M.: Defense-in-depth security strategy in Log4j vulnerability analysis. In: 2022 International Conference Advancement in Data Science, E-learning and Information Systems (ICADEIS), pp. 01–04 (2022). https://doi.org/10.1109/ICADEIS56544.2022.10037384
9. Goodin, D.: NSA-leaking shadow brokers just dumped its most damaging release yet. In: ArsTechnica (2017). https://arstechnica.com/information-technology/2017/04/nsa-leaking-shadow-brokers-just-dumped-its-most-damagingrelease-yet/. Accessed 09 June 2023
10. Gorbenko, A., Romanovsky, A., Tarasyuk, O., Biloborodov, O.: Experience report: study of vulnerabilities of enterprise operating systems. In: 2017 IEEE 28th International Symposium on Software Reliability Engineering (ISSRE), pp. 205–215 (2017). https://doi.org/10.1109/ISSRE.2017.20
11. Hiesgen, R., Nawrocki, M., Schmidt, T.C., Wählisch, M.: The race to the vulnerable: measuring the Log4j shell incident (2022). arXiv: 2205.02544 [cs.CR]
12. Kalyanam, R., Yang, B.: Try-CybSI: an extensible cybersecurity learning and demonstration platform. In: Proceedings of the 18th Annual Conference on Information Technology Education. SIGITE 2017. Rochester, New York, USA: Association for Computing Machinery, pp. 41–46 (2017). isbn: 9781450351003. https://doi.org/10.1145/3125659.3125683
13. Kuhn, R., Raunak, M., Kacker, R.: It doesn't have to be like this: cybersecurity vulnerability trends. IT Prof. 19(6), 66–70 (2017). https://doi.org/10.1109/MITP.2017.4241462
14. Morton, M. Werner, J., Kintis, P., Snow, K., Antonakakis, M., Polychronakis, M., et al.: Security risks in asynchronous web servers: when performance optimizations amplify the impact of data-oriented attacks. In: 2018 IEEE European Symposium on Security and Privacy (EuroS&P), pp. 167–182 (2018). https://doi.org/10.1109/EuroSP.2018.00020
15. Netcraft: May 2023 Web Server Survey. https://www.netcraft.com/blog/may-2023-web-server-survey/. Accessed 27 Oct 2023
16. NIST. CVE-2020-1472 Detail (2020). https://nvd.nist.gov/vuln/detail/CVE-2020-1472. Accessed 09 June 2023
17. Piantadosi, V., Scalabrino, S., Oliveto, R.: Fixing of security vulnerabilities in open source projects: a case study of apache HTTP server and apache tomcat. In: 2019 12th IEEE Conference on Software Testing, Validation and Verification (ICST), pp. 68–78 (2019). https://doi.org/10.1109/ICST.2019.00017
18. Puys, M., Thevenon, P.-H., Mocanu, S.: Hardware-in-the-loop labs for SCADA cybersecurity awareness and training. In: Proceedings of the 16th International Conference on Availability, Reliability and Security. ARES 21. Vienna, Austria: Association for Computing Machinery (2021). isbn: 9781450390514. https://doi.org/10.1145/3465481.3469185

19. Roth, S., Calzavara, S., Wilhelm, M., Rabitti, A., Stock, B.: The security lottery: measuring client-side web security inconsistencies. In: 31st USENIX Security Symposium (USENIX Security 22). Boston, MA: USENIX Association, pp. 2047–2064 (2022). isbn: 978-1-939133-31-1. https://www.usenix.org/conference/usenixsecurity22/presentation/roth
20. Sahin, M., Ünlü, T., Hébert, C., Shepherd, L.A., Coull, N., Lean, C.M.: Measuring developers' web security awareness from attack and defense perspectives. In: 2022 IEEE Security and Privacy Workshops (SPW), pp. 31–43 (2022). https://doi.org/10.1109/SPW54247.2022.9833858
21. van der Stock, A., Glas, B., Smithline, N., Gigler, T.: OWASP Top 10:2021 (2021). https://owasp.org/Top10/. Accessed 07 June 2023
22. Williams, M.A., Dey, S., Barranco, R.C., Naim, S.M., Hossain, M.S., Akbar, M.: Analyzing evolving trends of vulnerabilities in national vulnerability database. In: 2018 IEEE International Conference on Big Data (Big Data), pp. 3011–3020 (2018). https://doi.org/10.1109/BigData.2018.8622299
23. Woo, S.-w., Alhazmi, O.H., Malaiya, Y.K.: Assessing vulnerabilities in apache and IIS HTTP servers. In: 2006 2nd IEEE International Symposium on Dependable, Autonomic and Secure Computing (2006). https://doi.org/10.1109/DASC.2006.21

Assessing the Effect of the Lack of Essential Workforce on the Economic Sectors During a Pandemic

Stefano Bartolucci[1], Roberto Setola[1], Antonio Scala[2], Stefano Panzieri[3], and Gabriele Oliva[1(✉)] (iD)

[1] Universitá Campus Bio-Medico di Roma, via Álvaro del Portillo 21, 00128 Rome, Italy
g.oliva@unicampus.it
[2] ISC-CNR Physics Department, Università La Sapienza, Rome, Italy
[3] Department of Civil Computer Science and Aeronautical Technologies Engineering, University Roma Tre, Rome, Italy

Abstract. This study presents a dynamic modeling framework that combines epidemiological and Input-Output analyses to evaluate the impact of a pandemic on essential occupational sectors in a nation and to assess the downstream consequences of the unavailability of essential workforce, due to the presence of interdependency relations among infrastructures or sectors. In particular, the proposed approach relies on a compartmental SIR epidemiological model that considers different age classes. Based on such a model, the amount of unavailable essential workforce due to the pandemics is identified and fed into a Dynamic Inoperability Input-Output model (D-IIM), which in turn provides the dynamics of the degree of inoperability of the different sectors due to both the initial perturbation caused by the lack of essential workforce and to the effect of interdependency relations. The potential of the framework is demonstrated via a proof-of-concept simulation analysis for a scenario in Italy at the beginning of the COVID-19 pandemic, considering realistic data.

Keywords: Pandemic Impact · Dynamic Inoperability Input-Output Modeling · Epidemiological Analysis · Economic consequences · Essential Workforce

1 Introduction

Pandemics have long been recognized as formidable threats to human health and well-being, but their repercussions extend far beyond the realm of public health [2,12,16,25]. The devastating impact of pandemics on national economies and infrastructures has become increasingly evident, as witnessed by the recent global outbreaks of diseases such as the COVID-19 pandemic [10,19]. The unprecedented scale and speed at which pandemics spread present immense challenges, testing the resilience of economies and exposing vulnerabilities within critical infrastructures. Understanding the intricate dynamics between pandemics, economic systems, and infrastructural networks is paramount for effective crisis management and the formulation of proactive strategies.

This paper introduces a framework for modeling the impact of pandemics on essential occupational sectors within a nation, while also evaluating the downstream consequences arising from the unavailability of crucial workforce due to the presence of interdependency relations among infrastructures or sectors. The proposed approach combines epidemiological and Input-Output analyses. At its core, the framework employs a compartmental SIR (Susceptible-Infectious-Recovered) epidemiological model [13] that takes into account different age classes, thus allowing to identify the extent of essential workforce unavailability caused by the pandemic.

To capture the cascading effects of the unavailability of the essential workforce on various sectors, a Dynamic Inoperability Input-Output model (D-IIM) is employed [5], in order to take into account not only the initial perturbation caused by the lack of essential workforce but also the influence of interdependency relations among sectors. By feeding the identified amount of unavailable essential workforce into the D-IIM, the dynamics of the degree of inoperability across different sectors can be quantified.

To showcase the potential of this modeling framework, a proof-of-concept simulation analysis is conducted using realistic data from a scenario in Italy during the early stages of the COVID-19 pandemic. By incorporating actual data, the simulation provides tangible insights into the real-world consequences of the pandemic on essential sectors and the subsequent interdependencies among them. This demonstration serves as a valuable illustration of the framework's capabilities and its potential applicability in informing policymakers and stakeholders in their decision-making processes, enhancing preparedness for future pandemics, and guiding effective response strategies. In particular, we consider a realistic case study set in Italy in 2020, and we rely on epidemiological data for the COVID-19 outbreak. Notice that, wherever possible, real epidemiological and economic data has been used. However, given the difficulty to exactly assess some of the parameters, and given the limited scope of this study, the results provided here are intended as a way to show the potential of our framework, rather than as a tool to actually draw conclusions on the real situation in Italy for the simulated time span. Indeed, this analysis serves as a valuable illustration of the framework's capabilities and its potential to inform policymakers and stakeholders in decision-making processes, enhance preparedness for future pandemics, and guide effective response strategies.

1.1   Contribution with Respect to the State of the Art

In recent literature, several studies have analyzed the disruption of economic sectors and infrastructures caused by pandemics (e.g., by lockdowns). In particular, in [29] a model is developed to account for the disruption resulting from the extended shutdown of business operations. The model is based on a persistent inoperability input-output model (PIIM). Similarly, the approach in [22] amounts to a Leontief input-output model, which is used to assess the impact of COVID-19 on the U.S. economy. The model relies on the epidemical curves to estimate the ripple effects of workforce disruptions across interdependent sectors of the economy. In [3] a framework to predict the economic and environmental effects of the lockdowns is provided, based on the Input-output inoperability model. In particular, the model accounts for the reduced operability of some of the sectors due to lockdowns, In [26] a disaster economic consequence analysis framework is developed to estimate the economic impacts of COVID-19 in the U.S. In [23] an input-output model to perform an ex-post analysis of the COVID-19 pandemic workforce disruptions in the Philippines is provided. In [11] the dynamic inoperability input-output model is used to analyze the economic impact of COVID-19 in Shanghai in the first quarter of 2022.

With respect to these works, the main novelty of this paper is that, within the proposed model, we explicitly account for the dynamics of the epidemiological situation, considering several age classes. Moreover, we consider a modified epidemiological model where the probability of infection is influenced by the intensity of the lockdown measures put in place. These measures play the role of a control input. This allows us to assess how lockdown policies influence the infection in general, and to quantify the resulting unavailability of essential workforce. In turn, such unavailability is fed to a Dynamic Inoperability Input-Output model, in order to estimate how the different economic sectors or infrastructures are impacted, also accounting for interdependency and domino effects.

In this context it is worth mentioning the framework developed in [24], where a multiobjective mixed-integer linear programming formulation is proposed in order to attempt to minimize the epidemiological, social and economic impact. The model is based on a combination of epidemiological and economical models. However, the epidemiological model considered in [24] encompasses a single population class and does not adapt to a varying intensity of the lockdown policies, while in our paper we consider multiple age classes and we adapt the epidemiological model based on lockdown policies that may vary with time.

1.2   Paper Outline

The outline of the paper is as follows: Sect. 2 reviews and discusses the tools and methodologies adopted in this paper; Sect. 3 provides a case study aiming at demonstrating the potential of the proposed framework; Sect. 4 draws some conclusive remark and outlines possible future work directions.

2   Materials and Methods

2.1   Notation

In this paper, vectors are indicated by boldface lowercase letters and matrices with uppercase letters; moreover, the notation A_{ij} is used to refer to the (i,j)-th entry of a matrix A. Then, vectors with n components, all equal to zero and to one are represented by $\mathbf{0}_n$ and $\mathbf{1}_n$, respectively. Instead, the notation $0_{n \times m}$

and $1_{n \times m}$ are used to denote an $n \times m$ matrix with just zero and one entries, respectively. To denotate the arguments of a function, round brackets are used, e.g., the notation $f(x, y)$ is used to denote a function with arguments x and y; even if, where understood, for brevity a function of one or more arguments is abbreviated with $f(\cdot)$. The operator diag$[\cdot]$ applied to a generic vector $x \in \mathbb{R}^n$ allows to calculate the diagonal matrix $n \times n$ having diag$[x]_{ii} = x_i$. The symbol $\odot$ is used to indicate the Hadamard matrix product (i.e., entry-wise) between matrices A and B with the same dimensions, i.e., the matrix $C = A \odot B$ is such that $C_{ij} = A_{ij}B_{ij}$; analogously, the Hadamard product between $c = a \odot b$ between two vectors a, b is such that $c_i = a_i b_i$. Furthermore, it must be remembered that Hadamard product is commutative; moreover, notice that $a \odot b = \text{diag}[a]b = \text{diag}[b]a$.

2.2   SIR Epidemics Model

The section discusses the SIR Epidemics model, where the population is divided into compartments [28] (S, I, R) representing susceptible, infected, and recovered individuals, respectively, and individuals can transition between these compartments. Considering a population of N individuals divided in n classes (e.g., by age or geographical area), N_ℓ indicates the population in the ℓ-th class with $N = \sum_{\ell=1}^{n} N_\ell$. Moreover, $s_\ell(t), i_\ell(t), r_\ell(t)$ indicates the fraction of susceptible, infectious and removed individuals in the ℓ-th class at time t and with $s(t), i(t), r(t) \in \mathbb{R}^n$ the stack of such variables for all classes. In the following, it is assumed that $s(0), i(0), r(0) \in [0, 1]^n$ and $s(0) + i(0) + r(0) = 1_n$. Overall, the SIR equations for heterogeneous population classes are given by

$$\begin{cases} \partial_t s(t) = -s(t) \odot \mathcal{B}i(t) \\ \partial_t i(t) = s(t) \odot \mathcal{B}i(t) - \gamma \odot i(t) \,, \\ \partial_t r(t) = \gamma \odot i(t) \end{cases} \tag{1}$$

where $\mathcal{B}$ is the $n \times n$ transmission matrix, $\mathcal{B}_{ij}$ being the rate at which a susceptible individual of class i meets an infectious individual of class j and becomes infected. Instead, $\gamma \in \mathbb{R}^n$ collects the rates γ_i at which infectious individuals in the i-th class are removed from the infection cycle.

Notably, the above choice for the initial conditions guarantees that $s(t), i(t)$, and $r(t)$ all belong to $[0, 1]^n$ and $s(t) + i(t) + r(t) = 1_n$ for all time instants t.

Within the SIR model, an epidemic ends when $i(t) = 0_n$, i.e., when it holds $s(t) + r(t) = 1_n$; such states are also called end-of-epidemic states.

Social Distancing Interventions in SIR Model. The SIR model can be modified in order to take into account the effect of social distancing interventions. As noted in [20], such interventions can be modeled via coefficients that reduce the rate of contact between susceptible and infectious individuals (e.g., as a result of the social distancing). In particular, using $\mathcal{E}_{ij}(k) \in [0, 1]$ to model the intensity of social distancing measures between the i-th and the j-th population class, the static coefficients $\mathcal{B}_{ij}$ of the SIR model are replaced by $\mathcal{B}_{ij}(k) = \mathcal{B}_{ij}[1 - \mathcal{E}_{ij}(k)]$, i.e., the stronger is the intensity of social distancing the weaker is the probability of infection (and viceversa).

2.3   Input-Output Inoperability Model

The Input-Output Inoperability Model (IIM) [6] analyzes the interdependencies and cascading effects among interconnected infrastructures in the face of natural disasters or terrorist attacks.

Static Input-Output Inoperability Model. According to the economic equilibrium theory of Leontief [14], the static IIM model for h infrastructures/sectors is defined as

$$\delta x = A\delta x + \delta c, \tag{2}$$

where $\delta c \in \mathbb{R}^h$ denotes the reduction in the final demand denoted and is defined to be the difference between the as-planned and degraded final demands ($\delta c = c_0 - c_d$) where, this reduction in final demand consequently triggers a reduction in production denoted by $\delta x \in \mathbb{R}^h$, which is defined to be the difference between the as-planned and degraded productions ($\delta x = x_0 - x_d$). In order to move from a monetary value to a more abstract quantity modeling the *inoperability* of an infrastructure or sector, in [5] the following $h \times h$ transform matrix P is considered

$$P = (\text{diag}[x_0])^{-1}. \tag{3}$$

In this view, the inoperability of an infrastructure or sector, which represents its inability (expressed as a percentage) to operate correctly, is then obtained by applying the transformation matrix to the Eq. (2), thus obtaining the following equation

$$\underbrace{P\delta x}_{q} = \underbrace{PAP^{-1}}_{A^*}\underbrace{P\delta x}_{q} + \underbrace{P\delta c}_{c^*}, \tag{4}$$

where

$$q = (\text{diag}[x_0])^{-1}\delta x = P\delta x, \tag{5}$$

is the vector collecting the inoperability of each infrastructure or sectors,

$$A^* = (\text{diag}[x_0])^{-1} A (\text{diag}[x_0]) = PAP^{-1} \tag{6}$$

is the so-called *interdependency matrix*, and

$$c^* = (\text{diag}[x_0])^{-1}\delta c = P\delta c, \tag{7}$$

can be regarded as externally-caused inoperability due to a disruption. Assuming that the interdependency matrix A^* is Hurwitz stable (i.e., that it has eigenvalues with magnitude less than one), for a perturbation c^* the inoperability q can be calculated as follows

$$q = Sc^*, \tag{8}$$

where $S = (I - A^*)^{-1}$. Interestingly, assuming A^* is Hurwitz stable, the *operator norm* of S is smaller than one and thus S can be expressed in terms of the *Neumann Series* (e.g., see [27])

$$S = \sum_{k=0}^{\infty} (A^*)^k.$$

According to the above equation, S is the infinite sum of the terms A^{*k}, which model the k-th order effect of the interdependency (e.g., A_{ij}^* models the direct effect of i on j, while A_{ij}^{*2} is the indirect effect of i on j via all possible choices of a third infrastructure w). Therefore, S_{ij}^* models the long-term impact of a malfunction in sector j on sector i as a result of the domino effects linking them.

Dynamic Input-Output Inoperability Model. In [21], the static IIM has been extended in order to account for the dynamics of the inoperability propagation and recovery. Such an extension is given by

$$\delta \boldsymbol{x}(t) = A\delta \boldsymbol{x}(t) + \delta \boldsymbol{c} + B\delta \dot{\boldsymbol{x}}(t), \tag{9}$$

where the matrix $B \in \mathbb{R}^{h \times h}$ in Eq. (9), a square matrix of capital coefficients, shows the economy's readiness to invest in capital resources. Assuming B to be diagonal, in [21] the resiliency matrix $K \in \mathbb{R}^{h \times h}$ is defined as the $n \times n$ diagonal matrix such that $B = -K^{-1}$, i.e., such that $B_{ii} = -1/K_{ii}$ for all i. Based on such a definition, we have that Eq. (9) can equivalently be expressed as

$$\delta \dot{\boldsymbol{x}}(t) = K \left((A - I)\delta \boldsymbol{x}(t) + \delta \boldsymbol{c} \right), \tag{10}$$

Following the same path as in the static case, the matrix P defined in Eq. (3) can be applied to Eq. (10), leading to the dynamic IIM formulation, i.e.,

$$\dot{\boldsymbol{q}}(t) = K(A^* - I)\boldsymbol{q}(t) + K\boldsymbol{c}^*, \tag{11}$$

and it can be noted that, in case an equilibrium is reached we have that $\dot{\boldsymbol{q}}(t) = \boldsymbol{0}_h$, and the above equation reduces to Eq. (8).

Notice that, within the above model, it is possible to consider a perturbation $\boldsymbol{c}^*(t)$ that changes with time, thus obtaining a dynamics in the form

$$\dot{\boldsymbol{q}}(t) = K(A^* - I)\boldsymbol{q}(t) + K\boldsymbol{c}^*(t). \tag{12}$$

Tuning the Resilience Matrix K. In [15], a procedure to estimate the entries K_{ii} of the resilience matrix is developed. Specifically, in [15], K_{ii} is estimated as follows

$$K_{ii} = \frac{\ln \left(\frac{q_i(0)}{q_i(T_i)} \right)}{T_i S_{ii}}, \tag{13}$$

where $q_i(0)$ is the initial inoperability, T_i is the time at which the industry or sector i has recovered, $q_i(T_i)$ is the inoperability after the recovery phase has ended, and S_{ii} is the long-term effect of the inoperability of the i-th infrastructure or sector on itself, taking into account all the domino effects.

Mapping the Essential Workforce Unavailability into a Perturbation to D-IIM. In this paper, we focus on the effect of the unavailability of the essential workforce on the D-IIM model. To this end, there is a need to translate the epidemiological data into a perturbation $c^*(t)$ to be fed to the D-IIM model. Note that, since the focus is on the effect of the unavailability of the essential workforce, we set the i-th entry of $c^*(t)$ to zero, whenever the corresponding sector is not deemed essential as per the categorization adopted in a specific Decree of the President of the Council (DPCM) [17].

Conversely, for essential sectors, we set

$$c_i^*(t) = \beta_i \psi(t), \tag{14}$$

where β_i is a coefficient used to model the harm caused by the complete absence of essential workers while $\psi(t)$ is a parameter that shows the percentage of essential workers that are unavailable at a specific time instant. In order to define $\psi(t)$, let us consider the deaths $M_l(t)$ at time t of the individuals belonging to the working age classes, i.e.,

$$M_l(t) = \int_0^t \sum_{i \in \mathcal{J}} \alpha_i r_i(\tau) N_i d\tau, \tag{15}$$

where α_i is the death rate in the i-th class, $r_i(t)$ is the fraction of recovered individuals at time t, N_i is the population in the i-th class (hence $r_i(t)N_i$ is the number of recovered individuals at time t and, recalling that within the SIR model the recovered individuals also include deaths, $\alpha_i r_i(t)N_i$ are the deaths in the i-th population class at time t), and $\mathcal{J} \subseteq \{1, \ldots n\}$ is the subset of the classes that correspond to individuals in the working age range. Moreover, let us consider the total number of infected for the classes in $\mathcal{J}$, i.e.,

$$I_l(t) = \sum_{i \in \mathcal{J}} i_i(t) N_i. \tag{16}$$

Based on the above quantities, we define

$$\phi(t) = M_l(t) + I_l(t); \tag{17}$$

in other words, $\phi(t)$ amounts to the overall amount of individuals in the working age range that are either infected or dead at time t. Then, we define

$$\Psi(t) = \xi \eta \phi(t), \tag{18}$$

where ξ denotes the employment rate and η is the percentage of essential workers (hence $\xi\eta$ is the fraction of essential workers); $\Psi(t)$ essentially amounts to the number of essential workers that are unavailable at time t. Finally, in order to normalize $\Psi(t)$, we consider

$$\psi(t) = \frac{\Psi(t)}{\sum_{i \in \mathcal{J}} N_i} \in [0, 1], \tag{19}$$

where $\sum_{i \in \mathcal{J}} N_i$ is the number of individuals in the working age range.

3   Case Study

In this section, we consider a realistic case study set in Italy in 2020, and we rely on epidemiological data for the COVID-19 outbreak. Notice that, wherever possible, real epidemiological and economic data has been used. However, given the difficulty to exactly assess some of the parameters, and given the limited scope of this study, we reiterate that the results provided here are intended as a way to show the potential of our framework, rather than as a tool to actually draw conclusions on the real situation in Italy for the simulated time span.

Epidemiological Data. In this case study, we consider the age classes reported in Table 1 (the table also reports the death rates as of April 2012, which, for simplicity, we consider as constant throughout all the simulations).

Table 1. Population in the different age classes (Source: [8]) and Covid-19 death rates as of April 2021 (Source: [1]).

Age Class	Population	Death
00–04	2264538	0.10%
05–09	2627956	0.10%
10–14	2835060	0.10%
15–19	2871056	0.10%
20–24	2955888	0.10%
25–29	3128494	0.10%
30–34	3282441	0.14%
35–39	3572191	0.14%
40–44	4187464	0.26%
45–49	4749765	0.26%
50–54	4876704	0.57%
55–59	4537491	0.57%
60–64	3893350	2.73%
65–69	3471014	2.73%
70+	10388076	14.80%

Specifically, we consider the COVID-19 pandemic over the year 2020, and we assume that, as of January 1st, 2020, only a small fraction (i.e., 0.01%) of the age group in the 35–39 year group is initially infected. Notice that, in the following, time is expressed in days. Regarding the parameters, we follow the scenario outlined in [20], and we set $\gamma_i = 15$ days for all population classes.

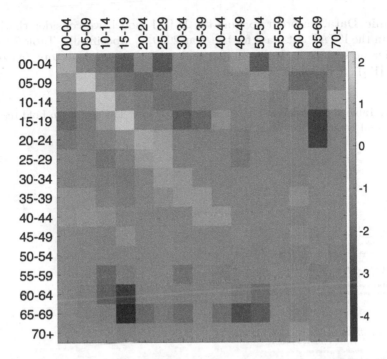

Fig. 1. Elements of the matrix $\mathcal{K}$ of physical contacts among age classes in Italy. For the sake of readability, the logarithms of the coefficients $\mathcal{K}_{ii}$ are reported. (Source: [18]).

Let us now discuss a way to tune the $\mathcal{B}$ matrix in terms of a *contact matrix* $\mathcal{K}$, whose entries $\mathcal{K}_{ij}$ are proportional to the probability of encounter between the i-th and j-th population class. In particular, following the approach in [20], we define the transmission matrix $\mathcal{B}$ as

$$\mathcal{B} = \lambda \frac{\mathcal{K}}{\|\mathcal{K}\|}, \tag{20}$$

where $\lambda = 3$ is the probability that a contact between two individuals results in an infection.

Figure 1 shows a heatmap describing the structure of the matrix $\mathcal{K}$ considered in [20], which is based on data developed in [18].

Notably, the original strain of the COVID-19 virus, which emerged at the end of 2019, was estimated to have a basic reproduction rate of about $\lambda = 3.0$-3.3; however, this value has significantly increased with the new variants; for instance, in [4], the value was estimated to be $\lambda = 18.6$. In order to model the increase in the basic reproduction rate of the virus, in this case study we assume λ is time-varying (hence $\mathcal{B}$ is also varying) and grows linearly from $\lambda(0) = 3$ to $\lambda(365) = 18.6$.

Finally, we have that the set $\mathcal{J}$ containing the age classes in the working age range spans from the 15–19 to the 60–64 age classes.

Economic Data. In order to tune the D-IIM model, we consider the input-output in the ISTAT database for the year 2020 [9]. Specifically, Table 2 reports the different sectors in Italy; in particular, non-essential sectors (as of the DPCM [17]) are highlighted in bold.

Table 2. Table of the different Italian economic sectors. The sectors in bold represent non-essential branches according to the DPCM [17].

N.° sectors	Name sectors
Sect. 1	Plant and animal production, hunting and related services
Sect. 2	Forestry and use of forest areas
Sect. 3	Fishing and aquaculture
Sect. 4	Mining activity
Sect. 5	Food, beverage and tobacco industries
Sect. 6	Textile industries, manufacture of clothing and leather items and the like
Sect. 7	Manufacture of wood and of products of wood and cork, except furniture; manufacture of articles in straw and plaiting materials
Sect. 8	Manufacture of paper and paper products
Sect. 9	Printing and reproduction on recorded media
Sect. 10	Manufacture of coke and petroleum refining products
Sect. 11	Manufacture of chemicals
Sect. 12	Manufacture of basic pharmaceutical products and pharmaceutical preparations
Sect. 13	Manufacture of rubber and plastic products
Sect. 14	**Manufacture of other non-metallic mineral processing products**
Sect. 15	**Metallurgical activities**
Sect. 16	**Manufacture of metal products, except machinery and equipment**
Sect. 17	**Manufacture of computer and electronic and optical products**
Sect. 18	Manufacture of electrical equipment
Sect. 19	Manufacture of machinery and equipment n.e.c.
Sect. 20	Manufacture of motor vehicles, trailers and semi-trailers
Sect. 21	Manufacture of other means of transport
Sect. 22	**Manufacture of furniture; other manufacturing industries**
Sect. 23	Repair and installation of machinery and equipment
Sect. 24	Supply of electricity, gas, steam and air conditioning
Sect. 25	Collection, treatment and supply of water
Sect. 26	Management of sewer networks; waste collection, treatment and disposal activities; recovery of materials; remediation activities and other waste management services
Sect. 27	Buildings
Sect. 28	Wholesale and retail trade and repair of motor vehicles and motorcycles
Sect. 29	Wholesale trade, excluding that of motor vehicles and motorcycles
Sect. 30	Retail trade, except of motor vehicles and motorcycles
Sect. 31	Land transport and transport via pipelines
Sect. 32	Sea and water transport
Sect. 33	Airplane transport
Sect. 34	Warehousing and transport support activities
Sect. 35	Postal services and courier business
Sect. 36	Accommodation services; catering service activities
Sect. 37	Editorial activities
Sect. 38	**Motion picture, video and television program production, music and sound recording activities; programming and broadcasting activities**
Sect. 39	Telecommunications
Sect. 40	Computer programming, consultancy and related activities; information services activities
Sect. 41	Provision of financial services (excluding insurance and pension funds)
Sect. 42	Insurance, reinsurance and pension funds, excluding compulsory social insurance
Sect. 43	Activities auxiliary to financial services and insurance activities
Sect. 44	Real estate activities
Sect. 45	Legal and accounting activities; head office activities; management consulting
Sect. 46	Activities of architecture and engineering firms; technical testing and analysis
Sect. 47	Scientific research and development
Sect. 48	**Advertising and market research**
Sect. 49	Other professional, scientific and technical activities; veterinary services
Sect. 50	**Rental and leasing activities**
Sect. 51	**Research, selection, supply of personnel**
Sect. 52	**Travel agency service activities, tour operators and booking services and related activities**
Sect. 53	Investigation and surveillance services; services for buildings and landscape; administrative and support activities for office functions and other business support services
Sect. 54	Public administration and defense; compulsory social insurance
Sect. 55	Instruction
Sect. 56	Health services activities
Sect. 57	Social care
Sect. 58	**Creative, artistic and entertainment activities; activities of libraries, archives, museums and other cultural activities; activities relating to betting and gambling houses**
Sect. 59	Sports, entertainment and leisure activities
Sect. 60	Activities of membership organizations
Sect. 61	Repair of computers and personal and household goods
Sect. 62	**Other personal service activities**
Sect. 63	Activities of families and cohabitation as employers for domestic staff; production of undifferentiated goods and services for own use by families and partnerships

Moreover, the heatmap in Fig. 2 shows the entries for the resulting A^* matrix for the considered sectors.

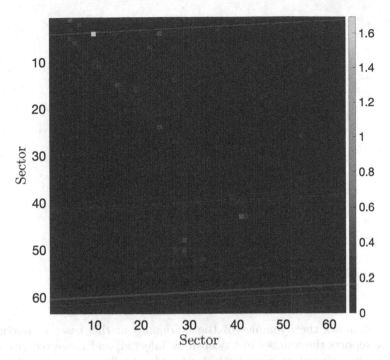

Fig. 2. Elements of the matrix A^* for the different sectors in Italy as of 2020 (Source: [9]).

Let us now discuss our choice of the resilience matrix K. Notice that we follow the approach in Eq. (13) and, for simplicity, we assume the entries K_{ii} all have the same value. In particular, we set $q_i(0) = 1$ (i.e., fully operable infrastructures) and $q_i(T_i) = 0.01$ (i.e., almost completely operative) and we assume that the time required T_i amounts to 15 days. Notably, instead of considering S_{ii} in Eq. (13), we take the average $\frac{1}{n}\sum_{i=1}^n S_{ii}$, thus obtaining $K_{ii} = 0.34$ for all i.

Regarding the employment rates, based on data provided by the Italian National Statistics Institute (ISTAT) [7,8], we set the employment rate to $\xi = 0.6563$ and the percentage of essential workers to $\eta = 0.8960$. Finally, for the sake of simplicity, we set the coefficients β_i all to the same value; in this case study, we assume $\beta_i = 0.75$.

3.1 Scenario #1: No Intervention

Let us consider a scenario where no containment measures such as lockdowns, restricting access to stores, or requiring the use of PPEs, are implemented, i.e., we assume $E = 0$ for the entire simulation time span.

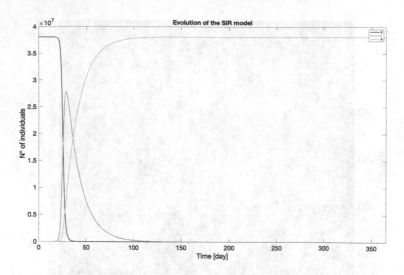

Fig. 3. SIR model results in the absence of lockdown.

Figure 3 shows the dynamics of the epidemics in this case; in particular, the figure reports the number of susceptible, infected, and recovered (we recall that this compartment includes both dead and actually recovered individuals) individuals belonging to the working age group (i.e., 15-64 years). Analyzing Fig. 3, we observe that the number of infected individuals begins growing with quite a steep trend, and reaches a peak around the 28-th day; after the peak, the curve begins to decrease with a slightly slower trend, until zero is reached.

Let us now discuss the repercussions of the above epidemiological scenario on the availability of essential workforce, and the cascading effects on the nation's infrastructures due to such an unavailability.

Figure 4 shows the inoperability of each sector (see Table 2 for the definition of the different sectors) as a result of the inoperability of the essential workforce. Notably, the curves exhibit a pattern that closely follows the epidemiological trend discussed above. It is evident, however, that the peak reaches different inoperability values depending on the sector under consideration. In particular, the most affected sectors are sectors n. 4 (Mining activity), 43 (Activities auxiliary to financial services and insurance activities), 46 (Activities of architecture and engineering firms; technical testing and analysis), and 50 (Rental and leasing activities, which is deemed not essential). Moreover, other sectors such as n. 5 (Food, beverage and tobacco industries) or n. 39 (Telecommunications) experience a significant degradation of operativeness, up to about 50%. Interestingly, the time required to reach the peak is essentially the same for each sector, despite the fact that the peak reached varies, as previously mentioned.

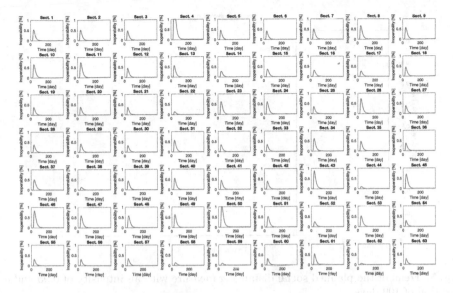

Fig. 4. Percentage of inoperability in each sector in the absence of lockdown.

3.2   Scenario #2: Intense Lockdown at the Beginning

Let us now consider a modified scenario and let us assume that, after an initial delay of 12 days where no intervention is put in place, an intense lockdown is enforced for 100 days (i.e., for $t \in [12, 120]$ we assume $E_{ij}(t) = 0.95$ for all i, j); Fig. 5 summarizes this intervention pattern. As a result of the intervention, Fig. 6 shows the modified epidemiological situation, while Fig. 7 reports the consequences on the different sectors of the unavailability of the essential workforce. Interstingly, according to Fig. 6 it can be noted that the lockdown has the only effect to delay the peak of infections. Similarly, as shown in Fig. 7, the inoperability peak, although delayed, is comparable with the uncontrolled case.

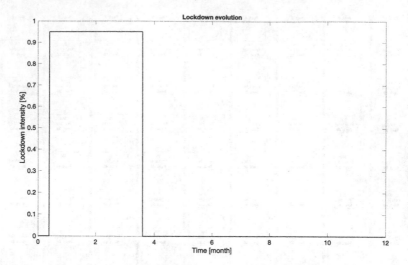

Fig. 5. Trend of the planned social distancing measure with an intensity of 0.95 and a duration of 100 days.

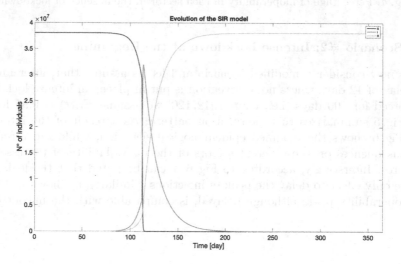

Fig. 6. SIR model results for in case of an initial intense lockdown.

3.3   Scenario #3: Progressive Lockdown

Let us now consider a scenario where a strict lockdown (with a peak value of $E_{ij}(t) = 0.98$) is gradually enforced, and subsequently gradually lifted. The pattern for the coefficients $E_{ij}(t)$ is reported in Fig. 8. Figures 9 and 10 show, respectively, the epidemiological situation and the corresponding inoperability due to the unavailability of the essential workforce. In particular, according to Figs. 9, the infection peak is both delayed and flattened; consequently, the effect

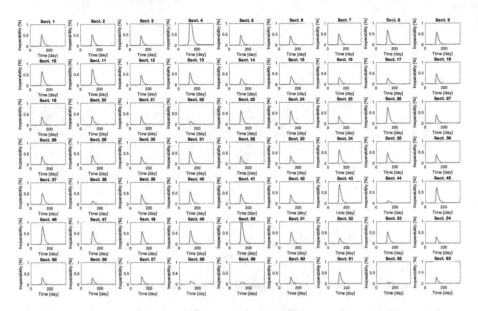

Fig. 7. Percentage of inoperability in case of an initial intense lockdown.

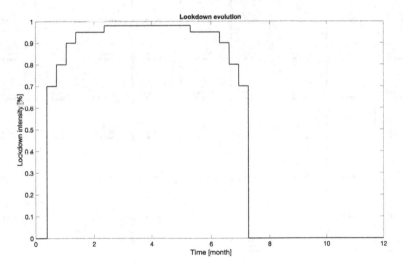

Fig. 8. Trend of the planned social distancing measure with symmetrical structure and maximum intensity reached equal to 98%.

of the lack of the essential workforce is delayed and reduced. Interestingly, we observe that sector n. 4 (Mining activity) still exhibits a large inoperability peak.

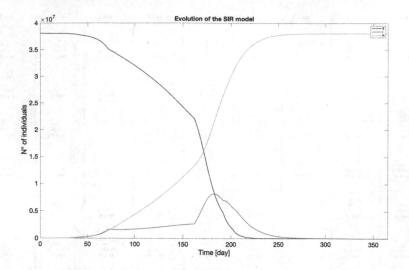

Fig. 9. SIR model results following the lockdown shown in Fig. 8.

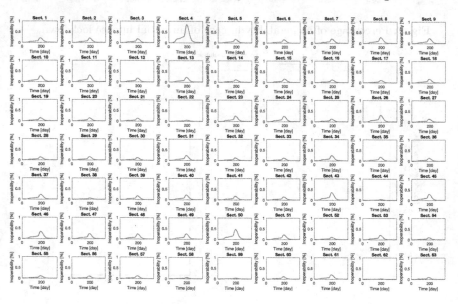

Fig. 10. Percentage of inoperability following the lockdown shown in Fig. 8.

4   Conclusions and Future Work

In this paper, we develop a framework to quantify the effect of the unavailability of the essential workforce of a nation on the infrastructures/sectors. In particular, we consider a compartmental SIR model with several age classes and with the possibility to enforce lockdown measures. Then, we feed the unavailable essential workforce (e.g., due to infection and/or deaths) to a D-IIM model, in order to assess the impact in terms of inoperability of the different sectors. In order to show the potential of the approach, the study is complemented by a realistic case study set in Italy, using real epidemiological and economic data.

Future works will be aimed to overcome some of the limitations of the approach. In particular, we will consider more realistic epidemiological models (e.g., SEIR model), we will account for dynamically changing populations (e.g., modeling phenomena such as births, hirings and retirements, which have been overlooked in this proof-of-concept study), and we will investigate the role of vaccination plans in the reduction of the infection peak. Moreover, we will investigate other dimensions that couple the epidemiological and economic models: for instance, we will quantify how lockdowns directly impact the production of goods and services.

References

1. RR Assessment: Coronavirus disease 2019 (Covid-19) in the EU/EEA and the UK– ninth update. European Centre for Disease Prevention and Control: Stockholm (2020)
2. Correia, S., Luck, S., Verner, E., et al.: Fight the pandemic, save the economy: lessons from the 1918 flu. Federal Reserve Bank of New York 5 (2020)
3. Cottafava, D., Gastaldo, M., Quatraro, F., Santhiá, C.: Modeling economic losses and greenhouse gas emissions reduction during the Covid-19 pandemic: past, present, and future scenarios for Italy. Econ. Model. **110**, 105807 (2022)
4. Esterman, A.: What to expect from a third Omicron wave in Australia (2023). https://www1.racgp.org.au/newsgp/clinical/what-to-expect-from-a-third-omicron-wave-in-austra. Accessed 2 June 2023
5. Haimes, Y.Y., Horowitz, B.M., Lambert, J.H., Santos, J.R., Lian, C., Crowther, K.G.: Inoperability input-output model for interdependent infrastructure sectors. I: theory and methodology. J. Infrastruct. Syst. **11**(2), 67–79 (2005)
6. Haimes, Y.Y., Jiang, P.: Leontief-based model of risk in complex interconnected infrastructures. J. Infrastruct. Syst. **7**(1), 1–12 (2001)
7. ISTAT: Regular and irregular employment by industry and population (2023). (in Italian). http://dati.istat.it/Index.aspx?DataSetCode=DCCN_OCCNSEC2010. Accessed 2 June 2023
8. ISTAT: Resident population in Italy on 1st January: By age group (2023). http://dati.istat.it/Index.aspx?DataSetCode=DCIS_POPRES1#. Accessed 2 June 2023
9. ISTAT: The Input-Output Table System - Years 2015–2018 (2023). (in Italian). https://www.istat.it/it/archivio/264985. Accessed 2 June 2023
10. Jallow, H., Renukappa, S., Suresh, S.: The impact of Covid-19 outbreak on united kingdom infrastructure sector. Smart Sustain. Built Environ. **10**(4), 581–593 (2021)
11. Jin, J., Zhou, H.: A demand-side inoperability input-output model for strategic risk management: insight from the Covid-19 outbreak in Shanghai, China. Sustainability **15**(5), 4003 (2023)
12. Katina, P.F., Pinto, C.A., Bradley, J.M., Hester, P.T.: Interdependency-induced risk with applications to healthcare. Int. J. Crit. Infrastruct. Prot. **7**(1), 12–26 (2014)

13. Kermack, W.O., McKendrick, A.G.: A contribution to the mathematical theory of epidemics. Proc. R. Soc. Lond. Series A, Containing Papers of a Mathematical and Physical Character **115**(772), 700–721 (1927)
14. Leontief, W.: Input-Output Economics. Oxford University Press, Oxford (1986)
15. Lian, C., Haimes, Y.Y.: Managing the risk of terrorism to interdependent infrastructure systems through the dynamic inoperability input-output model. Syst. Eng. **9**(3), 241–258 (2006)
16. Meltzer, M.I., Cox, N.J., Fukuda, K.: The economic impact of pandemic influenza in the United States: priorities for intervention. Emerg. Infect. Dis. **5**(5), 659 (1999)
17. Italian Government Presidency of the Council of Ministers: Decree of the president of the council of ministers (DPCM) (2020)
18. Mossong, J., et al.: Social contacts and mixing patterns relevant to the spread of infectious diseases. PLoS Med. **5**(3), e74 (2008)
19. Nicola, M., et al.: The socio-economic implications of the coronavirus pandemic (Covid-19): a review. Int. J. Surg. **78**, 185–193 (2020)
20. Oliva, G., Schlueter, M., Munetomo, M., Scala, A.: Dynamical intervention planning against Covid-19-like epidemics. PLoS ONE **17**(6), e0269830 (2022)
21. Ramos Carvajal, M.d.C., Blanc Díaz, M., et al.: The foundations of dynamic input-output revisited:¿ does dynamic input-output belong to growth theory? Documentos de trabajo (Universidad de Oviedo. Facultad de Ciencias Económicas) (2002)
22. Santos, J., Pagsuyoin, S.: The impact of "flatten the curve" on interdependent economic sectors. In: Linkov, I., Keenan, J.M., Trump, B.D. (eds.) COVID-19: Systemic Risk and Resilience. RSD, pp. 163–180. Springer, Cham (2021). https://doi.org/10.1007/978-3-030-71587-8_10
23. Santos, J.R., et al.: Uncertainty analysis of business interruption losses in the Philippines due to the Covid-19 pandemic. Economies **10**(8), 202 (2022)
24. Soltanisehat, L., Barker, K., González, A.D.: Multiregional, multi-industry impacts of fairness on pandemic policies. Risk Anal. (2023)
25. Tuncer, N., Le, T.: Effect of air travel on the spread of an avian influenza pandemic to the united states. Int. J. Crit. Infrastruct. Prot. **7**(1), 27–47 (2014)
26. Walmsley, T., et al.: Macroeconomic consequences of the Covid-19 pandemic. Econ. Model. **120**, 106147 (2023)
27. Watson, G.N.: A Treatise on the Theory of Bessel Functions, vol. 3. The University Press (1922)
28. Weiss, H.H.: The sir model and the foundations of public health. Materials matematics 0001–17 (2013)
29. Yu, K.D.S., Aviso, K.B., Santos, J.R., Tan, R.R.: The economic impact of lockdowns: a persistent inoperability input-output approach. Economies **8**(4), 109 (2020)

Ethics and the Threat to Infrastructure

Dieter Budde[✉], Marina Alonso-Villota[iD], and Stefan Pickl[iD]

Universität der Bundeswehr München, 85577 Neubiberg, Germany
budde.dieter.dr@t-online.de

Abstract. The study discusses the essential aspects of ethics and the threat to infrastructure. The threat and thus possible destruction of infrastructure can be made by different causers, such as friendly forces actors, internationally organized actors, non-state actors, state-backed actors, and state-military actors, as well as means and methods. Depending on the means available to the causers, a threat or destruction can be by mechanical, kinetic, chemical, biological, nuclear, hybrid, data-based, or AI-based. This is an intrusion into the quality of life or existence of people or societies. It affects material resources but can also result in the death of people. The actions of causers can be evaluated ethically. Three main theories are available for this purpose within the framework of ethics: virtue ethics, deontological ethics, and consequentialist/utilitarian ethics. The study deals with the application of these theories to moral action and shows the conditions of the possibilities to ethically evaluate the destruction of infrastructure. In doing so it becomes clear that consequentialist/utilitarian ethics can be a generally accepted way of evaluating moral action. Rule utilitarianism offers itself. Thus, it provides a framework for action and the possibility of an operationalized comparison and shows the conditions of the possibilities of a framework. Further essential criteria of evaluation are human dignity, human rights, double effect, the doctrine of war, and collateral damage. The study also makes clear that actors can face an aporia. The agent or non-agent must bear responsibility for his actions, and he may become culpable. He must give account of his own free and autonomous action or non-action and its consequences before an authority. It is shown that attacking perpetrators of infrastructure destruction usually act morally reprehensible, while defending perpetrators usually, but not always, act morally acceptable. This is exemplified by a case study/dilemma situation.

Keywords: Ethic · Morality · Deontology · Consequentialism · Utilitarianism · Human rights · Double Effect · Responsibility · Infrastructure

1 Introduction

This study considers the relationship between ethics and morality with respect to threats to and destruction of critical infrastructure. It does not consider the impact on society and the human suffering that destruction of infrastructure or critical infra-structure causes. Critical infrastructures are facilities with important significance for the state community and the people. They form the basis for the functioning of a society. They include, for

S. Pickl et al. (Eds.): CRITIS 2023, LNCS 14599, pp. 41–61, 2024.
https://doi.org/10.1007/978-3-031-62139-0_3

example, energy and water supply, transport, medical care, and data security. Ensuring the protection of critical infrastructures is a core task of government and corporate security. Their failure or impairment, threat, breakdown, or destruction leads to lasting supply shortages, significant disruptions to public safety, the functioning of society or parts of it, or other dramatic consequences. In this article, the threat to infrastructure is understood as the possibility of actors using various methods and procedures to influence and damage critical infrastructure.

Threats to and destruction of infrastructure can come from a variety of actors. They can be criminals, terrorists, partisans, or armed forces. They are individual perpetrators, groups, or organizations. They may act individually or together in time and/or space to threaten or destroy infrastructure. Actions often involve primary and secondary/collateral damage.

Threats can occur through a variety of means, including mechanical (through tools), kinetic (through weapon systems), chemical (through chemical agents), biological (through biological agents), nuclear (through nuclear agents), data-based (through hackers), or AI-based (through manipulation) (see Fig. 1). Destruction to infrastructure can occur by all the means separately or together. In this regard, the greatest structural destruction occurs through the attack of military forces, regardless of the means used.

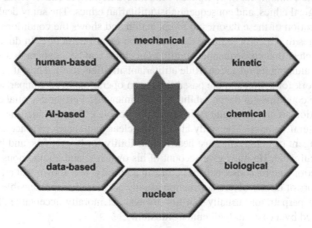

Fig. 1. Variety of means that can threat infrastructures

Among these, the greatest structural destruction occurs through attack by military forces, regardless of the means used. A threat can be made by internal and external measures, i.e., by societal, police or military means, structures, or organizations. This means the defense against actors up to the defense against a war of aggression. However, this also means the possibility of destroying one's own infrastructure as part of a defensive war.

Infrastructure includes fixed and permanent facilities, installations, and buildings. The technical, social, and material infrastructure is an essential and necessary component of human and social life. It enables the existence and well-being of societies at different stages of development. It thus covers a basic human need for life and survival. The threat or destruction of infrastructure is therefore an attack on society and the individual. Infrastructure has many different forms. It includes facilities, transportation systems, networks, utilities, and buildings. They form a system of material foundations of a society. The destruction of parts of the infrastructure is a disruption of the system and thus a systemic attack on society and individuals. Thus, the EU states, "critical infrastructure' means an asset, a facility, equipment, a network or a system, or a part of an asset, a facility, equipment, a network, or a system, which is necessary for the provision of an essential service" [1].

Another example of a definition is: "Critical infrastructures (CRITIS) are organizations and facilities of major importance for society whose failure or impairment would cause a sustained shortage of supplies, significant disruptions to public order, safety and security or other dramatic consequences" [2].

The European Parliament defines 11 areas as critical infrastructure: "energy, transport, banking, financial market infrastructure, digital infrastructure, drinking water, wastewater, food (including production, processing and delivery), healthcare, public administration and space" [3].

This critical infrastructure can be threatened or destroyed by different actors, means and methods. In addition to the conventional methods used in a war or armed conflict, methods of cyber war, artificial intelligence (AI), and the use of hybrid threats pose a challenge today. The most pressing question is how to prevent these threats or destructions. Since the coexistence of states, societies and people also requires ethical and moral aspects, it is necessary to ask how an action can be evaluated regarding this. In the following, it will be examined by which criteria and possibilities an action of this kind can be evaluated.

For example, Nitul Dutta states regarding "ethics" about cybersecurity: "The simple rule of ethics with respect to security. Do not do something wrong in a cyber-world where others have to pay in everyday life". There are no general rules specifying ethics; however, it is a moral responsibility of a user not to use of any malicious software, do cyberbullying, out hear the communication line (passive eavesdropper), use someone else's password for your benefit, and follow the copyright restriction while downloading movies, games, and software (ad-here to license) [4].

Due to current events and the increasing threat, also to the critical infrastructure, it seems necessary to develop a system for the assessment of corresponding actions. The reference to "Do not do something wrong in a cyberworld where others have to pay in everyday life" gives a clue to the possible destruction of infrastructure by cyber but is not sufficient to be operationalized. To this end, possibilities are identified below. To do this, it is necessary to be clear about the basic framework of ethics and morality. Furthermore, it is necessary to examine the possibility offered by ethical theories.

2 Ethics and Morals

Ethics and morality are often used synonymously in social discourse. Thus, the close connection between theory and practice in the context of human action and its evaluation becomes manifest. In the context of this study, both aspects are dealt with, and their interactions are considered. If threat and destruction are to be analyzed from an ethical point of view, ethics and morality must first be distinguished (see Fig. 2).

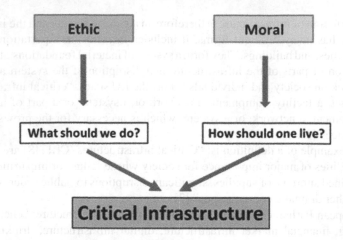

Fig. 2. Difference between ethics and moral

Ethics is the science, the practical philosophy, of specific and concrete questions about the actions and behavior of people and societies. It enables answers to good or bad, right, or wrong, virtuous, or vicious, acceptable, and unacceptable actions. It seeks answers to the question: what should we do? It also examines whether a particular canon of norms and precepts, moral philosophical teaching or positions have universal or relative significance. Historical, cultural, differentiated and division of labor developments have led to different ethics and fields of application, such as medical ethics, bioethics, or business ethics. If the contents of an ethic are applied in practical life and action, one speaks of morality and moral action.

Morality refers to all the norms and ideals of good and correct behavior recognized by a person or a society as right and important. These behavioral norms are also called morals (lat. mores). Moral rules and moral norms offer the possibility to judge how one should live. They also offer the possibility to judge one's own and others' behavior. Morality is therefore an action-effective and internalized basic understanding. This basic understanding also includes respect for self-determination and the attribution of rights, such as human rights or duties, as well as respect for universalistic, egalitarian, and inalienable human dignity. However, it is important to keep in mind that due to the historical and cultural diversity of people and societies, conceptions of morality vary.

The distinction between ethics and morality has significant influence on the evaluation of actions related to threats and destruction of critical infrastructure. Other elements that are significant in this context are human rights and human dignity. The destruction of critical infrastructure threatens the human rights and human dignity of those affected.

3   Human Rights and Human Dignity

Fundamental criteria for the ethical evaluation of threats to and destruction of infrastructure, especially critical infrastructure, are human rights and human dignity, which are thereby violated. This is especially true in the context of governmental action when it results in the destruction of critical infrastructure.

Human rights are fundamental rights. They are intended to protect human dignity and enable people to live together in a society and a state in freedom and autonomy. Human rights are superpositive rights that can be found in the various human rights declarations.

The UN Charter contains human rights provisions as a program for future action, and it provides the framework that is still filled out today by universal and regional human rights conventions. After the general reference to rights in Article 1, a list of human rights follows in Articles 2–4:

"Everyone is entitled to all the rights and freedoms set forth in this Declaration, without distinction of any kind, such as race, color, sex, language, religion, political or other opinion, national or social origin, property, birth or other status. [...] Everyone has the right to life, liberty, and security of person" [5].

The UN Charter refers to human rights in other places after the preamble.

The "International Covenant on Civil and Political Rights" (1966/1976) contains important steps towards the implementation and consolidation of human rights. It contains an extensive catalog of human rights, such as the prohibition of discrimination, the right to life, the prohibition of torture and cruel, inhuman, or degrading treatment or punishment, the right to personal freedom and security, and the right to freedom of movement (see Institute for Human Rights).

Human rights are universal. Their implementation is not equally respected or applied everywhere. The realization of human rights also depends on cultural and historical conditions.

Government action is based on the respective historical conditions and forms. It is the task of governments to implement the law and the internationally agreed human rights in their societies, and to ensure their observance. This also includes safeguarding the living conditions of the population. Critical infrastructure is an essential element of this. On a global scale, there are two fundamental opposing approaches to society: the one in which the individual is the basis of society and takes precedence over it, and the one in which society takes precedence and the individual must align himself with it. This has an impact on the formulation of civil and fundamental rights and thus also on the conception of human rights. The unequal implementation of human rights has an influence on the consciousness of people socialized in different cultures. Human rights are based on human dignity.

The concept of human dignity has a long tradition in different cultures. Its conceptual content has also developed differently over time. The concept of human dignity is traditionally used in two ways: as a characteristic or as a mandate. As an essential characteristic, it is the innate quality of the human being. As a creative mandate, it is the ethical challenge to develop his person, society, and the relationship of his person to society.

Thus, Kant distinguishes that which has a price and that which has a dignity: "In the realm of ends everything has either a price or a dignity. What has a price can also be replaced by something else, as an equivalent; what, on the other hand, is above all price, consequently, does not confer an equivalent, has a dignity" [6].

Therefore, dignity is independent of external determinations. This non-respect of dignity by agents is a moral transgression. In addition to the autonomy of dignity, there is the possibility of its violation in the reality of action.

It should be emphasized, however, that there are different conceptions of human dignity. In one, human dignity is understood as always being possessed by the human being and therefore independent of recognition by others. In the other, human dignity is understood as something that can be damaged and violated. The possession of human dignity is independent of recognition "by others" and cannot be taken away or diminished by them.

4 Ethical Theories

Four main ethical theories can be used to evaluate actions in the context of critical infrastructure destruction: deontological ethics, virtue ethics, consequentialist ethics, and utilitarianism (see Fig. 3).

Essential prerequisites for morality, its cognition and its implementation are reason, intellect, will, and freedom. It is about principles and norms as well as reasons and consequences of acting and the acceptance of acting in a social context. The relationship between reason, understanding, and will is important for the evaluation of an action as moral. Moral action requires that what is recognized as right by reason through the rational faculty is converted into action by the act of the will, taking into account the circumstances and the framework conditions.

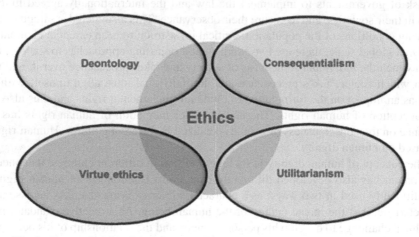

Fig. 3. Four main ethical theories to evaluate actions against critical infrastructures

Deontological ethics judges an action based on a principle. This principle can be either an objective standard based on reason, a commandment of God, or a law of nature. According to Kant, this principle is based on the autonomy of man, his moral self-legislation resulting from pure reason. This principle must be universalized and thus becomes a maxim, as formulated by Kant in the categorical imperative. Kant's categorical imperative can be used as an orientation rule to check whether an action can be universally thought of as a general law without contradiction and must therefore be observed. In its basic formula, this reads, "act only according to that maxim by which you can at the same time will that it become a general law" [7]. Moral action takes place in a legal system. "Law, then, is the epitome of the conditions under which the arbitrariness of the one can be united with the arbitrariness of the other according to the general law of freedom" [8]. Thus, human dignity and human rights can be translated into action in the recognition of the equality of human beings.

Virtue ethics comprises an internalized moral basic attitude of the actor. It determines attitudes and behavior, as well as attitudes and habits, which cause to act according to certain principles of the right. It is about character traits or attitude of the actor, which are manifested in his actions. It is based on catalogs of virtues that have changed throughout history.

Virtue ethics can be in two fundamentally different systems. One of the systems follows the Aristotelian approach, the other the Kantian approach. The Aristotelian approach sees the ethical virtues as grounded in the nature of human beings, in which individuals strive for the right middle ground between their affects, strivings of will, and rational insight. Thus, Aristotle notes, "virtue is therefore a habitus of choosing, which holds the middle measured according to us, and is determined by reason, and in such a way as a wise man is wont to determine it" [9]. The Kantian approach sees virtues not in man's nature, but in his reason-based adherence to maxims and will in deference to the moral law and overcoming his natural inclinations.

The virtue ethics as they were developed by Plato and Aristotle were principally developed and differentiated in the course of history. Well-known representatives of virtue ethics today are G. E. M. Anscombe and MacIntyre. MacIntyre defines: "A virtue is an acquired human quality the possession and exercise of which tends to enable us to achieve those goods which are internal to practices and the lack of which effectively prevents us from achieving any such goods" [10]. Trait, disposition and thus around character are to be acquired and developed by man in terms of virtue.

Consequentialist ethics determine the morality of an action based on the consequences. Not the intention of the action, but the practical effects of an action, its consequences, are the criterion. The realization of good consequences of action is the goal of the action. Good consequences can be achieved in several ways. These are either the increase of positive or the avoidance of negative consequences. The actor is not only responsible for the consequences, but also for the process of his considerations and the alternatives.

Utilitarianism is a form of consequentialism. The main theories are action utilitarianism, rule utilitarianism, and negative utilitarianism. Action utilitarianism evaluates the respective consequences of a single action for the greatest possible benefit. In rule utilitarianism, it is the reference to a rule, such as the preservation of human rights. In negative utilitarianism, the criterion of evaluation becomes not the maximization of utility but the reduction of suffering, such as injury or death to non-combatants or innocents. The moral value of an action is judged by its consequences. Utility considerations of consequences determine the morality of an action.

This is Mill's view: "The great majority of good actions are intended, not for the benefit of the world, but for that of individuals, of which the good of the world is made up; and the thoughts of the most virtuous man need not on these occasions travel beyond the particular persons concerned, except so far as is necessary to assure himself that in benefiting them he is not violating the rights - that is, the legitimate and authorized expectations - of any one else" [11].

Sidgwick emphasizes that utilitarianism is based on the foundation and rules of an existing society: "He must start, speaking broadly, with the existing social order, and the existing morality as a part of that order and in deciding the question whether any divergence from this code is to be recommended, must consider chiefly the immediate consequences of such divergence, upon a society in which such a code is conceived generally to subsist" [12].

Hare understands rule utilitarianism as follows: "This is the doctrine, [...], which says that we ought to inculcate and foster in ourselves and others, and in our actions cleave to, general principles whose cultivation is for the greatest good" [13]. These rules must apply universally. From an action recognized as right also follows the obligation to act accordingly. Rules and thus rule utilitarianism form for him a central role for moral action. Thus, rule utilitarianism forms a theoretic bridge between utilitarianism and deontological ethics. The dual justification of action, rules, and consequences can lead to a rule-following leading to unintended consequences or to the desired positive consequences requiring the breaking of rules. This problem is intrinsic and theoretically unsolvable.

The question arises as to which of the ethical theories can be applied regarding the destruction of critical infrastructure. Since destruction of critical infrastructure can also be caused by war and the associated collateral damage, these must first be examined.

5   Just War and Collateral Damage

The doctrine of just war has a long tradition in which it has been constantly modified and refined. The classical doctrine of just war permitted not only defensive war, but also offensive war. Today's proponents of the doctrine of just war only allow defensive warfare and humanitarian interventions under strict conditions to be considered legitimate.

Human dignity and human rights may be defended: "There are times when waging war is not only morally permitted, but morally necessary, as a response to calamitous acts of violence, hatred, and injustice" [14]. Should be noted: "Just war" is intended to contain means, arbitrariness to war, and the atrocities of war. It allows warfare under limiting conditions. Core elements are *ius ad bellum* and *ius in bello*, which are supposed to ensure the immunity of non-combatants and proportionality. However, there remains a need for clarification: It does not provide normative guidance for solving practical problems. Furthermore, it does not define "immunity", "non-combatants", and "proportionality". Nor does it indicate an ethical relation for the ratio of collateral damage to positive consequences.

One of the elements of just war is the doctrine of double effect. It refers to the way of dealing with certain moral issues regarding the killing of innocent people in a war, which has been developed since the Middle Ages. It targets non-intended side effects or collateral damage. In this context, collateral damage involves the acceptance of the deaths of non-combatants and innocents. The question arises whether the intention, motivation, or attitudes of a decision-maker or actor are important factors in determining the permissibility of a course of action. This doctrine should make it possible to limit the negative consequences of weapons effects in armed conflicts by not intentionally killing or injuring non-combatants and innocents.

McMahan and Walter point out a problem: "Just as it is often quite uncertain whether a war is a just one, so too can there be uncertainty about whether an individual act of war is permissible. Even when the rules of law are clear and explicit, they are inconsistent with the principles governing the morality of conduct in war. Occasionally they permit an action that would be wrong from a moral point of view, or they prohibit something that morality dictates. Thus, there may be considerable uncertainty about what morality commands, even if the order a combatant receives is obviously lawful [...]" [15].

The principle of double effect deals with moral dilemmas and is meant to offer a possible solution under certain conditions. In general, it also deals with the question of whether one's own actions, such as self-defense, are justified, whether it is permissible to accept that other non-involved people may come to harm, and whether and how this can be morally justified.

In modern times, the principle of the double effect is essentially treated under the aspects of intention and action. At the same time, the developments of modern international law of war and the Geneva Protocols have an influence on an ethical evaluation. Anscombe, for example, examines action not from the point of view of the goal of action and the object of action, but from the point of view of intentions. In her view, there is a close connection and interaction between action and intention. In one action there can be several intentions in sequence, that is, in chain. In this case, the last of the intentions is the actual intention with which the action is performed [16].

To be able to evaluate an action under the aspect of the principle of double effect or to apply it as a basis for action, criteria are needed. Magan has taken the following approach to this: "A person may licitly perform an action that he foresees will produce a good effect and a bad effect provided that four conditions are verified at one and the same time:

1. that the action in itself from its very object be good or at least indifferent;
2. that the good effect and not the evil effect be intended;
3. that the good effect be not produced by means of the evil effect;
4. that there be a proportionately grave reason for permitting the evil effect".

In both of these accounts, the fourth condition, the proportionality condition is usually understood to involve determining if the extent of the harm is adequately offset by the magnitude of the proposed benefit" [17].

Two conditions apply: all conditions must be met simultaneously, and the extent of the harm caused must be smaller in relation to the benefit generated.

As Coates points out, the principle of double effects makes it possible to analyze and evaluate an action in moral terms. To this end, Coates states: "Double effect is not itself a moral norm or principle, but an instrument of moral analysis, an aid in the application of moral principles to situations of extreme moral conflict, in which the pursuit of a legitimate and worthy objective threatens the violation of a fundamental moral norm"

[18]. In his view, this provides a way to analyze a decision in critical situations and moral dilemmas.

The principle of double effect can also be applied to the evaluation of acts of destruction of critical structure. Mangan's approach can be applied as essential criteria for evaluation. Although developed for war, it is possible to apply this to the realm of cyber, artificial intelligence, and hybrid war. Regardless of the methods or means of destruction, the actions of the actors are critical to ethical evaluation and morality. The essential determining element of action is intention. It determines means, procedures and the resulting relationship between benefit and the damage caused.

In an ethical consideration of the destruction of critical infrastructure the principle of double effects can be a further element. It remains to be examined how the intention of an actor can be recognized. Basically, there are two possibilities: before or after the action. In this case one depends on corresponding statements and their reliability.

In this context, the negative consequences of collateral damage must also be evaluated. Their severity also determines the impact on human rights and the human dignity of those affected.

6   Moral Evaluation of Threat and Destruction of Infrastructure

In the moral evaluation of threat and destruction of infrastructure, it is necessary to distinguish whether the destruction is done by criminals, terrorists, partisans, or armed forces. It must also be distinguished whether the threat and destruction occur in a normal state of the state and society, a war of aggression, or a defensive war. Furthermore, it must be clarified whether civilian and military infrastructure are involved.

The different ethical theories offer manifold ways of looking at and judging decisions and actions. The theoretical foundation of the individual ethics usually follows different norms and principles. Thus, they have in each case a special view on decisions and actions. The moral standards and evaluations result from this point of view.

Bases of the evaluation criteria: UN Charter, Geneva Convention, Additional Protocols to the Geneva Convention, Human Rights Conventions, Just War and Double Effect. Despite all the theoretical background and systems of justification, there is still the necessity to check whether an action is not only legal, but also legitimate.

If one tries to analyze the different ethical approaches that are relevant for an evaluation of a morally correct decision or action in terms of which of them can be applied in the practical execution of decisions and actions in the context of threats to or destruction of infrastructure, one can identify test criteria for a decision or action. These can be the basis for moral action (see Fig. 4).

For this purpose, one can proceed in the sense of action utilitarianism or rule utilitarianism based on the following test questions:

- Which rules are present and determine the actions?
- Are these rules consistent or do they contradict each other?
- Do these rules apply to the situation at hand?
- What are the consequences of the destruction of the infrastructure?
- Are human dignity and human rights taken into account?
- Are civilians, non-combatants, and innocent people affected?

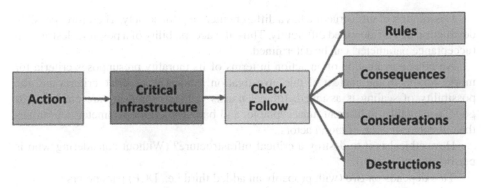

Fig. 4. Elements for the assessment of actions against critical infrastructure

- Is critical infrastructure being destroyed?

With these test questions, actions can be evaluated ethically. Uncertainties in the evaluation result from the real inner and outer conditions of the possible action, which cannot be avoided. Absolute certainty in the evaluation of moral action may be theoretically possible, but it is impossible to achieve in practice. The advantages of this approach are that decision makers at different levels must consider moral aspects in addition to political, legal, and operational requirements. The answers to each question provide an ethical system for decision and action. It should be emphasized that the application of this system is possible even under threat and stress.

6.1 The Threat

The assessment of threat and destruction of infrastructure, especially critical infrastructure, depends on the originator, the type of infrastructure affected, and the consequences of the destruction. The assessment is based on the consequences for the individual and society. It should be noted that it is the task of a sovereign state to ensure the foundations for the viability of society. The criteria according to which an evaluation can be made based on utilitarianism are the consequences of the destruction and the affectedness of the individuals and society. These are to be determined by violations of rights, violation of human rights and human dignity and thus on the right to life, security, and property of the people and of the society.

Within the framework of an evaluation model, a destruction of infrastructure could be evaluated. In an ethical evaluation, two areas must be distinguished: Acting and Tolerating. Acting is an action of one actor or several actors. Tolerating is a consequence of that action. Ethical evaluation requires a multidimensional approach. These dimensions consist of the type of infrastructure, the actors and the assignment of indicators, and various evaluation criteria. Furthermore, the actions of different actors must be taken into account. There is an ethical difference in whether an aggressor destroys critical infrastructure or a defender. For example, destroying an important bridge is a morally bad act for the aggressor. For the defender, if no other means of defense exists, this is a morally acceptable act.

Destruction of infrastructure has a different meaning for society. Therefore, possible destruction can be identified differently. Thus, the acceptability of a possible destruction (acceptance parameter) can be determined.

An ethical evaluation of an action in terms of its morality presupposes criteria for moral action. In the context of this investigation a linearity of these criteria and the possibility of scaling is assumed. Ethical norms (ethics parameter) are classified as good, acceptable, indifferent, unacceptable, and bad. The ethics parameter determines the ethical evaluation of moral actors.

How ethical is it to destroy a critical infrastructure? (Without considering who is performing the action).

This depends on two (with probably an added third i.e., DCP) parameters:

- Necessity Parameter (NP): how much the CI is needed (between 1 and 5). The lower the number, the more needed is the critical infrastructure. 1 = high necessity, 5 = low necessity (e.g., Hospital = 1; Bank = 4; the hospital is more needed than the bank).
- Destruction Acceptability Parameter (DAP): how acceptable the destruction of a CI is (between 1 and 5). The lower the number, the less accepted its destruction can be. 1 = low acceptance; 5 = high acceptance (e.g., Hospital = 1; Bank = 3; the destruction of the hospital is less acceptable than the destruction of a bank).
- Dependability Contextual Parameter (DCP): This parameter could be included in future lines of research in order to account for the differences between destroying a hospital that is in the middle of the city used by 1,000 people, vs. destroying a hospital that is in the middle of the forest used by 10).

These parameters can be defined as follows (see Table 1):

Table 1. Parameters for the assessment of the ethics behind destruction of critical infrastructure

Parameter							
Necessity Parameter		Destruction Acceptance Parameter		Affectedness Parameter		Tolerance Parameter	
NP	Value	DP	Value	BP	Value	TP	Value
highest	1	lowest	1	highest	1	lowest	1
high	2	low	2	high	2	low	2
medium	3	middle	3	medium	3	middle	3
low	4	high	4	low	4	high	4
lowest	5	highest	5	lowest	5	highest	5

It should be noted that the parameters may be weighted differently in each society. Societies and cultures have different risk and tolerance thresholds in relation to a threat situation. This results in different acceptance and tolerance behavior. Furthermore, the ethical evaluation of actions and endurance/suffering is subject to a variety of different factors and culturally changing influences.

In the destruction of critical infrastructure, one is essentially dealing with the following actors (see Fig. 5):

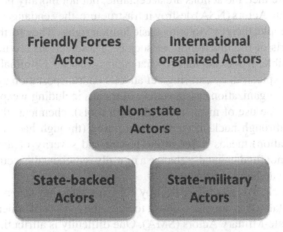

Fig. 5. Types of actors that take actions against critical infrastructures

The various actors, such as friendly forces actors, international organized actors, non-state actors, state-backed actors, and state-military actors, were selected because they are the ones that can threaten critical infrastructure in its various forms, both in the context of conflicts and operations.

When Friendly Forces Actors (FFA) destroy infrastructure in a defensive war, they do so as part of combat operations as a means to the end of defense. This can also lead to the destruction of critical infrastructure. This should be avoided as a matter of principle. However, it can also occur as part of unintended side effects. If such destruction occurs, it may be legal, but not legit. This means that the action is unacceptable or indifferent. The actor must decide between different, contradictory value structures. He finds himself ethically in an aporia. This is all the truer, since even a non-action cannot free him from this situation. He would thereby also get into a conflict that cannot be solved.

When partisans defend their country in an area occupied by a foreign power, there is usually also a destruction of infrastructure. Since partisans are directed against an occupying power and want to achieve or maintain the independence and functioning of their own society, their overriding goals are not their own infrastructure. In this respect, destruction is a non-causal, undesirable side-effect or collateral damage in the conduct of operations.

International Organized Actors (IOA) act on behalf of the United Nations or a regional security organization. If this operation is carried out with military means, it cannot be ruled out that the infrastructure of the state to be supported will be destroyed.

This is fundamentally reprehensible but must be assessed within the framework of a balancing of interests. In particular, the question of proportionality must be taken into account. This means that a legitimate goal must be pursued, the measures must be suitable, they must not go beyond that goal, and a balance must be struck between the consequences and the fundamental rights to be protected. This leads to a certain relation, as it is analogously located in the "just war". Destruction must by no means be a non-causal, undesirable side effect or collateral damage in the conduct of operations. If these conditions are met, the actions are acceptable, but not morally positive.

When Non-State Actors (NSA) destroy infrastructure, they endanger the lives, safety, and property of people, thereby violating basic human rights. They further endanger the functioning or parts of the functioning of society. These actions are unacceptable and morally reprehensible. It does not matter what means are used. Criminals often use tools and occasionally explosives by carrying out attacks on transportation systems and their facilities. Terrorist organizations use a variety of means including weapons, explosives, or other systems. The use of mechanical (through tools), chemical (through chemical agents), nuclear (through nuclear agents), data-based (through hacking), or AI-based (through manipulation) means differ in the nature and severity of the consequences. However, they do not fundamentally change a morally reprehensible action, even though the consequences can be catastrophic.

When State-Backed Actors (SBA) destroy infrastructure, they act on behalf of or with the approval of a state. They are thus subject to the same criteria of ethical evaluation for their actions as State-Military Actors (SMA). One difficulty is attributing the actions to individuals and their backing states. The evaluation of their actions in terms of morality can only be assessed from the outside based on the consequences of their actions and the way in which their actions are carried out.

When State-Military Actors (SMA) attack a country, they violate the UN Charter and thus the prohibition of a war of aggression. SMA destroy infrastructure, especially critical infrastructure in a war of aggression, this is part of the acts of war. A war of aggression is not only illegal under international law, but also immoral. Attacking military infrastructure as part of combat operations or destroying civilian infrastructure as unintended side effects or collateral damage is acceptable in principle, but morally unpalatable. Willful attack on civilian infrastructure, especially critical infrastructure, is not only a war crime but also morally reprehensible.

Often, war crimes occur in addition to the destruction of infrastructure. An attack of this kind can be directed primarily against the armed forces and infrastructure vital to the war effort but also against civilians and civilian infrastructure. In either case, it is morally reprehensible in terms of war of aggression. However, it is morally reprehensible in a causal relationship with the attack with respect to both types of combat. In this context, the killing of civilians and the destruction of civilian infrastructure is particularly morally bad.

These parameters of the actors can be defined as follows (see Table 2):

Table 2. Adjudicated values to each actor assessed

ACTOR		VALUE
Friendly	Friendly forces actors	1
Friendly/Hostile	International actors	2
Hostile	Non-state actors	3
Hostile	State-backed actors	4
Hostile	State-actors	5

The determination of the ethical evaluation is done by means of the parameters presented in graphical form. It should be noted that the area contents are the ethical factors. Thus, the ethical evaluation of an action becomes possible in a comparative form. Basically, it can be stated that the smaller the area, the morally better the action.

The following examples show this. The parameters were chosen according to an assumed social evaluation. Both the action and the toleration were taken into account. The parameters Necessity, Destruction Acceptance, Affectedness and Tolerance are considered. Further parameters are State Actors and Friendly Forces as well as State-backed Actors and Friendly Forces. Road Facilities (see Fig. 6) and Digital Infrastructure (see Fig. 7) are chosen as examples.

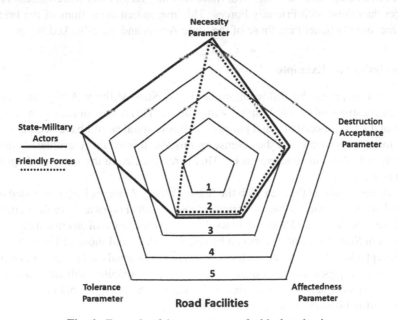

Fig. 6. Example of the assessment of ethical evaluation

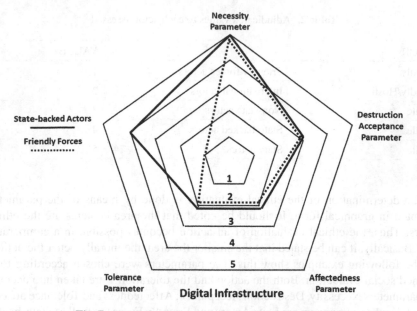

Fig. 7. Example of the assessment of ethical evaluation

It becomes clear that the areas with State-Military Actors and State-backed Actors are larger than those with Friendly Forces. This means that the actions of the Friendly Forces are morally better than those of the State Actors and State-backed Actors.

6.2   Analysis of an Example

The example assumes the following situation: A State-Military Actor intentionally attacks and destroys an enemy hospital with a drone. This results in the death of a large number of doctors, specialists, and patients. If this hospital would have been destroyed by own forces in the context of the defense by mistake, this would be evaluated ethically differently with the same consequences. This is represented in the network diagram as follows (see Fig. 8).

It becomes clear that the area with the State-Military Actors is larger than that of the Friendly Forces. This means that the actions of the Friendly Forces are morally better than those of the State Actors and State-Military Actors. In the context of an ethical evaluation, the actions of State-Military Actors can be rated as "Bad" and those of Friendly Forces as "Unacceptable". At this point, no legal or international legal evaluation will be made. Furthermore, the question of responsibility and possible culpability will not be addressed.

These actors not only destroy critical infrastructure by conventional means, but also use cyber, artificial intelligence (AI) and hybrid war.

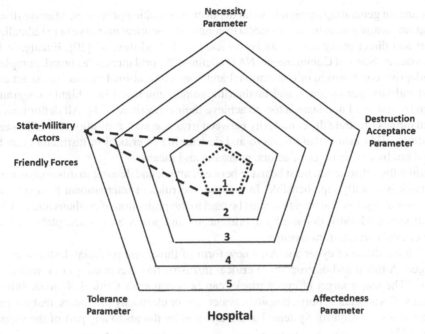

Fig. 8. Example of the assessment of ethical evaluation

7   Hybrid War and Cyber War

Hybrid war is about covert warfare. It combines different strategies, types and means of operational and tactical warfare. Hybrid wars are a mixture of irregular and conventional warfare that involve conventional, irregular, asymmetric, and criminal capabilities and activities. This is not a single entity, but both state and non-state actors can engage in hybrid warfare. Nevertheless, there is no generally binding definition of "hybrid threat". It therefore seems appropriate to highlight the essential elements, as it was done in the Lithuanian Annual Strategic Review 2017–2018: "In general, the concept of hybrid warfare refers to a much earlier developed concept of the fourth-generation war, the essence of which lies in the manipulation of mass media, execution of acts of terrorism, absence of a clear hierarchy and structure of the enemy, employment of military, economic, financial, energy-related and social pressure measures, use of asymmetric tactics, and the implementation of combined and coordinated, overt and covert military, para-military and civilian measures. [...] The term "hybrid" is often used while attempting to define everything that takes place in a non-conventional form or is more difficult to define by using traditional terms, for example, attributing a single hacker attack or employees protesting because of social problems to hybrid actions" [19].

The European Union defined "hybrid threats" as "the mixture of coercive and subversive activity, conventional and unconventional methods (i.e. diplomatic, military, economic, technological), which can be used in a coordinated manner by state or non-state actors to achieve specific objectives while remaining below the threshold of formally declared warfare. There is usually an emphasis on exploiting the vulnerabilities of the target and on generating ambiguity to hinder decision-making processes. Massive disinformation campaigns, using social media to control the political narrative or to radicalize, recruit and direct proxy actors can be vehicles for hybrid threats" [20]. Finally, in its 2016 Warsaw Summit Communique, NATO defined "hybrid threats "as broad, complex, and adaptive combination of conventional and non- conventional means, and overt and covert military, paramilitary, and civilian measures, employed in a highly integrated design by state and non-state actors to achieve their objectives" [21]. All definitions of hybrid threats illustrate the complexity between irregular and conventional conflicts and operations. This means that threats to and destruction of critical infrastructure can be carried out by a wide range of actors, measures and means.

Ethically, a distinction must be made between attack and defense in this area as well. An attack is morally reprehensible. In defense, the rules of international humanitarian law of war apply. Special attention must be paid to the protection of civilians and civilian infrastructure. Morally, defense by hybrid means and procedures is acceptable if they spare critical civilian infrastructure.

With the threat of cyber and AI, a new form of threat and potential destruction has emerged. A threat and destruction of critical infrastructure can come from a variety of actors. "The major target of cyber-attacks can be a country's Critical National Infrastructures (CNIs) such as ports, hospitals, water, gas or electricity producers, that use and rely on Industrial Control Systems but are affected by threats to any part of the supply chain" [22].

These threats come from private hackers, hackers acting on behalf of a state, state organizations (government ministries and agencies), state armed forces (state defense institutions), or militias (civilian and military reserve forces). Thus, a basic distinction can be made between criminal and military threats and destruction of objects. The targeting is directed at transportation systems, industrial infrastructure, information technology, nuclear reactors, water and sewage systems, energy, dams and water supply, critical production facilities, commercial facilities, or defense industrial base. It may also be directed against governmental entities or bodies, health care and public health, emergency services, or food and agriculture.

Several questions arise in the context of cyber and AI warfare: Is a cyberattack in response to a hostile conventional attack ever morally justified? Is a cyberattack in response to a hostile cyberattack ever morally justified? Is a conventional attack in response to a hostile cyber-attack ever morally justified? Is a cyberattack ever morally justified if the enemy has not conducted either a cyberattack or a conventional attack? What types of cyberattacks are morally justified once a war has begun? From a moral point of view, one must distinguish between an attack and a defense. An attack with cyber and AI is morally reprehensible. A defense with cyber is morally permissible under the international humanitarian law of war. However, civilian critical infrastructure must not be destroyed. The question arises on whether and how the different conditions of an ethical situation can be analyzed and evaluated by a framework.

Threats to and destruction of infrastructure and critical infrastructure can be assessed by utilitarianism/rule utilitarianism regarding the morality of actions. In addition to the consequences of the action, law, human rights, the system of just war, double effect and proportionality are used as a basis for evaluation. It should be noted that despite the consideration of these factors, an unambiguous ethical evaluation of moral actions is not always possible. This means that even in a CRITIS situation, an evaluation cannot be unambiguously moral. Only an approximation to the moral criteria remains possible. This is also determined by the legal, social, and ethical conditions of the actor and the affected parties. There is a certain relativity of the evaluations, which is not least determined by the culturally determined conditions of the possibilities.

Often there is an aporia in which the actor or non-actor is caught. This means that he must decide between different possibilities of acting without ethical theories being able to give him an instruction for acting in an ethically contradictory situation. Thus, he stands in Heidegger's "thrownness of being". If he must decide, he has no possibility to decide morally correct. Thus, depending on the view from the outside, he becomes guilty and must bear the responsibility. For example, he can stand between the order or the intention to destroy critical infrastructure and the ethical demand to preserve human rights and the dignity of those affected. Thus, he finds himself between two contradictory ethical systems without the possibility of resolving this contradiction.

Thus, he must bear responsibility for his actions, and he may become guilty. Guilt is established by an institution. Bonhoeffer, for example, states: "Whoever takes on guilt in responsibility - and no responsible person can escape this - ascribes this guilt to himself and to no one else and stands up for it, answers for it. He does not do it in the sacrilegious arrogance of his power, but in the recognition of this freedom - to be compelled and in it dependent on grace. Before other men, necessity justifies the man of free responsibility; before himself, his conscience absolves him; but before God, he alone hopes for grace" [23].

"Responsibility", however, is not a one-dimensional concept of assignment between decision and action or action and consequences, but a multidimensional concept of relation of different elements (see Fig. 9). An essential condition is the possibility of subjective and objective predictability of consequences.

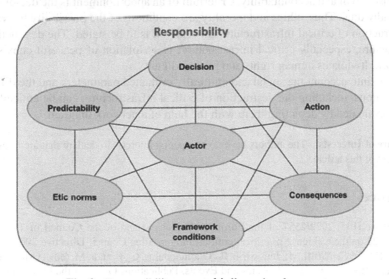

Fig. 9. Responsibility as a multi-dimensional concept

Only if the negative consequences can be recognized, a responsibility can be attributed to the deciding and acting party. A further prerequisite is free will, whereby the argument that one has only followed instructions or orders cannot justify immoral action. The classical concept of responsibility relates the responsibility to the deciding and acting person. In an increasingly complex society and its organizations based on the division of labor, the assessment of responsibility may change.

8 Resume

The ethical evaluation of moral actions of different actors depends on the condition of the action. Friendly Forces actors, International Organized actors, Non-State actors, State-Backed actors and State-Military actors are to be judged in their actions not only by the consequences but also by the law of their actions. Another essential element is whether an actor is attacking or defending itself, and whether it is destroying infrastructure or critical infrastructure.

The different ethical theories offer the possibility to evaluate decisions and actions ethically. They also enable the decider and the actor to become aware of the morality of his actions. Thus, they can behave morally.

Regarding the criteria according to which the decider and agent can act morally in practice, the view is taken here that law, in its formal and customary form, provides corresponding rules. Rules as such and their application, the proportionality of actions and means, human dignity and human rights, protection of civilians, non-combatants and innocent people form the basis for an ethical evaluation and the morality of actions. The theoretical, philosophical system, on which an evaluation can be based, is the rule utilitarianism. Based on the test questions, the agent can ethically evaluate his or her actions or the actions of an agent. The actor must answer for himself. Responsibility, however, is bound to different preconditions and criteria. Basic prerequisites are autonomy, freedom, reason, will and accountability. Criterium of an apportionment is the deciding and acting individual. Thus, ethics and morality are conditions of the possibility to evaluate the destruction of critical infrastructure. Basically, it is to be stated: The destruction of infrastructure, especially critical infrastructure, is a violation of peaceful coexistence and of law. It violates human rights and human dignity.

Taking into account the social and culturally evaluated parameters and the different actors, actions, including the destruction of critical infrastructure, can be ethically and morally evaluated by depicting them with the help of a network diagram.

Disclosure of Interests. The authors have no competing interests to declare that are relevant to the content of this article.

References

1. Directive (EU) 2022/2557 of the European Parliament and of the Council of 14 December 2022 on the resilience of critical entities and repealing Council Directive 2008/114/EC, page 176.In: Cardarilli, M., Jungwirth, R., Giannopoulos, G., Brandt, M. (eds.) Critical Infrastructure Resilience: News, Updates and Events. Publications Office of the European Union, Luxembourg, JRC131742 (2023)

2. Bundesamt für Sicherheit in der Informationstechnik: Was ist kritische Infrastruktur?. https://www.bsi.bund.de/EN/Home/home_node.html. Accessed 15 Apr 2023
3. Europäisches Parlament. Parlament nimmt neue Regeln zum Schutz kritischer Infrastruktur in der EU an. Pressemitteilung (22-11-2022) (2022). https://www.europarl.europa.eu/news/de/press-room/20221118IPR55705/parlament-nimmt-neue-regeln-zum-schutz-kritischer-infrastruktur-in-der-eu-an. Accessed 15 Apr 2023
4. Dutta, N.: Cyber Security. Issues and Current Trends. Studies in Computational Intelligence, vol. 995, p. 3. Springer, Singapore (2022). https://doi.org/10.1007/978-981-16-6597-4
5. UNRIC Regionales Informationszentrum der Vereinten Nationen für Westeuropa: Charta der Vereinten Nationen, Art. 2–4. http://www.unric.org/de/charta. Accessed 13 Sept 2023
6. Kant, I., Kraft, B., Schönecker, D.: Grundlegung zur Metaphysik der Sitten, p. 519. Meiner, Philosophische Bibliothek, Hamburg (1999)
7. Kant, I.: Werke in sechs Bänden, hrsg. von Wilhelm Weischedel, unveränd. Nachdr. der Sonderausgabe Darmstadt 1998, 7. unveränd. Aufl., p. 421. WBG 2011, Darmstadt (2011)
8. Kant, I.: Werke in sechs Bänden, hrsg. von Wilhelm Weischedel, unveränd. Nachdr. der Sonderausgabe Darmstadt 1998, 7. unveränd. Aufl., p. 337. WBG, Darmstadt (2011)
9. Aristoteles. Philosophische Schriften. In: sechs Bänden. Meiner, Hamburg 1107a (1995)
10. MacIntyre, A.: After Virtue. A Study in Moral Theory, 3rd edn., p. 191. University of Notre Dame Press, Notre Dame (2007)
11. Birnbacher, D., Mill, J.S. (eds.): Utilitarianism/Der Utilitarismus. [Lacher.], p. 57. Reclam (Reclams Universal-Bibliothek, 18461), Stuttgart (2010)
12. Sidgwick, H.: The Methods of Ethics, 7th edn., p. 474.: MACMILLAN and CO., Limited/The Mac Millan Company, New York/London (1907)
13. Hare, R.M.: Rules of war and moral reasoning. Philos. Public Affairs 1(2), 177 (1972)
14. Institute for American Values (IAV): What We're Fighting For. A Letter from America, New York (2002). http://americanvalues.org/catalog/pdfs/what-are-we-fighting-for.pdf. Accessed 03 Mar 2023
15. McMahan, J., Walter, A.: Kann Töten gerecht sein? Krieg und Ethik, p. 115. WBG Wiss. Buchgesellschaft, Darmstadt (2010)
16. Anscombe, G.E.M.: Intention, 2nd edn. Harvard University Press, Cambridge (2000). (First Harvard University Press paperback edition), paragraph 26, p. 46 (2000)
17. Mangan, J.T.: An historical analysis of the principle of double effect. Theol. Stud. X(1), 41–61 (1949). https://s3-us-west-2.amazonaws.com/ts-web-index-pdf-may22018/ts-pdf-index-tableofcontent-pdf/1949/volume10-issue-1.pdf. Accessed 13 Sept 2023
18. Coates, A.J.: The Ethics of War, p. 238. Manchester University Press, Manchester (1997)
19. Bajarunas, E., Kersanskas, V.: Hybrid threats: analysis of content, challenges posed and measures to overcome. Lith. Annu. Strategic Rev. 16(2017–2018), 125–126 (2019)
20. European Commission. Joint Communication to the European Parliament and the Council, Joint Framework on countering hybrid threats: a European Union Response, JOIN (2016) 18 final (2016)
21. NATO. Warsaw Summit Communique, Warsaw, 8–9 July 2016 (2016). https://www.nato.int/cps/en/natohq/official_texts_133169.htm. Accessed 21 Sept 2023
22. Maglaras, L., Janicke, H., Ferrag, M.A. (eds.): Cyber Security and Critical Infrastructures (2022)
23. Bonhoeffer, D.: Gewissen und konkrete Verantwortung, zitiert nach Ethik, DBW, vol. 6, p. 283 (1989). dietrich-bonhoeffer.net. Accessed 30 Mar 2023

Short and Long Term Vessel Movement Prediction for Maritime Traffic

Farshad Farahnakian(✉)⬚, Fahimeh Farahnakian⬚, Javad Sheikh⬚,
Paavo Nevalainen⬚, and Jukka Heikkonen⬚

Department of Computing, University of Turku, 20500 Turku, Finland
{farfar,fahfar,javshe,ptneva,jukhei}@utu.fi

Abstract. In maritime traffic management, the precise prediction of
vessel trajectories is paramount, given the industry's substantial dependence on vessel transportation for the transport of commodities, passen-
gers, and energy resources. This study proposes two innovative prediction
methodologies (short-term and long-term) for vessel movements. Furthermore, we introduce a novel evaluation metric designed to quantitatively assess the efficacy of the proposed short-term prediction method in
forecasting vessel trajectories. The presented methodologies were empirically tested, employing two-month Automatic Identification System
(AIS) data collected from the Baltic Sea to examine their performance.
Preliminary experimental outcomes indicate a superior level of accuracy
embodied in the short-term prediction method. On the other hand, the
long-term prediction method demonstrated enhanced performance metrics in the context of computational speed and memory utilization. These
observations underscore the potential of the proposed methodologies to
amplify efficiency and augment safety standards in marine traffic management.

Keywords: Maritime Traffic · Vessel Movement Prediction ·
Intelligent Transportation System · Machine Learning · Neural
Networks

1 Introduction

In the modern marine business, it is essential to accurately estimate how ships
will travel in the future. To handle maritime traffic effectively and safely, which
is necessary for the transfer of products, and people, it is necessary to be able to
predict the movements of vessels. A precise prediction of vessel movements also
enables the optimization of shipping routes, leading to lower fuel consumption
and reduced emissions, thus promoting sustainable shipping practices. In addition, predicting the future movement of vessels enhances the safety and security

This work is part of the AI-ARC project funded by the European Union's Horizon 2020
research and innovation programme under grant 96 agreement No. 101021271.

S. Pickl et al. (Eds.): CRITIS 2023, LNCS 14599, pp. 62–80, 2024.
https://doi.org/10.1007/978-3-031-62139-0_4

of maritime operations, as it facilitates the identification and mitigation of potential risks and hazards [1]. These factors contribute to the overall sustainability of the maritime industry and highlight the significance of developing effective vessel movement prediction methods.

The prediction of vessel movements is a challenging task due to the dynamic and complex marine environment with a large number of vessels navigating through various sea routes, so the amount of Automatic Identification System (AIS) data that needs to be processed and analyzed to predict vessel movements is exceptionally high accurately. This challenge is particularly significant given the statistics reported by the Organization for Economic Co-operation and Development (OECD) and the United Nations Conference on Trade and Development (UNCTAD), which indicate that approximately 90% of global trade was conducted through maritime transport in 2022 [2]. Moreover, the demand for global cargo is also expected to rise, leading to a projected tripling of naval trading by 2050 [3]. Figure 1 shows an example of heavy daily traffic by a graphical representation of the number of ships crossing Baltic Sea waterways as of April 20, 2023, taken from the MarineTraffic website. It shows the need to develop robust, innovative, efficient, and fast prediction methods that can address real-time and online data, as maritime traffic management systems require up-to-date and accurate vessel movement predictions to ensure the safety and efficiency of operations.

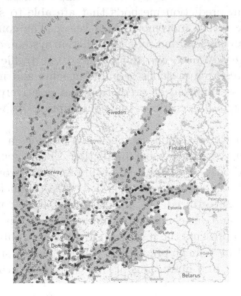

Fig. 1. Marine traffic map in Baltic Sea region (Red color indicators are oil/chemical tankers, blue color indicators are passenger ships, green color indicators are containers and orange color are fishing ships). (Color figure online)

In addition, the availability of maritime traffic data (AIS), advanced computing systems, and machine learning algorithms provides possibilities to develop advanced vessel movement prediction methods. However, the utilization of vast historical AIS data for vessel trajectory prediction remains an open and tricky topic. This is due not only to AIS technological restrictions, such as significantly irregular time sampling, imperfect data quality, and integrity, but also to the wide range of behaviors displayed by ships (depending on, for example, their size and ship type, navigational state, traffic regulations, and so on).

This study makes significant contributions to the field of vessel movement prediction in the context of maritime traffic management. Firstly, it introduces two novel prediction methods, short-term and long-term, for vessel movements. These methods address the challenges associated with the dynamic and complex maritime environment, providing valuable insights into vessel behavior and aiding in the optimization of maritime operations. Secondly, the short-term prediction method leverages machine learning techniques, specifically a feed-forward neural network, to accurately predict vessel movements based on user-defined time intervals. This approach enhances the efficiency and accuracy of prediction models, enabling effective maritime traffic management and decision-making processes. Additionally, the long-term prediction method employs sophisticated similarity measurement methods to identify similar ship trajectories within the same region, enabling the prediction of vessel movements based on historical patterns. Due to the use of similarity measurement techniques in the long-term prediction method, the system enables to provision of long-term vessel movement predictions for marine agents. Finally, we also implemented a novel evaluation metric for short-term prediction methods that are able to show how well the method predicts the future movements of a vessel. The combination of these approaches creates an efficient and robust prediction system, contributing to the development of more advanced and reliable maritime traffic management systems. Overall, this research provides valuable insights and methodologies that can revolutionize vessel movement prediction and positively impact maritime sectors such as coastguard operations, fuel consumption optimization, and shipping management.

The paper is structured as follows. Section 2 provides a review of previous studies conducted in vessel movement prediction. Subsequently, in Sect. 3, two novel prediction methods are introduced, outlining their theoretical foundations and underlying methodologies. Section 4 is dedicated to elucidating two crucial components: the dataset utilized, the pre-processing stage employed to prepare the data for analysis, and one compressing method used to simplify vessel trajectory points. Section 5 presents the results obtained from applying both methods to the task of vessel movement prediction. Finally, Sect. 6 summarises the key findings, contributions, and limitations of this study and future plans.

2   Related Work

The utilization of AIS data for the prediction of vessel movements has witnessed a substantial increase in recent years because of two significant factors: (1) the availability of AIS messages across commercial vessels navigating marine areas has facilitated access to comprehensive data sources for prediction purposes, and (2) AIS messages offer a range of features that prove instrumental in the task of trajectory prediction. Under Chapter V of the International Convention for the Safety of Life at Sea (SOLAS), vessels weighing over 300 tons have been mandated to install AIS transponders since 2004 [4]. These AIS messages contain three distinct types of data: (1) static data: including vessel-specific information such as ship name and type; (2) dynamic data: including encompassing position and movement-related information such as speed, course, latitude, and longitude; and (3) voyage-related data: including encompassing information concerning the vessel's current voyage, including the designated destination. Figure 2 shows ways of AIS transmission.

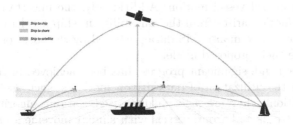

Fig. 2. AIS communication system in marine environment [5].

Existing methods using the AIS dataset for the vessel movement prediction task generally contain various approaches, including machine learning-based techniques, statistical models, and data driven techniques. Machine learning-based approaches, such as Neural Network (NN) [19] and Support Vector Machine (SVM) [20], have gained prominence due to their ability to learn patterns and relationships from historical vessel data, enabling accurate prediction of future movements. Statistical models, such as Markov models [21], utilize probabilistic methods to capture the stochastic nature of vessel movements, providing insights into transitional probabilities and aiding in trajectory forecasting. Data-driven methods, such as clustering algorithms, leverage unsupervised learning algorithms to identify common patterns and group vessels with similar movement characteristics, enabling the prediction of vessel movements based on observed patterns in historical data.

In [6], sequence-to-sequence vessel trajectory prediction models have been presented based on historical trajectory data. They combine Long Short-Term Memory (LSTM) and Recurrent Neural Networks (RNNs) for sequence modeling with intermediate aggregation layers to capture space-time dependencies. They used the AIS dataset from the Danish maritime authority to evaluate the effectiveness of the models. In [7], a Convolutional Neural Network (CNN) model is used to extract data on the relationship between various variables (for example, longitude, latitude, speed, and course over ground). Moreover, they used an LSTM in order to capture temporal dependencies. Finally, a squeeze-and-excitation (SE) [22] module is used to adaptively adjust the importance of channel features and focus on the more significant ones. To evaluate their proposed model, AIS messages of two cargo ships from 18 October 2022 to 23 October 2022 in the Yangtze River in China have been used. In another work [8], they proposed an offline SVM to predict vessel trajectory when there are a small number of AIS messages for target ships. Furthermore, they employed differential evolution [23] which is an optimization algorithm to find the internal model parameters to have higher speed and accuracy prediction.

Gaussian process regression [24] is one of the most popular probabilistic methods that captures vessel locations' stochastic nature (latitude and longitude) to estimate future vessel positions. Moreover, those types of methods are generally employed for long-term vessel movement prediction. In [9], a non-parametric Bayesian model employs a Gaussian process to characterize the uncertainty associated with lateral vessel motion. Additionally, the uncertainty pertaining to longitudinal motion arises from the variability in ship acceleration along the designated route. Three-month AIS data gathered by the coast of Portugal was used to evaluate their proposed model.

On the other hand, significant progress has been achieved in trajectory prediction through the utilization of data-driven methods, such as clustering and pattern recognition. They leverage unsupervised learning algorithms to identify common patterns and group vessels with similar movement characteristics, enabling the prediction of vessel movements based on observed patterns in historical data. In [10], the k-nearest neighbor method to predict vessel trajectories in the Gulf of Finland, employing an AIS dataset obtained from the Finnish transport agency. To enhance precision and focus on vessels moving from the observation zone to the prediction target zone, the raw data was filtered to obtain a subset of relevant information. The objective of the research was to forecast the timing of a boat's passage through the observation zone. Another work [11], employed a K-means algorithm to cluster AIS data, followed by training an NN model using the derived clusters to predict vessel trajectories. The lack of an advanced system that is able to predict short-term and long-term vessel prediction simultaneously is totally obvious for maritime management. This is a vital research gap that was brought to our attention, and we have developed an effective prediction system with a high potential of applied for different purposes from monitoring to optimizing costs for cargo companies.

3   Methodology

We propose a vessel movement prediction system including two distinct methods: short-term prediction, and long-term. In the following, two methods are introduced separately.

3.1   Short-Term Prediction Method

For short-term vessel movement prediction, we employed a feed-forward NN approach to analyze historical vessel movements. The objective was to identify patterns and trends within the data that could be utilized for making accurate predictions. By leveraging the capabilities of the neural network, this method enabled the prediction of vessel movements at specific time points or intervals, which could be customized based on the requirements of a maritime agent.

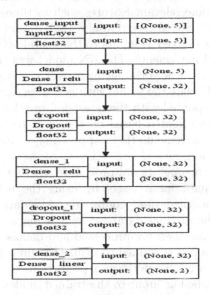

Fig. 3. The proposed NN architecture for the short-term vessel movement prediction.

As shown in Fig. 3, the proposed NN model consists of three hidden layers, the first layer contained 32 neurons and employed the rectified Linear unit (ReLU) activation function. This layer accommodated an input shape of (5,), aligning with the 5 input features. Subsequently, a dropout layer with a rate of 0.2 was introduced after the first layer to address potential overfitting concerns. The second layer, consisting of 32 neurons and utilizing ReLU activation, was succeeded by another dropout layer with an identical rate of 0.2. Finally, the output layer comprised two neurons, facilitating the representation of predicted latitude and longitude coordinates. The model was compiled with the Adam optimizer, incorporating a learning rate of 0.001. To select Adam and ReLU as an optimizer and activation functions, we experimented with other optimizers and activation functions. However, Adam and ReLU provided the best performance in our specific context. The Mean Squared Error (MSE) loss function was adopted, while supplementary evaluation metrics, such as Mean Absolute Error (MAE) and accuracy, were also assessed during the training process. The pre-processed training data and the corresponding target variables were utilized to train the model. In our model's training procedure which encompassed 100 epochs, the dataset was divided as follows: Initially, 20% of the entire dataset was set aside for validation. This validation data was kept separate and was not exposed to the model during training. Its sole purpose was to evaluate the model's performance after each epoch. 64% (which is 80% of the initial 80%) was used explicitly for training. The remaining 16% served as a test set to evaluate the model's generalization capability on unseen data.

To implement the methodology, historical vessel movement data were collected and preprocessed, ensuring its suitability for training NN. To train our model, we have used some relevant features such as timestamp, vessel location (latitude and longitude), Speed Over Ground (SOG), and Course Over Ground (COG). These attributes served as inputs to the neural network for learning and predicting future vessel movements. The NN model was trained using a supervised learning framework, where the historical vessel movements served as the training examples. To Update the model with new data, when new AIS messages come in, the model is updated with the latest information. For this reason, the trained model is always updated based on the most recent AIS messages and can handle any sudden movements that happen due to environmental factors or maritime traffic limitations.

Figure 4 illustrates the operational procedure wherein a maritime agent initiates a prediction request for a vessel by using the KAFKA platform [18]. Subsequently, a two-month dataset comprising AIS data pertaining to vessel A is extracted from the original database, employing a filtering process. The selected AIS messages are then pre-processed and denoised. Subsequent to the pre-processing stage, an NN is trained to utilize the prepared data, and its corresponding model is stored. To perform a prediction, the current AIS data of the target vessel is supplied as input to the trained model. Finally, the model is capable of estimating the future movements of vessel A.

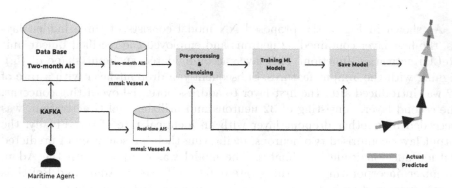

Fig. 4. The proposed methodology for short-term vessel movement prediction.

3.2   Long-Term Prediction Method

The similarity measurement technique is a pivotal component of our prediction system, enabling the estimation of future vessel trajectories over prolonged durations. Trajectory similarity measurement techniques can be broadly classified into three categories: spatial-based measures [12], temporal-based measures [13], and spatiotemporal-based measures [14]. In our approach, we utilized a spatial similarity measure, the Symmetrized Segment-Path Distance (SSPD) [15]. This measure evaluates the similarity between vessel trajectories focusing exclusively on spatial features: latitude and longitude. As illustrated in Fig. 5, the SSPD algorithm segments trajectories into shorter sub-paths, termed "segments". For every segment in trajectory S^1 (representing a specific ship's path), the algorithm identifies the most analogous segment in trajectory S^2 (another ship's path). The geometric attributes of these segments, like length and direction, determine this similarity. Subsequently, the SSPD calculates trajectory dissimilarity considering both forward and backward directions. It determines the shortest distance between segments in both orientations. Averaging these two distances provides the final similarity score:

$$D_{SSPD}(S^1, S^2) = \frac{D_{SPD}(S^1, S^2) + D_{SPD}(S^2, S^1)}{2} \tag{1}$$

Here, D_{SPD} denotes the segment-path distance in both forward and backward directions:

$$D_{SPD}(S^1, S^2) = \frac{1}{n} \sum_{i=1}^{n} D_{pt}(p_i, S^2) \tag{2}$$

$$D_{SPD}(S^2, S^1) = \frac{1}{n} \sum_{i=1}^{n} D_{pt}(p_i, S^1) \tag{3}$$

The term $D_{pt}(p_i, S^1)$ signifies the distance between two geographical points. This distance is ascertained using the Haversine formula [16]:

$$D_{ll} = 2r * sin^{-1}(sin^2(\frac{\Delta Lat}{2}) + cos(Lat_1).cos(lat_2).(sin^2(\frac{\Delta Long}{2}))) \tag{4}$$

It is important to emphasize that the spatial-based similarity measure or SSPD solely considers the spatial information of the trajectories when performing similarity evaluations. The general methodology of long-term vessel movement prediction is shown in Fig. 6. It consists of three steps as follows:

1. Vessel trajectory construction: initially, the vessel's trajectory is constructed using its AIS records, which contain relevant positional information.
2. Historical trajectories comparison: the constructed trajectory is then compared to the corresponding historical trajectories stored in the database, focusing on trajectories originating from the same departure ports.
3. Distance measures generation: the comparison process generates a set of distance measures, including the SSPD between the target trajectory and the historical trajectories.

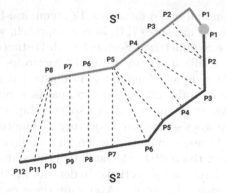

Fig. 5. Illustration of calculating SSPD for two different ships trajectories S1 and S2 departed from a port (green point). (Color figure online)

By applying these steps, the prediction system leverages the similarity measurement method to assess the resemblance between the target trajectory and the historical data, thereby enabling the estimation of future vessel movements. Eventually, the most similar trajectories are selected as the future movements of a target vessel.

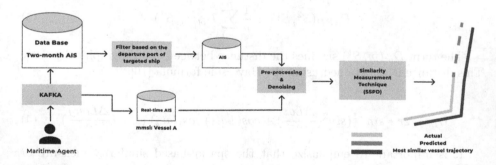

Fig. 6. The proposed methodology for long-term vessel movement prediction.

4 Experimental Setup

4.1 Dataset

AIS data, encompassing both static and dynamic information, was obtained from two open application programming interfaces (APIs). The Finnish transport infrastructure agency provided the marine information available on the "digitraffic.fi" website. These open data APIs offer various details, including marine warnings, harbor schedules, and vessel location AIS messages of vessels sailing in the Baltic Sea. In this study, AIS data collection commenced on 1st June 2022 and concluded on 31st July 2022, resulting in an approximate database size of 11 GB. The static and dynamic vessel features, extracted from separate APIs, were combined to ensure accurate interpretation. The International Maritime Organization (IMO) served as the foundation for integrating the data. Following the combination, the AIS data encompassed dynamic elements such as timestamps (year-month-day-time), latitude, longitude, SOG, COG, ship's heading, and COG, along with static elements such as MMSI (Maritime Mobile Service Identity), ship name or call sign, ship type, IMO number, drought, and physical characteristics like width and length. In this research, we more focused on cargo, tanker, and passenger ships as the number of these types of ships was high compared to other types.

4.2 Pre-processing

Data pre-processing serves as a crucial initial step in the data mining and analysis process, particularly for real-world AIS data. These data often exhibit missing, inconsistent, erroneous, or incomplete attributes. To address these issues and prepare the raw data for both short-term and long-term vessel movement prediction, various pre-processing methods were applied. Moreover, spatial and temporal segmentation has been applied to decrease computational sophistication and concentrate on specific regions or time intervals of interest. It means that the proposed methods only consider vessels' trajectories based on the time interval and research area determined by marine agents.

The two-month AIS dataset used in this research consists of approximately 8 million samples with 13 features. To reduce computational time, the data was first divided into weekly subsets. After that, invalid MMSI numbers, which should consist of 9 digits, were identified and corresponding rows were eliminated. Next, rows with more than five missing values were also removed. The focus was narrowed to specific ship types (cargo, tanker, passenger, fishing, tug, and dredging) for research purposes. Finally, samples with longitude values exceeding 180 or below −180, as well as latitude values exceeding 90 or below −90, were filtered out. In the final stage of cleaning and denoising, rows with invalid COG values (greater than 360 or less than 0) were discarded.

After cleaning the dataset and removing incorrect samples, we have also used Douglas-Peucker (DP) [17] to simplify the vessel's trajectory. It makes a vessel's trajectory smooth by reducing the number of data points while preserving the essential shape and characteristics of the original trajectory. DP algorithm works as follows:

– Given a series of points representing a vessel's locations (latitude, longitude), the algorithm begins by selecting the first and last points as the first approximation of the reduced route.
– It then determines the "farthest point," or the place that deviates the farthest from the line segment connecting the first and last locations (blue dashed line in Fig. 7).
– If the distance between the farthest point and the line segment is less than a certain threshold, the algorithm deems the line segment to be a sufficient approximation of the trajectory and discards all points between the first and last points.
– If the distance exceeds the threshold, the method repeats the second and third recursively to the two sub-trajectories generated by dividing the trajectory at the farthest point.
– The resulting simplified trajectory consists of the remaining points that were not removed during the recursive process.

In Fig. 7, the original trajectory is represented by solid lines, while the DP simplified trajectory is depicted by dashed lines.

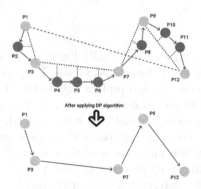

Fig. 7. Illumination of the DP algorithm performance.

If the vertical distance between P3 and P7 and the line defined by P1 and P12 exceeds the specified threshold, P3 and P7 will be retained. Conversely, if the vertical distances between P2 and the line defined by P1 and P3, between P4, P5, and P6 and the line defined by P3 and P7, between P8 and the line defined by P7 and P9, and between P10 and P11 and the line defined by P9 and P12 are smaller than the preset threshold, P2, P4, P5, P6, P8, P10, and P11 will be discarded. As a result, the original trajectory in the figure is simplified to P1, P3, P7, P9, and P12. After pre-processing explained in this section, the dataset prepared for the prediction methods comprised 7,221,049 samples with 13 features.

5   Results

The obtained experimental results are shown in two separate sub-sections for short-term and long-term prediction.

5.1   Evaluation of Short-Term Prediction Method

For short-term prediction, the two-month locations of the cargo vessel were initially filtered from the original dataset based on the MMSI number of six vessels with different types of ships. Table 1 shows the attributes of the selected vessels in detail. Subsequently, the study employed the following model architecture. The input features underwent normalization using the MinMaxScaler provided by the scikit-learn library. Attributes such as latitude, longitude, SOG, COG, draught, year, month, day, hour, and minute, constituting the historical data, were appropriately scaled using the aforementioned scaler.

Table 1. Information of selected vessels for the short-term vessel movement prediction evaluation part.

Vessel	MMSI	Name	Vessel Type	Call Sign
Vessel A	211833390	NILS HOLGERSSON	Cargo	DKLZ2
Vessel B	212499000	NILS DACKE	Passenger	5BEU4
Vessel C	245286000	CORAL IVORY	Tanker	PHPE
Vessel D	265610040	FOX LUNA	Tanker	SIJK
Vessel E	230041000	VIKING GLORY	Passenger	OJTO
Vessel F	230186000	MIDAS	Cargo	OIZZ

To facilitate the prediction process, the trained model utilizes the ten features encompassing the current AIS data of the target vessel as input. Consequently, the model exhibits a high degree of proficiency in estimating the future movements of the selected vessel. The performance metrics, loss, and accuracy, of the proposed neural network model on both training and test datasets for short-term prediction methodology across all vessels are shown in Fig. 8. After training models, these models were assessed individually on previously unobserved AIS messages to determine their robustness and performance fidelity. The obtained performance metrics including loss, Mean Absolute Error (MAE), and accuracy values for each vessel are succinctly tabulated in Table 2. Furthering this analysis, Fig. 9 graphically represents the selected vessels' forecasted geospatial coordinates, namely latitude, and longitude, over an imminent three-hour interval.

Furthermore, an evaluation metric named the Error Rate of Prediction (ERP) was developed to comprehensively assess the model's efficacy following each prediction. This metric effectively measures the disparity between the actual and predicted positions by computing the Haversine distance utilizing Eq. 4.

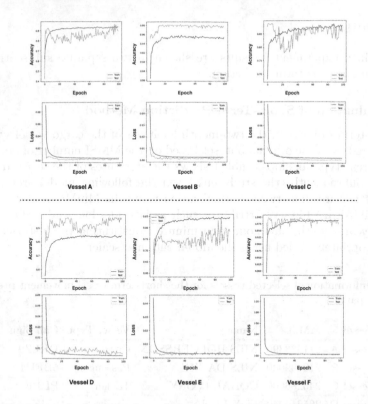

Fig. 8. The loss and accuracy plots of the proposed NN model for training and test datasets.

The ERP metric, through its calculation of the Haversine distance, provides a quantifiable measure of the accuracy and performance of our short-term method in predicting vessel movements. It serves as a valuable tool for evaluating and validating the effectiveness of the proposed approach. Figure 10 illustrates the variation of ERP over a three-hour prediction period for vessels. By observing the ERP values over time, trends, patterns, and any potential deviations from the desired accuracy can easily be identified and analyzed. One of the obvious things that we could realize from Fig. 10 is that the short-term prediction method is able to predict the vessel locations perfectly as the distance between real points and the predicted points ranges between 0–0.3 km.

Table 2. Comparative Evaluation Metrics (loss, MAE, and accuracy).

Vessel	Loss	MAE	Accuracy
A	0.03	0.13	0.86
B	0.01	0.08	0.98
C	0.006	0.6	0.89
D	0.002	0.04	0.99
E	0.005	0.06	0.82
F	0.04	0.05	0.98

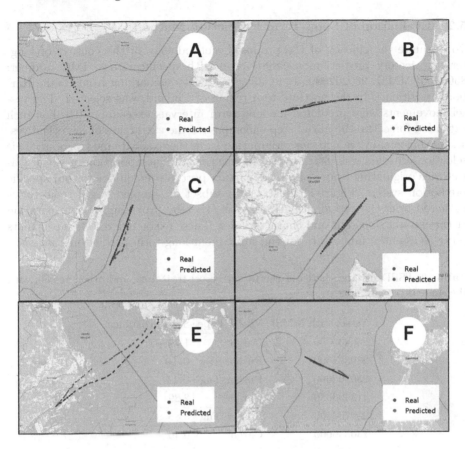

Fig. 9. Illustration of six vessels' real and predicted vessel movement locations.

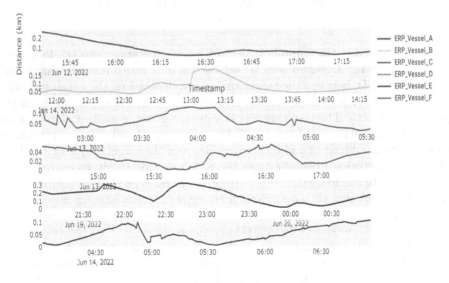

Fig. 10. ERP values over three-hour prediction.

5.2 Evaluation of Long-Term Prediction Method

To evaluate the efficacy of the proposed methodology in the context of long-term trajectory prediction, a cargo vessel with specifications - IMO number: 8503503, MMSI: 230202000, and Callsign: OIVR - embarking from Raahe Harbour, positioned in the northwestern region of Finland, was selected. The vessel movements were predicted for long-term intervals exceeding 10 h. For such extended forecasts, the initial step encompassed the extraction of historical vessel movements, or trajectories, originating from the exact Raahe Harbour. This selection criterion was instrumental in ensuring the incorporation of vessel trajectories originating from a shared departure port, a prerequisite for our specific prediction system. Figure 11 illustrates a subset of sampled vessel trajectories gathered from the two-month AIS dataset, thereby providing a representation of the dataset's content and characteristics. These extracted vessels movements serve as essential input data for the subsequent long-term prediction analysis.

Table 3. SSPD distance between the target vessel trajectory and other vessels with the same departure port.

Vessel with MMSI	Vessel Type	SSPD Distance
266435000	Cargo	1.77
230358000	Pusher Tug	**0.10**
230202000	Pusher Tug	**0.11**
413493080	Cargo	2.29
209732000	Pusher Tug	3.85
230336000	Cargo	0.40
305836000	Cargo	1.95
255805988	Cargo	4.97

Upon identifying the suitable trajectories for integration into the long-term prediction system, a comprehensive set of distance measures was calculated, specifically SSPD, between the target trajectory, denoted by the cargo ship with MMSI 230202000, and the historical trajectories of vessels departure from the same port (Raahe). The resulting SSPD values, serving as indicative metrics of trajectory similarity, are reported in Table 3. This tabulated data quantitatively assesses the dissimilarities and similarities between the target trajectory and the historical trajectories. In emphasizing the SSPD as a similarity measurement, it is noteworthy to elucidate that this particular metric is predicated entirely upon spatial characteristics, thereby strictly focusing on the spatial congruity between the studied trajectories. According to the obtained results in Table 1, two vessels with MMSI 230358000 and 230202000 are the most similar, so the trajectories of the two vessels with the most similarity are assigned to the future vessel movements for the targeted vessel. Eventually, we have visualized trajectories of vessels with the most similar target vessels together in Fig. 12.

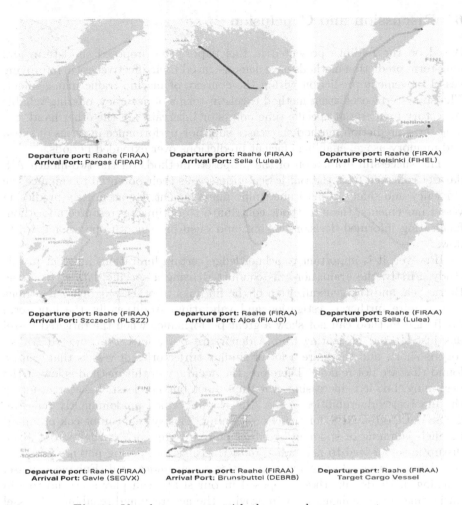

Fig. 11. Vessel movements with the same departure port.

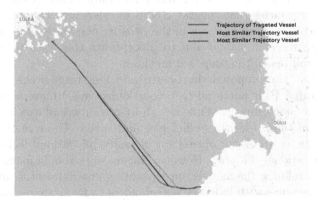

Fig. 12. Illustration of most similar vessel trajectories with the target vessel.

6   Discussion and Conclusion

Based on the findings presented in this paper, the proposed short-term and long-term prediction methods have demonstrated their effectiveness in improving vessel movement prediction within the context of marine traffic management. The short-term prediction method excels in terms of accuracy, offering reliable trajectory forecasts at specific time points or intervals. On the other hand, the long-term prediction method showcases superior performance in terms of speed and memory usage, enabling efficient predictions over extended periods.

The successful evaluation of the proposed methods on the two-month AIS dataset collected from the Baltic Sea underscores their potential to enhance the efficiency and safety of maritime traffic management. By accurately predicting vessel movements, these methods contribute to optimizing resource allocation, facilitating informed decision-making, and ensuring smooth operational work-flows.

However, it is important to acknowledge certain limitations inherent in this study. Firstly, the evaluation was conducted using a specific dataset from the Baltic Sea, and the generalization of the findings to other geographical regions may require further investigation and validation. Additionally, the long-term prediction method can not show a great performance when the targeted vessel has just started navigating from a departure port, since the targeted trajectory is short, and there are a lot of similar trajectories of vessels that can be found that are not reliable. Therefore, the accuracy of this method is low at the beginning, but it is increasing over time. Last but not least. It's worth noting the inherent vulnerabilities of the AIS system, which predominantly relies on GNSS data, often GPS, for vessel positioning. This system can be compromised through jamming or spoofing by either onboard crew or external actors. Such disruptions can lead to misleading data transmission, posing potential navigational hazards or allowing illicit activities to go undetected. Enhanced vessel tracking methods, like those proposed in our study, can play a crucial role in mitigating these challenges. By improving the accuracy and reliability of vessel movement predictions, we can better verify AIS data's authenticity, potentially identifying discrepancies that suggest GNSS interference. This further empha-sizes the importance of our research in the broader maritime safety and security context. Future research should aim to incorporate this issue to enhance the predictive capabilities of the proposed methods.

In conclusion, the proposed short-term and long-term prediction methods have demonstrated their potential to revolutionize vessel movement prediction in marine traffic management. While the short-term method excels in accuracy, the long-term method prioritizes efficiency and speed. These methods provide valuable insights and tools for optimizing resource allocation, decision-making, and overall operational efficiency. However, future work should focus on address-ing limitations, refining the models, incorporating environmental variables, and exploring partnerships with industry stakeholders to facilitate real-world imple-mentation.

References

1. Farahnakian, F., et al.: A comprehensive study of clustering-based techniques for detecting abnormal vessel behavior. Remote Sens. **15**(6), 1477 (2023). https://doi.org/10.3390/rs15061477
2. United Nations Conference on Trade and Development. "Review of Maritime Transport 2022, Chapter 1". https://unctad.org/system/files/official-document/rmt2022-en
3. Organization for Economic Co-operation and Development (OECD). "ITF Transport Outlook 2021". https://www.itfoecd.org/sites/default/files/transport-outlook-executive-summary-2021-english.pdf
4. International Convention for the Safety of Life at Sea (SOLAS) Chapter V: Safety of Navigation Regulation 19 December 2002. https://www.imo.org/en/OurWork/Safety/Pages/AIS.aspx
5. Cheng, Y.: Satellite-based AIS and its comparison with LRIT. TransNav: Int. J. Mar. Navig. Saf. Sea Transp. **8**(2), 183–187 (2014)
6. Capobianco, S., Millefiori, L.M., Forti, N., Braca, P., Willett, P.: Deep learning methods for vessel trajectory prediction based on recurrent neural networks. IEEE Trans. Aerosp. Electron. Syst. **57**(6), 4329–46 (2021)
7. Wang, X., Xiao, Y.: A deep learning model for ship trajectory prediction using automatic identification system (AIS) data. Information **14**, 212 (2023). https://doi.org/10.3390/info14040212
8. Liu, J., Shi, G., Zhu, K.: Vessel trajectory prediction model based on AIS sensor data and adaptive chaos differential evolution support vector regression (ACDE-SVR). Appl. Sci. **9**, 2983 (2019). https://doi.org/10.3390/app9152983
9. Rong, H., Teixeira, A.P., Soares, C.G.: Ship trajectory uncertainty prediction based on a Gaussian Process model. Ocean Eng. **15**(182), 499–511 (2019)
10. Virjonen, P., Nevalainen, P., Pahikkala, T., Heikkonen, J.: Ship movement prediction using k-NN method. In: 2018 Baltic Geodetic Congress (BGC Geomatics), pp. 304–309 (2018)
11. Gan, S., Liang, S., Li, K., Deng, J., Cheng, T.: Ship trajectory prediction for intelligent traffic management using clustering and ANN. In: 2016 UKACC 11th International Conference on Control (CONTROL), pp. 1–6). IEEE (2016)
12. Ranacher, P., Tzavella, K.: How to compare movement? A review of physical movement similarity measures in geographic information science and beyond. Cartogr. Geogr. Inf. Sci. **41**(3), 286–307 (2014)
13. Magdy, N., Sakr, M.A., Mostafa, T., El-Bahnasy, K.: Review on trajectory similarity measures. In: 2015 IEEE Seventh International Conference on Intelligent Computing and Information Systems (ICICIS), pp. 613–619. IEEE (2015)
14. Magdy, N., Sakr, M.A., El-Bahnasy, K.: A generic trajectory similarity operator in moving object databases. Egypt. Inform. J. **18**(1), 29–37 (2017)
15. Besse, P.C., Guillouet, B., Loubes, J.M., Royer, F.: Review and perspective for distance-based clustering of vehicle trajectories. IEEE Trans. Intell. Transp. Syst. **17**(11), 3306–17 (2016)
16. Maria, E., Budiman, E., Taruk, M.: Measure distance locating nearest public facilities using Haversine and Euclidean Methods. In: Journal of Physics: Conference Series, vol. 1450, no. 1, p. 012080. IOP Publishing (2020)
17. Yan, X., He, J., Ren, Q., Bai, C., Zhang, C., Wang, C.: Research on extraction method of multiple narrow channel vessel trajectory feature in Yangtze river based on VITS data. J. Adv. Transp. **9**, 2022 (2022)

18. Shree, R., Choudhury, T., Gupta, S.C., Kumar, P.: KAFKA: the modern platform for data management and analysis in big data domain. In: 2017 2nd International Conference on Telecommunication and Networks (TEL-NET), Noida, India, pp. 1–5 (2017). https://doi.org/10.1109/TEL-NET.2017.8343593
19. Mehlig, B.: Machine Learning with Neural Networks: An Introduction for Scientists and Engineers. Cambridge University Press, Cambridge (2021)
20. Pisner, D.A., Schnyer, D.M.: Support vector machine. In: Machine Learning, pp. 101–121. Academic Press (2020)
21. Ghahramani, Z.: An introduction to hidden Markov models and Bayesian networks. Int. J. Pattern Recogn. Artif. Intell. **15**(01), 9–42 (2001)
22. Hu, J., Shen, L., Sun, G.: Squeeze-and-excitation networks. In: Proceedings of the IEEE Conference on Computer Vision and Pattern Recognition, Salt Lake City, UT, USA, 18–23 June 2018, pp. 7132–7141. IEEE, Piscataway (2018)
23. Pant, M., Zaheer, H., Garcia-Hernandez, L., Abraham, A.: Differential evolution: a review of more than two decades of research. Eng. Appl. Artif. Intell. **1**(90), 103479 (2020)
24. Graser, A., Widhalm, P.: Modelling massive AIS streams with quad trees and Gaussian Mixtures (2020)

Managing Uncertainty Using CISIApro 2.0 Model

Chiara Foglietta[✉][ID], Valeria Bonagura[ID], Stefano Panzieri[ID],
and Federica Pascucci[ID]

University Roma Tre, 00146 Rome, Italy
{chiara.foglietta,valeria.bonagura,stefano.panzieri,
federica.pascucci}@uniroma3.it

Abstract. Critical infrastructures are large and complex systems showing physical, geographical, cyber, and logical interdependencies. Assessing the consequences of faults, cyber-attacks, or natural events on critical infrastructures is fundamental to mitigate the impact of these events and to improve the resilience of the entire "system of systems".

Modeling critical infrastructures is a way to understand how networks are interconnected and increase awareness. Our paper proposes a well-established framework for decomposing each infrastructure into its meaningful elements and their interconnections using the Mixed Holistic-Reductionist approach. CISIApro 2.0 is an agent-based simulator that implements the previous methodology.

In this paper, we improve the framework using possibility theory to handle epistemic uncertainty. In contrast to randomness, epistemic uncertainty is caused by incomplete, ambiguous, or inaccurate knowledge. This is a problem in the modeling of critical infrastructures, due to the complexity of the physical process, the vagueness of telecommunications, and imprecise information. Including possibility and necessity measures in the CISIApro 2.0 simulator allows us to handle uncertainty in the propagating information in the model. The synthetic model is composed of eight interconnected infrastructures. The model output demonstrates the reasonableness of the proposed approach, although there is a need for further improvements, especially with regard to parameter tuning.

Keywords: Epistemic Uncertainty · Possibility Theory · Critical infrastructure Interdependency · CISIApro

1 Introduction

Modeling critical infrastructures is a fundamental task to assess the consequences of different events: cyber-attacks, faults, natural events, and recovering actions. This problem usually shows a trade-off between the amount of information needed to implement a realistic model and the difficult to have a full disclosure of such data. Sometimes, neither the operators know the perfect functioning of their

S. Pickl et al. (Eds.): CRITIS 2023, LNCS 14599, pp. 81–99, 2024.
https://doi.org/10.1007/978-3-031-62139-0_5

infrastructure or which are the exact interconnections with other infrastructures. Predictions obtained by a model are also uncertain because their implementations are never entirely accurate but are only hypothetical. Other sources of uncertainty exist in addition to the intrinsic uncertainty of inductive reasoning, such as false model assumptions and noisy or inaccurate data.

Uncertainty is typically handled probabilistically, and such theory has been considered for a long time the gold standard for addressing uncertainty in disciplines such as statistics [12]. Conventional approaches to probabilistic modeling, which are essentially based on capturing knowledge in terms of a single probability distribution, may fail to distinguish between two inherently different sources of uncertainty, which are frequently referred to as aleatoric and epistemic uncertainty, without calling into question the probabilistic approach in general.

Aleatoric (or statistical) uncertainty refers to the notion of randomness, i.e., the variability in the output of an experiment caused by naturally occurring random effects [5]. The classic example is the coin toss, in which the data generation process has a stochastic component that cannot be reduced by any additional source of information, except Laplace's demon. Therefore, even the most accurate model of this process will only be able to offer probabilities and not a firm conclusion. Epistemic uncertainty, also known as systematic uncertainty, is the opposite of this: it refers to uncertainty brought by ignorance (of the best model). In other words, rather than referring to any underlying random phenomena, it refers to the agent's or decision-maker's ignorance or epistemic condition. However, epistemic uncertainty has a distinct nature, since it may quickly be eliminated. In other words, aleatoric uncertainty refers to the component of the (total) uncertainty that is irreducible, whereas epistemic uncertainty refers to the reducible part.

Modeling critical infrastructures and their interdependencies is a well-established field, which started from the seminal work of Rinaldi *et al.* [19]. Several surveys on critical infrastructure modeling techniques can be found in the literature [16,17,20,21,23]. The problem of modeling several interdependent infrastructures is still an open research topic that does not have a definitive and unique answer. Modeling interconnected infrastructures is fundamental to assess the consequences of large disaster events or very specific adverse events, causing the so-called domino effect.

Following the approach proposed in [21], the proposed modeling techniques are divided into three main categories depending on how they capture dependencies and interdependencies: dependency table-based models, interaction rule-based models, and data-driven approaches.

In dependency table models, each infrastructure is represented as an element in a table or a node in a graph. Most of these approaches gather experts' opinions about interconnections or take advantage of economic dependencies in their analyses. These approaches are useful when simulating random functionality recovery curves, the degree of correlation in a random sampling algorithm, or the economic consequences of faults or natural events.

Interaction rule models can model complex interactions using agent-based modeling, system dynamics simulation, or Bayesian networks. To obtain meaningful results, these methods require large amounts of data and large amounts of computation. These methods can be applied to planning or what-if analysis.

So far, only few researchers have employed data-driven techniques for interdependency assessments. This suggests that this type of interdependency modeling approach is still in its early stages, with low development maturity. Data-driven techniques can be computationally inexpensive or expensive, depending on the strategy used. Despite the limitations of no physical insights and potentially biased results, the availability of big data offers promising opportunities for using data-driven approaches to understand dependencies and interdependencies among infrastructure systems from various perspectives, ultimately supporting decision-making in disaster management in the coming decades.

Many interdependent infrastructure models either don't mention or don't mathematically describe system uncertainty [4]. While it would be difficult for a single model to identify and quantify every uncertainty affecting the coupled system, doing so would be questionable [1]. This implies that both the model output and inherent uncertainty may be quite high. We contend that this could have consequences for decision-makers who are unaware of the boundaries of understanding [18].

1.1 Contributions

In this paper, CISIApro 2.0 is exploited to analyze the consequences of adverse events in a complex scenario made of interconnected infrastructures. CISIApro 2.0 is an agent-based simulator where each infrastructure is decomposed into agents to describe complex behaviors and presented in Sect. 2.

The Mixed Holistic Reductionist (MHR) approach is a hierarchical approach to decomposing infrastructures into simple elements, granting several abstraction levels. CISIApro 2.0 is a simulator that implements MHR, exploiting an agent-based framework where interaction among simple agents leads to global emergent behavior. This paper improves CISIApro 2.0 to handle epistemic uncertainty using the possibility theory.

The uncertainty in the model is due to the complexity of the processes, but also to imprecise information. We consider the model generated from synthetic data representing the information of the Italian National Security Perimeter for Cyber [10]. In this case, the information is related to the different types of device that are critical for a specific service. However, we don't know if these devices are all necessary for the service, or among them, there are backups or additional devices that are exploited only during turn-off time. This framework is functional when dealing with threats and cyber-attacks to cope with the uncertainty of the trigger and the model.

1.2 Paper Organization

The paper is structured as follows. Section 2 is dedicated to the modeling approach to evaluate the impact of adverse events. Section 3 illustrates the mathematical background of the model presented. The case study of eight inter-connected infrastructures is described in Sect. 4 with the results. Finally, the conclusions and future work are discussed in Sect. 5.

2 Modelling Approach

In this section, the proposed modeling approach is presented. Initially, the MHR approach is described as a general framework for modelling interdependent critical infrastructures. Then we describe the CISIApro 2.0 simulator to assess the impact of adverse events on a complex scenario.

2.1 Mixed Holistic Reductionist (MHR) Approach

We provide a general framework for supporting the modeling process. The Mixed Holistic Reductionist (MHR) [6] approach combines the strengths of reductionist and holistic thinking. The MHR approach provides a practical road map for detailed modeling of Critical Infrastructures and their interdependencies.

Interconnected infrastructures are described as a series of networks in the MHR methodology. Each infrastructure is specified at several abstraction levels to capture the phenomena that arise at various granularities. The goal is to combine the benefits of the holistic approach with the reductionist one to minimize the downsides.

Holistic modeling considers infrastructures as discrete entities with precisely defined borders and functional properties, resulting in a full and global image. In this approach, several infrastructures can be easily identified and described. The quantity of data necessary for modeling processes is modest at this level, and it may be available in open databases.

The reductionist paradigm, on the other hand, emphasizes the need for thoroughly studying the functions and behaviors of specific infrastructure to completely comprehend the entire system. The reductionist method divides each component into input and output. At this level of abstraction, the relationships between the machinery and individual components may be easily identified.

The link between the two degrees of complexity, that is, holistic and reductionist methodologies, is the evaluation of service efficiency (referred to as "service"), which is a critical component for operators. This layer specifies the functional connections between infrastructures and components at various granularities.

Different systems demand varying levels of investigation, and their limits are lost in sophisticated case studies. Top-down or bottom-up examination of network interactions at multiple levels is possible using the MHR model. Given the amount of data available, it is also possible to depict infrastructure at many levels of abstraction.

To demonstrate how MHR can be used in real-world scenarios, we provided an example in Fig. 1 with the three separate levels portrayed as concentric circles. In general, the holistic layer elements are solely related to the service blocks, and

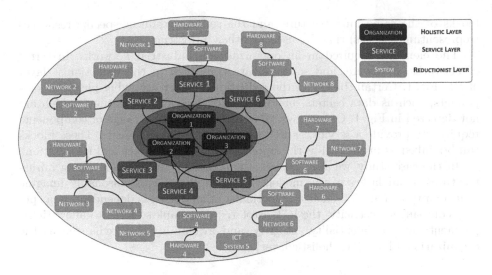

Fig. 1. The MHR representation of an example, where the dark gray nodes are in the holistic layer, the gray ones are part of an intermediate layer, and the light gray ones are in the reductionist level.

the reductionist elements are the same. As a result, the service blocks serve as links between reductionist and holistic parts.

We consider the case study of several interconnected infrastructures that produce essential services to their customers. The reductionist layers contain different types of telecommunication elements that are needed to produce the essential services.

The holistic layer includes all the blocks that represent organizations. The organization provides essential services to its customers and other organizations. Each service is produced by a set of networks, hardware and software, connected variously as depicted in Fig. 1.

Physical resources (such as electricity or water) and cyber risks are exchanged between the holistic blocks. This concept involves the evaluation of confidentiality, integrity, and availability (e.g., the CIA triad) related to cyber-attacks. In the IT (Information Technology) world, this concept is often associated with cybersecurity, and it has a difficult translation into the OT (Operational Technology) sector. In this paper, we exploit this concept to evaluate the impact of cyber-attacks such as ransomware in the industrial domain. For example, a data breach within one business has no direct influence on information availability, but it undermines a company's reputation at the whole level. When no other data is provided, the model might include blocks relating to the organization without providing other information.

The service layer comprises all the components required to provide essential services. Organization blocks are linked to services in two ways: the service of an infrastructure provides resources, faults, and cyber-attacks to the organization blocks of the same infrastructure; and the service produces specific resources (representing services) that are used by other infrastructures.

The elements required in an organization's industrial networks, in terms of networks, hardware, and software, are contained in the reductionist layer of the Fig. 1. Certain blocks in the reductionist layer are cyber-physical components, such as data centers, buildings, and electrical substations, which are not depicted in Fig. 1. Cyber-physical systems comprise a range of components required to provide a service, as well as certain ICT components. These blocks can be linked as in the real-world topology to share resources and information.

In the case study, we also consider the possibility of interconnecting infrastructures at all layers of the model: for example, we can reasonably imagine that an airport (considered as a reductionist component) is dependent on a specific company's electricity; the ICT asset requires bank services to allow ticket payment; and confidentiality, integrity, and availability are exchanged at the organizational level (i.e., holistic layer).

2.2 CISIApro 2.0 Simulator

CISIApro 2.0 (Critical Infrastructure Simulator by Interdependent Agents) [3, 11] is a simulator that is used to evaluate the consequences of adverse events in interconnected infrastructure. The simulator employs agent-based modeling, which consists of three major components: the agents, basic interaction rules, and the environment in which the agents are placed. Complex systems can be modeled by several agents working concurrently according to basic principles. There is no central control over the behavior of agents in this modeling technique. Following local rules results in output or aggregate behavior that adapts to the environment or responds to negative conditions. In its most basic form, an agent-based model is a collection of agents that obey relatively simple rules to produce collective behavior that results in an emergent property or behavior. Agent-based modeling needs a high degree of information to be predictive. As a result, the precision of this technique is determined by its detail.

CISIApro 2.0 is a simulator in which each infrastructure is split into agents with the same overall structure of inputs and outputs. Each agent gets resources, faults, and cyber-attacks from upstream agents and transmits them to downstream agents. Resources are supplies of materials, amounts, and other assets that an organization or operator relies on to work efficiently. A fault involves malfunctions and natural disasters that must be exploited to evaluate various outcomes based on the circumstances of the initial adverse event. Malicious operations that aim to capture, disrupt, deny, degrade, or destroy information system resources are called cyber-attacks. CISIApro 2.0 allows agents to share resources, faults, and cyber-attacks.

The operational level summarizes the agent's state as depicted in Fig. 2. Operational level denotes an agent's capacity to function and carry out its responsibilities. Every agent has internal state variables that determine behavior based on resource, fault, and cyber-attack evaluation. Depending on its operational level, each agent delivers resources, faults, and cyber-attacks to downstream agents.

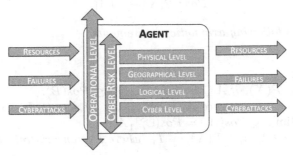

Fig. 2. The agent representation in CISIApro 2.0

The agent has an extra state variable called "cyber risk level" (Fig. 2) to better manage cyber-attacks and appropriately analyze their implications. This variable indicates how internal and external cyber-attacks influence the agent. The CIA (Confidentiality, Integrity, and Availability) triangle governs cyber risk. The CIA parameters may be challenging to use in the context of IACS (Industrial Automation and Control System). However, the terms are beneficial for dealing with information from a more traditional IT environment and disseminating information about cyber-attacks in the industrial sector. The CIA triad is significant in evaluating the impact of cyber-attacks on the IACS tied to communications networks.

The idea of operational level in CISIApro 2.0 captures the availability of information conveyed by a telecommunication network. The cyber risk level, on the other hand, identifies confidentiality and integrity. The two measures (operational and cyber risk levels, see Fig. 2) can be linked and partially overlapped.

To better represent reality, the model usually uses information related to back-up or redundant devices, services, or organizations. This information is fundamental to avoid the situation where a single point of failure means the collapse of the entire overall system. For this reason, handling the uncertainty of the interconnection among devices is needed.

3   Mathematical Background

In this section, we describe the mathematical background for handling epistemic uncertainty and how this theory can be exploited in the use case.

3.1   Possibility Theory

Possibility theory can be thought of as a subset of fuzzy measure theory [22]. Possibility theory is based on two dual semicontinuous fuzzy measures: possibility (lower semicontinuous) and necessity (upper semicontinuous). This theory can be defined in terms of these measures, which are often considered functions from a given universal set X's power set, $\mathcal{P}(X)$, to the unit interval $[0, 1]$ [14].

Definition 1. *Given a universal set X, a possibility measure, Pos is a function*

$$Pos : \mathcal{P}(X) \to [0,1] \tag{1}$$

that satisfies the following axiomatic requirements:

1. $Pos(\emptyset) = 0$;
2. $Pos(X) = 1$;
3. *for all* $A, B \in \mathcal{P}(X)$, *if* $A \subseteq B$, *then* $Pos(A) \leq Pos(B)$;
4. *for any increasing sequence* $A_1 \subseteq A_2 \subseteq \ldots$ *of sets in* $\mathcal{P}(X)$, *if* $\cup_{i=1}^{\infty} A_i \in \mathcal{P}(X)$, *then* $\lim_{i \to \infty} Pos(A_i) = Pos(\cup_{i=1}^{\infty} A_i)$;
5. *for any family* $\{A_i | A_i \in \mathcal{P}(X), i \in I\}$, *where I is an arbitrary index set*

$$Pos\left(\bigcup_{i \in I} A_i\right) = \sup_{i \in I} Pos(A_i) \tag{2}$$

Definition 2. *Given a universal set X, a necessity measure, Nec is a function*

$$Nec : \mathcal{P}(X) \to [0,1] \tag{3}$$

that satisfies the following axiomatic requirements:

1. $Nec(\emptyset) = 0$;
2. $Nec(X) = 1$;
3. *for all* $A, B \in \mathcal{P}(X)$, *if* $A \subseteq B$, *then* $Nec(A) \leq Nec(B)$;
4. *for any decreasing sequence* $A_1 \supseteq A_2 \supseteq \ldots$ *of sets in* $\mathcal{P}(X)$, *if* $\cap_{i=1}^{\infty} A_i \in \mathcal{P}(X)$, *then* $\lim_{i \to \infty} Nec(A_i) = Nec(\cap_{i=1}^{\infty} A_i)$;
5. *for any family* $\{A_i | A_i \in \mathcal{P}(X), i \in I\}$, *where I is an arbitrary index set*

$$Nec\left(\bigcap_{i \in I} A_i\right) = \inf_{i \in I} Nec(A_i) \tag{4}$$

From the previous definitions, some basic properties can be deduced: for any $A, B \in \mathcal{P}(X)$

- $Nec(A) \leq Pos(A)$
- $Pos(A \cap B) \leq \min[Pos(A), Pos(B)]$
- $Nec(A \cap B) \leq \max[Nec(A), Nec(B)]$

In view of the given facts, a necessity measure allows for justifiable degrees of conviction on each occurrence. The associated possibility measure assesses the extent to which an event may still be said to be feasible in the absence of any opposing evidence.

Despite its extreme simplicity, this framework is sufficiently generic to describe a wide range of information items, including numbers, intervals, consonant (nested) random sets, linguistic information, and uncertain equations in logical situations [7,8].

In practice, the degree of necessity is frequently seen as a lower probability bound and the degree of possibility as an upper probability constraint [2].

We consider every state variable in CISIApro 2.0 using the concept of possibility and necessity measures. In this way, the propagation algorithm in CISIApro 2.0 is a max-based consensus considering the possibility measures and a min-based consensus for the necessity measures. Furthermore, the main combination rules in possibility theory, minimum and maximum, may be interpreted with the "least commitment principle". A prudent method is to follow the "least commitment principle", which argues that you should never assume more beliefs than are reasonable [9].

Therefore, we can apply the classical combination rule of possibility theory. Let A_1 and A_2 be two sets on X the universal set, which we want to combine conjunctively into a new possibility and necessity measures. Applying the minimum rule, we get for all $x \in X$

$$A_{12}(x) = \min\left(A_1(x), A_2(x)\right), \tag{5}$$

Its related possibility measure is given by

$$Pos_{12}(A) = \max_{x \in A \subseteq X} Pos_{12}(x) \tag{6}$$

Its related necessity measure is given by

$$Nec_{12}(A) = \min_{x \in A \subseteq X} Nec_{12}(x). \tag{7}$$

3.2 Multi-layer Graph

We can formally define a graph (i.e., a single-layer network) as a tuple $\mathcal{G} = (\mathcal{V}, \mathcal{E})$, where $\mathcal{V}$ is the set of nodes and $\mathcal{E} = \mathcal{V} \times \mathcal{V}$ is the set of edges that connect pairs of nodes. If there is an edge between two nodes, they are said to be neighboring.

To model the Critical Infrastructure structure, we must add layers to the system's graph definition. Using the formalism of the multilayer networks [13], a complex system with d different types of layers is usually indicated as $\mathbf{L} = \{\mathcal{L}_a\}_{a=1}^d$.

We define a subset $\mathcal{V}_M \subseteq \mathcal{V} \times \mathcal{L}_1 \times \cdots \times \mathcal{L}_d$ containing only the corresponding node-layer combinations. Let u and α_i be the considered node and layer respectively, then $(u, \boldsymbol{\alpha}) \equiv (u, \alpha_1, \ldots, \alpha_d)$ represents the set containing the topological connection (u, α_i) between node u on the layer α_i.

We now introduce the edge set $\mathcal{E}_M \subseteq \mathcal{V}_M \times \mathcal{V}_M$, defined as the set of all possible node-layers pairings. It should be noted that alternative connections, such as self-node connections in different levels and multiple layer connecting, can be evaluated using this set.

Finally, we can define a *multilayer network* as a quadruplet

$$M = (\mathcal{V}_M, \mathcal{E}_M, \mathcal{V}, \mathbf{L}). \tag{8}$$

Note that a single-layer network is a special case of a multilayer network, in which $d = 0$ and $\mathcal{V}_M = \mathcal{V}$ are redundant. Furthermore, given a subset $D \subseteq \mathbf{L}$ of the layers of the *multilayer network* M, a special set of nodes that can be reached by any edge starting from a generic node v from any of the layers in D, is called *neighborhood* and is formally defined as $\Gamma(v, D)$.

CISIApro 2.0 structure is a directed multilayer network where each agent is a node that exists in at least one layer but can also be included in all the layers. CISIApro 2.0 also uses the convention to prevent multilayer network self-edges by avoiding self-edges in the underlying graph, i.e., $((u, \boldsymbol{\alpha}), (u, \boldsymbol{\alpha})) \notin \mathcal{E}_M$. CISIApro 2.0 structure connects each agent with the set of nodes identified by the same entity in different layers.

Each node $(u, \boldsymbol{\alpha})$ that occurs in at least one layer of M has a status vector $x_u(t)$ that defines the development of the u component at the time t. Each component's status vector is treated as driven by a nonlinear discrete dynamical equation, with the status changes for each u modified by its internal state $x_i(t)$ and the nearby data acquired. Each state variable is described using possibility and necessity measures.

Formally, the discrete-time nonlinear dynamics of the status vectors at time k are specified as follows:

$$\begin{aligned} x_u(t + 1) &= g_u \left(x_u(t), y_{\Gamma^+(u,\mathbf{L})}(t), z_u(t) \right) \\ y_u(t) &= h_u(x_u(t), z_u(t)) \end{aligned} \tag{9}$$

where g_u and h_u are nonlinear functions, $z_u(t)$ represents the external input of the node u and $y_{\Gamma^+(u,\mathbf{L})}(t)$ the data received from the incoming neighborhood. The incoming neighborhood of the node u is defined as:

$$\Gamma^+(u, \mathbf{L}) = \{v \in \mathcal{V}_M | ((v, \boldsymbol{\beta}), (u, \boldsymbol{\alpha})) \in \mathcal{E}_M, \boldsymbol{\alpha}, \boldsymbol{\beta} \in \mathbf{L}\} \tag{10}$$

Assuming that the topology of the communication network is fixed and that communication between the nodes takes place synchronously, that is, each node exchanges information with its neighbors simultaneously, the maximum (or minimum) consensus algorithm [15] is defined as follows:

$$Pos\left(x_i(k + 1)\right) = \max_{j \in \mathcal{J}_i} \left\{Pos\left(x_j(k)\right)\right\}, \qquad i = 1, \ldots, n \tag{11}$$

$$Nec\left(x_i(k + 1)\right) = \min_{j \in \mathcal{J}_i} \left\{Nec\left(x_j(k)\right)\right\}, \qquad i = 1, \ldots, n \tag{12}$$

where $\mathcal{J}_i$ is the set of predecessor nodes of node i and k is the communication event. We assume that $i \in \mathcal{J}_i, \forall i \in \mathcal{V}_f$, that is, there exists a self-loop only for source nodes.

4 Case Study and Results

To show the effectiveness of the suggested method, we describe a synthetic-generated scenario comprised of eight interconnected infrastructures: two communications providers, two distribution electricity providers, one railway business, one airline company, one bank, and one government department.

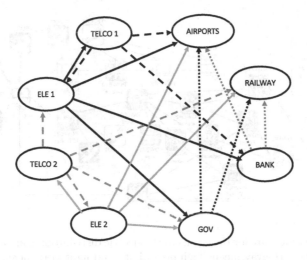

Fig. 3. The interdependency among the considered infrastructures

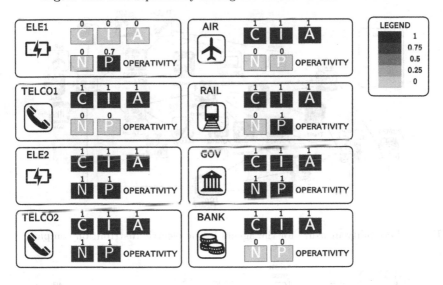

Fig. 4. Infrastructure synoptic view in case of ransomware attack on the electrical operator. The color scale indicates dark gray a value that is better than a light color.

Figure 3 depicts the interdependence among infrastructures. The two telecommunications carriers provide a range of services (including Internet access, mobile cellular networks, and backbone infrastructure) to the other infrastructures. Power is delivered to devices and components, as well as buildings, airports, and train stations, by electrical distribution companies. Banks handle airline and rail payments. The government agency (the Italian Ministry of Transport) issues rail transport permits and manages air traffic rights.

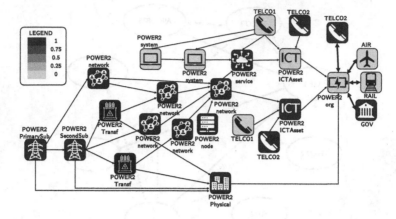

Fig. 5. Necessity measure for the agents in the electric distribution company 2 indicated by colors, where dark gray means high operativity and light gray means low one.

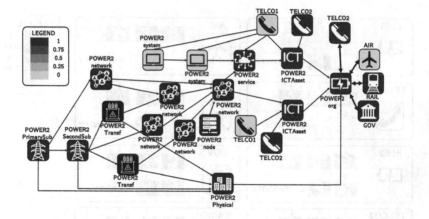

Fig. 6. Possibility measure for the agents in the electric distribution company 2.

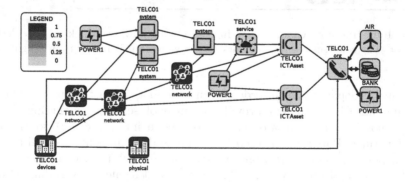

Fig. 7. Necessity measure for the agents in the telecommunication network.

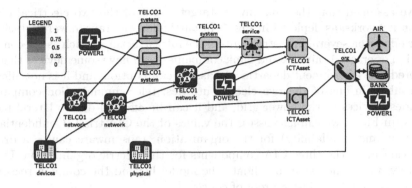

Fig. 8. Possibility measure for the agents in the telecommunication network.

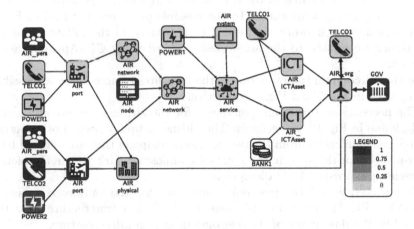

Fig. 9. Necessity measure for the agents in the airline company.

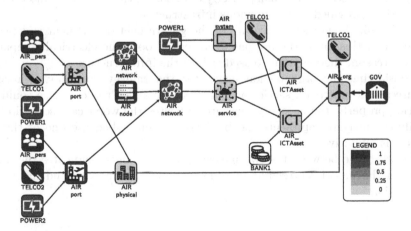

Fig. 10. Possibility measure for the agents in the airline company.

We assumed that the ransomware targeted one of the two electrical distribution networks, as depicted in Fig. 4. In particular, the ransomware attack can cause effects on several infrastructures: some infrastructures (such as telecommunication operator 1, airline, and bank companies) can have some devices that are powered; the government department has a backup option, and it is not affected by troubles in one of the two electric utilities; telecommunication company 2 provides services to the power grid, and it can be affected due to lateral movements. In Fig. 4, we can also assess the values of the CIA triad (Confidentiality, Integrity, and Availability) for the organization: ransomware causes a drastic reduction in all the three CIA components for the electric organization. Unfortunately, we are not able to validate the model beyond the common reasoning because the model is just a proof of concept.

In Fig. 5 and in Fig. 6, the necessity and possibility measures are depicted. The ransomware is located in the central software block. The three blocks that are dark gray in Fig. 6 are caused by the possible problems that could affect the telecommunication network, as we will demonstrate in the following pictures. The colors are related to the assessment realized using CISIApro 2.0 using a gray scale.

In the telecommunication network, the measures of necessity and possibility are reported in Fig. 7 and Fig. 8, respectively.

The necessity and possibility measures for the airline company are depicted in Fig. 9 and in Fig. 10, respectively. The airline company needs both electricity and telecommunication from the two previous company that are affected by the cyber-attack. For this reason, the agents are almost all dark gray in the pictures, representing a possible large disruption.

The necessity and the possibility measures for the railway company are depicted in Fig. 11 and in Fig. 12, respectively. This infrastructure is partially affected by the downgrade of the telecommunication infrastructure.

The bank's necessity and possibility measures are represented in Fig. 13 and in Fig. 14, respectively. The bank strictly depends on the electricity and telecommunications provided by the previous infrastructure.

In Fig. 15, the necessity measure of the government department is depicted. In this case, this infrastructure has been fed by both the electrical companies. For this reason, there is no increased risk in the infrastructure.

Considering the organization agent for the railway company, it receives resources from upstream service agents. Because at least one service could not function properly, the necessity measure indicates the worst-case scenario. The possibility measure represents the best-case scenario, because one of the two services is operative.

The distance between the two measures for each agent indicates the uncertainty in the model representation, due to reality complexity and incomplete information.

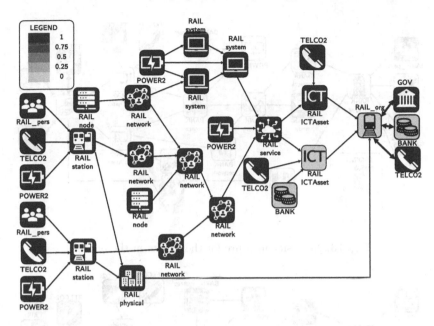

Fig. 11. Necessity measure for the agents in the railway company.

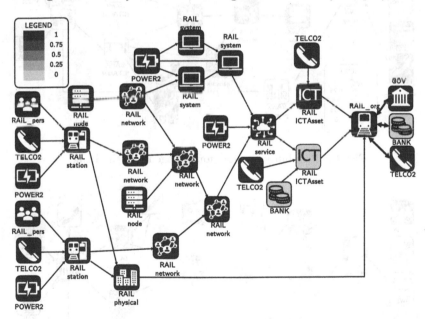

Fig. 12. Possibility measure for the agents in the railway company.

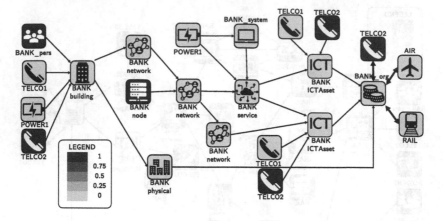

Fig. 13. Necessity measure for the agents in the bank.

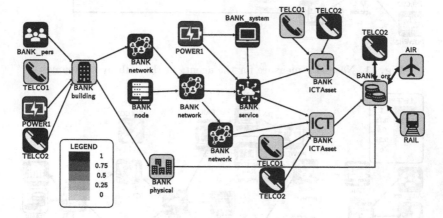

Fig. 14. Possibility measure for the agents in the bank.

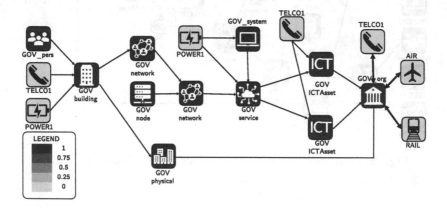

Fig. 15. Necessity measure for the agents in the government department.

5   Conclusions and Future Works

Cyberattacks on Critical Infrastructures are becoming increasingly widespread and can result in significant losses from a variety of perspectives, including operational, economic, and reputational. Infrastructure has its own regulations and best practices for avoiding them. However, the situation is more complicated because of unintended effects connected to CI interdependencies.

The proposed model assesses the consequences of adverse events or feasible restoration actions. Unfortunately, the problem of modeling an interdependent infrastructure is still an open issue and has no definitive answer due to its complexity.

We employ the Mixed Holistic-Reductionist (MHR) method to break down each infrastructure into distinct abstraction layers to capture the consequences of various unfavorable events. Using MHR, it is illustrated how CISIApro 2.0 may be utilized to simulate complex situations in the cyber-physical world using synthetic produced data. CISIApro is an agent-based simulator in which each element is an agent with a generic structure in common. The interchange of resources, errors, and cyber-attacks among agents results in an evaluation of repercussions across infrastructures.

The case study demonstrates that the suggested technique can measure ransomware effects on various infrastructures, especially when the knowledge information is not complete. In this case, the proposed methodology is very useful when dealing with devices or services that could be redundant. CISIApro 2.0 has been enhanced to deal with epistemic uncertainty in the model using possibility and necessity measures.

Furthermore, future work will be related to model revisions, considering increasingly interconnected infrastructures. The model may be enhanced by accounting for data propagation delays across infrastructures and considering both physical processes and ICT services. In addition, the model requires more time to confirm its conclusions, due to a better tuning of parameters within each block or entity.

References

1. Balakrishnan, S., Zhang, Z.: Modeling interdependent effects of infrastructure failures using imprecise dependency information. Sustain. Resilient Infrastruct. **7**(2), 153–169 (2022)
2. Baudrit, C., Dubois, D., Guyonnet, D.: Joint propagation and exploitation of probabilistic and possibilistic information in risk assessment. IEEE Trans. Fuzzy Syst. **14**(5), 593–608 (2006)
3. Bernardini, E., Foglietta, C., Panzieri, S.: Modeling telecommunications infrastructures using the CISIApro 2.0 simulator. In: Staggs, J., Shenoi, S. (eds.) ICCIP 2020. IAICT, vol. 596, pp. 325–348. Springer, Cham (2020). https://doi.org/10.1007/978-3-030-62840-6_16

4. Brown, T., Beyeler, W., Barton, D.: Assessing infrastructure interdependencies: the challenge of risk analysis for complex adaptive systems. Int. J. Crit. Infrastruct. **1**(1), 108–117 (2004)
5. Der Kiureghian, A., Ditlevsen, O.: Aleatory or epistemic? Does it matter? Struct. Saf. **31**(2), 105–112 (2009)
6. Digioia, G., Foglietta, C., Panzieri, S., Falleni, A.: Mixed holistic reductionistic approach for impact assessment of cyber attacks. In: 2012 European Intelligence and Security Informatics Conference, pp. 123–130. IEEE (2012)
7. Dubois, D.: Possibility theory and statistical reasoning. Comput. Stat. Data Anal. **51**(1), 47–69 (2006)
8. Dubois, D., Nguyen, H.T., Prade, H.: Possibility theory, probability and fuzzy sets misunderstandings, bridges and gaps. In: Dubois, D., Prade, H. (eds.) Fundamentals of Fuzzy Sets. FSHS, vol. 7, pp. 343–438. Springer, Boston (2000). https://doi.org/10.1007/978-1-4615-4429-6_8
9. Dubois, D., Prade, H., Smets, P.: New semantics for quantitative possibility theory. In: Benferhat, S., Besnard, P. (eds.) ECSQARU 2001. LNCS (LNAI), vol. 2143, pp. 410–421. Springer, Heidelberg (2001). https://doi.org/10.1007/3-540-44652-4_36
10. Foglietta, C., et al.: The Italian national security perimeter for cyber: assessing and modeling cyber threats in interdependent critical infrastructures with the cisiapro simulator. In: Seventeenth Annual IFIP WG 11.10 International Conference on Critical Infrastructure Protection (2023)
11. Foglietta, C., Panzieri, S.: Resilience in critical infrastructures: the role of modelling and simulation. In: Issues on Risk Analysis for Critical Infrastructure Protection. IntechOpen (2020)
12. Hüllermeier, E., Waegeman, W.: Aleatoric and epistemic uncertainty in machine learning: an introduction to concepts and methods. Mach. Learn. **110**, 457–506 (2021)
13. Kivela, M., Arenas, A., Barthelemy, M., Gleeson, J.P., Moreno, Y., Porter, M.A.: Multilayer networks. J. Complex Netw. **2**(3), 203–271 (2014)
14. Klir, G.J.: On fuzzy-set interpretation of possibility theory. Fuzzy Sets Syst. **108**(3), 263–273 (1999)
15. Nejad, B.M., Attia, S.A., Raisch, J.: Max-consensus in a max-plus algebraic setting: the case of fixed communication topologies. In: 2009 22nd International Symposium on Information, Communication and Automation Technologies, ICAT 2009 (2009)
16. Ouyang, M.: Review on modeling and simulation of interdependent critical infrastructure systems. Reliab. Eng. Syst. Saf. **121**, 43–60 (2014)
17. Pederson, P., Dudenhoeffer, D., Hartley, S., Permann, M.: Critical infrastructure interdependency modeling: a survey of us and international research. Idaho Natl. Lab. **25**, 27 (2006)
18. Reilly, A.C., Baroud, H., Flage, R., Gerst, M.D.: Sources of uncertainty in interdependent infrastructure and their implications. Reliab. Eng. Syst. Saf. **213**, 107756 (2021)
19. Rinaldi, S., Peerenboom, J., Kelly, T.: Identifying, understanding, and analyzing critical infrastructure interdependencies. IEEE Control Syst. Mag. **21**(6), 11–25 (2001)
20. Satumtira, G., Dueñas-Osorio, L.: Synthesis of modeling and simulation methods on critical infrastructure interdependencies research. In: Gopalakrishnan, K., Peeta, S. (eds.) Sustainable and Resilient Critical Infrastructure Systems, pp. 1–51. Springer, Heidelberg (2010). https://doi.org/10.1007/978-3-642-11405-2_1

21. Sun, W., Bocchini, P., Davison, B.D.: Overview of interdependency models of critical infrastructure for resilience assessment. Nat. Hazard. Rev. **23**(1), 04021058 (2022)
22. Wang, Z., Klir, G.J.: Fuzzy Measure Theory. Kluwer Academic Publishers, Norwell (1993)
23. Xiao, N., Sharman, R., Rao, H.R., Upadhyaya, S.: Infastructure interdependencies modeling and analysis-a review and synthesis. In: AMCIS 2008 Proceedings (2008)

Adaptable Smart Distribution Grid Topology Generation for Enhanced Resilience

Nataša Gajić$^{(\boxtimes)}$ ⓘ and Stephen Dirk Bjørn Wolthusen

NTNU, Trondheim, Norway
{natasa.gajic,stephen.wolthusen}@ntnu.no

Abstract. Whilst the robustness and resilience of power transmission networks including their susceptibility to attacks on measurements has been studied extensively, this is not the case for distribution networks. Although simpler in structure and instrumentation, these face increasing challenges from the integration of renewable energy and electric mobility, also increasing the attack surface for cyber attacks in the process. In this paper we therefore present a modelling mechanism allowing the representation of power distribution networks as well as communication and control networks with explicit parametric characterisation of their interconnection, capturing both current designs and allowing the study of future distribution networks. We then present initial results on resilience of distributed measurements based on topological properties.

Keywords: Topology Generator · Distribution Grid · Communication and Control Networks

1 Introduction

When considering attacks against the integrity of measurements and the management of power networks, the majority of attention has been devoted to transmission networks [15]. However, distribution networks are rapidly moving from being largely static and un-instrumented systems to active and intelligent part of power distribution. This is driven by factors such as electric mobility and bi-directional power flows with the deployment of residential and industrial renewable energy and storage, and requires the placement of large numbers of sensors and actuators at the edge of the power network where adversarial intervention is more easily achieved than in transmission networks.

This raises the question of how to determine the resilience of such intelligent distribution networks to faults and attacks, and the effects of changes to the topology of the network on the ability to detect and respond to these. The analysis of existing distribution networks offers only limited insight, as few documented smart distribution networks exist, and also because the dynamic elements of these networks are one of the key characteristics requiring further exploration.

© The Author(s), under exclusive license to Springer Nature Switzerland AG 2024
S. Pickl et al. (Eds.): CRITIS 2023, LNCS 14599, pp. 100–119, 2024.
https://doi.org/10.1007/978-3-031-62139-0_6

Real-time vulnerability assessments for power systems operation including distribution networks were studied by Biswas et al., [3] based on graph-theoretical formulations also to achieve enhanced situational awareness for power system operations, whilst other approaches seek to employ machine-learning approaches to detect possible attacks [25]. These, as well as the extension of detection algorithms for well-known false data injection attacks [8] all rely on a static topology of the underlying network for their analysis.

The modelling of distribution grids has remained relatively static with a number of models only considering power network aspects. Shi et al., [21] presents a method of generating topology of low voltage distribution grids. The modelling presented is based on the "transformer-branch box-meter box-meter" model which itself is based on the event of power outage in the low voltage network. Chen et al., [4] inspects differences between different topology models of distributed feeder automation in different international standards, such as IEC 61970 and IEC 61968. [1] also focuses on distributed feeders, but take approach of synthetic networks instead of looking at international standard. Their work is therefore somewhat restricted to generating topologies in the area where the research has been conducted because of the data they had available. Pisano et al., [17] models topologies of distribution grids on a larger areas in Italy and also uses synthetic approach which is based on different types of data (geographical, geological, electrical etc.) that is openly available to them. [2] researches topologies that underlie distribution grids by using fractal geometry.

Existing research on distribution networks mostly focuses on voltage sensitivity and state estimation of network parameters. For example, Wang et al. use state estimation to deal with the detection and localization of biased load attacks in smart grids by designing an internal observer [22], while Gómez-Peces et al. deal with location-based voltage sensitivities in distribution grids, focusing on the PV panels [10].

A mechanism for synthetically generating distribution network topologies where the structure of power network elements, measurement and control network controlling these more extensively in future distribution networks, and particularly their interconnection, can be configured dynamically is hence required to study both the resilience of such networks to attacks in particular, and also to enhance the understanding how re-configuration of such networks may aid in enhancing the resilience of the network. In this paper we therefore provide such a model and briefly demonstrate its utility for analysis.

1.1 Structure of the Paper

The remainder of this paper is structured as follows: After a brief problem description we review the related work on synthetic distribution networks before outlining our approach in Sect. 5. We describe algorithms alongside a complexity analysis and describe validation efforts in Sect. 8 before giving initial results on metrics to be used in the assessment of differently configured networks in Sect. 7. We then discuss ongoing and future work and give brief conclusions.

2 Motivation

Central motivation behind this work is developing topology generators that will generate (flexible) networks with 3 layers - distribution grid, information network overlay and adaptive interconnection layer - that can then be efficiently used as test networks for different protection algorithms. Larger scope of the project is to research how distribution grids can be protected from adversaries by studying their topological, that is, their graph structure. After that the plan for the future work is to develop algorithms and approaches for protection of the mentioned networks by the means of graph theory and combinatorial optimization. This will done by using dynamic analysis of the information overlay as well as the interconnection layer. That analysis along with the ability to re-configure the interconnecting overlay which is provided by the generators presented in this work Sect. 6, will be one of the central themes of our future work. Proofs of validity of these algorithms shall then be of a crucial importance in the future work as well as testing those protection algorithms on grids of different structures provided by the topology generators presented here Sect. 6. While the algorithms that will be presented in this work will be mainly used to improve distribution grids, these algorithms can be used in other areas of research, Thus, modelling of power flow is out of the scope of this work, as it impedes the flexibility and generalizations of the models presented here and instead deserves its own full work, which is planned in the part of future validation work.

3 Models of Distribution Grids are Insufficient to Capture Cyber Resilience

The main problems we address in this work are centered on the resilience of distribution grids (both in a sense of adversarial attacks as well as random failures). For that, there is a need to generate topologies which will model a wide range of different (yet sufficiently randomised) distribution grids. However, whilst models for these exist, it is commonly assumed that the information network for capturing measurements and sending control commands follows the same topology, which need not be the case and may in fact be exploited in the service of enhancing resilience.

Similarly, the placement of sensors and actuators as well as possible redundant mechanisms have so far not found entry into generative models.

Thus, we want to model valid structures for distribution grid with latitude for parameterised random variations. We augment this model with a modifiable information network overlay, connected to the distribution grid; whilst in the first instance these will mimic the topology of the underlying power network, we construct models where deviations of this approach can be explored dynamically. Making the mapping parameterized will ensure that a mapping will mostly preserve the structure of the distribution grid. It is important to note that such parameterisation is one of the factors that should be possible to change at any point. This is to capture the fact that a distribution grid and its connected information network overlay are not one and the same, or, in precise terms, the mapping from one to another is not a bijection. That, however, does not mean that they don't share large similarities, which is why the parameterisation of the mapping from distribution grid to information network overlay is done. If there is a need for the information network overlay to be even more different, that is, different on a more microscopic level (on the level of edges and vertices) than the distribution grid, additional changes to its edges and vertices can be made by making another mapping from the original information network overlay to the next "version" of it by using a new mapping with a new parameterization (another factor that should be possible to change and affect at any moment) for edges and vertices, respectively. Lastly, we introduce a join structure connecting the distribution grid model given information network overlay; this is achieved by choosing, with some pre-chosen parameterisation, matching nodes from both graphs and introducing possible cost-based variations on direct mappings; this also allows vertices in one graph (typically the power network) to have paths to multiple information network vertices.

We briefly identify the vertex and edge annotations in the following. Vertices in the generated graph have different semantics depending on the layer. In the distribution grid, the nodes can represent buses in electrical engineering terms, and may aggregate components such as substations or branching points. In the information network overlay, the nodes can represent smart parts of these buses (like sensors or actuators) or any other smart component in the vicinity that has communication abilities, such as cloud devices or telecommunication computing centers. In the interconnecting layer, while it is not usual to have nodes, there can exist vertices if needed and would likely reproduce some interconnection abstractions such as software-defined networking elements.

Edges in the generated graph also represent different entities depending on the layer. In the distribution grid, the edges would usually represent lines, i.e. physical cables. In the information network overlay, edges can represent any logical connections with a physical substrate. In the interconnecting layer, edges can be a little bit more abstract since if, for example, a substation has sensors inside it, an edge connecting the node that denotes the substation itself and the node denoting its smart part are both inside the same physical entity, so the edge between them would be inside the same physical entity as well, but it does not need to be the case if there is a way to connect, using the same example, that substation to a network cloud. Then that connection would be the edge between them.

4 Related Work

Two major approaches to topology modelling are dominant. The first relies on test networks of electrical networks. In [19], the authors list many different types of models of distribution grid such as IEEE Test Feeder or CIGRE Benchmark models as well as many other ones, which were used in this work to validate the ability to create equivalent power network topologies.

In [14] the authors generate a small-scale grid topology for smart low voltage distribution grids. Most such networks are themselves anchored in real test data such as [6], which presents benchmark low voltage networks based on data sets from German networks, while in [18], the authors describe benchmarks for integrating distribution grid in medium voltage distribution networks. Their proposed benchmark is meant to be representative of a real network while it is also designed for ease of use. However, instead of having the freedom and the wide range of different possibilities with models of distribution grids, these existing test networks focus on making networks with specific and therefore rigid requirements, which is the opposite of what is needed in this work.

The other major approach is based on synthetic networks. Synthetic networks have also been made for other levels of power networks. For example, in [23], the authors felt the similar need for topology generators as we do and have developed the means for producing power grids with scalable size and randomly generated topologies. They have made these as ensembles of networks and propose to use them as statistical tools to study the scale the performance of the combined electric power control. However, they have focused on large scale power networks (such as transmission grids) and use it as an ensemble rather than one interactive tool that this research needs. But this approach of synthetic networks has also been used in distribution grids as well. For example, as explained in [16], the authors created an open-source Matlab Toolbox by the name *TDNetGen*, which generates synthetic models of combined transmission and distribution grids. They have made this to be able to analyse the interactions between transmission and multiple distribution grids at once and analyse primarily voltage behaviours in them. While this is very useful for the needs of their work, it doesn't suit the needs of this research because, not only it adds the element of transmission grids, which is out of the scope of this work, but also did not validate the mapping of their synthetic model to real networks.

Another example is the DiNeMo (Distribution Network Models) [7] platform which focuses on modelling distribution grids of different communities, cities or regions. However, at the time of writing this paper, the platform is currently non-operational since the people behind it are working on a new version, thus, making it unsuitable for this research. But, wanting to have a better understanding of their approach, we looked at their previous work in [9] which was their first case study where the authors used the Croatian city of Varaždin to test their platform and then use it to analyse voltage fluctuations that appear in the network. This approach was also shown to be unsuitable for the purposes of this research since they use city maps to build their distribution grids, which, while it can be seen as graph-like, doesn't have the level of randomness or the flexibility this research needs, but focuses on a single real city, which is the opposite of what this research needs - many different topologies which are sufficiently random and different from one another to be able to properly use them as test networks in the future work.

An additional problem with both of these approaches is that neither have the information overlay that is needed for the purposes of this work.

From our literature review, there is another problem for why there aren't really all that many topology generators today being built. In this work from 2016 [24], authors argue that today, due to the increasing number of distributed energy resources (or DERs), it is hard to know the exact topology of distribution grid. Further, that the known topology gets outdated quickly because distribution grid changes very frequently (think new buildings, new EV charging stations, new gas stations etc. get built during the time). Because of that, the authors propose, instead of a topology generator, a so called *Topology Reconstruction Algorithm* based on probabilistic methods and historical data. This paper is of unique interest for this work because it actually takes into account both distribution grid *and* information overlay. However, it focuses on historical data which makes it both less flexible and less general than this work needs.

5   Methods

A distribution grid be interpreted as a graph consisting of two different types of substructures or topologies: open structures (tree-like structures aka radial form) and closed structures (aka meshes). That means that there should be higher degree of redundancies in the networks in urban centers than in the rural areas. Which then further means that it will be easier to alleviate the problems that arise in urban centers (faults or attacks in the network) compared to the problems that arise in rural areas. Tree graphs are open, tree-like, graphs that have no loops. Closed structures, like meshes or rings, are defined by them having loops, or in other words redundancies.

5.1   Importance of Redundancies Aka a Little on Attacks

This section presents the plan on how to include attack lines in the future work. It will also give motivation as for why is it important for this research to have robust (or as robust as possible) redundancies in generated graphs.

First of all, the plan is to define an attack in the further research as any adversary action (or multiple actions) in the distribution grid that works to disturb and destroy stability of energy supply in electrical network. Thus, from mathematical and abstract point-of-view, the plan is to include in this definition of adversary both actual hackers and intruders as well as faults in the system, since in the mathematical sense both of these can be modeled in a similar way as well as develop protective algorithms in the similar ways. That modelling of adversaries will also be a part of future work.

The main way to stop an adversary from spreading damage in a network is to "quarantine" them by shutting down the energy supply in their closest vicinity, or as close to them in the network as possible. And it is necessary for the future developed protection algorithms to be able to do that while impacting as few citizens as possible. But if a power company shuts down the power along one edge of "infected" graph to stop an adversary, an innocent user that might be on one side of that edge will lose their electricity as well. Unless there is another way, that is, another edge to bring electricity to them. Which is why redundancy of some level in distribution grids is important.

5.2   Problem with the Missing Redundancy

In the country where this research is being conducted, level of redundancy is significantly lower than it would be optimal for the sake of system protection. According to an expert, who has kindly agreed to share some of their time and expertise to help the authors understand better how distribution grids actually look like (in the country where this research takes place). The expert has explained that while *some level* of redundancy in distribution grids does exist, it is certainly not nearly a mesh - level connectivity. The expert has also explained that

1. When a redundancy happens in a distribution grid, it happens exclusively on the level of substations
2. There is no rule by which a redundancy in the grid can appear, because it can be there because of multitude of reasons, most of which are historical (and some geographical). And those reasons do not follow any sort of pattern.

Thus a statistical and randomized approach was deemed as an optimal and these points were taken into account.

Therefore, the need to use information network overlay becomes even more imperative because having it improves the redundancy and thus the robustness of the network. Specially, it is cheaper to add more sensors in the information network than in the distribution grid. Or, in other words, the density of the information network graph is likely much higher than the distribution grid graph because of that cheapness (or, it is easier to make the density of it much higher). To improve the robustness, that is, redundancy level even further, it would also be possible to use other networks, such as radio network, for example.

5.3   How Redundancy Should Work in a Distribution Grid

The state of redundancy of the country where this research is being conducted power networks being what it is, we still believe that it is worth it to say a few words regarding the *how redundancy should work in distribution grid*, if nothing else, for the sake of the future city planning projects. If we are looking at it from the point of view of protection from both adversaries and random power failures in the system, having a good level of redundancy both in urbane and rural areas would make it easier to both better protect the information flow (f.e. because of popularization of ideas of smart homes and smart buildings, look, for example at this paper [11] from 2020 which deals with the state of the art regarding smart cities or at this one [20] from 2021 where the authors explore an intelligent home automation system that allows the user to monitor electrical appliances of the home) and better ensure the supply of energy to the users even in the events of adversaries attacks on the grid or random failures in the grid (f.e in an event when a tree would fall on the power line and damage it - having another branch to supply the power to the customers would certainly simplify the problem). Therefore, security wise, in both sense of that word in power engineering world, it would be preferable if in the future the professionals that plan cables setups would take more care to think of redundancy and why is it important.

6   Algorithms

In this part, three algorithms that are the central part of this research's topology generators will be presented. The first one generates *Distribution Grid*, the second one generates *Information Network* and the third one connects them by generating an *Interconnection Layer*.

In Algorithm 1 a *distribution grid graph* is defined as a graph that is both tree-like and has loops (that is, closed forms or meshes) in parts of its structure. Configuring branching factor is taken into account as input via two different input probabilities, one which will denote whether, during a creation of a node, a node stays a node and the other one which decides what kind of a (more) complex structure should be in a place of a node (that is, how the graph is branching be it a tree/radial form or a closed form/mesh), in a scenario that instead of a node, due to the first probability, it was decided that there will be a more complex structure there. We call it a distribution grid graph because it models the grid structure of distribution grids.

Algorithm 1: Given the size n, branching factor $branchingFactor$ and the probabilities $pNode$ and $pTree$, where $pNode$ is a probability that in a creation of our graph, a node stays a node, while $pTree$ is a probability that in a creation of our graph, a node turns into a more complex structure and $pNode \leq pTree$, the algorithm makes a connected distribution grid graph.

Additionally, $nodesNumber$ is a counter of the current number of nodes in the graph. $newNode$ is the node that shall be next node in the graph. It is a list that contains all of its neighbors. G is the graph. It is a vector of nodes and it grows throughout the algorithm. $makeANewNode(G, n)$ is a temporary function that makes a new node for the given graph G of length n. $randomNumber(n)$ is a temporary function that returns random number between 1 and n. $update(G)$ is a temporary function that updates all the nodes that have connections with the newest node in 2 steps: by updating their number of connections and by growing them by adding the newest connection in the following manner: $node = [nodenewconnection]$, where $node$ is the current node and $newconnection$ is its newest connection. $MakeATreeGraph$ is function that generates a tree of a given size and branching factor. $MakeAClosedGraph$ is a function that generates a closed form/mesh of a given size and probability that denotes density of connections in it.

Algorithm 1. Makes a random distribution grid

1: **function** MAKEADISTRIBUTIONGRID($n, pNode, pTree, branchingFactor$)
2:   ▷ Makes a random distribution grid
3:     $nodesNumber \leftarrow 1$
4:     $newNode \leftarrow [nodesNumber, 0]$
5:     $G \leftarrow newNode$
6:     **while** $nodesNumber < n$ **do**
7:         $p \leftarrow pNode$
8:         **if** $p \leq pNode$ **then**   ▷ Case: added node is an actual node
9:             $nodesNumber \leftarrow nodesNumber + 1$
10:             $newNode \leftarrow makeANewNode(G, nodesNumber)$
11:             $G \leftarrow update(G)$
12:         **end if**
13:         **if** $p > pNode$ & $p \leq pTree$ **then**   ▷ Case: added node is a tree graph
14:             $nTree \leftarrow randomNumber(n - nodesNumber - 1)$
15:             $GTree \leftarrow MakeATreeGraph(nTree, branchingFactor)$
16:             $nodesNumber \leftarrow nodesNumber + nTree$
17:             $G \leftarrow [G, GTree]$
18:         **end if**
19:         **if** $p > pTree$ **then**   ▷ Case: added node is a closed graph
20:             $nClosedGraph \leftarrow randomNumber(n - nodesNumber - 1)$
21:             $GClosedGraph \leftarrow MakeAClosedGraph(nClosedGraph, pTree)$
22:             $nodesNumber \leftarrow nodesNumber + nClosedGraph$
23:             $G \leftarrow [G, GClosedGraph]$
24:         **end if**
25:     **end while**
26:     **return** G
27: **end function**

In Algorithm 2 an *information network overlay* is defined as a graph that is similar enough to the provided distribution grid graph, yet with more connections since it contains both cable, aka physical and wireless connections.

Algorithm 2: Given the distribution grid graph DG, its size nDG, and probabilities $pNodeLimit$, $pConLimit$, $pErase$, $pEraseLimit$, where $pNodeLimit$ denotes the probability limit of when the algorithm should stop making nodes, $pConLimit$ denotes the probability limit of when the algorithm should stop making the connections between the nodes, $pErase$ denotes the starting probability to erase connections, while $pEraseLimit$ denotes the probability limit of when the algorithm should stop erasing connections, the algorithm creates an information network connected graph overlay by, first, making a copy of DG, and then, with the provided probabilities, edges of some of the nodes will change.

Additionally, G is a graph, which is a vector of nodes and it grows throughout the algorithm. $pRandomNode$ denotes starting probability decided by a temporary function $startingProbability(p)$ that decides a starting probability depending on the provided probability limit p probability. $connection$ is a label of a node which has a connection to the current node in the graph, $numberOfConnections$ is a number of connections of the current node $currentNode$. $randomNumber(n)$ is a temporary function that returns random number between 1 and n. $pCon$ is a probability that denotes a probability of making an additional connection between the nodes. $decreasingProbability(n)$ is an additional function that tells the algorithm how to decrease the initial probability. $tempConnection$ is a new number that denotes one of the connections of the current node, which the algorithm decides whether it should be erased or not. $oldNode$ is then the node that corresponds to $tempConnection$. $EraseConnection(node, connection)$ is an additional function that erases the provided connection, $connection$ from the given node, $node$. $update(G)$ is a temporary function that updates all the nodes that have connections with the newest node in 2 steps: by updating their number of connections and by growing them by adding the newest connection in the following manner: $node = [nodenewCon]$, where $node$ is the current node and $newCon$ is its newest connection. $newCon$ is a number that denotes the new connection node $newNode$ that, if the conditions are satisfied, will replace the old $tempConnection$ with the new one using an additional function $ReplaceConnection(tempconnection, newCon, tempnode)$ that replaces an old value in the current node with the new one. This means that it uses search to find the old connection inside the node (which is a vector). This gives it a linear complexity. Lastly, GIN denotes generated information network overlay.

Algorithm 2. Makes an information network

1: **function**   MAKEINFORMATIONNETWORK($DG, nDG, pNodeLimit, pConLimit,$
    $pE, pELimit$)
2:    ▷ Makes information network from provided distribution grid, f.e. a graph made
    by 6
3:    $G \leftarrow DG$
4:    $pRandomNode \leftarrow startingProbability(pNodeLimit)$
5:    **while** $pRandomNode > pNodeLimit$ **do**   ▷ Changeable condition
6:        $pRandomNode \leftarrow decreasingProbability(pRandomNode)$
7:        $connection \leftarrow randomNumber(nG - 1)$
8:        $currentNode \leftarrow G(connection)$
9:        $pConnection \leftarrow startingProbability(pConLimit)$
10:        **while** $pCon > pConLimit$ **do**
11:            $pCon \leftarrow DecreasingProbability(pCon)$
12:            $tempCon \leftarrow currentNode(2 + randomNumber(currentNode(2)))$
13:            $oldNode \leftarrow G(tempCon)$
14:            **if** $pErase < pEraseLimit$ **then**
15:                $currentNode(2) \leftarrow currentNode(2) - 1$
16:                $currentNode \leftarrow EraseConnection(currentNode, tempCon)$
17:                $G \leftarrow update(G)$
18:                $DG \leftarrow update(DG)$
19:            **else**
20:                $newCon \leftarrow randomNumber(nDG - 1)$
21:                $newNode \leftarrow G(newCon)$
22:                $currentNode \leftarrow ReplaceConnection(tempCon, newCon,$
    $currentNode)$
23:                $G \leftarrow update(G)$
24:            **end if**
25:        **end while**
26:    **end while**
27:    $GIN \leftarrow G$
28:    **return** GIN
29: **end function**

Now that both distribution grid and information network overlay that follows distribution grid closely enough have been generated, next there is a need for an algorithm that connects the two, so that the final desired structure - the multilayered graph that consists of distribution grid, information network overlay and the interconnecting layer - is generated. Algorithm 3 is the algorithm that connects those two graphs.

Algorithm 3: Given the distribution grid graph DG, information network graph IN, their individual sizes n and the probabilities $pNode$ and $pTree$, where $pNode$ is a probability that in a creation of the graph, a node stays a node, while $pTree$ is a probability that in a creation of the graph, a node turns into a more complex structure and $pNode \leq pTree$, the algorithm creates a connected adaptive communication layer graph by first making a distribution grid graph (by calling Algorithm 1 (Sect. 6)) between them. By choosing $pNode$ and $pTree$ to be 1, we will get only connections without nodes in the adaptive communication layer. *neighborhoodFactor* is a number that defines what is a neighborhood of a node and it is used to generate a probability density function which decides how to connect a node from distribution grid to a neighbor of its corresponding node in the information layer.

Additionally, *Network* is the structure that we are looking for, *tempNode*, *tempNode*1 and *tempNode*2 denote temporary nodes, *lenght(tempNode)* is a function that returns length of *tempNode*. *nodesNumber* is a counter of the current number of nodes in the graph. *ReturnNeighbor(i, neighboorhoodFactor)* is a temporary function that separately generates a probability density function using the *neighborhoodFactor* which it then uses to return a neighbor of the node in the information layer that corresponds to the node i in distribution grid to which that node i should connect to. *updateNode(node, k)* is a temporary function that updates the node *node* by updating its number of connections and adding the new connection to its list of connections. *update(G)* is a temporary function that updates all the nodes that have connections with the newest node in 2 steps: by updating their number of connections and by growing them by adding the newest connection in the following manner: *node* = [*nodenewconnection*], where *node* is the current node and *newconnection* is its newest connection.

Algorithm 3. Makes an adaptive communication layer

1: **function** MAKEADAPTIVELAYER($n, DG, IN, neighborhoodFactor$)
2:     $G \leftarrow DG$
3:     $GIN \leftarrow IN$
4:     $Network \leftarrow G$
5:     **for** $i \geq 1$ & $i \leq n$ **do**
6:         $tempNode \leftarrow GIN(i)$
7:         **for** $j \geq 1$ & $j \leq length(tempNode)$ **do**
8:             **if** $j \neq 2$ **then**
9:                 $tempNode(j) \leftarrow tempNode(j) + n$
10:            **else**
11:                $tempNode(j) \leftarrow tempNode(j)$
12:            **end if**
13:        **end for**
14:        $Network(i + n) \leftarrow tempNode$
15:    **end for**
16:    $nodesNumber \leftarrow 2n$ ▷ since $2n$ is the total number of nodes in DG and IN
17:    **for** $i = 1 : n$ **do**
18:        $tempNode1 \leftarrow Network(i)$
19:        $tempNode2 \leftarrow ReturnNeighbor(i, neighborhoodFactor)$
20:        $tempNode1 \leftarrow updateNode(tempNode1, n + i)$
21:        $tempNode2 \leftarrow updateNode(tempNode2, i)$
22:        $Network \leftarrow Update(Network)$
23:    **end for**
24:    **return** $Network$
25: **end function**

---

7   Results

Here an example of comparison between a model made by one of the presented algorithms and a real distribution grid will be presented. In the Fig. 1 it is shown how our model compares to the study case used in [26]. The distribution grid model on the right hand side was made by Algorithm 1, Sect. 6, with the branching factor of 3 and the number of nodes equal to the number of nodes in the study case. Comparing the pictures, it can be seen that our algorithm can make a model of a real distribution grid that is close enough (close enough meaning taking into consideration the inherent randomness of Algorithm 1 which it inherits from the probability density function, which is in turn generated by the provided branching factor, and which is used to generate branches). Additionally, due to the flexible and interactive properties of our models, there is a degree of freedom of changing our network at different stages.

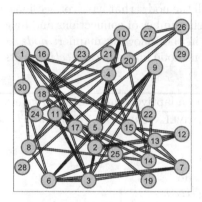

Fig. 1. The picture shows a distribution grid made by the Algorithm 1 with the branching factor = 3. This example is made as a comparison to the study case (Fig. 2) in the paper [26]. It is important to note that a DSO (Distribution System Operator) would have actual, real life parameters, which, when provided, would improve the precision of the Algorithm 1.

In the Fig. 2, the comparison between the same model network visualised both in Matlab and in Arena3D, [13] is shown. Arena3D is a visualization tool made by the authors of [13] and which is used to generate visualizations of large and complex graphs. These visualizations can be presented in different ways and an as many layers as needed. In our specific case there is a need for two distinct layers - distribution grid and information overlay as well as a clear way to present the connections between those layers. Matlab is used to visualize smaller networks, since Matlab has greater node interactivity than Arena3D, however, visualization in Arena3D is used in those cases of larger networks because the visibility in it is better in those cases, when compared to visualization of the same large networks in Matlab.

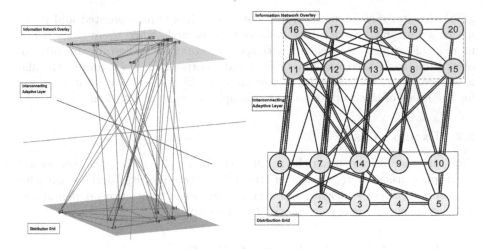

Fig. 2. On the left side a small network of 20 nodes as visualized in Arena3D is shown, while on the right hand side the same network visualized in Matlab is shown.

8   Validation

In this part, there will be a two part validation of what we have done in this work so far. In the first part there will be a validation of whether the developed algorithms can reasonably recreate real distribution grid and in the second part, a two-case example will be presented where the advantages of having an information network overlay are, compared to what happens when there is no information overlay. More thorough examination is planned for the future work, where a grid lab will test how well the algorithms presented here can approximate their grid simulation as well as how well these algorithms can adapt and follow the changes in the grid.

First, let us take a look at the left hand side of the Fig. 1 that has been presented in the Sect. 7. This is a model used in the study case [26]. The right hand side of the picture represents the model made by Algorithm 1 with the same number of nodes as the study case and the branching factor of 3 and a probability density function chosen in such a way that the resulting distribution grid is dense. Still, the grid made by the Algorithm 1 is good enough approximation for the future parts of this research, since the number of connections and branching factor is one of the factors that set to be flexible. Obviously, with an accurate probability density function provided by a grid company with exact data, distribution grid model made by Algorithm 1 would be a much closer approximation.

8.1   Graph Metrics

There are different graph metrics that can be used on the graphs generated by the presented algorithms. Some of them, such as size of graph, degree of graph,

graph density, shortest path and all paths are already incorporated and in use in our algorithms. In the future parts of this research, when there is a need for more localized metrics or metrics with specific properties for certain optimization algorithms, such metrics will be defined and incorporated. For example, the plan is to incorporate and make use of flow metrics [12] in the future work. However, for the needs of this work, these listed simple metrics are sufficient.

8.2   Example Case

Here, an example case using the result from the Fig. 2 will be presented as well as graph density, average path length and shortest metrics to showcase what happens to the graph density and average number of connections depending on whether or not the information overlay is present.

8.3   Case 1: Information Overlay Is Not Present

Let us suppose in this case that the graph from the Fig. 2 doesn't have information overlay and consists only of 10 nodes in the distribution grid. In that case, its graph density will be $density(DG) = \frac{2*E}{V*(V-1)} = \frac{2*15}{10*9} = 0.33$, where DG denotes our distribution grid, E is the number of its connections (or edges or lines) and V is number of its nodes (or vertices or buses). Also, in this case, its average number of connections will be $k = \frac{s}{n} = 1.5$, where s is its number of all connections and n is the number of vertices. To showcase the usage of shortest path metric, let us set one arbitrary node as a starting point. For the sake of simplicity, lets say that the node 1 is the starting point. The shortest path and its length will then be measured from the starting node to the rest of the nodes in the graph. To calculate the shortest paths (and their lengths), Dijksta's algorithm is used, which can be found, among other places, in [5]. The algorithm gives the shortest path to each of the other nodes as well as all of the paths, which can be seen in the left hand side of the Fig. 3. It is important to note that the metric used here is node/vertex independent, which ensures that there are no loops in the paths found. That the metric is vertex independent also ensures that there are only finite number of paths, which is important when there is a need to list all of the paths (f.e. when one of the vertices or one of the edges is made unreliable by an adversary). Using the provided results, it is then easy to show that the average path length, when using the node 1 as a starting point is 2.11.

8.4   Case 2: Information Overlay Is Present

Let us suppose now that the graph from the same example now includes information overlay as well as its interconnecting layer and therefore consist of 20 nodes (10 nodes in the distribution grid and 10 nodes in the information overlay). In that case, the density of the graph will be $density(DG) = \frac{2*E}{V*(V-1)} = \frac{2*51}{20*19} = 0.27$. Also, in this case, its average number of connections will be $k = \frac{s}{n} = 5.15$. For the shortest paths, the same Dijkstra algorithm will be used. To have a

Dij =

1	0	0
2	1	1
3	2	2
4	3	3
5	2	7
6	2	7
7	1	1
8	2	7
9	3	8
10	3	5

Dij =

1	0	0
2	1	1
3	2	2
4	2	14
5	2	7
6	2	7
7	1	1
8	2	7
9	2	11
10	3	5
11	1	1
12	2	2
13	3	3
14	1	1
15	2	14
16	2	7
17	1	1
18	2	2
19	2	11
20	3	15

Fig. 3. On the left side the result of Dijksta's Algorithm for only distribution grid part of the graph from Fig. 2 is shown, while one the right side, the same result is shown, but for the both distribution grid and information overlay. In both cases, nodes are in the first column, while the third column contains the penultimate node in its path. That third column contains actual paths, while the second column contains their lengths.

good comparison between two provided cases, the same starting node - node 1 - is used. The results can be seen on the right hand side of the Fig. 3. And the average shortest path in this case is then easily calculated to be, when considering node 1 as the starting node, 1.89.

8.5   Case 1 vs Case 2

As we can see, by including information overlay and interconnecting layer, even in this small (in the sense of number of nodes) and simple example with only 20 nodes the average number of connections has been increased almost 3.5 times in the case 2 and it is trivial to see that if the number of connections in the interconnecting layer grows, the number of connections would grow and the average path length would shorten (as it was shown in both cases, with the average path length in the first case being 2.11 and in the second case 1.89). Now, considering graph density, while this small example (which has been showcased because denser cases are worse off in a sense of visual representation) shows that the graph is sparser if the information layer is included, but that only happens in such a small case as this, as it is obvious that the more connections there are in the interconnecting layer, the denser the graph will be and therefore, for any sufficiently larger or more complex example, graph density of the case 2 will be larger than the density of case 1.

This is important because in the future work the methods for preventive measures (that is, algorithms) against both adversaries and faults in the network will be explored in detail. Thus, having denser graphs, more connections and shorter paths to an adversary or a fault will help mitigate and/or prevent the damage done by an adversary or a fault.

8.6   Validation Example

Let us make a small example for the sake of validation. Let us suppose that in our example from the Fig. 2 there exist a static adversary in the node number 3.

Stopping the adversary from making damage would mean shutting down all its connections. Let us also suppose that the electricity provider for our example of distribution grid is located in the node number 5. In the case 1, where there is no information overlay, that would mean shutting down 4 connections, which means lowering the density of the graph from 0.33 to 0.24 as well as lowering the average number of connections from 1.5 to 1.1, which means that for a equally sparse, but larger graph, there is a significant risk of some nodes (that is, users) ending up without electricity, since there is only one connection per node (on average), which means that if that connection is shut down for the sake of protection of the rest of the network, that node and user will be left without electricity. On the other hand, in case 2, where information overlay does exist, the changes in graph density and average number of connection are as follows: graph density goes down from 0.27 to 0.24 and the average number of connections goes from 5.15 to 4.9. This shows that with the information network overlay, the whole graph becomes more robust and thus more resilient to adversaries because the average number of connections and its density doesn't change much even if all of the direct neighborhood of adversary is shut down.

This has been just a small example and this will be researched in detail in the future work. There, we will also look at more complex metrics that include shared and independent paths, since independent paths are the one which are most endangered by an adversary.

Following 2 points are also of significant importance - having a (dense) information overlay helps shorten the path of information. This is important because, if there is an adversary, such as in our validation case, it is important that the information relaying there existence (or, more precisely, information showcasing that there is a disturbance in distribution grid) reaches one of the nodes with the power of decision, which can then deal with the situation as soon as possible. That is why shortening the path of information flow is of significant importance. The second important point would be that having information overlay provides different paths that can be independent of an edge infected by an adversary.

9   Conclusions

Future distribution grids will need to perform far more tasks than traditional unintelligent distribution networks owing to the need to obtain far more measurement points both internally and interfacing with advanced metering infrastructure, and will also need to actively manage loads and power flows in the presence of more variable loads such as those resulting from electric mobility, storage, renewable energy production at the grid edge. This increased complexity and particularly the additional communication and control, unfortunately, also bring with it a larger attack surface for cyber attacks.

We consider it imperative to be able to study the resilience of future distribution networks, but as existing models focus primarily on power networks, this opens a lacuna in the ability to understand the resilience of such networks and how they may be configured in a way to support robustness and resilience in the face of both faults and attacks.

In this work we have hence laid foundation for the modelling of intelligent distribution grids and particularly the ability to study the effects of modifying cyber elements of the resulting cyber-physical system. We note that these resilience measures will apply to faults in networks by e.g. studying the effect of re-routing measurements and control traffic. To this end we have created a set of configurable topology component generators capable of replicating existing distribution network designs, but also offer sufficient flexibility to study extensive variations. Our main contribution, however, lies in the creation of a joined network structure containing three layers:

Distribution Grid. Constructed of sub-components configured by way of probability density functions derivable from a user-provided branching factor

Information Network. Derived from the distribution grid by a modified mapping with parameterised distortion, reflecting co-location of active and passive components of the information network

Connecting Adaptive Layer. Interconnecting the distribution and information networks in a configurable manner, also allowing bounded deviations from direct mappings.

We have provided the required algorithms along with complexity analysis and in this paper provide a small selection of graph metrics for illustration purposes and provided examples of the resulting models, including different interconnection mechanisms.

9.1 Future Work

As part of our ongoing and future work, we are studying the susceptibility of different intelligent distribution networks to various faults and attacks and will create algorithms for both detecting such incidents as well as possible reconfiguration approaches which may require the integration of redundancy in the information and adaptive layers. As such protective algorithms must operate in a variety of circumstances it is important that these are functional not only in a limited number of test cases, but also when networks are under attack and have had to disconnect buses or individual loads and generators. We also aim to integrate our models with power flow analysis models to study further dynamic effects.

References

1. Ali, M., Prakash, K., Macana, C., Raza, M., Bashir, A., Pota, H.: Modeling synthetic power distribution network and datasets with industrial validation. J. Ind. Inf. Integr. **31**, 100407 (2023)
2. Barakou, F., Koukoula, D., Hatziargyriou, N., Dimeas, A.: Fractal geometry for distribution grid topologies. In: 2015 IEEE Eindhoven PowerTech, pp. 1–6 (2015). https://doi.org/10.1109/PTC.2015.7232496

3. Biswas, R.S., Pal, A., Werho, T., Vittal, V.: A graph theoretic approach to power system vulnerability identification. IEEE Trans. Power Syst. **36**(2), 923–935 (2021). https://doi.org/10.1109/TPWRS.2020.3010476

4. Chen, R., Lu, J., Liu, M., Ying, J., Chen, Y., Yue, Y.: Distribution network topology model generation method for distributed feeder automation. In: 2019 IEEE Innovative Smart Grid Technologies - Asia (ISGT Asia), pp. 1057–1062 (2019). https://doi.org/10.1109/ISGT-Asia.2019.8881765

5. Daintith, J., Wright, E.: A Dictionary of Computing. Oxford University Press, Oxford (2008)

6. Dickert, J., Domagk, M., Schegner, P.: Benchmark low voltage distribution networks based on cluster analysis of actual grid properties. In: 2013 IEEE Grenoble Conference, pp. 1–6 (2013). https://doi.org/10.1109/PTC.2013.6652250

7. Dinemo. https://ses.jrc.ec.europa.eu/dinemo. Accessed 12 Oct 2022

8. Fahmeeda, S., Bhagyashree, B.K.: Detection and prevention of false data injection attack in cyber physical power system. In: 2021 IEEE International Conference on Mobile Networks and Wireless Communications (ICMNWC), pp. 1–5 (2021). https://doi.org/10.1109/ICMNWC52512.2021.9688471

9. Grzanic, M., Flammini, M.G., Prettico, G.: Distribution network model platform: a first case study. Energies **12**(21) (2019). https://doi.org/10.3390/en12214079. https://www.mdpi.com/1996-1073/12/21/4079

10. Gómez-Peces, C., Grijalva, S., Reno, M.J., Blakely, L.: Estimation of PV location based on voltage sensitivities in distribution systems with discrete voltage regulation equipment. In: 2021 IEEE Madrid PowerTech, pp. 1–6 (2021). https://doi.org/10.1109/PowerTech46648.2021.9494762

11. Inibhunu, C., Carolyn McGregor, A.: A privacy preserving framework for smart cities utilising IoT, smart buildings and big data. In: 2020 IEEE 22nd International Conference on High Performance Computing and Communications; IEEE 18th International Conference on Smart City; IEEE 6th International Conference on Data Science and Systems (HPCC/SmartCity/DSS), pp. 1096–1103 (2020). https://doi.org/10.1109/HPCC-SmartCity-DSS50907.2020.00197

12. Kalman, L., Krauthgamer, R.: Flow metrics on graphs (2021). https://doi.org/10.48550/ARXIV.2112.06916

13. Kokoli, M., et al.: Arena3Dweb: interactive 3D visualization of multilayered networks supporting multiple directional information channels, clustering analysis and application integration. bioRxiv (2022). https://doi.org/10.1101/2022.10.01.510435. https://www.biorxiv.org/content/early/2022/10/05/2022.10.01.510435.1

14. Krontiris, A., Pfeffer, S., Neukamp, T., Jeromin, I., Pfeffer, M.: Smart grid lab Hessen - a real-life test environment for active distribution grids. In: 2021 9th International Conference on Modern Power Systems (MPS), pp. 1–5 (2021). https://doi.org/10.1109/MPS52805.2021.9492637

15. Liu, Y., Ning, P., Reiter, M.K.: False data injection attacks against state estimation in electric power grids. In: Jha, S., Keromytis, A.D. (eds.) Proceedings of the 16th ACM Conference on Computer and Communications Security, Chicago, IL, USA, pp. 21–32. ACM Press (2009). https://doi.org/10.1145/1653662.1653666

16. Pilatte, N., Aristidou, P., Hug, G.: TDNetGen: an open-source, parametrizable, large-scale, transmission, and distribution test system. IEEE Syst. J. **13**(1), 729–737 (2019). https://doi.org/10.1109/JSYST.2017.2772914

17. Pisano, G., et al.: Synthetic models of distribution networks based on open data and georeferenced information. Energies **12**(23) (2019). https://doi.org/10.3390/en12234500. https://www.mdpi.com/1996-1073/12/23/4500

18. Rudion, K., Orths, A., Styczynski, Z., Strunz, K.: Design of benchmark of medium voltage distribution network for investigation of dg integration. In: 2006 IEEE Power Engineering Society General Meeting, p. 6 (2006). https://doi.org/10.1109/PES.2006.1709447

19. Sarajlić, D., Rehtanz, C.: Overview of distribution grid test systems for benchmarking of power system analyses. In: 2020 AEIT International Annual Conference (AEIT), pp. 1–6 (2020). https://doi.org/10.23919/AEIT50178.2020.9241140

20. Shabber, S.M., Bansal, M., Devi, P.M., Jain, P.: iHAS: an intelligent home automation based system for smart city. In: 2021 IEEE International Symposium on Smart Electronic Systems (iSES), pp. 48–52 (2021). https://doi.org/10.1109/iSES52644.2021.00023

21. Shi, Z., Liang, Y., Wang, X., Li, S.: Research on low voltage distribution network topology generation method based on "transformer - distribution box - meter box - meter" model. In: 2022 3rd International Conference on Computer Vision, Image and Deep Learning & International Conference on Computer Engineering and Applications (CVIDL & ICCEA), pp. 1–4 (2022). https://doi.org/10.1109/CVIDLICCEA56201.2022.9824305

22. Wang, X., Luo, X., Zhang, M., Jiang, Z., Guan, X.: Detection and localization of biased load attacks in smart grids via interval observer. Inf. Sci. **552**, 291–309 (2021)

23. Wang, Z., Thomas, R., Scaglione, A.: Generating random topology power grids. In: 41st Hawaii International Conference on System Sciences, p. 183 (2008). https://doi.org/10.1109/HICSS.2008.182

24. Weng, Y., Liao, Y., Rajagopal, R.: Distributed energy resources topology identification via graphical modeling. IEEE Trans. Power Syst. **32**(4), 2682–2694 (2017). https://doi.org/10.1109/TPWRS.2016.2628876

25. Yavuz, L., Soran, A., Önen, A., Muyeen, S.: Machine learning algorithms against hacking attack and detection success comparison. In: 2020 2nd International Conference on Smart Power & Internet Energy Systems (SPIES), pp. 258–262 (2020). https://doi.org/10.1109/SPIES48661.2020.9243033

26. You, Y., Li, H.: Coordinate scheduling approach of integrating transmission grid with distribution grid including intermittent energy resources. In: 2018 IEEE Power & Energy Society General Meeting (PESGM), pp. 1–6 (2018). https://doi.org/10.1109/PESGM.2018.8585799

Business Continuity Management– Building Block of Dynamic Resilience

Hytönen Eveliina(✉) ⓘ and Ruoslahti Harri ⓘ

Laurea University of Applied Sciences, Ratatie 22, 01300 Vantaa, Finland
{eveliina.hytonen,harri.ruoslahti}@laurea.fi

Abstract. Today's organizations face almost constant exigencies and disruptive events such as natural or manmade disasters, technological innovations, public relations crises, and cyber-attacks, which have led many of them to reconsider their approaches to their business continuity management processes and practices. Organizations may lack resilience and lose critical functions or interrupt operations if they encounter a disruption. Adverse events causing loss of functionalities may also affect stakeholders and society. Therefore, business continuity management is essential for enhancing dynamic resilience. This case study research uses qualitative methods to collect and analyze the data. The data were collected by conducting 28 interviews of Finnish continuity management practitioners and experts. Then a cross-case analysis of the data was conducted. The results of the study show that business continuity principles are recognized and utilized in the organizations' security management work to a varying extent. Emphasis is put on dynamic continuity planning, including continuous risk assessment and exercises and open communication. By following these principles flexibly and by adapting to the changing environment, the organizations may be able to build and enhance dynamic resilience.

Keywords: Dynamic Resilience · Business Continuity Management · Disruptive Events

1 Introduction

Cyber incidents and business interruptions rank as the foremost business risks according to the Allianz Risk Barometer 2023 [1]. Today's organizations may almost constantly face exigencies and disruptive events such as natural or manmade disasters, technological innovations, public relations crises, and cyber-attacks, which have led many of them to reconsider their approaches to their business continuity management processes and practices. Also, people, organizations, and society are increasingly reliant upon complex and interconnected cyber systems, and their connections to conduct the activities of daily life. Thus, the increasing number and complexity of cybersecurity threats and attacks have become a significant reality in everyday life and have also become one of the biggest risks to threaten business continuity [25]. Critical infrastructures and services may easily lose critical functionalities when hit by an adverse event [21], as

S. Pickl et al. (Eds.): CRITIS 2023, LNCS 14599, pp. 120–134, 2024.
https://doi.org/10.1007/978-3-031-62139-0_7

critical services such as transportation, healthcare, and energy often lack resilience [30]. Continuity management strategies for critical infrastructure operators and their networks, such as other organizations rely on other interrelated networks and can be considered being part of a system of systems, and resilience and continuity can be enhanced by studying and improving interconnectivity between these relevant networks [21].

Building resilience is a collaborative process between social networks [37]. Resilience and continuity management have wide impacts on society and are especially important for critical infrastructure operators [31]. Organizational resilience provides tools and conditions that help understand and reduce risks and mitigate crises [37]. Important factors that can help manage continuity and improve resilience are identifying risks, critical activities, key personnel, creating guidelines and procedures, and open communication [31].

The research question of this study is: How can the principles of business continuity management aid in building dynamic resilience?

2 Business Continuity and Dynamic Resilience

The concepts of Business Continuity and Business Continuity Management (BCM) have evolved from the 1970s as a response to technical and operational risks that threaten an organization's recovery from adverse events and disruptions [11]. According to ISO22301:2019 [18], business continuity means the "capability of an organization to continue the delivery of products and services within acceptable time frames at predefined capacity during a disruption" (p. 9).

2.1 Business Continuity

BCM can be defined as a management process that aims at holistically identifying threats and their impacts to an organization. The BCM process provides a framework for building organizational resilience and enables an effective response in case of an adverse event, at the same time safeguarding the interests of stakeholders, reputation, brand, and value-creating activities [3, 18]. Savage [33] describes BCM as a cyclical process, where a well-executed Plan-phase prepares the organization and its personnel to phases Absorb and Recover from disruptive events, while the Adapt-phase promotes feedback used to enhance future operations and planning. The Plan-phase can be divided into three sub-phases: prepare, prevent, and protect, especially when developing continuity management against cyber threats [14].

One traditional BCM approach provides a Plan-phase process: 1) producing a business impact analysis (BIA), 2) setting recovery time targets (RTO, RPO), 3) conducting a risk assessment (RA), 4) obtaining explicit executive support, 5) testing the process, and 6) delivering training and creating awareness [20]. BCM can thus be seen to promote knowledge management and dynamic capabilities that can enhance organizational performance and resilience against unforeseen adverse events [10]. For BCM to become holistic and strategic, the scope of BC needs to be broadened from value preservation to value creation [27].

The organizational capabilities for business continuity planning can be identified as 1) adequate and serious management commitment, 2) clear continuity strategy, 3) regular plan development and execution, 4) training and counselling, and 5) periodic reporting [24]. Lindstedt and Armour [20] criticize some of the traditional approaches to BCM and propose a flexible Adaptive Business Continuity (ABC) approach that works towards continuous improvement of an organization's recovery capabilities with the focus on continued delivery of services. The ABC approach is based on nine principles: 1) deliver continuous value, 2) document only for mnemonics, 3) engage at many levels within the organization, 4) exercise for improvement, not for testing, 5) learn the business, 6) measure and benchmark, 7) obtain incremental direction from leadership, 8) omit the risk assessment and business impact analysis, and 9) prepare for effects, not causes [20].

2.2 Dynamic Resilience

On an organizational level, the term 'resilience' describes the inherent characteristics of an organization to respond quicker, recover faster, or develop more unusual ways of conducting its business under pressure than other organizations [36].

Niemimaa et al. [27] propose a dynamic view of resilience, where business continuity capabilities are broadly defined and approached as the socio-technical ability of an organization to proactively respond to and recover from contingencies. Building continuity and resilience requires collaboration within social networks, where risks can only be reduced, but not be avoided totally [37]. Resilience is built through sharing values and norms, and through collaboration and constant communication that helps recalibrate the situation [38].

Dynamic perspectives on resilience have been discussed in various research; Resilience has been described as the maintenance of a positive adjustment in changing and challenging situations [35, 36]; Herbane [12] emphasizes the dynamic view on resilience by defining it as the capacity to absorb the pressure caused by internal and external threats and disruptions and to recover from them; and Hollnagel [15] defines resilience as dynamic from the resilience engineering point of view as "an intrinsic ability of a system to adjust its functioning prior to, during or following changes and disturbances" (xxxvi). The dynamic capabilities approach to organizational resilience defines it as the combination of anticipation, coping and adaptation phases. The dynamic capabilities are sets of organizational abilities to anticipate, survive, and thrive in turbulent environments, thus leading to organizational resilience [8].

Weick and Sutcliffe [38] state that instead of technical control measures and formal procedures, cultural features contribute to how well organizations achieve resilience. The cultural features they define as 'mindful organizing' include principles e.g., general preoccupation with failure, reluctance to simplify, sensitivity to operations, commitment to resilience, and deference to expertise. These principles may become enabled by different organizational practices.

Resilience can be understood as flexibility in business, endurance, and ability to recover from adverse events; and to adapt to a new normal after a crisis or a critical event [29]. Resilience is a dynamic construct, where organizations that are considered resilient can either take an anchored or an adaptive mindset approach to resilience [17]. Anchored-resilient organizations, when faced with a trigger event "are surprised but prepared, think about how to maintain their identity, and quickly look for a return to normalcy" (p. 192). Adaptive-resilient organizations, "understand disruptions as part of their process, view change as normal, and look forward to how they can adapt" (p. 192) [17].

Resilience can be measured as the organizational ability to minimize negative impacts, where resilient organizations can quickly adapt to wide systemic changes that occur in the organization, its value network, environment, or society [28, 29]. Figure 1 shows how system performance may change across event management cycles of resilience [22].

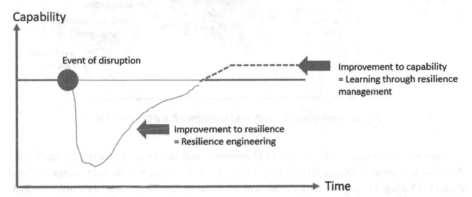

Fig. 1. System performance across event management cycles of resilience, Modified: Linkov et al., [22].

Resilient organizations or networks have organizational agility and a culture that promotes situational awareness to detect and identify clues that may indicate the realization of risks for appropriate mitigation and reaction [29]. Conz and Magnani [6] propose a conceptual framework that adds to the dynamic perspective on the resilience of firms by conceptualizing resilience as "a dynamic process made of absorption- and adaptation-related capabilities" (p. 401). Organizational resilience should be approached as a dynamic process that needs to be developed with the understanding of the different types of capacities that contribute to resilience.

2.3 Resilience Management

The four phases of the event management cycle by The National Academy of Sciences [26] help maintain resilience: 1) The plan-phase prepares the set-up of procedures that help keep services available and assets functioning, 2) the absorb-phase includes activities such as maintaining the most critical assets and their functioning and service availability while fighting disruption, 3) during the recover-phase the organization aims at restoring assets and their functions and service availability, and 4) the adapt-phase consists of gaining knowledge from the event for learning and changing of procedures, configuring the system, and re-training the personnel. The goal of resilience management is to learn from unwanted events and thus improve the system's capability.

Figure 2 presents how the holistic BCM process identifies potential threatening impacts on the organization and provides a framework for developing resilience and the ability to respond effectively to protect the system and the interests of the key actors [16]. The goal of resilience engineering is to improve resilience by reducing the drop in capability and speeding up recovery [34].

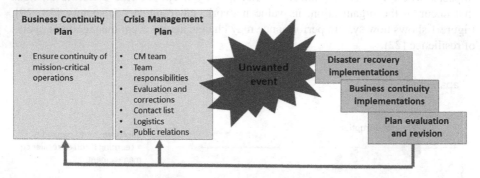

Fig. 2. Business continuity and resilience management [16]

Hiermaier, Scharte and Fischer [14] propose measuring and managing resilience of socio-technical systems with five phases: prepare, prevent, protect, respond, and recover. During 1) prepare and 2) prevent phases information about possible hazards and risks is collected, assessed, and managed, while potential disruptions become modelled and simulated, the 3) protect phase aims at minimizing the drop in performance e.g., by establishing protective structures and monitoring potential quick responses for the response phase, the 4) respond phase is the most critical as situation awareness is needed to make appropriate decisions and take actions, such as securing affected people and systems, disaster management, and even rescue work, the final 5) recovery phase aims at re-establishing the original level of performance and adapting to the experienced disruption.

2.4 Business Continuity Principles in Practice

Earlier research has through theoretical and empirical studies investigated the implementation of BCM principles and their contribution to business continuity as well as their relation to resilience. Earlier studies have also identified critical success factors and best practices of BCM.

Management support, organizational preparedness, and embeddedness of continuity practices are critical success factors of BCM. It is essential that senior management initiates, authorizes, and sponsors a relevant business continuity program from the initial stages of its implementation [5, 19]. Organizational preparedness involves understanding different recovery methods and risk mitigation, creating, and maintaining business continuity plans, forming crisis management teams, and establishing redundancy among key personnel [13, 23].

Embeddedness of continuity practices means that practices are integrated into organizational processes, and that staff and senior management are highly committed to work. To foster the integration of the BCM process, organizations can utilize many ways to communicate and emphasize the significance of BCM, including awareness-raising, training, and addressing the varying requirements for different target groups. [13]. The main approaches or strategies to business continuity management arise from collaborative work and effective communication between stakeholders. Collaboration and communication, enable monitoring the context and establishing trustworthy relationships, thus supporting the development of collective responses during times of crisis. Leaders and managers should cultivate a collaborative culture within the organization and with its stakeholders, and actively engage in daily operations to bolster employee dedication and demonstrate unwavering support [32].

According to Buzzao and Rizzi [4] the ambition to fulfil the business continuity requirements depends on the dynamic organizational capabilities to improvise and coordinate the use of its assets: people, technologies, premises, information when encountering critical events. Leveraging these dynamic capabilities can improve the implementation of BC practices. Fischbacher-Smith [10] highlights the key elements of BCM that can and should be incorporated into the BCM agenda, such as management processes, integration of risk management into BCM, and the development of dynamic capabilities.

BCM requires a systemic and holistic approach where the business continuity requirements are perceived as interrelated and indivisible, where several of the dynamic capabilities are present and affect BC by raising awareness and drawing attention towards its improvement [4]. Also, for the BCM to be effective, a holistic approach to handling the issues that organizations encounter should be adopted. The managerial processes are essential for the development of a holistic approach and for the performance of the BCM practices [10].

3   Method

This research with its research question (How can the principles of business continuity management aid in building dynamic resilience?) uses an academic approach to focus on the views and experiences of BCM practitioners and experts. According to Baskerville and Myers [2] "academic work is usually synchronous with practitioner interests" (p. 648). This is case study research that uses qualitative methods of data collection and analysis [e.g., 7, 39]. The data for this study were collected by conducting 28 interviews. Master's students contributed to the practical collection of the sample data by each conducting an interview during the spring term of 2023, as part of their studies in Continuity Management. Each participating student chose an interviewee, who they thought a relevant and suitable expert in business continuity or resilience measures. The students were given a semi-structured interview template that was prepared by the researchers, to ensure that every interviewee was asked the same questions. The data of this study consist of answers to one question within the interview: What are the essential elements and means of BCM that you employ and recommend for managing continuity? The interviews were held face-to-face in Finnish. The interviews were recorded on the interview template, and answers were extracted to an analysis table.

In line with the demands of research ethics, each interviewee was told before the start of each interview that their responses may be used for student assignments and for research, such as this study, and were then asked for their informed consent for anonymous usage of their responses.

The cross-case analysis of this data was conducted by the authors in the spring of 2023. The analysis is based on first narrowing the sample to a Data Extraction Table (DET), designed for this study based on the research question. The data were then further analyzed thematically. The frequency of the mentioned themes was also noted in the analysis. The themes that emerged from the sample data, and the frequency of their occurrence are presented in the Results section and discussed further in the Conclusions section.

4   Results

This Results section aims at answering the research question of this study: how can the principles of business continuity management aid in building dynamic resilience? The results are based on 28 interviews of Finnish continuity management practitioners and experts. The interviewees represented different fields of expertise: 21 were experts in BCM or risk assessment (RA), three in cybersecurity, and four in general management. Eleven interviewees work in a public authority organization, 14 interviewees in the private sector, and three in the education sector.

Based on the analysis of the data, the basic principles of business continuity: identify risks, and critical activities and facilities, key personnel, and competencies, and develop guidelines and procedures, and promote open communication across the organization and its major stakeholders, when employed actively, adaptively, and dynamically within organization, can help in pursuing resilience.

4.1   Business Continuity Management Practices

Identify Risks.   The respondents noted that identifying risks is essential. The theme was mentioned fifteen (15) times. Risk assessments and impact analyses should be conducted on a regular basis or whenever needed, and risk identification should be active and dynamic. Respondents also stated that preparing for the most probable and recognized risks and creating contingency plans should be in the core of business continuity management. However, acknowledging also unlikely risks and creating plans for them, was mentioned in the interviews. Creating and updating a situational picture, while always maintaining situational awareness and on all levels of the organization, is also shown in the results. Risks such as power outages and water damage, as well as threats to backups and backup storage were mentioned.

Critical Activities and Facilities.   The respondents stated that critical functionalities should be identified. This theme came up eighteen (18) times in the data. A realistic view of critical functions, and of functions that can endanger or even stop operations, is important. Impact analyses that show weaknesses in the operations were mentioned as part of business continuity management. Anticipating and thinking beforehand which services can be produced in all kinds of circumstances was also mentioned in the interviews.

As part of continuity planning organizations look for new products and ways to generate revenue. A few respondents' organizations analyze their current facilities and equipment to identify critical assets and functions. Up-to-date maintenance contracts and ensuring self-sufficiency in e.g., electricity was seen essential for continuity management. Insurance contracts must be up to date and suitable for company operations, and other financial issues should also be considered, and the relationship with the bank taken good care of. One respondent also stated that developing continuity management requires investments.

Key Personnel and Competencies. This BC principle was discussed widely in the interviews. Three sub-themes emerged from the interview data: embedding the BCM to the work in the organization, leadership and management practices and support, and exercises. Based on the fifteen (15) mentions in the responses, to embed the BCM into the work in the organization, the risk management thinking needs to be inculcated in everyday work in the organization, contingency work needs to be part of all activities, and contingency plans should be implemented to all levels of organization. Motivating personnel to participate to the risk management work was seen essential. This can start with observing the quality of one's own work and reporting deviations, which creates a situational picture for the safety management department. One interviewee also emphasized that the whole organization needs to participate in the strategy work and be committed to the work. Continuous and up-to-date training of the personnel was seen important. One respondent stated that all individuals create security, and therefore, everyone's competencies matter. Increasing, for example, the amount of IT-systems training was also noted to be beneficial for everyone in the organization even though not in the core of their role. This can help in the case of disruption and ensure continuity of operations. Understanding new technologies and their use was brought up by one respondent. Continuity planning can be approached from the viewpoint of an adaptable organization and persons; there must be people and systems that can withstand the change and are able to resolve changes and make decisions. Another respondent approached continuity management from the perspective of individual resilience, which should be more focused on. An individual's ability to function in different situations should be enhanced, which can improve the tolerance of uncertainty and ensure continuity.

Leadership and management practices and support were mentioned by the interviewees altogether seven (7) times. The role of leadership and management was seen essential to the security work in the organization. Leaders and managers need to show support for the security work. Two interviewees stated that for example contingency plans need to be approved by the management for BCM to be effective. The management system and practices need to function under any kind of circumstances, and it must be ensured that leaders and managers are skillful and capable to work in a crisis.

The theme of exercising was mentioned eight (8) times. The respondents emphasized the role of practical exercises and testing of contingency plans together with management and personnel, and with value chain partners when needed. Exercises should be conducted in settings that are as realistic as possible. Exercises can motivate personnel and help enhance collaboration between units to build knowledge on how to prepare for disruptions. Exercises and participation in everyday risk management and safety work were noted to create skills and competencies needed to build resilience. Workshops as an effective method to enhance personnel competencies was also mentioned by two interviewees.

Guidelines and Procedures. This theme was covered eleven (11) times in the interview data. The respondents stressed the importance of up-to-date contingency plans with clear roles and responsibilities, knowledge of the organization, its security, and activities for building business continuity in both everyday life and in case of any disruptions. The risk assessments and contingency plans should be dynamically and actively updated and regularly tested. Analyzing past disruptions and monitoring organizational security procedures, evaluating the functioning of systems, and auditing were mentioned as ways to build continuity. Documenting the security work and creating guidelines for different scenarios was mentioned by a couple of interviewees, too.

Open Communication. This theme was mentioned eighteen (18) times in the interviews. The respondents emphasized open communication and collaboration as key elements for continuity planning and management. Open communication is needed all the time to build and update the situation awareness of the personnel and stakeholders. The security department must cooperate with the entire organization. Internal and external relationships need to be well taken care of. Open networking and discussion with cross-administrative stakeholders and partners, and authorities can create a broader understanding of BCM and enhance it. The respondents also noted the importance of communication in creating transparency of operations and increasing trust. Informing personnel and partners and customers about possible threats and how to cope with them is also important for continuity management and planning. Open communication can also create new collaboration possibilities.

4.2 Key BCM Practices Build Dynamic Resilience

The results of this study show that the basic BCM principles and practices are utilized in the organizations of the interviewees. The principles were recognized and viewed as important for structuring continuity management (see Table 1.).

Table 1. Overview of results and literature

	Results of the study	Frequency of mentions	Earlier research
Identify risks	- Creating contingency plans - Risk assessments and impact analyses - Active dynamic risk identification -Preparing for the most probable and recognized risks -Continuous situation awareness -Acknowledging also unlikely risks and creating a plan for them - Risk assessment for all new projects - Realistic risk identification	15	A Plan-phase process in the traditional BCM approach includes e.g., producing a business impact analysis, setting recovery time targets, conducting a risk assessment [20]. Organizational preparedness involves understanding different recovery methods and mitigating risks, such as creating and maintaining business continuity plans, and forming crisis management teams [23, 13]
Critical activities and facilities	- Identifying critical functionalities - Anticipating and anticipating which services can be produced under any circumstances - Analyzing the current facilities and equipment to identify critical assets and functions - Evaluating the current situation and looking for new products and ways to generate revenue, investing - Up-to-date maintenance contracts and insurance contracts, ensuring self-sufficiency in fuel and electricity - Ensuring sufficient resources	18	Continuity can be enhanced by analyzing and improving interconnectivity between critical activities [21]. BCM approach consists of two parts: value preservation, i.e., sustaining the continuity of the company business model, and value creation, i.e., evaluating and modifying the business model [27]
Key personnel and competences	Embedding the BCM to the organization- Inculcating risk management thinking in everyday work of the whole organization- Contingency work needs to be part of all activities- Implementing contingency plans to all levels of organization- Motivating personnel to participate to the risk management work. The whole organization needs to participate in the strategy work and become committed to the work- Training the personnel- People and systems that can withstand the change and are able to resolve changes and make decisions- Individual resilience i.e., ability to function in different situations should be enhanced	15	BCM can be seen to promote knowledge management and dynamic capabilities that can enhance organizational performance and resilience against unforeseen adverse events [10]. Resilient organizations have a culture that promotes situational awareness to detect and identify risks and to prepare for appropriate mitigation and reaction [29]. The Resilience Matrix has been developed to facilitate focusing on creating shared situational awareness and decentralized decision-making [22]

(continued)

Table 1. (*continued*)

	Results of the study	Frequency of mentions	Earlier research
	Leadership and management- The role of leadership and management is essential to security work- There needs to be management support for the security work- Contingency plans need to be accepted by the management- The management system needs to function under any kind of circumstances- Ensuring that leaders and managers are skillful and able to work in a crisis	7	The managerial processes are essential for the development of a holistic approach and for the performance of the BCM practices [10]Embeddedness of continuity practices means that practices are integrated into an organization's processes, and that staff and senior management are highly committed to work [13]
	Exercising and practicing - Exercising regularly and enough - Exercising with real life simulating scenarios - Up-to-date training - Workshops to enhance personnel competences	8	Leaders and managers should cultivate a collaborative culture in the organization and with the stakeholders. They should actively engage in daily operations to show support [32]
Guidelines and procedures	- Go through and update risk assessments and contingency plans dynamically and actively - Systematic development work and monitoring the security procedures - Defining clear roles and responsibilities - Plans should be regularly tested - Analyze past disruptions - Document and create instructions	11	The organizational capabilities for BCM include also regular plan development and execution, training and counselling, and periodic reporting [24]. Leveraging the dynamic capabilities, such as the use of organizational assets, i.e., people, technologies, premises, and information, can improve the implementation of BC practices [4]
Open communication	- The security unit needs to collaborate with everyone in the organization - Creating possibilities for new collaboration - Open communication is needed all the time - Internal and external relationships need to be well taken care of - Open networking and discussion with cross-administrative stakeholders and partners, and authorities - Creating transparency of operations through communication - Increasing trust through open communication - Regular meeting and going through the situation - Communicating instructions and guidelines for disruptions to the personnel and to the stakeholders - Keeping personnel up to date with the situational picture by communicating	18	Building continuity and resilience requires collaboration within social networks [32]. Resilience is built through sharing values and norms, and through collaboration and constant communication that helps recalibrate the situation [38]. To foster the integration of the BCM process, organizations can utilize various ways to communicate and emphasize the significance of BCM [13]. Through collaboration and communication, it is possible to monitor the context and establish trustworthy relationships, thus supporting the development of collective responses during times of crisis [32]

The results indicate that the organizations of the interviewees mostly follow the Plan-phase process by e.g., conducting risk assessment and impact analyses, by obtaining executive support, testing, and monitoring the process, and organizing training and creating awareness [e.g., 20, 24]. They also seem to build organizational preparedness by mitigating risks through risk assessments, and business continuity plans [e.g., 23, 13].

Critical activities and facilities identification and evaluation seems to be quite self-evident for the interviewees as a key element of continuity work. For BCM to be dynamic, it should be approached from two perspectives: the value preservation, i.e., sustaining the continuity of the company business model, and value creation, i.e., evaluating and modifying the business model [27].

The results imply that the BCM principle of key personnel and competencies is seen critical for the success of BCM work. The organizations aim at embedding continuity practices into their processes and creating commitment to the BCM and security work among employees and management [e.g., 13]. By inculcating risk management thinking in everyday work, implementing contingency plans across the organization, motivating, and training personnel, and enhancing also individual resilience, the organization can build a culture that supports resilience. Resilient organizations have a culture that promotes situational awareness to detect and identify risks and to prepare for appropriate mitigation and reaction [29].

The managerial processes are essential for the development of a holistic approach and for the performance of the BCM practices [e.g., 10]. Leaders and managers should cultivate a collaborative culture in the organization and with the stakeholders. They should actively engage in daily operations to bolster employee dedication and demonstrate support [e.g., 32]. Also in this study, the interviewees stated that support and approval from the management team enables BCM work within the organization. The role of training was also recognized as part of BCM. Training promotes knowledge management and dynamic capabilities that can enhance BC, organizational performance, and resilience [e.g., 10].

The results suggest that guidelines and procedures are recognized as a key element of contingency planning, even though it was not discussed that explicitly and in detail in the interviews. The interviewees implied that procedures that are necessary for BCM are for example regular evaluation and updates of risk assessments and contingency plans, documenting the security work and creating instructions, and testing the plans. Based on the results, the need for dynamic procedures as part of BCM is acknowledged; according to the interviewees procedures should be systematic, proactive, and dynamic. Leveraging the dynamic capabilities, such as coordination of processes and information, can improve the implementation of BC practices [e.g., 4].

The results imply that open communication and collaboration are regarded as crucial for an organization to manage continuity. Building continuity and resilience requires collaboration within social networks [e.g., 37]. Resilience is built through sharing values and norms, and through collaboration and constant communication that helps recalibrate the situation [e.g., 38]. Based on the results, open communication and collaboration are needed all the time for creating transparency of operations, increasing trust, building situation awareness, sharing information and knowledge, and opening new possibilities for networking and collaboration. The integration of the BCM process can be enhanced with different means of communication, and this way also emphasizing the significance of BCM [e.g., 13]. Collaboration and communication enable monitoring situation and establishing trustworthy relationships, consequently supporting the development of collective responses during times crises [e.g., 32].

5   Conclusions

This study set out to investigate security experts' views and experiences on continuity management, and to understand how key elements or principles of BC could aid in building dynamic resilience. The findings indicate that the nature of BCM and the key practices are recognized, and viewed as active, continuous, systematic, dynamic, and adaptive. The organizations of the interviewees employ many key elements of BCM continuously. They identify risks proactively, maintain situational awareness all the time, and regularly monitor the BCM. They also aim at and recommend embedding BCM into the whole organization, engaging in many levels within the organization, gaining and providing management support, exercising for improvement, and collaborating within different networks, and focusing on constant internal and external communication.

The results of this research suggest that BCM can aid pursuing and building dynamic resilience. Adopting the BCM principles to a continuous, active, and systematic process of business continuity management, enables organizations to identify and create conditions for building dynamic resilience. The principles, if followed systematically but with flexibility, can help and enable an effective response and recovery in case of an adverse event, hence contributing to building dynamic resilience.

Based on the results, an important topic for further research would be communication and communication management in different phases of resilience since communication has an important role in enabling business continuity management activities and possibly in enhancing dynamic resilience. Also, further study is recommended to better understand the business continuity management and specifically cybersecurity related risks, needs and relevant technical and human factors of different organizations and critical sectors such as energy, health care and maritime. Increased understanding can help the successful adaptation of business continuity principles and the dynamic resilience framework to the needs of different sectors.

Acknowledgements. This study has received funding by the European Union project DYNAMO [9], under grant agreement no. 101069601. The views expressed are those of the author(s) only and do not necessarily reflect those of the European Union. Neither the European Union nor the granting authority can be held responsible for them.

References

1. Allianz Risk Barometer 2023, Allianz Global Corporate & Specialty (AGCS), https://www.agcs.allianz.com/news-and-insights/news/allianz-risk-barometer-2023-press.html. Accessed 28 May 2023

2. Baskerville, R.L., Myers, M.D.: Fashion waves in information systems research and practice. Mis. Quart., 647–662 (2009)
3. British Standards Institution BS 25999–1 Code of practice for business continuity management. British Standards Institution, London (2006)
4. Buzzao, G., Rizzi, F.: The role of dynamic capabilities for resilience in pursuing business continuity: an empirical study. Total Qual. Manag. Bus. Excell. **34**(11–12), 1353–1385 (2023)
5. Chow, W.S.: Success factors for is disaster recovery planning in Hong Kong. Inf. Manag. Comput. Secur. **8**(2), 80–87 (2000)
6. Conz, E., Magnani, G.: A dynamic perspective on the resilience of firms: a systematic literature review and a framework for future research. Eur. Manag. J. **38**(3), 400–412 (2020)
7. Denzin, N.K., Lincoln, Y.S.: The Sage Handbook of Qualitative Research. SAGE Publications, Thousand Oaks (2005)
8. Duchek, S.: Organisational resilience: a capability-based conceptualization. Bus. Res. **13**(1), 215–246 (2020)
9. DYNAMO homepage, https://horizon-dynamo.eu/. Accessed 28 May 2023
10. Fischbacher-Smith, D.: When organisational effectiveness fails: business continuity management and the paradox of performance. J. Organ. Effectiv. People Perform. **4**, 89–107 (2017)
11. Herbane, B.: The evolution of business continuity management: a historical review of practices and drivers. Bus. Hist. **52**(6), 978–1002 (2010)
12. Herbane, B.: Exploring crisis management in UK small-and medium-sized enterprises. J. Contingencies Crisis Manage. **21**(2), 82–95 (2013)
13. Herbane, B., Elliot, D., Swartz, E.M.: Business continuity management: time for a strategic role? Long Range Plan. **37**(5), 435–457 (2004)
14. Hiermaier, S., Scharte, B., Fischer, K.: Resilience engineering: chances and challenges for a comprehensive concept. In: Handbook on Resilience of Socio-Technical Systems, pp. 155–166, Edward Elgar Publishing (2019)
15. Hollnagel, E. (ed.): Resilience Engineering in Practice: A Guidebook, Ashgate Publishing Ltd, Farnham (2013)
16. Hytönen, E., Rajumaki, J., Ruoslahti, H.: Managing variable cyber environments with organizational foresight and resilience thinking. In: Wilson, R.L., Curran, B. (eds.): Proceedings of the 18th International Conference on Cyber Warfare and Security, vol. 18(1), pp. 162–170 (2023)
17. Ishak, A.W., Williams, E.A.: A dynamic model of organizational resilience: adaptive and anchored approaches. Corp. Commun. **23**(2), 180–196 (2018)
18. ISO 22301:2019. Societal security - Business continuity management systems - Requirements. Finnish Standards Association SFS, Helsinki
19. Järveläinen, J.: IT incidents and business impacts: validating a framework for continuity management in information systems. Int. J. Inf. Manage. **33**(3), 583–590 (2013)
20. Lindstedt, D., Armour, M.: Adaptive Business Continuity: A New Approach. Rothstein Publishing (2017)
21. Linkov, I., et al.: Changing the resilience paradigm. Nat. Clim. Chang. **4**(6), 407–409 (2014)
22. Linkov, I., et al.: Measurable resilience for actionable policy. Environ. Sci. Technol. **47**(18), 10108–10110 (2013)
23. Lindström, J., Samuelsson, S., Hägerfors, A.: Business continuity planning methodology. Disaster Prev. Manag. **19**(2), 243–255 (2010)
24. Maurer, F., Lechner, U.: From disaster response planning to e-resilience: a literature review. In: Proceedings of the 27th Bled eConference: cEcosystems; Bled eCommerce Conference: Vorarlberg University of Applied Sciences, Bled, Slovenia (2014)

25. Michel, M.C.K., King, M.C.: Cyber influence of human behavior: personal and national security, privacy, and fraud awareness to prevent harm. In: 2019 IEEE International Symposium on Technology and Society (ISTAS), pp. 1–7. IEEE (2019)
26. National Research Council 2012. Disaster Resilience: A National Imperative. The National Academies Press. Washington, DC (2012). https://doi.org/10.17226/13457
27. Niemimaa, M., Järveläinen, J., Heikkilä, M., Heikkilä, J.: Business continuity of business models: evaluating the resilience of business models for contingencies. Int. J. Inf. Manage. **49**, 208–216 (2019)
28. Palma-Oliveira, J.M., Trump, B.D.: Modern resilience: moving without movement, in Resource Guide on Resilience, EPFL International Risk Governance Center, Lausanne (2016). https://www.irgc.org/irgc-resourceguide-on-resilience/
29. Palomäki, S., Roschier, S., Gilbert, Y., Pokela, P.: Kestävän tuotannon resilienssi: kuinka varautua kriiseihin ja kasvaa kestävästi, Business Finland, Helsinki (2020)
30. Ruoslahti, H., Rajamäki, J., Koski, E.: Educational competences with regard to resilience of critical infrastructure. J. Inf. Warfare **17**(3), 1–16 (2018)
31. Ruoslahti, H.: Business continuity for critical infrastructure operators. Ann. Disaster Risk Sci. ADRS **3**(1) (2020)
32. Sánchez, M.A., De Batista, M.: Business continuity for times of vulnerability: empirical evidence. J. Contingencies Crisis Manag. **31**(3), 431–440 (2023)
33. Savage, M.: Business continuity planning. Work Study **51**(5), 254–261 (2002)
34. Thoma, K., Scharte, B., Hiller, D., Leismann, T.: Resilience engineering as part of security research: definitions, concepts and science approaches. Eur. J. Secur. Res. **1**(1), 3–19 (2016)
35. Trim, P.R.J., Lee, Y.: A strategic marketing intelligence and multi-organisational resilience framework. Eur. J. Mark. **42**(7/8), 731–745 (2008)
36. Vogus, T.J., Sutcliffe, K.M.: Organizational resilience: towards a theory and research agenda. In: IEEE International Conference on Systems, Man and Cybernetics (2007)
37. Vos, M.: Communication in Turbulent Times: Exploring Issue Arenas and Crisis Communication to Enhance Organisational Resilience, vol. 40. Jyväskylä University School of Business and Economics (2017)
38. Weick, K., Sutcliffe, K.: Managing the Unexpected: Sustained Performance in a Complex World. Wiley, Hoboken (2015)
39. Yin, R.K.: Case Study Research, Design and Methods, 3rd edn. Sage, Thousand Oaks, USA (2003)

Evasion Attack Against Multivariate Singular Spectrum Analysis Based IDS

Vikas Maurya[1]([⊠])[iD], Rachit Agarwal[1,2][iD], and Sandeep Shukla[1][iD]

[1] Indian Institute of Technology Kanpur, Kanpur 208016, India
{vikasmr,rachitag,sandeeps}@cse.iitk.ac.in
[2] Merkle Science, Bangalore 560102, India

Abstract. Machine learning-based intrusion detection systems (IDS) are being developed to detect industrial control systems (ICS) attacks. Such IDSs monitor sensor measurements to detect abnormal structural changes in the behavior of physical dynamics of the ICS. State-of-the-art IDS are based on the multivariate singular spectrum analysis (MSSA) technique that detects structural changes in the timeseries of sensor measurements. However, adversaries can exploit MSSA. We focus on the attackers who aim to compromise the most critical component of ICS and remain undetected by IDS. As critical components of ICS are the most secure, it is difficult for the attacker to manipulate the critical sensor measurements to conceal his attack from IDS by performing a replay attack. In this paper, we propose an evasion attack technique against MSSA-based IDS. In an evasion attack, an attacker manipulates a few sensor measurements that are easily manageable instead of manipulating sensors in the critical components as a replay attacker does. To perform such a task, we develop a crafting method that crafts successive measurements which reduce the departure score of the MSSA. Further, we consider both accessibility and manipulation constraints for a realistic evaluation. We use the TE-process simulator to generate two attack scenarios for validating the evasion attack technique: stealthy attack (SA) and direct damage attack (DDA). Our experimental results show that manipulating measurements of only 13 and 20 sensors are enough to conceal SA and DDA, respectively.

Keywords: Evasion Attack · Industrial Control System · Intrusion Detection System · Multivariate Singular Spectrum Analysis · Critical Infrastructure Security

1 Introduction

An industrial control system (ICS) operates and automates the industrial process with the help of a supervisory control and data acquisition (SCADA) system. Due to ICS's importance in critical infrastructure (CI), attackers have always targeted it. To secure the ICS, a process-level intrusion detection system (IDS)

S. Pickl et al. (Eds.): CRITIS 2023, LNCS 14599, pp. 135–154, 2024.
https://doi.org/10.1007/978-3-031-62139-0_8

is deployed on top of SCADA, whose objective is to monitor the sensor measurements and raise an attack alarm when any attack-induced abnormality is detected. An attacker performing an attack to damage the physical devices or resources causes behavioral changes in the sensor (also called **abnormal sensors** for future references) measurements [27]. The IDS monitoring sensor measurements detect anomalies in the sensor behavior. To evade the detection, attacker aims to conceal the attack-induced abnormalities from IDS.

A replay attack is a popular method an attacker uses to conceal his attack. During the attack, attacker replays sensor's normal measurements [18]. However, a replay attack is cumbersome in critical component. Further, attackers try to exploit the ICS's most **critical components** to maximize harm, but such critical components are secured with high priority. Therefore, manipulating measurements of critical component sensors and performing a replay attack is more difficult for the attacker. An alternative approach to replay attack is an **evasion attack**. Here, the attacker does not manipulate critical component sensor measurements. Instead, he conceals his illicit activities by manipulating a few other non-critical sensors (also called **adversarial sensors** for future references), which are easily manipulable to him. Therefore, he manipulates the adversarial sensor measurements in such a way that it evades the IDS detection mechanism without any change in the abnormal sensors.

In recent years, many state-of-the-art IDSs [1,2,5] have leveraged the **multivariate singular spectrum analysis (MSSA)** [11]. MSSA's efficient computation cost and noise cancellation property make it a promising IDS technique. It is a multivariate extension of SSA [22] that is able to process multiple sensor's measurement to be more accurate at a low computation cost. However, the proposed work shows that an MSSA-based IDS is vulnerable to evasion attacks. In this paper, we thoroughly analyze the evasion attack against MSSA-based IDS to introduce the ICS community about its adverse effects.

To perform the evasion attack, we develop a novel **crafting method (CM)** to craft adversarial measurements. Using CM, the attacker can craft and replace the adversarial sensor measurements to reduce the departure score (also called anomaly score) produced by MSSA-based IDS. The IDS fails to detect such attacks if the departure score is reduced below a threshold. The attacker needs to adhere accessibility and manipulation constraints of the CM technique to appear legitimate. The accessibility constraint restricts attacker (known as a greybox attacker) from accessing the IDS parameters. The manipulation constraint restricts the attacker from crafting a measurement within the normal range.

Using the proposed CM, the attacker predicts measurements for adversarial sensors, which aim to minimize the IDS departure score. When the subsequent measurements are generated, the attacker replaces actual adversarial sensor measurements with the estimated ones. The IDS installed on top of SCADA evaluates smaller departure score than the actual. Since manipulations are constrained to be legitimate, one adversarial sensor manipulation can slightly decrease the departure score and lower the alarm count. Manipulating enough adversarial sensors causes to conceal the attack from IDS. To reduce effort, the attacker traces departure score constantly so that score is always less than his estimated threshold (calculated at the attacker's end). He manipulates when the departure score exceeds the estimated threshold at a particular instance.

Our evasion attack technique can be applied in every multi-component-based sensor network (IoT, IIoT, or cloud computing-based monitoring systems), which are monitored by a central monitoring system. Such applications include ICS, CIs, self-driving cars, UAV drone recognition, vehicle recognition, human activity recognition, smart office, smart city, etc. Critical industries mostly rely on the ICS. The ICSs are primarily distributed in nature, consisting of multiple modules with different security levels. Therefore, we consider ICS a use case to explain the practicality of the attack model.

The IDS monitors the physical process data generated by sensors connected to various distributed control systems in ICS. Every sensor or controller cannot be equally critical in terms of cyber security. Critical components of ICS are usually highly protected by state-of-the-art methods. However, with fast-changing technology and ICS components being distributed in a large area, it is hard to maintain and upgrade non-critical components leading to outdated components having no encryption and authentication support [12]. Such less protected components, therefore, induce vulnerabilities in the ICS. Several methods discussed in [8,13,23,25] are used by an attacker to manipulate the communication between SCADA and sensors. Thus, the attacker can perform man-in-the-middle attack to manipulate the adversarial sensor measurements.

A CI may consist of thousands of sensors. We have explained that the developed evasion method is invariant with the number of sensors present in the CI (cf. Sect. 4.3). Our method uses a few adversarial sensors from a lesser secure workstation to neutralize the attack-induced abnormality in the more critical workstation. However, we have an experimental limitation of the number of measured variables (representing timeseries of sensor measurements) to experiment. We use the Tennessee-Eastman (TE) process simulator [6] which consists of 41 cross-correlated MEAsured vaiiableS (XMEAS) and generate two sophisticated attack scenarios to validate our evasion attack technique. The attack scenario belongs to stealthy attack (SA) and direct damage attack (DDA) categories [3,16]. We experimentally show that our evasive technique can conceal these attacks. Using our evasion attack technique, manipulating measurements of only 13 and 20 adversarial sensors during SA and DDA attacks, respectively, leads to concealment of corresponding attacks. For the evaluation, we perform both whitebox and greybox experiments. Both whitebox and greybox scenarios produce similar results showing that alarm count is inversely correlated to the number of adversarial sensors. The correlation coefficient between alarm count and the number of adversarial sensors is -0.95 and -0.82 for the SA and DDA attack scenarios, respectively.

The major contributions of our work are listed as follows:

- We introduce an evasion attack against MSSA-based IDS that effectively evades the IDS to conceal the attack-induced abnormality in the sensor measurements without manipulating them. To the best of our knowledge, no evasion attack technique has been developed against any MSSA-based IDS.

– We develop a crafting method for performing an evasion attack that crafts measurements for a few easily manipulable sensors. Manipulating the subsequent measurements of such sensors with the crafted measurements decreases the departure score of MSSA-based IDS. An attacker can hide the attack when he controls a significant number of sensors.
– Our crafting method adheres to accessibility and manipulation constraints to appear legitimate.
– We use our evasion attack technique to hide two attack scenarios: SA and DDA. We perform both whitebox and greybox analysis while considering different sets of adversarial sensors. The results suggest that raising the number of adversarial sensors reduces alarm frequency. A sufficient number of adversarial sensor manipulation (13 sensors for SA and 20 sensors for DDA, respectively) causes the attacks to be concealed.
– We theoretically and empirically discuss our evasion technique's computational complexity, which shows its implementation practicalities.

The rest of the paper is organized as follows: first, we discuss the necessary background knowledge in Sect. 2. Then, Sect. 3 describes the attack model and how an attacker can compromise CI to execute the evasion attack, along with its accessibility and manipulation constraints. Section 4 discusses our crafting method against the MSSA-based IDS. In Sect. 5 we discuss the TE-process generated dataset used for validation. Section 6 presents the experimental evaluation results of the proposed method. Section 7 discusses evasion attack-related work. Finally, Sect. 8 concludes our paper with a discussion.

2   Background

This section discusses the background needed to explain the proposed method.

2.1   Industrial Control System (ICS)

ICS operates and automates the cyber-physical systems (CPS) that integrate hardware and software with the Operational Technology (OT) network to control and manage industrial processes. In an ICS, programmable logic controllers (PLC), actuators, and sensors are mutually connected hardware components. Sensors and actuators connect physical components (such as grinder speed and flow level) with the cyber world. PLCs are pre-programmed industrial computers that send commands to the physical device through actuator, and sensors send physical component's response back to PLC. Large ICSs are usually implemented with SCADA systems. The SCADA is networked with multiple PLCs through a wireless OT network with the help of remote terminal unit (RTU) and master terminal unit (MTU) components. The data communication between the cyber components (such as sensors, actuators, and PLCs) of ICS is supported by OT communication protocols such as Modbus, dnp3, Profibus, IEC 870-5-101, IEC 61850 [12,25]. Data availability is the top priority among CIA triad in OT networks, unlike IT networks, where confidentiality is on top. Therefore, most OT communication protocols do not allow encrypted communications and data authentication.

2.2 Evolution of MSSA-Based IDS

Several process level IDS methodologies detect the abnormal activities induced by attacker's actions or errors in the physical device. In [17], for developing an IDS, authors addressed the challenges raised due to the unrealistic assumption that the system-generated data is noiseless. Noisy data causes lots of false alarms by a non-robust IDS. Further, an attacker can take advantage to hide his stealthy attack within noise margin. Singular spectral analysis (SSA) [22] is one of the popular timeseries analysis technique to develop IDS for ICS, as it is robust to noise and captures the structural skeleton of timeseries. However, SSA has limitations. It is univariate and applied to one timeseries at a time. Thus, developing a large-scale IDS needs many SSA models and is computationally expensive. SSA also misses the correlation between different sensors resulting into accuracy loss. To resolve this issue, multivariate singular spectrum analysis (MSSA) is introduced [11]. MSSA considers multidimensional timeseries (sequence of measurements from multiple sensors) and has better performance in terms of accuracy and computation cost [1,2]. The MSSA (or SSA) is not meant for IDS only. It has various other applications as well, such as timeseries forecasting and gap-filling. Recently in [1,2,5], authors used MSSA to detect structural changes in the multidimensional timeseries and depicted its various IoT and IIoT-based security application areas such as ICS, CIs, self-driving cars, UAV drone recognition, vehicle recognition, human activity recognition, smart office, and smart city.

2.3 MSSA-Based IDS: Offline Training

Let there be[1] N sensors in ICS network, and $X^{(n)}$ be a real-valued timeseries generated by n^{th} sensor, each consisting of K measurements collected during normal operation is used for training. MSSA performs the following steps to train the IDS:

1. Normalize each training timeseries $X^{(n)}$ using standard score as $(X_t^{(n)} - \mu^{(n)})/\sigma^{(n)}$. Where $\mu^{(n)}, \sigma^{(n)}$ are mean and standard deviation of sensors measurement during the training period.
2. Transform each sensor timeseries in the Hankel matrix using a lag parameter L. Let $M^{(n)}$ be a Hankel matrix for n^{th} sensor timeseries $X^{(n)}$ then $M^{(n)}$ is a $L \times (K - L + 1)$ dimensional matrix.
3. All Hankel matrices are stacked to form another bigger matrix $\mathbf{M} = [M^{(1)}, M^{(2)}, \cdots, M^{(N)}]$, where the shape of $\mathbf{M}$ is $L \times N(K - L + 1)$.
4. Perform Singular Value Decomposition (SVD) on $\mathbf{M}$ to get R ($R << L$) leading eigen vectors $U = [U_1, U_2, \cdots, U_R]$ of $\mathbf{MM}^T$. Here, the shape of U is $L \times R$.

---

[1] Note: summary of notations/symbols used in this paper are listed in the Table 1.

Table 1. Notations and their description

Notation	Description
$\mathbb{R}$	set of Real numbers
$\mathbb{I}$	set of Integers
N	number of sensors; $\in \mathbb{I}$
K	number of training measurements; $\in \mathbb{I}$
L	lag parameter; $\in \mathbb{I}$
R	dimension of signal subspace; $\in \mathbb{I}$
θ	threshold; $\in \mathbb{R}$
$X_t^{(n)}$	measurement of nth sensor at timestamp t; $\in \mathbb{R}$
$X^{(n)}$	timeseries of nth sensor
X_t	vector of sensor measurements at timestamp t; $\in \mathbb{R}^N$
$\hat{c}$	centroid; $\in \mathbb{R}^R$
$M^{(n)}$	Hankel matrix of nth sensor; $\in \mathbb{R}^{L \times (K-L+1)}$
$\mathbf{M}$	matrix of N Hankel matrices; $\in \mathbb{R}^{L \times N(K-L+1)}$
U	transpose of projection matrix; $\in \mathbb{R}^{L \times R}$
T	aggregated timeseries
m_t	t^{th} measurement of T; $\in \mathbb{R}$
w_t	lag vector, $w_t = [m_{t-L}, \cdots, m_{t-1}, m_t]^T$; $\in \mathbb{R}^L$
D_t	departure score at timestamp t; $\in \mathbb{R}$
y	a vector of intermediate computation; $\in \mathbb{R}^R$
abn	indices of abnormal sensors, attack induced abnormality
adv	indices of adversarial sensors, used for manipulation
nor	indices of normal sensors, neither adv or abn
$\overline{adv}$	other than adversarial sensors, i.e. abn and nor

5. Use U^T as a projection matrix to project any lag vector $w \in \mathbb{R}^L$ into an R-dimensional noise-free signal subspace: $U^T w \in \mathbb{R}^R$.
6. Determine $\hat{c}$ and θ. Here, $\hat{c}$ is centroid of the normal cluster formed in signal subspace. Threshold θ is the distance of the farthest point in signal subspace from $\hat{c}$.

2.4 MSSA-Based IDS: Online Detection

The projection matrix U^T is derived from every sensor-generated timeseries that projects the aggregated timeseries (cf. step 2) of all the sensors. To test the recent measurements, it prepares a lag vector $w \in \mathbb{R}^L$ (cf. Step-3) using the recent aggregated measurements and projects w using the projection matrix U^T into the signal subspace. The projected vector is compared with a threshold to check if it is normal or an anomaly.

Consider an ICS consisting of N sensors where n^{th} sensor generates measurement $X_t^{(n)}$ at time t. MSSA-based IDS performs the following steps for an online attack detection by collectively analyzing all the sensors measurements at time t.

1. Normalize each test measurements $X_t^{(n)}$ using standard score as $(X_t^{(n)} - \mu^{(n)})/\sigma^{(n)}$. Where $\mu^{(n)}, \sigma^{(n)}$ are computed during training.

2. Compute aggregated measurement $m_t = ||X_t||$ where $X_t = [X_t^{(1)} \cdots , X_t^{(N)}]^T$. Over time, we get an aggregated timeseries $\mathcal{T}$ such that $\mathcal{T} = [\cdots , m_t, \cdots]$.
3. Compute L length lag vector w using recently aggregated measurements in $\mathcal{T}$; $w_t = [m_{t-L+1}, \cdots , m_{t-1}, m_t]^T$.
4. Compute the departure score as $D_t = ||\hat{c} - U^T w_t||^2$ and check if $D_t > \theta$, then raise the alarm.

2.5   Evasion Attack

An adversarial machine learning (AML) evasion attacker aims to fool the ML classifier by crafting an input feature that looks legitimate [4,7]. Let $f(.)$ be the IDS classifier function such that for input feature vector x, $f(x) = 0$ represents 'Normal' and $f(x) = 1$ represents 'Attack'. Let x be an attack input ($f(x) = 1$), then the attacker aims to hide his attack by crafting x to $x* = x + \delta$ such that $f(x*) = 0$. In [4,7], the authors suggest that an adversary needs the knowledge of quad $(\mathcal{D}, \mathcal{X}, f, \phi)$. Here, $\mathcal{D}$ is the training data, $\mathcal{X}$ is the input feature, f is the learning algorithm, and ϕ is model parameters (such as weight vectors and threshold). There are two extreme AML attackers based on the capabilities: **whitebox** and **blackbox**. A whitebox attacker has a complete knowledge of $(\mathcal{D}, \mathcal{X}, f, \phi)$, while a blackbox attacker does not know $(\cancel{\mathcal{D}}, \cancel{\mathcal{X}}, \cancel{f}, \cancel{\phi})$. And, a greybox attacker needs partial quad information.

3   Attack Model, Capabilities, and Constraints

In this section we describe the attack model preceded by attacker capabilities and followed by attackers constraints.

3.1   Accessibility

Data availability is the top priority in the OT network among CIA (confidentiality, integrity, and availability) triad. While confidentiality is on top priority in the IT network. The high availability priority for the OT network allows only non-encrypted communication via protocols such as Modbus, dnp3, Profibus, IEC 870-5-101, IEC 61850 [12,25]. A man-in-the-middle attacker can eavesdrop the communications. Therefore, spoofing OT network communication is not a challenging task for an adversary [8]. In this scenario, an IDS cannot detect the eavesdrop until sensor measurements are not being changed.

3.2   Manipulation Capability

An attacker can manipulate the adversarial sensors by performing man-in-the-middle attack. Stuxnet [23] is a well-known example of an ICS attack where the attacker changed the motor rotation rates of nuclear centrifuges while spoofing the cyber component reported sensor readings through a man-in-the-middle attack. In [8], the authors proposed a HARVEY rootkit deployed within the PLC firmware to spoof and manipulate communications. In [13], the authors discussed an insider threat scenario where a victimized employee caused damages to the CI. If an insider performs any evasion attack, it would be more catastrophic for the critical components. In [25], the authors discussed various vulnerabilities reported related to OT networks. They found that ≈83% of the vulnerabilities violate OT network communication and are leveraged by evasive attackers for manipulating the data communication.

3.3 Attack Model

An attacker spoofs normal sensor measurements, specifically from the sensors he plans to attack. During the attack, he replaces the abnormal measurements with the spoofed normal measurements [18]. This trivial way to hide an attack is called a replay attack. A critical component (such as the chemical dosing component of a water treatment plant) of an ICS is relatively more secure, thus difficult to manipulate. Although the attackers cannot achieve much by targeting non-critical components (such as raw water supply stations of a water treatment plant) but it is easier to access. Therefore, the attacker aims to target critical components by leveraging non-critical components to maximize damage.

In proposed attack model, the attacker does not need to manipulate critical sensors. It enables the attacker to conceal his illicit activities by taking control of only a few adversarial sensors that are an easy target for him. This flexibility gives a more suitable attack model from an attacker's perspective.

Consider an ICS consisting of multiple components connected via multiple sensors. A high-level architecture of the attack model is shown in Fig. 1. Here, an attacker performs malicious activities to damage a critical component where the attack causes structural changes in sensor's normal behaviors. If the IDS processes these changes, the attack (without evasion) will get detected. Therefore, the attacker performs evasion attack to hide his malicious activity. In the evasion attack, attacker uses accessibility and manipulation capabilities to manipulate sensor measurements of the adversarial component (an easily accessible non-critical component) by performing a man-in-the-middle attack. He uses proposed CM to craft successive sensor measurements of adversarial component's sensors and waits for the subsequent measurement to be generated. When the associated sensor generates measurements, the attacker drops the actual measurement and forwards the crafted measurements to the SCADA. He continues the manipulation until departure score is above an estimated threshold during his attack.

3.4 Constraints

A realistic attacker should follow the following constraints:

Accessibility Constraints: In Sect. 2.5, we discuss the accessibility of quad information $(\mathcal{D}, \mathcal{X}, f, \phi)$ for a whitebox, blackbox, and greybox attackers. The whitebox attack needs all quad information. While the blackbox attacker does not require any quad information to perform the attack. However, the greybox attacker needs only partial quad information. Our greybox attack does not require training data and IDS parameters, i.e. $(\cancel{\mathcal{Z}}, \mathcal{X}, f, \cancel{\emptyset})$ to perform the attack. We consider both whitebox and greybox attackers in our experiments and compared them.

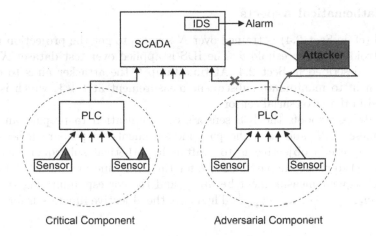

Fig. 1. Attack model: An adversarial attacker wants to conceal his abnormal activities reflected in the sensors of a critical component, but he cannot manipulate them. Therefore, he performs a man-in-the-middle attack to manipulate measurements of the adversarial component's sensors. He uses the proposed CM to generate adversarial measurement during the attack. When the successive measurement is generated, attacker replaces the actual with pre-generated adversarial measurement.

Manipulation Constraints: The evasive attacker aims to manipulate the measurement in order to conceal abnormalities in the critical sensors and appear legitimate on the sensors he has chosen to manipulate. Therefore, he adheres to two manipulation constraints in the proposed evasive technique.

- The manipulation of a sensor's measurement must be within the normal range of timeseries.
- The aggregation of manipulated measurement must be within the normal range of the aggregated timeseries.

4   Crafting Method

The crafting method's (CM) objective is to craft measurements that are used for manipulating subsequent measurements (measurements generated at the next timestamp) (cf. Sect. 1). We develop the CM method by optimizing the departure score (cf. Eq. 1) such that the aggregated timeseries's departure score is minimized for the latest measurement. Solving the objective function gives the manipulation formula (cf. Eq. 4), which takes the IDS parameter and historical measurements as input to craft the future aggregated measurement. The detailed mathematical aspects of the crafting method is discussed in Sect. 4.1, implemented using Algorithm 1 in Sect. 4.2, and the complexity analysis is provided in the Sect. 4.4.

4.1 Mathematical Aspects

The IDS (cf. in Sect. 2.4) is trained over N sensors to get the projection matrix U^T, centroid $\hat{c}$, and threshold θ. The IDS is applied over test dataset X using four steps described in Sect. 2.4. At timestamp t, the attacker aims to craft a measurement to manipulate subsequent measurement at $t + 1$, which is to be generated in the adversarial sensors.

The attacker spoofs the ICS sensor's communication to prepare an aggregated timeseries $\mathcal{T}$ and uses the past measurements to prepare a lag vector w_t. The attacker's objective is to craft a hypothetical subsequent measurement $(\hat{m}_{t+1})$ to reduce departure score for the next time instance. Let the predicted subsequent measurement be m'_{t+1}, and the corresponding lag vector be $w'_{t+1} = [m_{t-L+2}, \cdots, m_t, m'_{t+1}]^T$. Therefore, the objective function is formalized as Eq. 1.

$$\hat{m}_{t+1} = \arg \min_{m'_{t+1}} \left(D'_{t+1} \right) \tag{1}$$

To solve the objective function, we express the hypothetical departure score D'_{t+1} in the form of variable m'_{t+1} in Eq. 2.

$$\begin{aligned} D'_{t+1} &= ||\hat{c} - U^T \cdot w'_{t+1}||^2 \\ &= ||\hat{c} - (U[1:L-1]^T \cdot w'_{t+1}[1:L-1] + U[L] * w'_{t+1}[L])||^2 \\ &= ||y - U[L] * m'_{t+1}||^2 \\ &= ||U[L]||^2 m'^2_{t+1} - 2(y^T \cdot U[L])m'_{t+1} + ||y||^2 \end{aligned} \tag{2}$$

where,
$$y = \hat{c} - U[1:L-1]^T \cdot w'_{t+1}[1:L-1] \tag{3}$$

Here, operator '$\cdot$' represents matrix and vectors multiplication, '$*$' represents scalar to vector multiplication, and no operator between variables represents scalar to scalar multiplication. Since the objective function with variable $\hat{m}_{t+1}$ is a convex function (cf. Eq. 2), minima exist for it. When solving the Eq. 2 for a minima, we find a function (cf. Eq. 4) to get the next optimal measurement. Equation 4 solely depends on the past data and IDS parameters which are used to predict $\hat{m}_{t+1}$.

$$\hat{m}_{t+1} = \frac{y^T \cdot U[L]}{||U[L]||^2} \tag{4}$$

Replacing the actual subsequent measurement with $\hat{m}_{t+1}$ decreases departure score of the aggregated timeseries. Although $\hat{m}_{t+1}$ is a derived measurement, the attacker manipulates adversarial sensor's measurements while they are being communicated to SCADA. The manipulated sensor measurements at time $t+1$ is expected to be $||X_{t+1}|| = \hat{m}_{t+1}$. Let adv be the indexes of the adversarial sensors and $\overline{adv}$ be the index of remaining other sensors (referred as non-adversarial sensors) in the matrix X. Then $||X_{t+1}|| = \hat{m}_{t+1}$ can be broken in adversarial and non-adversarial sensors as follows.

$$||X_{t+1}[\overline{adv}]||^2 + ||X_{t+1}[adv]||^2 = \hat{m}_{t+1}^2 \tag{5}$$

Since X_{t+1} is unknown to the attacker and successive measurement of the ICS slowly increases or decreases. We can assume $X_{t+1} \approx X_t$ and use the current measurements $(X_t[\overline{adv}])$ to estimate $X_{t+1}[adv]$. Therefore, the adversarial sensors at time $t+1$ are manipulated according to the following equation.

$$||X_{t+1}[adv]||^2 = \hat{m}_{t+1}^2 - ||X_t[\overline{adv}]||^2 \tag{6}$$

4.2   Implementation

We present the pseudocode[2] implementation of proposed crafting method as Algorithm 1. The input model parameters $(U^T, \hat{c}, \theta)$ in the pseudocode are actual IDS parameters for the whitebox experiment and same estimated parameters for the greybox experiments. At step-9 of Algorithm 1, attacker uses currently available measurements of aggregated timeseries to prepare a $L-1$ length vector x at timestamp t. The algorithm estimates the next measurement $\hat{m}_{t+1}$ of the aggregated timeseries at step-11. Estimated measurement $\hat{m}_{t+1}$ is projected on the normal range of $\mathcal{T}$ to follow the manipulation constraints. Then the attacker appends the estimated measurement $\hat{m}_{t+1}$ to the $L-1$ length vector x at step-16 to estimate a departure score at step-17. To reduce the effort, attacker does not perform any changes if the departure score is less than the estimated threshold θ' at step-18. Otherwise, it distributes the estimated measurement to the adversarial sensor using function $getManipulatedArray()$. The estimated $\hat{m}_{t+1}$ is then used to manipulate the index adv sensors using function $getManipulatedArray()$ (step-19). According to Eq. 6, the function $getManipulatedArray()$ uses current measurements X_t to distribute an opposite share of non-adversarial sensors $(\overline{adv})$ into adversarial sensors (adv) such that the IDS performing the aggregation at timestamp $t+1$ generates the aggregated measurement equivalent to $\hat{m}_{t+1}$. Step-22 estimates the remaining share (rs) of other than adv sensor measurements in aggregated measurement at timestamp t. Step-23 computes to distribute rs into every adversarial sensor (currently using the same value to manipulate every adversarial sensor). It returns the same scalar value to replace every adv index sensor at timestamp $t+1$. Since the IDS performs sum of the square to aggregate, we return the square root value to balance the Eq. 6. If $(\hat{m}^2 - rs)$ is negative, $\sqrt{\hat{m}^2 - rs}$ is not a real number; therefore we return the minimum value zero.

---

[2] Note: the first index of an array is '1'.

Algorithm 1: Pseudocode of Crafting Method

---

    input : Model Parameters: Projection matrix U^T, Centroid $\hat{c}$, Threshold θ
               Input data: Multivariate timeseries X
    output: Manipulated multivariate timeseries X_m

1    $adv \leftarrow$ Initialize adversarial sensor's indices
2    $X_m \leftarrow$ Initialize an empty matrix of shape X
3    $\mathcal{T} \leftarrow agregrated\ X$ ▶(cf. Sect. 2.4)
4    $min, max \leftarrow getminmax(\mathcal{T})$ ▶normal range of $\mathcal{T}$
5    $\mu \leftarrow mean(\mathcal{T})$
6    $\theta' \leftarrow \theta/2$ ▶estimated threshold for attacker
7    $L \leftarrow len(U)$ ▶get lag parameter
8   **for** $t \leftarrow 1$ **to** *attack duration* **do**
9        $x \leftarrow \mathcal{T}[t - L + 1 : t]$
10      $y \leftarrow \hat{c} - U[1 : L - 1]^T \cdot x$ ▶eq. (4)
11      $\hat{m}_{t+1} \leftarrow \dfrac{y^T \cdot U[L]}{||U[L]||^2}$ ▶crafted measurement
12   **if** $\hat{m}_{t+1} > max$ **then**   ▶project at max
13        $\hat{m}_{t+1} \leftarrow max$
14   **if** $\hat{m}_{t+1} < min$ **then**   ▶project at min
15        $\hat{m}_{t+1} \leftarrow min$
16      $w'_{t+1} \leftarrow x.append(\hat{m}_{t+1})$
17      $D'_{t+1} \leftarrow ||\hat{c} - U^T \cdot w_{t+1}||^2$ ▶estimated departure score
18   **if** $D'_{t+1} \geq \theta'$ **then**   ▶manipulate only higher DS
19        $X_m[adv, t+1] \leftarrow getManipulatedArray(X[:, t], \hat{m}_{t+1}, adv)$
20   **return** X_m

21 **Function** getManipulatedArray($X_t, \hat{m}, adv$):
22    $rs \leftarrow ||X_t[\overline{adv}]||^2$ ▶ $\overline{adv}$ is complement of adv
23   **return** $\sqrt{\dfrac{MAX(\hat{m}^2 - rs, 0)}{len(adv)}}$ ▶distribute same to every adv sensor

---

4.3 Effect of Normal Sensors

A sophisticated attacker induces abnormality only in a few sensors to reduce its chance of being detected; we call these abnormal sensors (referred as *abn*). The attacker modifies a few sensors called the adversarial sensors (*adv*) to hide the attack-induced abnormality in *abn*. A CI may consist of thousands of sensors, most of which are normal (referred to as *nor*). In this section, we explain that the number of normal sensors would not affect the proposed evasion method. We rewrite the Eq. 6 as below.

$$||X_{t+1}[adv]||^2 = \hat{m}_{t+1}^2 - ||X_t[abn]||^2 - ||X_t[nor]||^2 \tag{7}$$

The aggregated timeseries $\mathcal{T}$ has a normal pattern for a single normal sensor. For two normal sensors, $\mathcal{T}$ will form a different timeseries but will still be normal. Similarly, $\mathcal{T}$ is normal for any number of normal sensors, and the departure score of IDS remains below the threshold. Therefore, $||X_t[nor]||^2$ in Eq. 7 is a known value which is a constant for the tth timestamp. The abnormal sensors ($||X_t[abn]||^2$) are modified, which affects $\hat{m}_{t+1}^2$. As the attack model does not allow manipulation $\mathcal{T}$ directly using $\hat{m}_{t+1}^2$. The adversarial sensors are used to adjust $\mathcal{T}$ to lower the departure score. Therefore, the changes in $||X_t[abn]||^2$ are adjusted by $||X_{t+1}[adv]||^2$. The normal sensor measurements ($||X_t[nor]||^2$) are used as a time dependent constant for estimating $\hat{m}_{t+1}^2$. It is a constant for any length of nor.

4.4 Complexity Analysis

Implementation of the CM method is expected to quickly crafts the measurements so that they can replace next measurement as soon as it gets generated. The main computation cost of our CM implementation lies in computing $\hat{m}_{t+1}$ (cf. steps 10 and 11 in Algorithm 1). Step-10 performs a $(R \times L - 1)$ dimensional matrix to $(L-1)$ dimensional vector multiplication to generate an R dimensional vector y, the computation cost is $O(RL)$. And Step-11 performs R dimensional vector dot products that cost $O(R^2)$. In addition, step-17 computes the departure score, which is a similar computationally expensive step and again costs $O(RL)$. Therefore, the computational complexity of our CM is $O(RL)$. Similarly, for the space complexity, the maximum memory needed to perform matrix to vector multiplications is $O(RL)$.

The MSSA-based IDS and CM have the same time and space complexity of $O(RL)$. Therefore CM is also computationally efficient. Further, the experimental computation cost is shown in Sect. 6.5.

5 Attack Scenarios and Dataset

We leverage direct damage attack (DDA) and stealthy attack (SA) attack datasets [3,16] with Tennessee-Eastman (TE) process simulator [6] to generate more sophisticated attack scenarios (cf. Sect. 6.2). In **DDA** [3], the attacker does not try to be stealthy. He aims to quickly achieve an abnormal state, damage the physical devices, and interrupt services. The measurements of the sensors generated during DDA go beyond the normal range. Therefore, this attack must be detected as soon as possible. We reset the TE-process simulator's reactor pressure sensor XMEAS(7) to zero for generating this attack scenario. In response, the controller initiates additional chemical reactions to maintain reactor pressure. As a result, the reactor's pressure rises. The unexpected pressure increase harms the reactor, eventually halting the process. In **SA** [16], the attacker wants to be stealthy and remain unnoticed. He hides his abnormal activities within the noise margin to slowly damage the ICS and stay undetected for an extended period. This dataset is generated by simulating the purge valve to be opened 28%, which is 2% more than normal.

Each scenario dataset is a timeseries of 41 XMEAS. The dataset is gathered during a 48-h period. The first 40 h are during normal operation, and the last 8 h

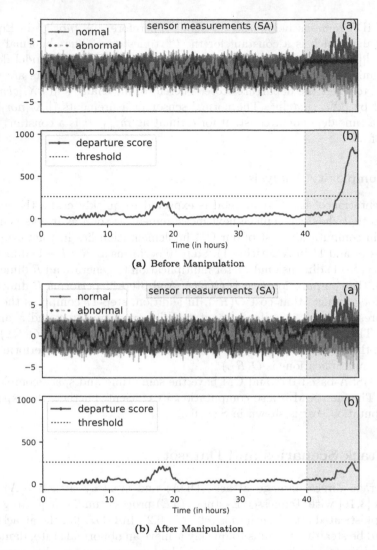

Fig. 2. We demonstrate evasion attack on the stealthy attack scenario present in fig (a). We manipulate 13 adversarial sensors without affecting the under-attack sensors. The manipulations cause the IDS to fail to detect the attack. Because of manipulation constraints, manipulated green points appear legitimate in fig (b).

are during attack. The measurements are produced regularly. It takes an hour to create 100 measurements.

6   Evaluation

In this Section we evaluate our evasion attack technique using the two attack scenarios (cf. Sect. 5). Assumption: To perform experiments, we assume that the sensors showing attack-induced abnormalities are the part of critical components that an attacker cannot manipulate. And a subset of normal sensors is considered adversarial, which are manipulable.

6.1 Greybox Experiment

A greybox attacker (cf. Sect. 3.4) describes accessibility constraints to restrict IDS access. The IDS parameters need to be estimated at the attacker's end. He can eavesdrop on the regular traffic to collect a normal dataset to estimate the IDS parameters $(U^T, \hat{c}, \theta)$. To evaluate the greybox experiment, we use the remaining normal data that are not used in training the actual IDS and different lag parameters $L = \{50, 100, 200, 300, 400, 500\}$. We use the estimated parameter in Algorithm 1 for crafting the adversarial measurements under greybox setting. However, the whitebox evaluation uses the actual IDS parameters.

6.2 Data Preparation and Normalization

An attacker usually targets an ICS component that causes structural changes only in a few sensors related to the component. In a naive attack, almost every sensor in the two attack scenarios shows structural change. An intelligent attacker never shows structural changes everywhere and gets caught. We ensure an attack scenario to be abnormal in only a few sensors. Hence, we collect completely normal measurements for every sensor of the TE-process simulator and replace four main abnormal sensors (cf. subfigure (a) of Figs. 2a and 3a) with the corresponding sensors. Further, we normalize each sensor $\forall i\ X_t^{(i)}$ using the standard score. We apply normalized dataset to the IDS described in Sect. 2.4. The IDS successfully detects the attacks cf. subfigure (b) of Figs. 2a and 3a).

6.3 Adversarial Sensor Selection and Manipulation

We select the adversarial sensors from a few normal sensors (other than the abnormal sensors) to experiment with the evasion attack. Then we apply the CM to manipulate adversarial sensors during an attack to conceal the abnormal activities. CM returns a manipulated array dataset. We then apply the manipulated data to the IDS described in Sect. 2.4 to check alarm count. To generalize the manipulation capabilities of CM, we select different sets of adversarial sensors and check the corresponding alarm count (cf. Figs. 4a and 4b). The remaining sensors which are neither abnormal nor adversarial are normal sensors.

6.4 Results

We evaluate CM by selecting the number of adversarial sensors that increase from zero to thirty (an extended number of adversarial sensors until the alarm counts drop to zero). Zero adversarial sensor means that the attacker does not manipulate any sensors, i.e., the actual alarms count by IDS while detecting

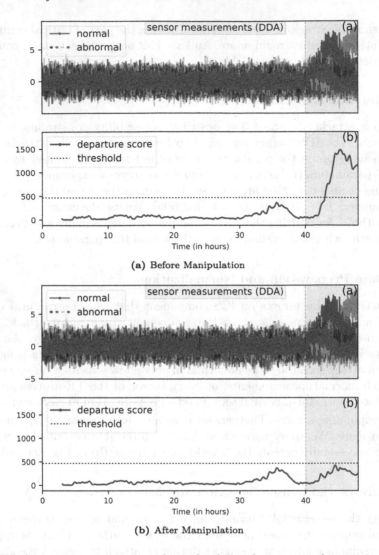

(a) Before Manipulation

(b) After Manipulation

Fig. 3. We demonstrate evasion attack on the direct damage attack scenario present in fig (a). We manipulate 20 adversarial sensors without affecting the under attack sensors. The manipulations causes the IDS to fail to detect the DDA. Because of the manipulation constraints, manipulated green points appear legitimate in fig (b).

the actual attack. When there is no manipulation, the departure score produced by IDS is high enough to cross the threshold during attack period (cf Figs. 3a and 2a). Therefore, 261 and 505 attack alarms are raised for the 800 attack measurement of SA and DDA, respectively.

Whitebox: Figures 4a and 4b (the red line shows the whitebox results) show the alarm count for increasing the number of adversarial senors. In the SA scenario (cf. Fig. 4a), the alarm counts decrease while increasing the number of adversarial sensors with a correlation coefficient of −0.95. When we manipulate 13 or more adversarial sensors, no alarms are raised. Similarly, in the DDA attack scenario (cf. Fig. 4b), the correlation coefficient is −0.82, and the alarm count reaches zero when we manipulate 20 or more adversarial sensors. All sensor measurements (attack, adversarial and normal) and departure scores for the no alarm raised scenario are shown in Figs. 2b and 3b, where manipulation (13 and 20 adversarial sensors manipulation, respectively) forces to keep the departure score below the threshold, thus causing no attack alarm. Since the manipulations are constrained to be within normal range, manipulated measurements of the adversarial sensors look similar to those of normal sensors.

Greybox: We perform the greybox experiment for different lag parameters (cf. Figs. 4a and 4b). The smaller lag parameters estimate an equivalent CM to the whitebox, but a higher lag parameter estimated model needs more manipulations to cause no attack alarm, especially in the DDA scenario. Figures 4b and 4a shows that every greybox model decreases alarm count with an increasing number of adversarial sensors, and enough manipulations evade IDS for both SA and DDA attack scenarios.

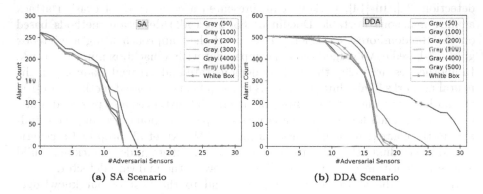

(a) SA Scenario   (b) DDA Scenario

Fig. 4. Number of alarms raised (y-axis) when an adversary manipulates 0-to-30 sensors (x-axis). Figures show the SA and DDA attack scenarios for whitebox, and greybox with different lag parameters. In every scenario, the alarm count decreases when the number of adversarial sensors increases. The greybox gives a close result to whitebox.

6.5   Parameters and Computation Cost

This section provides the necessary parameters to regenerate the result. There are two main parameters needed to train the IDS: lag L and dimensionality of signal space R. We use the guideline in [2] to select L and R and use L = 300 and R = 5. In the greybox estimation, we use different lags around the actual interval of 100. Since the alarm count decreases with the decreasing lag, we use a smaller (lag = 50) until the alarm counts stop falling.

To show computational feasibility, we observe computation cost of our crafting method takes an average of 53.7 μs to craft adversarial measurements at a timestamp. All experiments are computed using Intel(R) Core(TM) i7-4770 CPU @ 3.40 GHz processor, 64-bit Ubuntu 16.04 LTS, 16 GB RAM, and Python 3.6.5.

7   Related Work

Recent studies have shown that ICS security provided by machine learning-based IDSs are vulnerable to evasion attacks. In [7], Erba et al. introduced an evasion attack in the ICS, which is only applicable to reconstruction-based, multivariate, and deep learning-based IDS [9,21]. They used an auto-encoder model to craft some sensor measurements evading the IDS. Afterward, Jiangnan et al. carried out research in [15] to evade deep learning-based IDS by increasing perturbation accuracy at lower computation cost. They use an iterative method to generate adversarial examples with linear physical constraints. To the best of our knowledge, only the evasion attack strategies outlined above are suggested for use in the ICS sector.

Apart from ICS, the evasion attack has been introduced in multiple application scenarios such as face recognition [26], voice recognition [19], and malware detection [24]. In [14], Laskov et al. presented a case study of evasion attack against malicious Portable Document Format (pdf) detection methods based on the RandomForest classifier. They tested their approach using a whitebox gradient-based evasion method and compared it with a blackbox mimicry attack. In another research [20], the authors demonstrated adversarial examples in the neural networks. This shifted the focus to Deep Learning-based methods. In [10], the authors investigated the causes of adversarial instances and provided a fast gradient approach for performing adversarial perturbations, proving their findings in the context of image classification. In [24], Xu et al. proposed a generic method to evaluate the robustness of malware classifiers under attack and build a genetic algorithm that crafts PDF files to evade the malware detector.

Based on the above literature survey and to the best of our knowledge, no evasion attack technique has been developed against state-of-the-art MSSA-based IDS. We are the first to introduce an evasion attack against an MSSA-based process-level intrusion detector and experimentally show that our proposed method successfully conceals attack-induced abnormal activities.

8   Conclusion and Discussion

Securing each component of an ICS as a top priority is a challenging task. If an attacker utilizes the weaker component to harm the critical component, it becomes more dangerous and may negate the security of the critical component. In this paper, we inform the ICS community about such attacks where an attacker hides his attack induced in critical components by manipulating any other component sensors. This is the first work that evaluates the evasion attack technique against MSSA-based IDS. We reverse engineer the MSSA-based IDS to get a crafting method that an attacker uses even without any knowledge of the IDS parameters. Also, we constrain our CM to craft a measurement that looks legitimate to make a sophisticated attack so that he does not get detected.

There are many IDS security applications (IoT, IIoT, or cloud computing-based monitoring systems) where attackers can access less secure sensors and intend to conceal their attack in the most critical sensor. The proposed attack model can apply to all such applications. The larger industries are being operated by ICSs, which are always the target of attackers as they play a crucial role in any country and society. The ICSs mostly consist of multiple distributed components that have different security levels. Therefore, we consider ICS a usecase where the attacker aims to exploit the most critical component to maximize the loss.

Acknowledgement. We thank to the C3iHub (Technology Innovation Hub on Cyber Security and Cyber Security for Cyber-Physical Systems) at IIT Kanpur for partially funding this research project. We extend our heartfelt gratitude to our fellow lab mates, Miss Nanda Rani and Mr Virendra Nishad, for their constructive criticism toward improving the manuscript. We also thank the anonymous reviewers for their insightful comments.

References

1. Alanqary, A., Alomar, A., Abdullah, D.S.: Change point detection via multivariate singular spectrum analysis. In: Advances in Neural Information Processing Systems (2021)
2. Aoudi, W., Almgren, M.: A scalable specification-agnostic multi-sensor anomaly detection system for IIoT environments. Int. J. Crit. Infrastruct. Protect. **30**, 100377 (2020)
3. Aoudi, W., Iturbe, M., Almgren, M.: Truth will out: departure-based process-level detection of stealthy attacks on control systems. In: ACM SIGSAC Conference on Computer and Communications Security. ACM, Toronto (2018)
4. Biggio, B., Roli, F.: Wild patterns: ten years after the rise of adversarial machine learning. Pattern Recogn. (2018)
5. Chen, N., Chen, Y.: Anomalous vehicle recognition in smart urban traffic monitoring as an edge service. Future Internet **14**, 54 (2022)
6. Downs, J., Vogel, E.: A plant-wide industrial process control problem. Comput. Chem. Eng. **17**, 245–255 (1993)
7. Erba, A., et al.: Constrained concealment attacks against reconstruction-based anomaly detectors in industrial control systems. In: Annual Computer Security Applications Conference, Austin, USA (2020)
8. Garcia, L., Brasser, F., Cintuglu, M., Sadeghi, A., Mohammed, O., Zonouz, S.: Hey, my malware knows physics! Attacking PLCs with physical model aware rootkit. In: NDSS, San Diego, USA (2017)
9. Goh, J., Adepu, S., Tan, M., Lee, Z.: Anomaly detection in cyber physical systems using recurrent neural networks. In: 18th International Symposium on High Assurance Systems Engineering. IEEE, Singapore (2017)

10. Goodfellow, I.J., Shlens, J., Szegedy, C.: Explaining and harnessing adversarial examples. arXiv preprint arXiv:1412.6572 (2014)

11. Hassani, H., Mahmoudvand, R.: Multivariate singular spectrum analysis: a general view and new vector forecasting approach. Int. J. Energy Stat. **1**, 55–83 (2013)

12. Huitsing, P., Chandiaaa, R., Papa, M., Shenoi, S.: Attack taxonomies for the Modbus protocols. Int. J. Crit. Infrastruct. Protect. **1**, 37–44 (2008)

13. Kovacevic, A., Nikolic, D.: Cyber attacks on critical infrastructure: review and challenges. In: Handbook of Research on Digital Crime, Cyberspace Security, and Information Assurance (2015)

14. Laskov, P., et al.: Practical evasion of a learning-based classifier: a case study. In: 2014 IEEE symposium on security and privacy. IEEE (2014)

15. Li, J., Yang, Y., Sun, J.S., Tomsovic, K., Qi, H.: ConAML: constrained adversarial machine learning for cyber-physical systems. In: Proceedings of the 2021 ACM Asia Conference on Computer and Communications Security (2021)

16. Maurya, V., Agarwal, R., Kumar, S., Shukla, S.K.: EPASAD: ellipsoid decision boundary based process-aware stealthy attack detector. arXiv preprint arXiv:2204.04154 (2022)

17. Mo, Y., Sinopoli, B.: On the performance degradation of cyber-physical systems under stealthy integrity attacks. IEEE Trans. Autom. Control (2015)

18. Mo, Y., Sinopoli, B.: Secure control against replay attacks. In: 2009 47th Annual Allerton Conference on Communication, Control, and Computing (Allerton). IEEE (2009)

19. Sharif, M., Bhagavatula, S., Bauer, L., Reiter, M.K.: Accessorize to a crime: Real and stealthy attacks on state-of-the-art face recognition. In: Proceedings of the 2016 ACM SIGSAC Conference on Computer and Communications Security (2016)

20. Szegedy, C., et al.: Intriguing properties of neural networks. arXiv preprint arXiv:1312.6199 (2013)

21. Taormina, R., Galelli, S.: Deep-learning approach to the detection and localization of cyber-physical attacks on water distribution systems. J. Water Resour. Plann. Manage. (2018)

22. Vautard, R., Ghil, M.: Singular spectrum analysis in nonlinear dynamics, with applications to paleoclimatic time series. Phys. D Nonlinear Phenom. **35**, 395–424 (1989)

23. Weinberger, S.: Is this the start of cyberwarfare? Last year's Stuxnet virus attack represented a new kind of threat to critical infrastructure. Nature **474**, 142–146 (2011)

24. Xu, W., Qi, Y., Evans, D.: Automatically evading classifiers. In: Proceedings of the 2016 Network and Distributed Systems Symposium, vol. 10 (2016)

25. Yadav, G., Paul, K.: Assessment of SCADA system vulnerabilities. In: 2019 24th IEEE International Conference on Emerging Technologies and Factory Automation (ETFA). IEEE (2019)

26. Zhang, G., Yan, C., Ji, X., Zhang, T., Zhang, T., Xu, W.: DolphinAttack: inaudible voice commands. In: Proceedings of the 2017 ACM SIGSAC Conference on Computer and Communications Security (2017)

27. Zheng, X., Julien, C., Kim, M., Khurshid, S.: Perceptions on the state of the art in verification and validation in cyber-physical systems. IEEE Syst. J. **11**, 2614–2627 (2015)

Vulnerability Analysis of an Electric Vehicle Charging Ecosystem

Roland Plaka(✉) ⓘ, Mikael Asplund, and Simin Nadjm-Tehrani

Department of Computer and Information Science, Linköping University, Linköping,
Sweden
{roland.plaka,mikael.asplund,simin.nadjm-tehrani}@liu.se

Abstract. The increase of electric vehicles has exacerbated the need
for adequate security measures in the electric vehicle charging ecosystem
(EVCE). Integrating IT services into the electric vehicle charging infrastructure exposes it to several new attack vectors. In this paper, we apply
a vulnerability analysis method to assess the current security posture of
the internet-connected EVCE components. Our method is based on penetration testing principles using open-source cybersecurity search engines.
Using this method, we gathered security-related information apparently
associated with eight charging station vendors and three management
systems, and we found 13 vulnerable technologies containing 81 vulnerabilities. Based on the information provided by vulnerability databases,
we classified the threats according to the STRIDE model and analyzed
the potential consequences of the vulnerabilities in terms of the security
properties that can be violated.

Keywords: EV charging · cybersecurity · vulnerability analysis

1 Introduction

Integrating IT services in the electric vehicle charging stations introduces several
attack surfaces to this domain, threatening the security of the vehicle, the charging station, and potentially the grid. The rapid deployment of electric vehicle
charging stations (EVCSs) has contributed to the electric vehicle (EV) ecosystem's lack of proper security measures. Evidence of cyberattacks at EV charging
stations illustrates increasing cybersecurity risks for critical energy and transportation infrastructures. For example, there are reports that some charging
stations in Russia were hacked[1], and electric vehicle users in the U.K. reported

---

[1] https://www.utilitydive.com/news/putin-hacks-of-ev-electric-vehicle-charging-
stations-cybersecurity-preparations/634547/.

Supported by Vinnova through the project Sustainable Energy with Adaptive Security
(2021-01683) and RICS Centre on Resilient Information and Control Systems financed
by Swedish Civil Contingencies Agency (MSB).

seeing videos with inappropriate content playing on public charging stations[2]. The electric vehicle charging infrastructure is an important part of the smart grid, so such cyberattacks could potentially impact the electrical grid, ranging from localized, relatively minor effects to long-term national disruption [6].

Previous research [21] has shown that several Electric Vehicle Charging Management Systems (EVCMSs) exhibit internet-facing ports and assets with exploitable vulnerabilities. However, we are not aware of any studies that have focused on the internet-facing charging stations (EVCSs) themselves. Since both the management systems and the charging stations are connected to the internet, they are likely to be targeted by an adversary to gain access to the system. Thus, there is a need to complement existing research on the security posture of electric vehicle management systems based on insights on the state of security of the charging stations. While the management system can operate in a cloud environment with associated security protection mechanisms, the charging stations are essentially IoT devices with limited capacity and lack of security monitoring services. Moreover, the potential impact of a security breach at the charging station is high since it might negatively affect the vehicle and even the electrical grid if coordinated with other compromised charging stations [17].

In this work, we investigate the current security state for the electric vehicle charging ecosystem. This ecosystem consists of electric vehicles, mobile applications accessed by the EV user, charging stations, charging management systems, and web applications. Our focus is on the internet-connected EV charging stations (EVCSs) and charging management systems (CMS), whereas the vehicle's connection to the CS using protocols such as ISO 15118 is outside our scope. We analyze the relevant components to identify protocols, services, and vendor-specific information. We then use existing cybersecurity search engines to collect information about internet-connected charging stations and discover which ports, services, and technologies are provided by the hosts. We perform a vulnerability assessment using standard vulnerability databases based on this public information. Moreover, for each found vulnerability we classify it according to Spoofing, Tampering, Repudiation, Information disclosure, Denial of Service, and Elevation of Privilege (STRIDE) threat model to better understand the security property that might be violated if the vulnerabilities were to be exploited. Finally, we perform an initial assessment of the potential impact of such attacks if performed against the EV charging components.

Our results show that many analyzed hosts expose relatively complex software services like the Apache web server and interactive web applications. We identify a total of 78 vulnerabilities in 8 charging stations and 3 vulnerabilities for 3 charging management systems. We disclose the identified issues by making responsible disclosures and discussing vendor responses. Our threat analysis of these vulnerabilities reveals that most are related to information disclosure, but other threats exist, such as spoofing and denial of service.

To summarize, our contributions in this paper are as follows.

– Identify and analyze 81 vulnerabilities in internet-facing electric vehicle charging stations and charging management systems. Identifying these

---

[2] https://www.bbc.com/news/uk-england-hampshire-61006816.

vulnerabilities seems to indicate that the security level of the vehicle charging infrastructure is still relatively weak.
- Threat classification and initial impact analysis according to the STRIDE model for EV charging infrastructure attacks potentially possible given the identified vulnerabilities.

In the rest of this paper, we first introduce the charging infrastructure components and technologies to visualize and clarify the focus of our work. We also briefly discuss the security aspects of each component, its limitations, and the threats they may face. In Sect. 3, we describe the application of the vulnerability analysis method for detecting and analyzing vulnerabilities in EV charging systems and the results. Section 4 classifies the observed vulnerabilities according to the STRIDE model and details some of the most interesting aspects of the vulnerabilities. In addition, we discuss the impacts of the threats being exploited, identifying the potential risks that may affect the components of the EV charging ecosystem. Section 5 discusses the identified issues by making responsible disclosures and discussing vendor responses. Section 6 presents the related work in this domain, and Sect. 7 concludes the paper.

2   Charging Infrastructure Components

This section deals with the shortcomings of security in the EV charging ecosystem. As shown in Fig. 1 the charging ecosystem's architecture and common components. Earlier papers have presented similar architectures [6]. It presents the information flow marked with blue arrows and the power flow marked with red arrows. Attacker pathways to the charging stations are not limited to physical attacks but also include web-based attack vectors. If these succeed, attackers can change the operation of devices, switch on or off the charging sessions, and so on. Assuming that attackers may have access to a large number of charging stations, one can imagine them simultaneously triggering the termination of all active charging sessions, potentially causing harm to energy utilities and damage to equipment due to the sudden change in electrical load [31].

The Open Charge Point Protocol (OCPP) supports communication between the charging stations and the management systems. This protocol has adapted to the changing security requirements due to earlier concerns with weak authentication, end-to-end security, non-repudiation, and weak encryption. However, securing OCPP itself does not resolve all security problems in these systems. Physical security of the CSs, EV charging applications, hardware, and software-related security also need better understanding. In the remainder of this section, we discuss each of the architecture's main components and security issues related to these components.

Electric Vehicle (EV). Electric vehicles are what motivates the existence of the charging infrastructure. Data exchange across the EV charging infrastructure is enabled through various communication protocols. The communication between the EV and EVCS is mainly provisioned through the following standards:

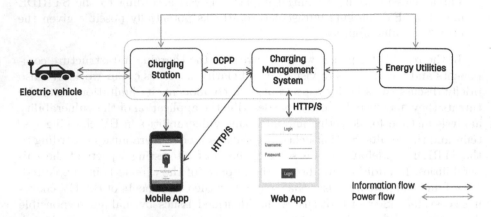

Fig. 1. EV charging ecosystem

- International Electromechanical Commission (IEC): IEC defines multiple standards that address different aspects of EV charging, including IEC 62169 and 61851.
- International Standardization ISO (ISO): ISO 15118 details the communication infrastructure within the charging environment and supports power flow from EVs.

Our work does not investigate the security posture of the communication between the EV and EVCS, focusing rather on the EVCS and CMS components.

Charging Station. Charging stations act as an interface or a high-wattage access point between the EV and the power grid. CSs are IoT devices running firmware and are located in close vicinity of the charging site. Charging stations can provide authentication based on RFID access tags and, in some cases, exhibit a payment terminal for credit card payments. CSs are controlled by the Charging Management System (CMS), which creates the messages that declare the power limits and the operational state of the CS. The CS can be compromised directly via on-site interactions or remotely through communication interfaces. An attacker who controls many CSs and EVs can, for instance, attempt to disrupt the power grid with synchronized charging loads. Notably, control over a large enough number of CPs and EVs would be gained via remotely exploitable vulnerabilities. Charging stations typically have internal charger ports, external maintenance ports, and wired ports. Physical ports are available for CS vendors to debug the equipment; however, these ports are often left open in production equipment, which may allow adversaries to monitor or disrupt equipment operations. Charging stations commonly host Telnet, SSH, or local website services, allowing the owner to configure the device or collect/maintain data [14].

EVCS-CMS. The Open Charge Point Protocol leads the effort towards a standardized communication protocol for this domain. OCPP facilitates the exchange of data between the CS and CMS, and it is used to manage the schedule of charging EVs, secure the logs of EV users and their charging, and maintain the status of the EVCS itself. Different versions of this protocol have been developed, starting from version OCPP 1.2, followed by 1.5, 1.6, and up to the latest OCPP 2.0. Attackers may undesirably exploit the compromised EVCS station to jeopardize the supply-demand balance of a grid by remotely controlling the charging behaviors of the station through a large-scale compromise. Each EV generates critical info (location, charging time, and average power consumption per hour) at the charging station, which can be subject to misuse. Attackers can cause a sustained, significant spike in demand, resulting in cascading disconnection of power supply from the grid and abnormal operation performance (load shedding). As a consequence of these attacks, the power plants would be forced into restart conditions, causing widespread brownouts or blackouts and grid instability. This situation can threaten the security and stable operation of the power systems. Identifying and securing the entry points that the threat actors can exploit is critical to controlling unintended access to the CS infrastructure. Therefore, cyber-physical security concerns of the EV charging ecosystem and the possible detection and mitigation measures must be addressed to ensure safe, secure, and resilient charging.

Charging Management System. CMSs typically are hosted on a cloud server and manage all operations of the public CSs. This system directs users to the available CS, schedules and manages charging sessions, and logs EVCS utilization data. The CS management system can send the CS-specific control signals related to the duration of the charging session, charging rate, beginning and termination commands, etc. CMS's main tasks are to communicate with the CS, to define the service parameters taking into account the user input, and the EV and the power grid status, to collect and store the charging system data, to host the user application, and to maintain a booking registry for the service. OCPP protocol bears a major responsibility in the communication processes between the CSMs and CSs. OCPP supports smart-charging policies and allows the CMS to implement customized profiles for the charging processes. OCPP allows open communication between an internet-connected charging station and the cloud-based backend, where the operators can easily manage accessibility, remotely upgrade firmware, monitor stations, bill users, optimize charging, and other extended functions.

The CMS can provide discrete grid services (peak shaving, voltage control, demand-side management, demand charge reduction, and emergency demand response). It receives charging requests from EVs/CSs and various grid service requests from utility control centers. It is used to provide common access to CSs from different vendors over OCPP with the goal of open and interoperable EV charging. Charging management systems consist of the aggregator server, the monitoring clients, and the personal computer, which can be used for information exchange, e.g., battery status and charging information.

Mobile and Web Applications. These are web or smartphone applications through which users can interact with the management system over the internet (in case of a public EVCS) or directly to the charger over a LAN (in case of a private EVCS). These services allow users to reserve and control charging sessions, pay for public charging, control charging rates, start/terminate charging sessions, and monitor the status of the EV. The user's actions, the user device's vulnerabilities, and the user's application add data and parameters to the service, indirectly affecting the charging operations and security.

Energy Utilities. EVCSs are typically connected to the power grid and, as such, can greatly impact the grid's security and stability. The distribution system operator (DSO) is the organization responsible for distributing electricity to the end-users. The DSO allows or prohibits the power flow to the charging site and, based on the EV's data feedback, ensures balance and decongestion in the grid [24].

3   Vulnerability Identification in the EV Charging Ecosystem

Our goal is to identify vulnerabilities in electric vehicle charging stations and electric vehicle charging management systems accessible from the internet to demonstrate the potential risks facing the EV charging ecosystem. In this section, first, we describe the method we used to identify and assess vulnerabilities, and then we discuss the results.

3.1   Vulnerability Analysis Method

Figure 2 shows an overview of our method. Each step in the process is described below.

Search Engine Selection. We start with the engine selection in order to reuse known data on internet-facing devices. A survey done in 2020 on cyberspace engines [3] shows that Shodan, Censys, BinaryEdge, ZoomEye, and Fofa are leading regarding the number of detectable devices and services. We use Shodan, Censys, and BinaryEdge in this step of our analysis. ZoomEye and Fofa are used in a later stage.

Keyword Selection. We need to know what to search for to focus on relevant protocols, components, vendors, and services related to charging stations and charging management systems. To collect instances of potentially vulnerable internet-facing EV services, we select 35 relevant keywords, including "OCPP",

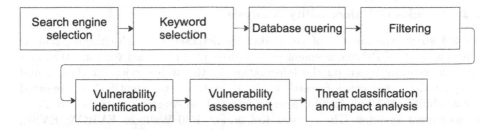

Fig. 2. Overview of vulnerability analysis method

"Charging Interface", "Charging station", "EV charging", "OCPP interface", and several vendor names.

Database Querying and Search Refinement. Using the keywords and the selected databases, we discover hundreds of IP addresses, some of which are deemed irrelevant. Combining several keywords helps to restrict the search results. As a result, we narrow down to 35 IP addresses with a relevant technology running behind. For each IP address we collect information such as the server type, location, port, network equipment information (i.e., router or switch), and protocol used.

Filtering. We further filter the selected services to exclude non-interactive web pages. This leaves us with web management interfaces that are used for configuring and maintaining CSs and CMSs. As a result, we decrease the number of IP addresses to 11.

Vulnerability Identification. We leverage search engines ZoomEye and Fofa to passively collect security-related information about the selected IP addresses. As a result, we get security status records, such as vulnerabilities in the form of Common Vulnerability Exposures identities (CVE-ID) and exploitation information.

Vulnerability Assessment. There are cases when the CVE-ID is missing for an output from the engines. Therefore, we search for more information in the National Vulnerability Database (NVD), which provides the CVE as well as Common Vulnerability Scoring System (CVSS) information. We also use other databases such as Tenable and CVE details database, that combine NVD data with information from other sources, such as the Exploit database.

Threat Classification and Impact Analysis. To evaluate the impact of each vulnerability, we consider the security properties that are violated according to the STRIDE threat model. The security properties we consider are authentication, integrity, non-repudiation, confidentiality, availability, and authorization. We analyze the vulnerabilities individually by considering the possible impact on the electric vehicle charging ecosystem, including the affected component.

3.2 Results of Vulnerability Analysis

Table 1 shows the number of vulnerabilities detected for each charging station interface and OCPP management system used by the named vendors. We identify the vendors based on the information in the web service interface found through the cybersecurity search engines. In total, we identified 81 reported vulnerabilities. 63 vulnerabilities were detected on charging stations and 25 on management systems. The vendors KeContact P30 Wallbox, EVBOX, EVSE, ENSTO Chago EVF200, Mennekes, Teltonika, EVTEC, and ETREL are charging station interfaces connected to the internet. SECWIN, CIRCONTROL, and CIRCUTOR are OCPP management systems deployed on cloud computing technology. Besides, we represent the total number of vulnerabilities and their risk level referring to the CVSS v3.1. These results reveal that the system identified by our method as being connected to KeContact30 P30 Wallbox contains the most significant vulnerabilities.

Note that we have not verified that the vulnerable instances are really running legitimate and updated software versions from the charging station vendors. We perform the analysis based on the information gathered by public sources and any errors or misattributions in those sources would also be reflected in our results. Methodologically, it is difficult to assess this information as there are potential legal and ethical obstacles with digging too deep into the services linked from cybersecurity search engines (as these services might not be meant for public access).

Table 2 shows the number of vulnerabilities detected on each technology. Our vulnerability analysis approach identified ten vulnerable technologies listed under the Product column. In the second column of this table, we list the vulnerabilities detected in each technology, which comprise eighty-one vulnerabilities. With technologies relying on the Apache server, we identified sixteen vulnerabilities making this technology the most vulnerable and exposed on our list.

4   Threat Classification and Impact Analysis

In the previous section we discussed a number of vulnerabilities seemingly present in connected EV charging systems. However, the criticality assessments of these vulnerabilities as retrieved from vulnerability databases are not necessarily made in connection to EV charging systems. Many of the vulnerabilities are in fact related to web services, and therefore the criticality is typically determined based on a generic system model. In this section, we take a closer look at the vulnerabilities to classify them in relation to what the attacker can accomplish if the vulnerability is exploited. Moreover, we discuss how these attacks could impact the EV charging ecosystem. There are several threat modelling frameworks [25] such as PASTA [30], OCTAVE [15], and LINDDUN [29]. In this work, we use the STRIDE methodology developed by Microsoft. STRIDE is one of the most mature threat modeling approaches that can help evaluate and identify system threats.

Table 1. The number of vulnerabilities detected for each type of charging station interface and OCPP management system

Charging station interface/OCPP MS	Critical	High	Medium	Total
KeContact P30 Wallbox	–	11	4	15
EVBOX	2	6	2	10
EVSE	–	6	1	7
ENSTO Chago EVF200	–	5	6	11
Mennekes	–	6	–	6
Teltonika	–	10	1	11
EVTEC	–	4	–	4
ETREL	–	14	–	14
SECWIN	–	1	–	1
CIRCONTROL	1	–	–	1
CIRCUTOR	–	1	–	1

Table 2. The vendors and vulnerabilities detected on each technology

Product	Count of Vulnerability
Apache server	31
DNS server	5
Dropbear server	2
Gateway	4
GoAhead webserver	2
gSQAP toolkit	3
Microsoft IIS httpd	13
OpenSSH server	11
OpenWrt httpd	1
nginx	1
PHP server	8

To accomplish our goal, we evaluate the information provided by the vulnerability databases such as CVE details[3], and NVD[4]. We aim to identify which security property of the assets is threatened by which threat. Finally, we map the impact information to the violated security property. The mapping is done as follows: threats that violate the authentication property expose the technology discovered to spoofing attacks; the threats that violate integrity reveal tampering attacks; non-repudiation-related threats expose to repudiation; confidentiality-related threats expose to information disclosure; availability-

---

[3] https://www.cvedetails.com/.
[4] https://nvd.nist.gov/.

related threats expose to denial of service, and authorization related threats expose to the elevation of privilege attacks. The chart in Fig. 3 presents our findings using the STRIDE model. We proceed by selecting and describing some of the more interesting vulnerabilities in each category.

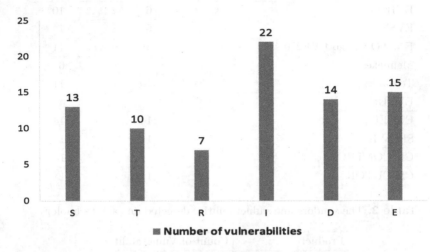

Fig. 3. Threat classification according to the STRIDE model. The characters in the x-axis stand for Spoofing (S), Tampering (T), Repudiation (R), Information disclosure (I), Denial of Service (D), and Elevation of Privilege (E)

Spoofing. As mentioned above in STRIDE, the authentication violation may lead to spoofing attack scenarios. There are 13 vulnerabilities with spoofing affecting authentication. One of the services exhibits a FreeSSHd Authentication Bypass vulnerability, which allows remote attackers to bypass authentication via a crafted session (CVE-2012-6066). When an actor claims to have a given identity, the software does not ensure the claim is correct. Concerning our EV charging ecosystem architecture, an attacker may masquerade as a legitimate user and compromise the user's identity, potentially leading to energy theft and privacy violation. Similar attacks have been discussed by Gottumakkala et al. [10].

Tampering. Integrity is the security property that is threatened by tampering attacks. There are 10 vulnerabilities with tampering affecting integrity. Among these, we can mention an "HTTP verb tampering" vulnerability, in which an attacker modifies the HTTP method to bypass access restrictions. This allows the attacker to access data that should otherwise be protected. The vulnerability may affect the OCPP communication messages in the CSs and CMSs. Another possible threat can be tampering with the configuration values. This can happen if an attacker gains access to the CS or CMS and alters the credentials, installs malware within the updates, deletes logs, and tampers with charging time to desynchronize the energy monitoring [2]. Even worse, Nasr et al. setup and conduct simulation experiments to illustrate the feasibility of leveraging a botnet of exploited EVCS to carry out frequency instability attacks against the power grid and its operations [22].

Repudiation. Repudiation is the user's ability to reject or deny the claims against them for performing something, and the victim cannot verify the truth of the claim. Threats to non-repudiation are due to the absence of system or application logs. There are 7 vulnerabilities affecting repudiation. Among these, a vulnerability PEPPERL+FUCHS WirelessHART-Gateway (CVE-2021-34559) may allow remote attackers to rewrite links and URLs in cached pages to arbitrary strings. Exploiting this vulnerability can propagate with an HTTP Cross-Site Request Forgery attack that forces users to execute unwanted actions on a web application they're currently authenticated to use. In older versions of OCPP, where digital signatures are not forced, repudiation attacks may arise (as well as tampering). If messages between CM and CMS are not properly audited, the system may not determine the responsible entity when an error occurs [2].

Information Disclosure. Confidentiality is the security property threatened by information disclosure. In our analysis, 22 vulnerabilities affect confidentiality. We observed several OpenSSH vulnerabilities, such as (CVE-2020-15778), (CVE-2018-15473), and (CVE-2023-25136) in different vendor products. Successful exploitation of these could allow a remote attacker to disclose sensitive information (or modify files). Leaking sensitive information may affect the reputation of the vendor. In addition, attackers can potentially extract internal IP addresses, back-end office URLs, security credentials, telemetry data, energy consumption, charging status of CSs, and software versions used. A cybersecurity report by Sandia National Laboratories [13] mentions a scenario where a threat actor illicitly may remotely exploit the vulnerabilities and cause information disclosure and loss of privacy.

Denial of Service. Denial of service attacks threaten the availability of CSs and CMSs. If threat actors exploit certain vulnerabilities, they can disrupt service communication with the authentication server, interrupting the real energy charge in EVs requested by the EV users. We found 14 vulnerabilities that potentially lead to a DoS attack. One vulnerability (CVE-2023-25136) allows an attacker to cause a denial of service through excessive CPU utilization in the server. Also, we observed presence of CVE-2017-9765, which allows remote attackers to execute arbitrary code, which may lead to DoS after tampering. Other DoS variants discussed in literature [11] are UDP or TCP/IP flood, low-rate DOS, ping flood, or ICMP flood. These attacks can take down a charging station or other nodes in the charging station ecosystem. In these attacks, an adversary targets the CMS or associated components to overload the network, preventing it from providing services to legitimate users. Such an attack can have severe consequences, affecting grid stability.

Elevation of Privilege. To gain unauthorized access to CS, CMS, and other components, attackers start by finding weak points through which they may first penetrate the network. They then attempt to escalate privileges to gain further permissions or access other sensitive subsystems [2]. The security property threatened by the elevation of privilege attacks is the authorization property. We noted 15 vulnerabilities that threaten authorization, e.g., a root privilege escalation vulnerability (CVE-2019-0211) that with a successful exploit provides access to the server. We observed another vulnerability (CVE-2022-31793), which if successful, enables an attacker to access the device's configuration, including access to passwords. A third vulnerability (CVE-2023-28231), if successfully exploited, could result in the execution of arbitrary code with administrative privileges.

Summary. From Fig. 3, it is obvious that threats relevant to information disclosure and privilege escalation are more prevalent, and threats of repudiation are seen to a lesser extent in this ecosystem. The most alarming observations are the instances of elevation of privilege. The massive use of such threats can enable actions that can further impact the other components of the ecosystem, including the grid operations. The absence of non-repudiation is also alarming. However, even from an individual perspective, the disclosure of information may be as relevant. Also, spoofing and tampering can lead to more serious instances like the elevation of privilege.

5   Responsible Disclosure

We performed responsible disclosure of our findings for all 11 vendors and their associated vulnerabilities. While all vulnerabilities were previously known, these still show up in search engine databases. We reported our findings via the official email addresses and contact forms of the vendors. Two vendors responded. One vendor stated that:

> "Fortunately for KEBA charging stations, all of the CVE entries can be considered as "false-positives". Most of the mentioned software solutions are not in use for charging stations and the related infrastructure components. Of course, it could be possible that a customer uses the mentioned software solutions for managing/accessing our products. But this scenario is out of scope for our risk assessment".

Another vendor (Mennekes) stated:

> "The interface behind the mentioned IP address indeed seems to show one of our products. ... However, besides the fact that these systems should not be connected to the public internet, the system uses a very old software version (v4.61).

We had a comprehensive security audit and penetration test in the meanwhile. ... Finally, the CVEs mentioned still do not really match the software used in these products, no matter which version is used".

Based on the vendor response regarding the false positive CVE entries, additional verification of cybersecurity search engine data seems to be a relevant direction for future work. It is possible that they report inaccurate information regarding the software running on the detected devices, as well as regarding the vulnerabilities present. We are not aware of any existing independent assessment of the quality of the data provided by these search engines. Another possibility suggested by both vendors is that a customer uses software solutions for managing/accessing their product that were not intended or foreseen by the vendors. Such unforeseen usage of the products by the customers may indicate that the identified vulnerabilities do exist for some EV charging components "in the wild", and that they are thus not being covered by security updates and audits by the vendors.

The services running on the IP addresses we analyzed are web management portals using CSs and CMSs software. From the outside, it is difficult to determine which entities that are responsible for taking care of identified vulnerabilities in these services. It can be argued that there is a shared responsibility between the EV charging component vendors, the software vendors that create the underlying technologies (e.g., web servers) and the owners and operators of the equipment. Upcoming regulations such as the European Cyber Resilience Act (CRA) are likely to increase the responsibility of the vendors to ensure that their products are secure throughout the entire lifecycle.

Given the second vendor's response that the system should not be connected to the public internet and the use of outdated software we see two possible explanations. Either the owners of the EV charging components have intentionally or unintentionally (e.g., through misconfiguration) connected these products to the public internet in a way that was not intended, or we may be dealing with honeypots and not with real systems.

6 Related Work

We divide the description of related work into two parts. First, we discuss threat modeling and risk analysis techniques related to EV charging systems, and then we survey other works that assess the security posture of the EV charging infrastructure.

6.1 Threat Modeling and Risk Analysis in EV Charging Systems

Casola et al. [5] propose an approach to support the security analysis of an IoT system using an almost entirely automated process for threat modeling and risk assessment, which also helps to identify the security controls to mitigate existing security risks. Baggot et al. [4] review the literature and present a risk-based framework in which they underscore the need for a coordinated U.S. cybersecurity effort toward formulating strategies and responses to protect the nation against attacks on the electric power grid. Shevchenko et al. [25], discuss twelve threat modeling methods from various sources and target different parts of the process. They do not recommend a threat modeling method over another; the decision of which method(s) to use should be based on the needs of the system and its specific concerns. Müller et al. [20], systematically formulate threat scenarios for the Cyber-Physical Systems (CPS) within Flexibility Markets (FM), revealing remaining security challenges across all domains. Based on threat scenarios, unresolved monitoring requirements for the secure participation of distribution system operators in FM are identified, eliciting future works that address these gaps. Granadilla et al. [9] propose a dynamic risk management response system consisting of proactive and reactive management software aiming at evaluating threat scenarios in an automated manner and anticipating the occurrence of potential attacks. They apply their system to a real case study of a critical infrastructure with multiple threat scenarios. We note that a systematic vulnerability-attack-impact analysis e.g. through the STRIDE classification that we adopt here would be useful.

Shrestha et al. [26] propose a methodology called Smart Grid Security Classification which aims to assign a system to a security class based on scores given to the various exposure aspects of the system and the respective protection mechanisms implemented without considering attackers. Kure et al. [18] present an integrated cybersecurity risk management framework to assess and manage the risks. Their approach enables the identification of critical CPS assets and assesses the impact of vulnerabilities that affect assets. Heiding et al. [12], investigate the cybersecurity of devices commonly located in connected homes: smart door locks, smart cameras, smart car adapters/garages, smart appliances, and miscellaneous smart home devices. They discover vulnerabilities that could lead to severe consequences for residents, such as an attacker gaining physical access to the house. Heading et al. [28] provides a four-stage IoT vulnerability research methodology built on top of four key elements: logical attack surface decomposition, a compilation of the top 100 weaknesses, lightweight risk scoring, and step-by-step penetration testing guidelines. Other works describe research about modeling and risk analysis techniques meant for EV charging systems. Lee et al. [19] analyze the security vulnerabilities of ISO/IEC 15118 and propose countermeasures to safely communicate between electric vehicles and power charging infrastructure. Gottumukkala et al. [10] present EVSE (electric vehicle supply equipment) as a cyber-physical system, then discuss and summarize cybersecurity-based vulnerabilities, threats, and consequences. In addition, they present methods and future research directions to improve the CPS security of charging stations. These works are all in other CPS domains, and our work complements these for the EVCS domain.

6.2   Security Posture on EV Charging Infrastructure

Zhdanova et al. [31] analyze conditions under which Vehicle to Grid (V2G) insecurity can lead to grid collapse. They use quantitative analysis and dynamic simulations of a typical European suburban grid to determine the scope and impact of EV charging manipulation. They review shortcomings of existing V2G protocols, analyze attack strategies able to cause overloads and validate known attacks based on experiments with off-the-shelf products. Lastly, they show that it is critical to consider the impact of known and unknown attacks and possible mitigations and fallback positions. Johnson et al. [14] survey publicly disclosed electric vehicle supply equipment vulnerabilities, the impact of EV charger cyberattacks, and proposed security protections for EV charging technologies. Bandurova et al. [27] analyze cyber security challenges of smart cities with a particular focus on the intelligent integrated and interconnected EV charging infrastructure. The analysis indicates that not all solutions have adequate cybersecurity protection. It is intended to lay a foundation for securing EV charging infrastructure by analyzing the problem context and the data to be protected, presenting some attack surfaces, cybersecurity threats, and vulnerabilities in the EV ecosystem. Our work confirms the lack of security protection and identifies individual components and vendor equipment in the current EV ecosystem.

Kern et al. [16] propose a framework for simulating and analyzing the impact of e-mobility-based attacks on grid resilience. They derive e-mobility-specific attacks based on the analysis of adversaries and threats and combine these attacks in their framework with models for grid and e-mobility to perform simulation-based outage analysis. The results show the scope of increased vulnerability during peak load hours, enabling attacks even with a small number of attacks in progress. They further discuss potential protection mechanisms for different resilience objectives, including detection, prevention, and response approaches. Nasr et al. [21] propose a novel multi-stage framework, ChargePrint, to discover Internet-connected EV charging management systems (EVCMS) and investigate their security posture. This framework leverages identifiers of EVCMSs to extend the capabilities of device search engines through iterative fingerprinting and a combination of classification and clustering approaches. Their security analysis highlights the insecurity of the deployed EVCMS by uncovering 120 0-day vulnerabilities. This sheds light on the feasibility of cyber attacks against the EVCS, its users, and the connected power grid. Their main focus is on the EVCSMS and the paper does not detail any EVCS-related vulnerabilities which is the focus of our work.

Ghafari et al. [8] investigate whether the abundance of Electric Vehicles can be exploited to target the stability of the power grid. They present a realistic coordinated switching attack that initiates interred oscillations between areas of the power grid. The threat model is formulated to illustrate the possible consequences of the attack. Finally, to protect the grid from this attack, a framework is proposed to detect and prevent this attack even before being executed. Gautam et al. [7], describe the concept of Smart Charging Management System (SCMS) and provide a comprehensive review of cybersecurity issues of EVSEs and SCMSs with their possible impacts on the power grid. Some insights on research gaps and vulnerabilities associated with currently commercially available SCMS technologies are also provided. Acharya et al. [1] describe and analyse cyber vulnerabilities and point to the current and emerging gaps in the security of the EV charging ecosystem. They list and characterize all backdoors that can be exploited to seriously harm either EV and EVCS equipment or the power grid. Our work makes the causal chain between the vulnerabilities, attacks, and security violations concrete in the EVCS context.

Sayed et al. [24] examine the EV ecosystem from vulnerability to attacks and solutions. They suggest several patches for the existing vulnerabilities but their focus is on methods to detect EV attacks. Sarieddine et al. [23] study the security posture of the EV charging ecosystem against a new type of remote access that exploits vulnerabilities in the EV charging mobile application as an attack surface. They leverage static and dynamic analysis techniques to analyze the security of widely used EV charging mobile applications. Their focus is user/vehicle verification and improper authorization for critical functions, which allow adversaries to remotely hijack charging sessions and launch attacks against the connected critical infrastructure. Nasr et al. [22] devise a system lookup and collection approach to obtain a representative sample of widely deployed EVCSMS; they leverage reverse engineering and penetration testing techniques to perform a comprehensive security and vulnerability analysis of the identified EVCSMS and their software/firmware implementations. They simulate the impact of practical cyber attack scenarios against the power grid, which result in possible service disruption and failure in the grid. Our work is similar to this but studies the vulnerability-attack chain from the EV charging station perspective.

7   Conclusions

As a part of the smart grid, the EV charging ecosystem is also connected to the internet, potentially making it vulnerable to cyber-attacks. In this paper, we investigate parts of the EV charging infrastructure through a vulnerability analysis method based on penetration testing techniques. We classify the potential security issues using the STRIDE threat modeling approach and trace 81 vulnerabilities to systems that appear to be running several popular charging station products. Although we cannot for sure know how many of these vulnerabilities exist in current commercial deployments, we believe that these results motivate further investigation into how such vulnerabilities can potentially affect end-users and the electrical grid (assuming large-scale attacks). We perform an initial analysis of potential impact by relating to the EV charging ecosystem and also discuss the identified vulnerabilities in the context of the STRIDE classification. Information disclosure is one of the more common vulnerability types, which can lead to loss of privacy and business-sensitive information. However, privilege escalation is one of the major categories that enables an attacker to gain control of the charging stations and traverse the network. These types of attacks can potentially cause substantial damage to the target system unless discovered in time.

Our work indicates that there are plenty of opportunities for attackers to utilize this new kind of infrastructure for malicious purposes. While awareness-raising efforts are an obvious step after the discovery of threat vectors, future research must also identify the defense-in-depth approaches to this new infrastructure and create means to protect the systems. At the same time, the vendor responses points to some threats to data validity. The first threat we identified is that we base our results on the outcome of search databases at face value. Some potential errors in vulnerability databases may not have been updated with the latest changes, and some of the systems we analyzed could even be security honeypots.

To improve the security of the EV charging infrastructure, future research should develop better tools and techniques to analyze and strengthen the security of the smart grid. This approach will help to expand the scope and depth of EV charging ecosystem security, and further explore the impacts of potential attacks.

References

1. Acharya, S., Dvorkin, Y., Pandžić, H., Karri, R.: Cybersecurity of smart electric vehicle charging: a power grid perspective. IEEE Access **8**, 214434–214453 (2020)
2. Alcaraz, C., Cumplido, J., Trivino, A.: OCPP in the spotlight: threats and countermeasures for electric vehicle charging infrastructures 40. Int. J. Inf. Secur. 1–27 (2023)
3. Ashley, T., Gourisetti, S.N.G., Brown, N., Bonebrake, C.: Aggregate attack surface management for network discovery of operational technology. Comput. Secur. **123**, 102939 (2022)
4. Baggott, S.S., Santos, J.R.: A risk analysis framework for cyber security and critical infrastructure protection of the us electric power grid. Risk Anal. **40**(9), 1744–1761 (2020)
5. Casola, V., De Benedictis, A., Rak, M., Villano, U.: Toward the automation of threat modeling and risk assessment in IoT systems. Internet Things **7**, 100056 (2010)
6. ElHussini, H., Assi, C., Moussa, B., Atallah, R., Ghrayeb, A.: A tale of two entities: contextualizing the security of electric vehicle charging stations on the power grid. ACM Trans. Internet Things **2**(2) (2021). https://doi.org/10.1145/3437258
7. Gautam, M., Bhusal, N., Benidris, M.: Concept of smart charging management system and its consensus on cybersecurity (2020)
8. Ghafouri, M., Kabir, E., Moussa, B., Assi, C.: Coordinated charging and discharging of electric vehicles: a new class of switching attacks. ACM Trans. Cyber-Phys. Syst. (TCPS) **6**(3), 1–26 (2022)
9. Gonzalez-Granadillo, G., et al.: Dynamic risk management response system to handle cyber threats. Futur. Gener. Comput. Syst. **83**, 535–552 (2018)
10. Gottumukkala, R., Merchant, R., Tauzin, A., Leon, K., Roche, A., Darby, P.: Cyber-physical system security of vehicle charging stations. In: 2019 IEEE Green Technologies Conference (GreenTech), pp. 1–5. IEEE (2019)
11. Hamdare, S., et al.: Cybersecurity risk analysis of electric vehicles charging stations. Sensors **23**(15), 6716 (2023)
12. Heiding, F., Süren, E., Olegård, J., Lagerström, R.: Penetration testing of connected households. Comput. Secur. **126**, 103067 (2023)

13. Johnson, J., et al.: Cybersecurity for electric vehicle charging infrastructure. Technical report, Sandia National Lab. (SNL-NM), Albuquerque, NM (United States) (2022)
14. Johnson, J., Berg, T., Anderson, B., Wright, B.: Review of electric vehicle charger cybersecurity vulnerabilities, potential impacts, and defenses. Energies **15**(11), 3931 (2022)
15. Katsikas, S., et al.: A hybrid dynamic risk analysis methodology for cyber-physical systems. In: Katsikas, S., et al. (eds.) ESORICS 2022. LNCS, vol. 13785, pp. 134–152. Springer, Cham (2023). https://doi.org/10.1007/978-3-031-25460-4_8
16. Kern, D., Krauß, C.: Analysis of e-mobility-based threats to power grid resilience. In: Proceedings of the 5th ACM Computer Science in Cars Symposium, pp. 1–12 (2021)
17. Kern, D., Krauß, C.: Detection of e-mobility-based attacks on the power grid. In: 2023 53rd Annual IEEE/IFIP International Conference on Dependable Systems and Networks (DSN), pp. 352–365 (2023). https://doi.org/10.1109/DSN58367.2023.00042
18. Kure, H.I., Islam, S., Razzaque, M.A.: An integrated cyber security risk management approach for a cyber-physical system. Appl. Sci. **8**(6), 898 (2018)
19. Lee, S., Park, Y., Lim, H., Shon, T.: Study on analysis of security vulnerabilities and countermeasures in ISO/IEC 15118 based electric vehicle charging technology. In: 2014 International Conference on IT Convergence and Security (ICITCS), pp. 1–4. IEEE (2014)
20. Müller, N., Heussen, K., Afzal, Z., Ekstedt, M., Eliasson, P.: Threat scenarios and monitoring requirements for cyber-physical systems of flexibility markets. In: 2022 IEEE PES Generation, Transmission and Distribution Conference and Exposition–Latin America, pp. 1–6. IEEE (2022)
21. Nasr, T., Torabi, S., Bou-Harb, E., Fachkha, C., Assi, C.: ChargePrint: a framework for internet-scale discovery and security analysis of EV charging management systems (2023)
22. Nasr, T., Torabi, S., Bou-Harb, E., Fachkha, C., Assi, C.: Power jacking your station: in-depth security analysis of electric vehicle charging station management systems. Comput. Secur. **112**, 102511 (2022)
23. Sarieddine, K., Sayed, M., Torabi, S., Atallah, R., Assi, C.: Investigating the security of EV charging mobile applications as an attack surface (2022). https://dl.acm.org/doi/10.1145/3609508
24. Sayed, M.A., Atallah, R., Assi, C., Debbabi, M.: Electric vehicle attack impact on power grid operation. Int. J. Electr. Power Energy Syst. **137**, 107784 (2022)
25. Shevchenko, N., Chick, T.A., O'Riordan, P., Scanlon, T.P., Woody, C.: Threat modeling: a summary of available methods. Technical report, Carnegie Mellon University Software Engineering Institute (2018)
26. Shrestha, M., Johansen, C., Noll, J., Roverso, D.: A methodology for security classification applied to smart grid infrastructures. Int. J. Crit. Infrastruct. Prot. **28**, 100342 (2020)
27. Skarga-Bandurova, I., Kotsiuba, I., Biloborodova, T.: Cyber security of electric vehicle charging infrastructure: Open issues and recommendations. In: 2022 IEEE International Conference on Big Data (Big Data), pp. 3099–3106. IEEE (2022)
28. Süren, E., Heiding, F., Olegård, J., Lagerström, R.: PatrIoT: practical and agile threat research for IoT. Int. J. Inf. Secur. **22**(1), 213–233 (2023)
29. Tuma, K., Scandariato, R.: Two architectural threat analysis techniques compared. In: Cuesta, C.E., Garlan, D., Pérez, J. (eds.) ECSA 2018. LNCS, vol. 11048, pp. 347–363. Springer, Cham (2018). https://doi.org/10.1007/978-3-030-00761-4_23

30. UcedaVelez, T., Morana, M.M.: Risk Centric Threat Modeling: Process for Attack Simulation and Threat Analysis, 1st edn. Wiley, Chicester (2015)
31. Zhdanova, M., Urbansky, J., Hagemeier, A., Zelle, D., Herrmann, I., Höffner, D.: Local power grids at risk–an experimental and simulation-based analysis of attacks on vehicle-to-grid communication. In: Proceedings of the 38th Annual Computer Security Applications Conference, pp. 42–55 (2022)

Decision Support System for the Monitoring and Risk Analysis of National Critical Entities

Vittorio Rosato[1,2,3] ⓘ, Fabio Pistella[3] ⓘ, Salvatore Stramondo[4] ⓘ,
Paolo Clemente[2,3] ⓘ, Diego Righini[5], Maurizio Pollino[2] ⓘ, and Roberto Setola[1(✉)] ⓘ

[1] Department of Engineering, University Campus Bio-Medico of Roma, Via Alvaro del Portillo, 21, 00128 Rome, Italy
r.setola@unicampus.it
[2] ENEA, Casaccia Research Centre, Via Anguillarese 301, 00123 Rome, Italy
[3] European Infrastructure Simulation and Analysis Centre, Italian Node, Rome, Italy
[4] Italian National Institute for Geophysics and Volcanology, Via Vigna Murata 605, Rome, Italy
[5] ITW LKW Geotermia Italia spa, Via di Porta Pinciana 6, Rome, Italy

Abstract. The EU Directive "Critical Entity Resilience" (CER Directive) has clearly indicated the need for a change of paradigm in the domain of protection and resilience enhancement of Critical Infrastructures. On the one hand, it has extended the set of Infrastructure having the right to be considered as "critical" and, accordingly must be coherently managed and protected, as it were a unique "system of systems". On the other hand, the removal of the terms "protection" and "infrastructure" to leave room for the terms "entity" and "resilience" provides further evidence that, besides a complete interdependence among the physical systems (the "infrastructure"), a considerable role and relevance are played by the stakeholders, the operators which have a critical role in infrastructure's management. The present work highlights the major issues needed to comply with the cited changes of paradigm implied in the CER Directive and the description of technological results allowing the implementation of these changes into an operational contest. The operational implementation of these strategies and technologies in Italy has been designed to be cast into a best practice, currently under further development, which might constitute a driver initiative that could be replicated in other EU Member States. An example of the capabilities of the technologies purposely realized to implement the strategy will be given.

Keywords: Critical Infrastructures · Resilience · Decision Support Systems · Risk management · Risk scenario

1 Introduction

Critical Infrastructures (CI) are technological systems that ensure the production and delivery of primary services to citizens. For this reason, they must be protected and their operational continuity granted with respect to the possible occurrence of perturbations from different origins (technological, natural, anthropogenic), which can engender their

S. Pickl et al. (Eds.): CRITIS 2023, LNCS 14599, pp. 174–185, 2024.
https://doi.org/10.1007/978-3-031-62139-0_10

integrity and reduce (or interrupt) their functioning [1]. Infrastructures nowadays constitute an entangled "system of systems" as they provide services to each other (see [1] for evidence of the relevance and timings of perturbation spread from one infrastructure to another). There is a vast amount of literature [2–5] both on the role that such functional dependence (and interdependence), induced by service sharing, plays in determining a further intrinsic vulnerability and on the resulting reduction of global resilience that these functional links can produce [6, 7]. These two issues (a larger set of infrastructures with respect to those previously considered as "critical" and the unavoidable presence of interdependencies forcing their "systemic" management) have been clearly posed by the European Commission through the issuing of the CER Directive [10]. The Directive has suitably received the inputs from the scientific and technological communities provided during the revision process of the previous Directive in this domain, the EU Directive 114/2008 [14], which focused only on energy and transportation infrastructure.

Currently, the threats scenario has sensibly worsened, due to the looming presence of cyber risks, on both Operational Technology (OT) and Information Technology (IT) structures, and to the intensification of natural events induced, for instance, by climate changes. Whereas the national legislation on cyber security has been solicited and regulated through EU Directives NIS [15] and NIS2 [16], an appropriate concern to protect CI in face of physical threats and natural events is still lacking; this is, in fact, the objective of the CER Directive, which is established to become effective in the second half of 2024.

To ensure the support of technological systems to comply with the translation into actions of CER Directive indications, a large deal of effort has been devoted, since long, by the scientific and technological communities to realize operational tools which can be able to support national strategies to be translated into actions for enabling the adoption of the Directive at the time of need. This is the goal of a Joint Agreement among two of the major public national Agencies in Italy, ENEA (National Agency for New Technology, Energy and Sustainable Economic Development) and INGV (Italian National Institute for Geophysics and Volcanology); the first committed in research and application dealing with technological systems (i.e. the infrastructures) and the latter acting as national centre for the territorial analysis and monitoring. The combination of the two areas of competence has allowed the realization of a national technological ICT platform to be used to support Italian government, Regional Public Entities and industrial operators to implement the national resilience strategy.

In the next sections, we will highlight the basic principle for implementing such a strategy and the technological tools purposely conceived and realised to this purpose.

2   Emergent Risk Scenario

In the late 1990s, the need for a paradigm shift in CI protection became increasingly evident. The deregulation and the urgency to update legacy systems in response to the Y2K issues brought to attention the significance of these systems and their vulnerabilities. The vulnerabilities primarily originate, as noted in [11], from the growing complexity of the infrastructure which contributed to their fragility. According to Perrow, a system becomes inherently fragile when multiple discrete failures can interact unexpectedly, making protective measures ineffective [11].

This fragility has only escalated over time, as the regional monopolies of infrastructure operators has been replaced by an arena where a number of industrial players compete, each with their own limited perspective and, at times, conflicting interests. Furthermore, the rapid rise of IT has transformed these infrastructures from peripheral components to elements indispensable for the proper functioning of any infrastructure. These systems are now commonly referred to as Cyber-Physical Systems (CPS), significantly amplifying the exposure to operational technology-related cyber threats. As a result, an all-hazard approach has become necessary, encompassing both intentional malicious actions and natural/accidental threats, while considering both the physical and cyber dimensions of an infrastructure.

The risk landscape has become increasingly intricate due to further complex drivers to modifications and adaptations aiming at facing the combined impacts of climate change, energy transition, and digital transformation. These factors have concurred to create a risk scenario that could be described as a generalized "compound event" [12] where concurrence of multiple natural threats could impact on enhanced vulnerabilities created by paradigmatic changes or model transition.

Within this intricate scenario, the geopolitical dimension has also emerged, involving not only the current Russo-Ukrainian conflict, but also other areas of tension. It has become evident that infrastructures serve as attractive targets for perpetuating persistent tension through various actions, including hybrid[1] tactics [13].

Moreover, the presence of a number of interdependencies, many of which are poorly understood or completely unknown, coupled with the novelty of the evolving phenomena, has reduced the effectiveness of traditional time series analysis. Consequently, there is an urgent need to develop methodological and analytical tools capable of effectively analysing and addressing these emerging risks. Whereas the prediction and the management of real-time risks are already accounted for by the technologies which have been purposely realized, the task of supporting new infrastructure engineering (with new gauges and parameters adapted to new scenarios foreseen by climate change predictions) are still underway. To tackle this challenge, a number of projects (among whom the DRIVERS project [8]) are currently undertaking the development of a comprehensive platform that aggregates information from diverse sources, encompassing both internal data within a facility and external data from the internet using Open-Source Intelligence (OSINT) techniques. While the project specifically focuses on E-PRTR facilities [9], its approach can be applied more broadly. The platform leverages on dynamic Bayesian analysis and incorporates stakeholder experiences to provide a robust solution for identifying and assessing risks. By integrating information collection from the field and the internet, the project aims to create a powerful tool to enhance risk identification and management processes.

---

[1] Hybrid tactics (and hybrid threats) are attacks whose perturbation profile mixes up the damage to physical integrity of structures with that coming from the use of their cyber vulnerability, by exploiting them simultaneously (i.e., cyber attacks issued after some physical perturbation to infrastructure produced by some natural event.

3 The EU CER Directive and its Goals

The major driver of the CER Directive is identified in the security of the internal EU market: CI which provides services and functions to it, are market's most direct emanations and must be protected in their operations. Member States (MS) are called to carry out more proactive monitoring and risk analyses of those infrastructures (or part of them), which are more critical for the functioning of the whole system of systems. Then, is necessary to evaluate the impacts of any negative event which might affect their integrity by weighting its consequences on the population, also considering interdependencies, cascading and cross-border effects. It has been underlined the need for a greater coordination between MS, without any prejudice to the responsibility for the protection of their own infrastructures. A major point which has been underlined is that the implemented strategies should not interfere with the security or be in conflict with the national interests of MS, which will not be required to share information that could be detrimental to national interests. [17] in particular against sabotages and/or hybrid actions.

The major source of contingent problems is identified in the current geo-political situation, which would require greater attention also to the infrastructures located outside the MS territories and with a specific attention to the protection of the *"undersea and offshore energy infrastructure"* [17], in particular against sabotages and hybrid actions [13] to which EU will have to provide a united and resolute response.

CER Directive enhances the primary objective to be attained, being the enhancement of the infrastructure resilience in relation to the most relevant risks, such as cascading effects, impacts on logistics chains, impacts from events resulting from climate change, the presence on the market of *"unreliable vendors and partners"* [17]. The infrastructures with greater transnational impacts are identified as the ones towards which a more effective protective action should be implemented.

There would be an interest in the unification and the creation of homogeneous protective measures (physical, cyber) both in the energy/transport domain (covered by Directive 114/2008) and on other networks and telecommunications systems covered by Directive 1148/2016. In the CER Directive, these sectors are unified as well as added to those of the financial market, healthcare system with its connected services, and the logistic chain, other than having integrated within the domain of the water resources and supply.

The strategic relevance of the CER Directive has been stressed by the EU Council Recommendation (2023/C 20/01) [17] which, moving from the sabotage of NordStream2 pipeline, asked MS to consider also High-Impact/Low-Probability (HILP) events, by performing, in parallel to risk assessment, specific stress-tests to analyse the capability of the different infrastructures to deal with critical scenarios. The developed technologies allow to perform scenario analysis by synthetically inserting initial conditions resulting from HILP events (either from natural origin, as earthquakes or flooding, and or anthropic origin, as deliberate attacks against elements of critical infrastructure) [18–20].

A greater in-depth analysis of the issues is entrusted to the "National Experts" and to the creation of the Critical Entity Resilience Group (needed to be implemented at MS level) capable of providing operational indications in agreement with the Directive and the Recommendations.

The Directive asks for MS to elaborate a national resilience strategy on the basis of a national multi-hazard risk assessment process. To perform such task, it is mandatory to have a national database containing data of Critical Entities to be used to merge information provided by the relevant stakeholders, implemented with the capabilities to perform impact analysis, to identify relevant interdependence and critical elements, to support the identification of effective countermeasures and to design significant stress test scenarios.

To fulfill the Directive indications, it is mandatory to create a national platform able to merge information related to CI with territorial characteristics and risk mapping. Indeed only in this way it is possible to perform a national-level risk assessment, taking into account cascade and interdependence phenomena. Such a platform should include a constantly updated database containing data about Critical Entities, and the capability to generate synthetic and actual incident scenarios, in order to constantly prove the level of security and resilience. This is the primary objective of the Italian EISAC.it initiative (European Infrastructure Simulation and Analysis Centre): to create a technological platform that, in accordance with CER Directive requirements, can enable a national-level assessment of the resilience of critical entities, in order to identify the major criticality and to support the design and the implementation of an effective national resilience strategy.

4   The Italian EISAC.it Initiative

The EISAC idea has been conceived at the time of the EU FP7 project CIPRNet (2013–2017) [21]. At that time, the scientific community (and, in particular, that supporting CIPRNet as a leading edge of that community) recognized that the direction to be followed, in CI Protection, is to adopt a "holistic" (or "systemic"[2]) vision of infrastructures, to take over a "vertical-type" protection, by realizing, and suggesting the adoption of technological tools enabling a global monitoring and a coherent control of infrastructures all together. Dependency and interdependency issues cannot be neglected anymore and the need of providing all CI operators (which have the ultimate responsibility of managing and protecting their assets) a coherent set of information concerning the state of risk of all other infrastructures [22] was mandatory for improving the effectiveness of their actions. Moreover, a strong emphasis has been also given to proactivity, and to the capability of predicting and preventing the impact of events, as an effective measure to improve overall resilience. These new strategies have resulted the only capable of providing effectiveness to all phase of risk management and resilience enhancement[3].

---

[2] The two terms are, in this context, used to indicate the need to have comprehensive information on all possible threat sources and all possible CI. Whenever possible, this is achieved by accessing "dependency maps" providing the capability of estimating the process of functional perturbation spreading across different infrastructures due to functional dependence - or interdependence - mechanisms.

[3] The strategy for enhancing preparedness actions has been exploited, for instance, for enhancing resilience of electrical distribution networks by predicting its improvement by realizing ad hoc implementation of automatic controls along a large and complex existing network (the case of the electric distribution network of the city of Rome) [23].

The proposed strategy, designed, demonstrated, and supported by EISAC, can be resumed in the following actions which would constitute the pillars for a new strategy for protection and resilience enhancement:

1. **National CI database.** There will be a strong pressure on Operators and P.A. Offices (e.g., Ministries) committed in the infrastructure protection in order to realise their own Database (as required by the CER Directive) constantly updated. Central technologies should access these data of the components of the different CI, in order to have information about their location, their functionalities, their vulnerabilities, and to be used for the risk analysis scenarios;

2. **National Context Risk database.** Gathering, in a comprehensive nationwide database, a large number of geospatial/geolocated information layers of different typologies (from the territorial to the socio-economic data, from the maps risk and historical events to the location of strategic assets, their components and the characteristics). These data are usually stored in a multitude of separate Database (managed by P.A. and private entities) and are rarely used in combination for understand and analyse territorial hazards and risks. This will avoid the proliferation of a multitude of information sources; the use of only certified sources to perform risk analysis will sensibly increase the reliability of the result. The presence of only certified public sources will also improve and ease the update of this information, as soon as new data are released by the appropriate public data owners;

3. **Tool to analyse dependence and interdependence effects.** The presence of the above-mentioned CI database will allow us to estimate the cascading effects due to territorial and functional dependencies. Access to dependency maps is the straightest way to approach the problem of understanding and predicting the generation of cascading effects;

4. **Real time situation awareness.** For a situational real-time analysis, there is the need of gathering all relevant territorial and environmental real-time data (weather forecast and nowcasting, data from sensors on the territory, simulation of flooding events, rapid link with providers of data on the occurrence of seismic events, etc.) for appropriate management of the prediction and early elaboration of the current impact scenario (e.g., in the case of an earthquake, when it is extremely important to provide a rapid qualitative assessment of the expected damage scenario). This is an extremely important preparedness action, to be performed in ordinary time, before the pressure deriving from the occurring event and the resulting possible unavailability of resources, which can interfere with the prompt activation of the emergency tasks. Moreover, emphasis must be given to providing suggestions that comply with the current understanding of climatic changes. "Occurring" events can be substituted, as input data, with synthetic events (e.g., expected earthquakes, stronger precipitation, etc.) to provide the further platform capability of producing what-if analysis.

5. **What-if analysis.** The platform should be used for performing *what-if* simulations, by introducing expected or possible events and establishing the resulting chain of events (impacts, damages, responses). Such analysis may be performed also with respect to HILP events in order to support stress tests.

All these requirements have been considered to design and realize a comprehensive Decision Support System (DSS) to be used by CI Operators and other stakeholders, entrusted with infrastructure management and emergency activities, as a value support for a better fulfillment of their roles. The proposed solution does not (and cannot) substitute the operation control of the infrastructures. It is meant to provide *global and coherent information to all players* who, in situation of emergency (as well as in ordinary time operations), must make decisions that have to be the most "situation-aware" and shared as much as possible among the other players, in order to maximize their efficiency and effectiveness.

5   The CIPCast DSS

CIPCast (Critical Infrastructure Protection risk analysis and forecast) is an advanced Decision Support System (DSS) that attempts to provide an answer to the real-time identification of the risks of different origins, to whom elements of CI present in a given territory, are subjected on the bases of a thorough constant inspection of the environment. The CIPCast DSS has been more detailed described elsewhere [24]. In particular, CIPCast has been conceived and implemented as a 24/7 operational tool for: i) CI monitoring; ii) CI vulnerability and risk assessment; and iii) CI evaluation of physical and functional impacts induced on CI by severe natural events (e.g. earthquakes, floods, heavy rainfalls, etc.). Thanks to its user-friendly WebGIS front-end, CIPCast is able to store and manage geospatial data and, consequently, it can also support risk analysis

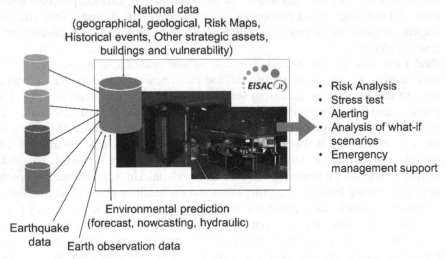

National data
(geographical, geological, Risk Maps,
Historical events, Other strategic assets,
buildings and vulnerability)

EISAC.it

- Risk Analysis
- Stress test
- Alerting
- Analysis of what-if scenarios
- Emergency management support

Environmental prediction
(forecast, nowcasting, hydraulic)

Earthquake data

Earth observation data

Fig. 1. Architectural and operational scheme of EISAC Centre. On the right, is the number of data whose availability must be granted; data are inserted in the CIPCast Database, becoming the basis on which data analyses are performed. The CIPCast Database will also contain a large set of national data on several domains and receive real-time data from weather forecasts, earthquakes, results of river hydraulic simulation and also data from sensing devices. Results provide risk analysis, stress tests of specific artworks or infrastructure, and scenario analysis in what-if mode. The system can also provide support in Emergency Management as it can provide, to operators on the field, a number of information and data helpful for their work.

and mapping [27]. In addition to the specific WebGIS interface, CIPCast data can be accessed via the web by using OGC standards (WMS, WFS and WCS) [25] (Fig. 1).

In this sense, the core of CIPCast architecture is represented by its large GeoDatabase, in which a large number of maps (more than 400) and information layers are stored and constantly updated. Here follows a list of the main types of data archived and managed:

- It is based on a GIS server boosted by an unprecedented DataBase
- Basic data and maps describing the territory;
- Environmental hazard maps (floods, landslides, earthquakes);
- Data about the location and topology of the main National CI systems and networks (i.e., High Voltage, gas, highway and roads, railway, etc.) (Fig. 2);

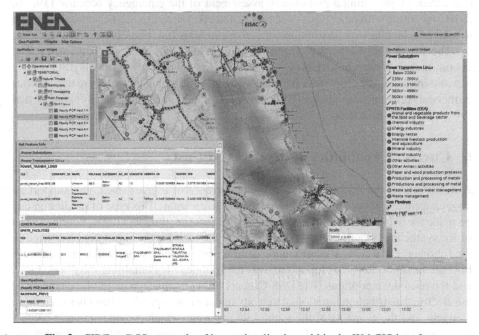

Fig. 2. CIPCast DSS: example of layer visualisation within the WebGIS interface

- Outputs from forecast models (weather, nowcasting, flooding);
- Real-time seismic data (source: INGV National Earthquake Observatory) and meteorological data (National Civil Protection);
- Data from distributed sensors (ground sensing) located on specific CI.

CIPCast can run both in "operational" mode (on a 24/7 basis, as an alert system) [18] and in "simulation" mode by performing hazard/risk assessments and/or simulating events [19, 20]. In the operational mode, CIPCast gets data from external sources and repositories (e.g., seismic network, meteo/hydrological models), to set the current conditions and elaborate an expected "damage scenario" for an area of interest where CI are located [18, 24]. In the simulation mode, CIPCast can be employed as a GIS-based tool to perform risk mapping and assessment for each element of the CI considered

[23, 28], depending on the type of event expected (e.g., earthquake) and the specific vulnerabilities [20, 26]. A major functionality is constituted by a module to simulate the impact of earthquakes on buildings and infrastructures. The simulation model, after being input with the characteristics of a just-occurred seismic event (or with those of a synthetic one) simulates its propagation in the area by estimating Peak Ground Acceleration (PGA) and/or Peak Ground Velocity (PGV) values, also accounting for local site-effects in terms of amplification factors (if the seismic microzonation is available). Crossing PGA values with seismic vulnerabilities of all infrastructures (buildings and others), the simulation model can assess the occurrence of damages or disruptions in these objects. In addition, the intersection with buildings damages with local population and social data allows to estimate the number of expected casualties and people to be evacuated, by providing a preliminary assessment of the emergency scenario [19, 20, 29]. Concerning with other types of scenarios (attacks) several activities have been made to simulate simultaneous disruptions of active elements (i.e. transformers).

The whole DSS CIPCast platform is submitted to appropriate security issues. The operational platform is hosted in a location with stringent security protocols (ISO 27001) to avoid intrusion, data breach. A particular care is given to the interaction to third parties (either data providers or end-users). Their respective links are established by using Virtual Private Network protocols.

6 Current Capabilities of the DSS CIPCast

A major aim of the DSS is to predict the occurrence of a given event and support an *ex-ante* estimate of the impact it might have in given areas. This type of prediction can be made for both really-incoming predictable events (i.e. thunderstorms, flooding, etc.) or for synthetically-built events (HILP). This is the case for the simulation (reported in the following) of a crisis scenario in the central area of a city submitted to a (synthetic) bi-centennial flooding. The input data was the (public) file containing the flooded area and the related water drains. The DSS CIPcast DB contains data on all the elements of the electrical distribution function of that city and the corresponding links between these elements and the elements of the mobile tlc network (which provides the tele-control functionality to many of the electrical stations). Moreover, the DB also contains the dislocation of the most important buildings of the city (Hospital, Defense Compounds, buildings of the Public Administration etc.). Once activated on the scenario, CIPCast identifies the number of electrical stations that, due to their position, could be subjected to damage from the flooding. A simulation model present in the platform estimates the blackout extent in the area (in terms of electrical cabins and parts of the electrical medium tension network disconnected. Thanks to the knowledge of the dependence map between the electrical and tlc networks, the simulation model identifies which among the tlc aerial would be disconnected (in the worst case) due to the loss of an electrical supply and will be thus unavailable for telecontrol operation for the restoration of the electrical network. The simulation results allow to estimate, with some advance, the lack of power supply in the different relevant buildings in the disconnected areas, thus allowing the taking of preparedness actions by the respective Emergency Managers (Fig. 3).

7   Conclusion and Perspectives

The EISAC initiative, when was launched during the CIPRNet project, was meant to replicate itself in the different EU MS, giving place to national initiatives to be subsequently federated into a EU-wide association, with a constant link with the EU authorities, for providing rapid, coherent and interoperable solutions to be applied at each MS level. Such a development schema complies with the requirement that all MS implementation of the EISAC initiative, although being coherent with their national institutional settings, must be interoperable each other, in a way they could grant interoperability in case in their joint deployment in case of possible transnational crises.

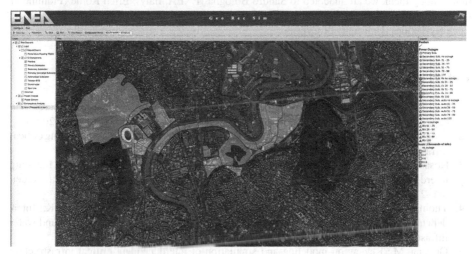

Fig. J. Area of the city disconnected after a flooding. Different colors represent the KPI given by the product of the number of disconnected users times the disconnection time. In a further layer the position and the extent of the blackout of the different relevant buildings is provided.

In Italy, EISAC.it has taken the legacy of the EISAC challenge and has pursued and achieved the task of building and consolidating the main tools (e.g., CIPCast and its linked applications) at the regional and national scale. Technologies and institutional settings can be of support for other MS aiming to provide a common direction to their efforts for endorse the CER Directive. Italy, as widely known, is particularly exposed, due to its geographical position and geomorphological characteristics, to a large number of natural threats which made it an ideal "laboratory" for developing, testing a validating technologies for the analysis and the protection of the territory and the asset located therein.

A further indication which has emerged in the last years, which in Italy again can assume a remarkable valence, is that the methods for the resilience analysis of critical entities could be effectively deployed in favour (and for the protection) of the vast national Cultural Heritage, represented by historic centres, monuments, places of worship, and many relevant artworks. Although they do not belong, *stricto sensu* to the CI set (nor their inclusion has been predicted in the EU CER Directive), nevertheless they represent remarkably relevant entities for the Italian history, culture and civilisation that, as such, as well as CI, must be *de facto* protected and preserved for the next generations and for the sake of human kind.

Acknowledgments. The work has been partly supported by project DRIVERS ("Combined data driven and experience-driven approach in the analysis of the systemic risk") funded by INAIL through a Contract provided to one of us (V.R.) and performed within a MoU between ENEA (Italian Agency for New Technologies, Energy and Sustainable Economic Development), INGV (Italian National Institute for Geophysics and Volcanology) and the Italian Ministry of Infrastructure and Transports. Several colleagues have been fundamental in conceiving ideas, formulating the appropriate strategies, and collaborating in developing technologies for their implementation: among them, we are indebted to Sandro Bologna (ENEA, Italy), Erich Rome (Fraunhofer Gesellschaft, Germany), Erik Luiijf and Marieke Klaver (TNO, The Netherlands) and to the late Elias Kyriakides (University of Cyprus).

References

1. Luiijf, E., Klaver, M.: Analysis and lessons identified on critical infrastructures and dependencies from an empirical data set. Int. J. Crit. Infrastruct. Prot. **35**, 100471 (2021)
2. Rinaldi, S.M., Peerenboom, J.P., Kelly, T.K.: Identifying, understanding, and analyzing critical infrastructure interdependencies. IEEE Control. Syst. Mag. **21**(6), 11–25 (2001)
3. Rosato, V., Issacharoff, L., Tiriticco, F., Meloni, S., De Porcellinis, S., Setola, R.: Modelling interdependent infrastructures using interacting dynamical models. Int. J. Crit. Infrastruct. **4**(1–2), 63–79 (2008)
4. Thompson, J.R., Frezza, D., Necioglu, B., Cohen, M.L., Hoffman, K., Rosfjord, K.: Interdependent Critical Infrastructure Model (ICIM): an agent-based model of power and water infrastructure. Int. J. Crit. Infrastruct. Prot. **24**, 144–165 (2019)
5. Ouyang, M.: Review on modeling and simulation of interdependent critical infrastructure systems. Reliab. Eng. Syst. Saf. **121**, 43–60 (2014)
6. Linkov, I., Trump, B.D., Hynes, W.: Resilience-based strategies and policiesto address systemic risks resilience strategies and approaches to contain systemic threats. In: OECD Conference,17–18 September 2019. OECD Conference Centre SG/NAEC (2019)
7. Johansen, C., Tien, I.: Probabilistic multi-scale modeling of interdependencies between critical infrastructure systems for resilience. Sustain. Resilient Infrastruct. **3**(1), 1–15 (2018)
8. DRIVERS. https://www.emergentrisk.it/index.php/en/
9. European Pollutant Release and Transfer Register (E-PRTR). https://www.eea.europa.eu/data-and-maps/data/member-states-reportingart-7-under-the-european-pollutant-release-and-transfer-register-e-prtr-regulation-23/european-pollutant-release-and-transfer-register-e-prtr-data-base
10. EU Directive 2022/2557 on the resilience of critical entities (CER Directive). https://eur-lex.europa.eu/legalcontent/EN/TXT/PDF/?uri=CELEX:32022L2557
11. Perrow, C.: Normal Accidents: Living with High Risk Technologies. Princeton University Press (1999)
12. Zscheischler, J., et al.: Future climate risk from compound events. Nat. Clim. Chang. **8**(6), 469–477 (2018). https://doi.org/10.1038/s41558-018-0156-3
13. Hybrid Warfare. Security and Asymmetric Conflict in International RelationsMikael Weissmann (Anthology Editor), Niklas Nilsson (Anthology Editor), Björn Palmertz (Anthology Editor), Per Thunholm (Anthology Editor) Bloomsbury Publishing (2023). ISBN 9781350429093

14. EU Directive 2008/114/EC on the identification and designation of European critical infrastructures and the assessment of the need to improve their protection (ICE Directive). https://eur-lex.europa.eu/LexUriServ/LexUriServ.do?uri=OJ:L:2008:345:0075:0082:en:PDF
15. EU Directive 2016/1148 concerning measures for a high common level of security of network and information systems across the Union (NIS Directive). https://eurlex.europa.eu/legal-content/EN/TXT/?uri=celex:32016L1148
16. EU Directive 2022/2555 on measures for a high common level of cyber security across the Union (NIS 2 Directive). https://eur-lex.europa.eu/eli/dir/2022/2555
17. EU Raccomandation 15623/22 on a Union-wide coordinated approach to strengthen the resilience of critical infrastructure. https://data.consilium.europa.eu/doc/document/ST-15623-2022-INIT/en/pdf
18. Taraglio, S., et al.: Decision support system for smart urban management: resilience against natural phenomena and aerial environmental assessment. Int. J. Sustain. Energy Plann. Manage. 24 (2019)
19. Matassoni, L., Giovinazzi, S., Pollino, M., Fiaschi, A., La Porta, L., Rosato, V.: A geospatial decision support tool for seismic risk management: Florence (Italy) case study. In: Gervasi, O., et al. (eds.) ICCSA 2017. LNCS, vol. 10405, pp. 278–293. Springer, Cham (2017). https://doi.org/10.1007/978-3-319-62395-5_20
20. Pollino, M., Di Pietro, A., La Porta, L., Fattoruso, G., Giovinazzi, S., Longobardi, A.: Seismic risk simulations of a water distribution network in southern Italy. In: Gervasi, O., et al. (eds.) ICCSA 2021. LNCS, vol. 12951, pp. 655–664. Springer, Cham (2021). https://doi.org/10.1007/978-3-030-86970-0_45
21. ciprnet.eu
22. Setola, R., Rosato, V., Kyriakides, E., Rome, E.: Managing the Complexity of Critical Infrastructures: A Modelling and Simulation Approach. Springer, Cham (2016). https://doi.org/10.1007/978-3-319-51043-9
23. Tofani, A., et al.: Operational resilience metrics for complex inter-dependent electrical networks. Appl. Sci. 11, 5842 (2021)
24. Di Pietro, A., Lavalle, L., La Porta, L., Pollino, M., Tofani, A., Rosato, V.: Design of DSS for supporting preparedness to and management of anomalous situations in complex scenarios. In: Setola, R., Rosato, V., Kyriakides, E., Rome, E. (eds.) Managing the Complexity of Critical Infrastructures. SSDC, vol. 90, pp. 195–232. Springer, Cham (2016). https://doi.org/10.1007/978-3-319-51043-9_9
25. OGC Standards and Resources. https://www.ogc.org/standards. Accessed 22 May 2023
26. Buffarini, G., Clemente, P., Giovinazzi, S., Ormando, C., Pollino, M., Rosato, V.: Preventing and managing risks induced by natural hazards to critical infrastructures. Infrastructures 7, 76 (2022)
27. Pollino, M., Cappucci, S., Pesaresi, C., Farrace, M.G., Morte, L.D., Vegliante, G.: Multi-hazard analysis and mapping of infrastructure systems at national level using gis techniques: preliminary results. In: Gervasi, O., Murgante, B., Misra, S., Rocha, A.M.A.C., Garau, C. (eds.) ICCSA 2022. LNCS, vol. 13377, pp. 153–168. Springer, Cham (2022). https://doi.org/10.1007/978-3-031-10536-4_11
28. Guarino, S., Oliva, G., Pietro, A.D., Pollino, M., Rosato, V.: A spatial decision support system for prioritizing repair interventions on power networks. IEEE Access 11, 34616–34629 (2023)
29. D'Agostino, G., et al.: Earthquake simulation on urban areas: improving contingency plans by damage assessment. In: Luiijf, E., Žutautaitė, I., Hämmerli, B. (eds.) CRITIS 2018. LNCS, vol. 11260, pp. 72–83. Springer, Cham (2019). https://doi.org/10.1007/978-3-030-05849-4_6

GNSS Signal Monitoring and Security of Supply of GNSS-Based Services

Mika Saajasto[1]([✉])(iD), Sanna Kaasalainen[1](iD), Maija Mäkelä[1,2](iD),
M. Zahidul H. Bhuiyan[1](iD), Hannu Koivula[1](iD), Martti Kirkko-Jaakkola[1,2](iD),
and Heidi Kuusniemi[1,3](iD)

[1] Finnish Geospatial Research Institute, Espoo, Finland
{mika.saajasto,sanna.kaasalainen,maija.makela,zahidul.bhuiyan,
hannu.koivula,martti.kirkko-jaakkola}@nls.fi, heidi.kuusniemi@uwasa.fi
[2] Nordic Inertial Oy, Akaa, Finland
[3] School of Technology and Innovations, University of Vaasa, Vaasa, Finland

Abstract. The global GNSS markets are expected to grow considerably in future, thus the number of threats against GNSS services will also increase. Understanding how GNSS services are utilized on a national level is crucial for the resilience, safety and quality of these services.

This study summarises interviews of authorities and specialists in the given GNSS segments, national and international research on related GNSS markets and analysis of related technologies. We provide an introduction to the current state of GNSS-based services, important shortcomings related to security of supply, and the GNSS user needs in relation to GNSS security of supply. We discuss ways to mitigate threats aimed against GNSS services, for example GNSS monitoring and provide suggestions to improve the security of supply of GNSS services. The GNSS markets are becoming increasingly vulnerable to interference, thus resilient navigation and timing solutions are needed. The authentication services of the Galileo-system are aimed to solve these problems, but they are not fully operational. The security of supply and the safety of the GNSS-based services should become a key feature in national cybersecurity planning.

Keywords: GNSS · Security of Supply · Critical Infrastructure

1 Introduction

The need for resilient Positioning, Navigation, and Timing (PNT) has been steadily increasing. This particularly applies to services and applications related to critical infrastructure requiring precises time synchronisation, such as power grids, telecommunications, and financial transactions. The need for resilience is also evident in services that require precises location information such as search and rescue (SAR) and aviation. The COVID-pandemic introduced a new category of apps that are aware of context. To help fight the spread of the virus,

S. Pickl et al. (Eds.): CRITIS 2023, LNCS 14599, pp. 186–207, 2024.
https://doi.org/10.1007/978-3-031-62139-0_11

authorities started to utilise anonymous location data to track areas where people moved, to create hot-spot maps. These maps were then used by applications to warn people and help them to avoid crowded areas [8]. Context-aware features can also be used in financial services for secure authentication. Utilising user location information it is possible to see if, for example, an online purchase was done in a typical region for the user. A purchase from another country can then be labelled a possible fraud, increasing the protection for both customer and the company providing services [23].

PNT-solutions are commonly obtained from Global Navigation Satellite Systems (GNSS), because of the ease of use and availability. However, the vulnerability of GNSS systems has also been globally increasing as a result of interference from different sources [10,13,26]. These events and their mitigation have been widely studied [55,58,65] and it has been shown that there is no single source behind the interference events [5]. Interference can result from ionospheric variations, other (possibly faulty) equipment operating at Radio Frequencies (RF) close to satellite navigation signals, or malicious RF-interference. The intentional Radio Frequency Interference (RFI) events can be divided into two categories: signal jamming, where the GNSS signal is completely or partially obfuscated by noise [37], and spoofing, i.e., broadcasting a counterfeit signal [57]. The effects caused by GNSS jamming depend on the strength of the jamming signal, a weak signal will decrease the signal to noise of the measurements, increasing the uncertainty of the computed location or time solution. A more powerful jamming signal, for example from a military grade jamming device, is aimed to completely deny the use of GNSS signals. While both weak and strong jamming attacks can target several, or all, available GNSS signals, the more common weaker jamming attacks are typically caused by small hand held devices installed in cars or trucks and usually only target one frequency band.

The aim of a spoofing attack is fundamentally different compared to a jamming attack. Jamming is meant to deny service, but a spoofing attack tries to force a receiver to show incorrect location or time information. In recent years, the most common incidents attributed to GNSS spoofing have been related to illegal activities, for example by passing transport sanctions [2]. However, as seen in the incident from Shanghai, where several ships were spoofed to report them following a circular pattern, the aim of the spoofing attack is not always clear. As discussed in the article, there might be criminal intent involved, or it might be a test campaign for state level electronic warfare. However, a spoofing attack of this magnitude demonstrated high theoretical understanding and technological capabilities of the attackers [36,46].

To protect the end users, the European GNSS service Galileo offers different services to secure or authenticate the navigation signal [22]. These services will be available for both civilians in the form of Open Service Navigation Message Authentication (OSNMA) and Commercial Authentication Service (CAS), and for governmental agencies or other safety-critical services via the Public Regulated Service (PRS). In spite of these security measures, GNSS could still be compromised by, e.g., a strong space weather event (see [9,68] for potential effects of such events) or because of a system-wide malfunction, such as the event in 2014, where GLONASS satellites were sending incorrect broadcast messages. This system level malfunction caused some receiver types to also lose the GPS signals, causing total loss of PNT [29]. Therefore, positioning based on other sensors or hybrid navigation solutions is an active fields of research, especially in the automotive industry [62]. In addition to resilient and precise location information, many critical infrastructures are increasingly dependent on precise time synchronisation, which is crucial for telecommunication networks, power grids, and financial sector [39,53]. This increases the need for precise and resilient PNT solutions. In particular, security of supply has become a concern in the Arctic region, where there are strong ionospheric phenomena and the GNSS signal strength is weaker, because satellite orbits are not optimised for use at high latitudes. The need for improved resilience is further emphasised with the advance of intelligent transportation and the growing number of applications utilising the Internet of Things (IoT) [38]. Many of the IoT solutions have been focusing on consumer products, like wearable electronics, but industrial applications, for example controlling lighting or machine operations, logistical applications, for example tracking of goods, or even agricultural applications for tracking livestock, are becoming increasingly common. In the 3rd Generation Partnership Project (3GPP), it has been estimated that 75% of the IoT applications would require or benefit greatly from positioning information [1]. The required accuracy depends on the application, but typical ranges are from a few meters to hundreds of meters. Meter level accuracy would be easily achieved with a GNSS chip set, but for IoT devices, the typical power consumption of these chips can be too high. However, there are emerging novel solutions to enable GNSS for low-power IoT devices, for example assisted GNSS technologies where for example satellite ephemeris data is transferred over cellular network [24].

The advancements in satellite technology have given rise to small, cost effective satellites, that are mainly deployed to the Low Earth Orbit (LEO) instead of the Medium Earth Orbit (MEO) typically utilized by communication and navigation satellites. Because of the lower altitude, any satellite constellation operating at LEO needs to have a higher number of satellites compared to constellations at MEO. The increased number of satellites and the closer proximity to the receivers provides a higher signal strength and better satellite geometry coverage, which are expected to increase the accuracy and robustness of PNT-services. However, the LEO-PNT concept is still under research and no real LEO-PNT systems are currently available [56]. In addition to the currently missing LEO-systems, there are currently no dedicated LEO-PNT signals. However, three possibilities exists. The first option is to use the LEO signals as signals of opportunity, and no PNT information is transmitted. In this case the angle of arrival of the signal or the Doppler shift can be used to estimate position. Secondly, it is possible to transmit a GNSS like signal, possibly in another frequency band, since current GNSS bands are heavily used. The third option is to create a dedicated LEO-PNT signal that would be optimised for LEO constellations. The challenges and possibilities provided by these approaches are evaluated in [56].

The vulnerability of different critical infrastructures to GNSS disruptions has been an increasing concern also beyond Finland. [34] has mapped the needs for PNT in critical infrastructures and services in the United States, ranging from agriculture to emergency services in terms of positioning and navigation, and from electricity grids to financial services in terms of timing. The estimated costs of a long term GNSS outage are estimated to be more than 1 billion dollars a day. The report states that mitigating long term disruptions is very challenging as no single alternative PNT approach is sufficient to meet the positioning requirements of different critical infrastructures. They recommend that temporary short-term disruptions are mitigated by PNT users, and encourage adaptation of alternative PNT sources and resilience by system design in order to be prepared for long term GNSS outages. Also United Kingdom is exploring new ways to protect critical infrastructures [28]. Similarly, the International Civil Aviation Organization (ICAO) urges addressing GNSS interference, as it has a significant impact on flight operations and air traffic management [35].

Several GNSS interference monitoring approaches have been proposed as means for dealing with harmful interference. GNSS reference networks can be used to monitor the signal on a large scales [51], and machine learning approaches can be used to detect more subtle signal phenomena [38]. Also crowd-sourcing [47,50] with smartphones and interference detection using Low Earth Orbit (LEO) satellites [49] could be suitable for large scale wide area GNSS monitoring. Current approaches for spoofing detection focus on methods based on receiver signal processing [57]. Project STRIKE3 [65] has defined standardized way to report GNSS interference events in terms of event date, duration, region, frequency band etc. This standard can be adapted also for crowd-sourcing approach [47].

The occurrence of interference events is very common. A monitoring campaign within STRIKE3 project in 21 different countries and 48 different sites observed interference at all sites [4], located in city areas and nearby major roads. The interference incidents occurred more often than anticipated, even though they were often short in duration and only low power.

As GNSS disruptions can have serious consequences, for example airplane crash [35], and thus, critical infrastructure and operations need protection. By utilising signal monitoring and alert systems, GNSS end users can be more resilient towards disruptions in PNT.

The accuracy needs and other requirements, for example availability of navigation signals, are typically well know within specific industry, for example aviation, but these requirements might not be well known for other industries. The lack of collective overview of the needs and requirements of the GNSS sector and markets as a whole can become problematic especially for policy makers or companies trying to enter the markets.

Secondly, an overview providing a deeper understanding of the needs of critical infrastructure can be used to streamline future purchases of equipment that is required to maintain sufficient positioning or time synchronisation accuracy on a national level. Comprehensive and detailed market reviews for GNSS subfields are available, but the information is still scattered and there is a clear lack of a collective overview of the users needs and requirements over the GNSS field as a whole. Furthermore, reports from specific GNSS sectors do not necessarily take into account specific needs of individual member states. For example, the arctic region presents certain challenges that require specific response from Nordic policy makers to ensure safe and efficient operations.

The aim of this article is to provide a collective overview of the GNSS user needs and requirements from the viewpoint of the security of supply. We have carried out an extensive end user survey to map the GNSS accuracy and availability needs in different sectors in Finland and combine this information with European and international scenarios from EGNSS (European Global Navigation Satellite System) market reports and existing literature. We will demonstrate the need and benefits of a situational awareness service with a jamming case study in Finland, to find out how a GNSS signal quality monitoring service can contribute to the security of supply of GNSS services. We will also assess the next steps and future work needed to improve the situation. The paper is organized as follows: the end user perspective and the security of supply are discussed in Sect. 2. A case study of GNSS monitoring and threat identification in Finland is presented in Sect. 3, followed by a discussion and conclusions in Sects. 4 and 5, respectively.

2   GNSS Security of Supply

The European Union Agency for Space Program (EUSPA) has been collecting information from GNSS user segment by organising a User Consultation Platform (UCP), which aims to promote discussion within various fields on their needs for PNT solutions, and the required accuracy. As a part of the ongoing REASON project (Resilience and security of geospatial data for critical infrastructures) [38], the Finnish GNSS experts and stakeholders were interviewed to better understand the unique requirements and user needs in the Finnish context. The user groups that were interviewed consisted of private companies working in the GNSS segment, for example receiver manufacturers, but also companies that utilise GNSS as a part of their appliances or sell added value services, for example precise point positioning (PPP) corrections. In addition to GNSS industry, governmental institutes and companies involved in maintaining critical infrastructure were also interviewed. This group included, for example telecommunication and power grid operators and emergency services. Finally, scientific experts from research institutes and universities were interviewed to better understand the direction of research and educational readiness. As many of the interviewed entities operate in safety critical operations or are directly involved in national security, we will use the answers anonymously. All of the interviewed private companies provided their answers as industry standards and not as their own needs and requirements, thus the results are given anonymously. Furthermore, the user needs and requirements in many fields are very similar with those reported in the UCP, thus we present a collective summary which combines both the UCP reports and the interview results gained during the REASON project.

2.1   Accuracy and Reliability Needs of GNSS User Segment

Because of the availability of GNSS services and the new opportunities provided by technological advancements, the needs and requirements of the end users have become more specific. In the following sections, overviews on the specific needs and requirements of the various fields are discussed and the required PNT accuracy is listed in Table 1.

We also discuss applications that might not need time synchronisation, but accurate time is crucial to ensure, for example, continuous telecommunication operations. On the other hand, in certain fields the precision needs are secondary, while continuous availability of GNSS has become the priority. Information on possible interference or service blackouts was a re-occurring need in the inter-views of the Finnish GNSS field, and was reported as an operation critical service for companies. An early warning system could be used to prepare for temporary blackouts or to give valuable time to deploy the secondary backup systems. In the interviews from the REASON project, many of the end users also expressed the increasing need of resilient GNSS services, mainly because of strict tolerance requirements. For example in construction sector, the accuracy tolerance can be within 5 cm level, thus even a small disturbance in the availability of precises GNSS solution can bring the construction project to a halt.

The next generation GNSS services currently under research and development, can address the needs of many users, however, adopting these new technologies might not be straight forward. For example in aviation domain, any new technological implementations have to go through rigorous testing and validation process, and often requiring changes in legislation, which can be time consuming. For example, although the LEO-PNT concepts are expected to improve availability of navigation signals, and thus increase the security, their adaption to aviation domain will take time.

Time and Synchronization. The timing and time synchronization sector cover many critical operations of a modern society: electricity grids, telecommunications, and financial sector (banking and stock exchange). Several other heavily used applications have become more reliant on accurate time over the recent years: for example public transportation, wastewater systems, and television broadcasts [20].

Because of the variety of different applications and systems that require timing or synchronization services, the level of accuracy required for the services varies from one application to another. However, for the operators working in critical infrastructure, for example power grids operators, the required time synchronisation over the grid is at a micro second level. Thus, because of the known vulnerabilities, these operators should have their own emergency systems [27,60,67]. In Finland the telecommunication operators and electricity transmission stations maintain their own grand-master clocks to ensure sufficient time synchronization in case the national time service is inoperative. The need of accurate time has been identified as a critical requirement and for example investigations carried out in Great Britain and the United States have recommended that the national time should not be maintained by a single laboratory, but rather a system of interlinked time laboratories is recommended [27,60,67]. Based on the investigation, a interlinked system of four time laboratories is currently under development in the Great Britain, and a similar system of decentralised time synchronisation services is used in Sweden.

- Telecommunication networks - Considering 5G systems, the time needs to be synchronized to an accuracy of 1.1 µs over the entire network with additional requirements of compensating for delay variation and jitter [20]. A synchronization accuracy worse than 1.1 µs will also affect the availability of the older network types (4G, 3G). Time synchronization of 100 ns is required for fibre-networks to detect defects that cause asymmetry in the optics and a similar accuracy of 100 ns is required for in certain satellite communication systems. The International Telecommunication Union (ITU) has documented a recommendation G.8272 (ITU G.8272/Y.1367 (11/18) and G.8272/Y.1367 (2018) Amendment 1 (03/20)) stating that the reference time signal of the network should be accurate to within 100 ns, when compared against a primary time standard, such as the Universal Coordinated Time (UTC). The recommendation also places requirements for the stability of the used time signals. Because of the need for high synchronization accuracy, any services that can detect and warn about GNSS interference are recommended to secure continuous operational stability.
- Finance - In the European Union, the time synchronization required by banks and stock exchanges is regulated by the MiFID2 directive (Directive 2014/65/EU), which places strict requirements for timestamps and time synchronization [20]. The exact time requirements depend on the nature of the trade operations in question. For example, in high frequency trading, HFT, the number of transactions can reach hundreds of thousands per second, which requires a high timing accuracy in the range of [100, 200] ns. On the other hand, for more conventional trading options the legally required granularity of the timestamps is 1 µs. The finance sector are legally required to be able

to trace their time back to UTC time, but GPS time is not fully traceable to UTC [20]. Thus, NTP and PTP server time solutions are used.

– Electricity transmission - The GNSS time is used for measurements of the network status, but also to probe for possible faults along a transmission line [20]. For the current needs of the transmission networks, the GNSS time accuracy of 1 μs is sufficient. For applications using NTP/PTP protocols, and possibly for future upgraded technologies, it is recommended to deploy several GNSS receivers in the network sub-stations. Because of the importance of the electricity transmission, it is advised to deploy a backup system for the time synchronization.

Positioning. The availability of GNSS positioning has helped to define rules and safety regulations, for example in aviation and enabled the development of new technologies, such as autonomous vehicles. The required positioning accuracy will naturally vary from one application to another, but the need for centimetre level accuracy has significantly increased. At the same time, GNSS solutions have become more common in our everyday lives: many sports equipment track the position and velocity, and other services, such as augmented reality games (for example Pokemon GO) rely on user position to show specific content. Because the vast number of different applications and user needs, the entries are presented on a general level.

– Aviation - Although safe flying is possible without any GNSS systems, the efficiency and available capacity of the airports will be compromised and smaller airports cannot operate without GNSS support [16]. For example, a flight from the city of Tallin, Estonia, to Savonlinna in Finland had to be canceled several times in spring 2023, because of degraded GNSS signal availability. Because of its small size, the Savonlinna airport relays on GNSS equipment for landing operations, and without backup systems, safe landing could not be guaranteed. The EU decree 2018/1048 obliges member countries to move towards using GNSS at airports, but for example in Finland the change is still on strategic planning level (TRAFICOM publications 12/2021). The importance of GNSS is evident during landing and lift-off, but the required positioning accuracy can be on meter scale. On the contrary, precise time information can be crucial especially for large airports, not only for scheduling purposes but also for possible backup electricity grids and other safety critical applications. During flight, the positioning accuracy is relaxed to a few hundred meters [33]. However, continuous availability of location solution is expected with availability from 95% up to 99.999%.
A new emerging trend in civil use of airspace are drones. Although there are some rules and regulations that limit where and how the drones can be flown, for example flying BVLOS, Beyond Visual Line of Sight, and no-fly zones around airports, the regulatory space, even on EU-level, is still evolving. The requirements on GNSS services are therefore unclear, but it is likely that they will reflect the general requirements of civil aviation.

– Maritime - GNSS systems are commonly used in maritime operations, and with increasing research on autonomous ships, the need for location services will increase in the future [17]. There are several auxiliary systems in use ranging from optical viewing to sonar systems. Therefore, failures in GNSS will not completely stop maritime traffic, as the auxiliary systems are sufficient for navigation, especially at open sea, where distances are larger and typical sailing speeds provide several minutes of reaction time. Accurate GNSS positioning and velocity information is needed in coastal waters and harbours, where accurate traffic control is required to assure safety of operations. The accuracy ranges from 100 m in open ocean conditions to 1 m in port operations and closed water ways but can be as high as 0.1 m for marine engineering needs. The vessels are also required to update their heading periodically, up to every 2 s depending on the sailing speed. Because of the increasing need for accurate GNSS information, there are initiatives to utilize EGNOS (European Geostationary Navigation Overlay Service) in maritime operations. In Finland, the FGI (Finnish Geospatial Research Institute) and the FTIS (Finnish Transport Infrastructure Agency) are supporting ESSP (European Satellite Services Provider) to study the performance of EGNOS in the Gulf of Finland. EGNOS services will provide additional benefits for cargo optimization, as altitude information can be used for more efficient cargo distribution on-board transport vessels [42].

– Road users - GNSS and related services are widespread among the road users, although mobile phone applications have replaced integrated systems in many day-to-day situations [19]. The constant influx of positioning data transferred over networks have allowed new services that provide road user with real time information of road conditions or traffic jams. The need for accurate and resilient location information has thus become an everyday need, which will soon increase with self-driving cars. For safety systems such as collision avoidance, an accuracy of 1 m is generally sufficient. However, for automated solutions the location information has to be accurate to a level of ∼20 cm [19,43]. The need for resilient positioning services has become apparent, as detailed by the Finnish Transport and Communications Agency (TRAFI-COM), who have estimated that a severe interference in GNSS can stagnate land transportation. If 10% of all cars will be autonomous within 10 years, a GNSS interference that causes these cars to stop will partially halt the road traffic. The need of cybersecurity for road users was further underlined when the taxi services of a major city were hacked in early September 2022. A cyberattack against the online services of one of largest taxi companies operating in the area sent dozens of cars to a single location, causing a significant traffic jam [7].

– Railroads - The EU railway control systems are being updated with modern digital ones [18]. As a part of the digitisation, the 3rd level of the European Rail Traffic Management System (ERTMS) control systems utilize GNSS to provide accurate positioning. The use of GNSS in rail traffic was suggested in the account written by the European Parliament: satellite navigation could especially be used for tracking rail traffic to improve rail safety, and it should thus be a high priority for member states. The ERTMS system should be operational throughout the EU before 2040. For tracking applications, an accuracy in range of 1 to 10 m is often enough, whereas structural monitoring and infrastructure surveying require centimetre level accuracy. The new GNSS systems for rail roads should also take into account GNSS interference, which could cause significant delays. In Finland, the Digital rail road (Digirata) [59] project is piloting approaches for train traffic control with GNSS and new 5G solutions.

– Construction and Agriculture - The availability of GNSS and the advances in receiver technology have opened new revenues for precision agriculture [15]. For example, the path of a farm machine can be programmed to follow the shape of the field in specific patterns or the planting of crops can be controlled in a predefined efficient way. On larger scales, GNSS can be used to control the daily operations of all farm machines in ways that optimize productivity. For construction workers, GNSS can be used to position the foundations of buildings or to precisely control the operating hand of heavy machinery. The applications that utilize GNSS positioning have different needs for positioning accuracy, but for both agriculture and construction work, there are applications where centimetre level accuracy is needed. The research on autonomous cars will likely reflect on both agriculture and construction, with autonomous operations further increasing the need for accurate positioning services.

Table 1. GNSS user requirements and needs. The values are based on the EUSPA market reports and Finnish GNSS end user interviews.

Industry	Users	Positioning	Timing
Telecom	Telecommunications, data transfer	–	100 ns–1 μs
Finance	Banks, stock exchange	–	100 ns–1 μs
Electricity	Digital electricity stations	–	1 μs
Aviation	Civil aviation	~1 m	–
Maritime	Shipping industry	1–10 m	2 s
Road user	Navigation, autonomous driving	10 cm–1 m	–
Rail roads	Civil transportation, rail transport	1–10 m	–
Constr. Agri	Precision agriculture, construction sites	1 cm–1 m	–

3   Case Study: Finland

Following the trends of recent years, the number of companies that either provide or utilize GNSS-based services has been steadily increasing. Therefore, it is only natural to expect that the demand for robust location or timing services will also continue to increase. This increasing trend is not only seen in Finnish markets, but it is a global phenomenon (markets expected to grow to 405 B € by 2031 from the 150 B € revenue estimated for 2021 [21]). It is evident that the companies involved in GNSS markets have a solid understanding of the needs of their customers and the required know-how to provide, for example, nature friendly positioning devices utilizing solar power.

It is noteworthy that in Finland companies operating in the GNSS and related fields are often strongly involved with the public sector, supporting governmental agencies on different levels, and providing scientific research. Thus, governmental support and understanding of the needs, capabilities, and requirements of these companies are crucial to ensure the growth of the market segment. Some solutions have already been provided, such as the GNSS-Finland service [52], but the need for new services is expected to increase in the near future. The free collaboration among different stakeholders working with positioning and timing solutions, and to a larger extent, the whole Finnish space segment, allows effective planning and development of new projects and services. The opportunities provided by new GNSS services, for example the Galileo PRS service, are being utilized, and there is a growing interest into research and development of new kind of receivers. The PRS service is expected to greatly improve the security of GNSS-based positioning and timing services throughout Europe. However, the PRS-service is only available for governmental entities, but Galileo OSNMA and CAS are available for general public. Although OSNMA and CAS are not as secure as PRS, they will offer increased security and robustness for many everyday PNT-services.

The National Land Survey of Finland maintains a GNSS situational awareness service, GNSS-Finland [52]. The GNSS-Finland service [51] was developed to provide 24/7 signal quality monitoring using the permanent FinnRef GNSS network [44]. The idea of using reference stations is similar to that in the COLOSSUS (Crowd-Sourced Platform for GNSS Anomaly Identification, Isolation and Attribution Analysis) project funded by the European Space Agency (ESA) [31]. Integrity monitoring using reference stations is often based on the measurement of the Carrier-to-Noise density Ratio (CNR), which is a simple parameter derived as receiver observable and available in all GNSS receivers [45].

3.1   GNSS Threats in the Finnish Context

The number of GNSS jamming incidents has been steadily increasing during the recent years, especially those involving small personal privacy devices (PPD). These devices are meant to conceal, e.g., personal location data to be used by employers. The range of the devices can be wide resulting in collateral damage. Several incidents of PPD's used in cars driving next to airports have been reported, which have caused delay in airport operations. Large-scale GNSS interference is relatively uncommon, but based on aviation pilot reports, hot spots of GNSS interference can be identified near European borders [12].

A similar trend of increasing small-scale GNSS interference has been reported in Finland, but there have only been two major interference events during the last few years. In the fall of 2018 [63], reports from northern Finland stated difficulties in gaining a location fix and the authorities issued a NOTAM (Notice To Airmen) warning covering most of Northern Finland. Another large-scale GNSS incident was in the spring of 2022, affecting large areas of eastern Finland [32,64]. For several days, GNSS signals were degraded to a level that prevented smaller airports from operating and caused personal sportswear to report illogical exercise routes [14]. An airline was reported to have cancelled several flights. The lack of GNSS prevented safe landing operations, as the destination airport was small and did not have alternative navigation equipment. Based on these reports, it is evident that eastern Finland was affected by large scale jamming and spoofing. Although the impact was considerable for small airports, the impact of a large-scale GNSS interference event on a major airport like Helsinki-Vantaa would not completely deny planes from landing. It would still make it more difficult to operate safely, causing significant delays and loss of revenue.

A key benefit of GNSS signal monitoring is in improving the resilience against threats targeting critical infrastructure. Attacks against GNSS can place human life at risk or lead to significant financial loss, further underlining the need of signal monitoring to understand the possible threats. For example, most goods transported to Finland are carried via waterways, which are mostly narrow, especially in the Archipelago Sea. Therefore, a spoofing attack on a cargo ship can have catastrophic results: loss of human life, environmental damage, loss of revenue, and a potential block of the shipping route. Spoofing attacks on vessels have been reported before. In an incident at Black Sea [30], several ships reported their GPS receivers to indicate them to be at a nearby airport while sailing at open sea. Another example is from Shanghai [48], where the captain of an American container ship reported that the ships AIS showed a nearby vessel jumping from one position to another. A visual observation revealed that the jumping ship was stationary at the dock. Further research on the AIS data from all nearby vessels showed that the locations of the vessels had been spoofed following a circular pattern. In total over 300 vessels had been affected on the same day that the American ship made the report. Furthermore, to exclude possible problems with the AIS of the American container ship, the researchers used data from a smartphone fitness app that records user location. The data showed the user location to follow a similar circular pattern as seen in the AIS data, pointing to a large-scale spoofing attack. However, a recent study on the cybersecurity of the AIS has shown that the system is vulnerable against attacks utilising radio frequency links, and that the attack can be carried out with a low cost setup [41].

In addition to accurate location, critical infrastructures of a modern society depend on precise time information. Smart power grids, telecommunication, and stock exchanges all require time synchronisation at microsecond level. It is therefore evident that these applications are vulnerable against spoofing or time synchronisation attacks. In a recent paper, [69] studied different spoofing based attacks, and how to defend against them in the context of smart power grids. It was found that a defence-in-depth method is necessary to provide sufficient level of protection, as none of the defensive precautions suggested could provide good results against all of the attack methods studied. In the Finnish context, VTT MIKES (Technical Research Centre of Finland, metrology centre) provides the official Finnish realisation of the UTC (Universal Time Coordinated) time. The UTC is a 24 h time standard, which is kept to a high synchronisation globally by national time laboratories utilising extremely precise atomic clocks and taking into account for example the Earth's rotation. Thus the generation of the UTC time is a international effort coordinated by the International Bureau of Weights and Measures (BIPM). The UTC time 0:00 is defined as midnight at Earth's zero meridian, which passes through Greenwich in England, linking the UTC with the Greenwich Mean Time (GMT) system.

National time laboratories distributes their own realisation of the UTC time which in the Finnish context is called UTC(MIKE). The time difference between the UTC time and the national Finnish time is plus 2 or 3 h, depending on the daylight saving time. The official Finnish time is distributed from a single laboratory, but for example, telecommunication operators maintain their own grand master clocks. These clocks are required to operate independently for two weeks in a case of an emergency. To increase the robustness of the time synchronisation services, a model where the official time is maintained with an interlinked system of several time laboratories would be beneficial. An interlinked system has been developed in Sweden [60], where the Swedish national time UTC(SP) is distributed from several different locations. In the United Kingdom, a system of several interconnected time laboratories is currently under development [27] and a similar system for time distribution was also recommended by a research done in the United States of America [67].

As the use of GNSS-based services is increasing, the number of interference events is growing as well. However, the currently available technology to localize interference signals is both costly and unwieldy. More research and development are needed to make the equipment more widespread. Combining small and light consumer grade detectors with the GNSS-Finland service could be a solution to create a denser monitoring network, which would allow a more robust and accurate detection system. Such a network could also be used to monitor and model space weather, separate local and large-scale phenomena, and give predictions of the possible cause (man-made versus natural). Long term continued monitoring would also improve our response against severe space weather, and other possibilities not yet been realised are likely to turn up.

3.2   Interference Monitoring with GNSS-Finland

An example of interference detection provided directly by the GNSS-Finland service is presented in Fig. 1, which shows the CNR (Carrier-to-Noise density Ratio) of Glonass G1 frequency recorded at one of the FinnRef stations in 2021. There is a significant decrease in the CNR at 9.30AM local time, which was detected by the service. An alert was issued when the CNR reached a threshold value pre-set by the service user. This time, the Glonass G1 was the only frequency band with problems, while the rest of the systems were functional.

A similar incident was recorded two weeks later, and the data combined with information from CCTV surveillance cameras showed the cause to be a truck approaching the site, first at 100 m and then at 10 m distance from the receiver (both incidents are visible in Fig. 1).

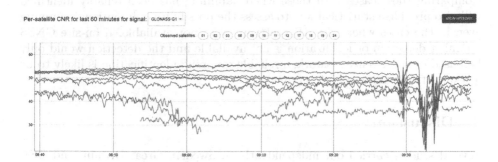

Fig. 1. Carrier-to-Noise density Ratio vs. time of Glonass G1 signal showing the significant decrease in CNR right after 9.30AM local time, as seen in the data directly provided by the GNSS-Finland Service.

The incident in Fig. 1 is an example of a typical use case of a GNSS situational awareness service. The cause of the interference is not available from the CNR-plot, and more information is required to determine the cause, i.e., whether it is intentional or caused by a natural phenomenon or by a malfunctioning device. In this case, additional information from the CCTV was enough to solve the case, but in most situations, it would be necessary to analyse the frequency spectrum to identify the sources of intentional interference. A database of frequency spectra has been collected in the STRIKE3-project to enable a classification scheme [11]. Antenna arrays and information from other sensors (such as in this case) have also been used to localize the source [3].

GNSS interference is mainly detected from the Automatic Gain Control (AGC), CNR, or by analysing the frequency data when available [6, 25]. Antenna solutions, such as Directional antennas or Controlled Reception-Pattern Antennas (CRPA), can also be used to mitigate interference. To be able to identify a jamming signal, the RF spectrum of the signal should be available, but CNR-based detection is so far mostly provided by reference stations. For an improved characterization and identification of error sources, the following parameters usually available in reference station data would provide more information:

- Comparison of position and time information (to estimate the positioning performance)
- Satellite orbit information for monitoring system performance [40]
- Dual frequency positioning for estimating ionospheric errors (cf. [61])
- AGC values have been shown to correlate with GNSS jamming (e.g., [45]). A reduced AGC value was also defined as an event detection criterion in the STRIKE3 project [65].

– Sudden changes in the RTK (Real-Time Kinematic) correction values should also be monitored
– Historic information on past interference events would also help to classify an incident

Comparing these cases with those where jamming has been reliably identified will also provide a statistical way to assess the possibility of intentional jamming even in the cases where the RF spectrum were not available. If on-site GNSS jamming detection or localization is not available and the detection would only be based on a reference network, a reliable jamming identification is likely to be a result of a combination of parameters.

4   Discussion

Several studies carried out independently in Sweden, Great Britain, and USA [27,60,67] have reached a similar conclusion: modern societies are extremely dependent on accurate positioning and especially time information provided by GNSS systems. Power grids and financial sector require nanosecond level accuracy to operate. At the same time, GNSS satellites are vulnerable against natural phenomena, such as solar storms, for which the occurrences and strength are difficult to predict. A major solar storm that strikes the Earth can potentially black out all GNSS systems and services. There is also an increase in local occurrences of GNSS jamming as a result of the crisis in the Eastern Europe [32]. In such events, it is critical to have a working network of back-up systems that can secure the critical infrastructure. Typically these secondary or back-up systems are used alongside GNSS or they can be used to provide sufficient positioning accuracy if GNSS is unavailable. Another method is to monitor the GNSS signals to better understand typical errors and develop mitigation techniques based on these observations.

4.1   Mitigating GNSS Vulnerabilities

There is a wide range of backup systems from terrestrial radio beacon networks (enhanced long range navigation, eLORAN) to sensor and hybrid positioning. A recent addition to the terrestrial radio network solution was presented by [66], who propose a two component system for providing a PNT solution in dense urban environments where GNSS signals suffer degradation caused by multi path effects and blocked signal due to high buildings. The proposed system uses a wide band radio signal for ranging and a optical fiber link between the ground stations to distribute accurate time information. The results are promising, but the system is still in prototype phase, but could offer a regional solution for accurate PNT.

The studies led by Great Britain and USA proposed a terrestrial radio beacon network, eLORAN, as the most cost-effective back-up system for GNSS-based navigation (e.g., [27] and references therein). With the advances in both receiver technologies and signal design, eLORAN could achieve a navigation accuracy of ~8 m and a timing accuracy below 1 μs. The timing accuracy can be further improved to ~100 ns by applying differential corrections [54]. Although the positioning accuracy is not comparable with modern GNSS-based solutions, eLORAN can provide a sufficient backup solution for many applications. A widespread eLORAN network could also be used as an auxiliary system in support of GNSS, for example as DGNSS stations.

In addition to auxiliary systems, monitoring the quality of the GNSS signal can help in mitigating the vulnerabilities of GNSS systems. The COLOSSUS (Crowd-Sourced Platform for GNSS Anomaly Identification, Isolation and Attribution Analysis) project that started 2017 aims at global GNSS error mapping with CORS (Continuously Operating Reference Stations) networks [31]. The detected errors and the related information will be uploaded to a database, which can be used to study the regional differences of GNSS errors. As the COLOSSUS project aims to create a global network of stations, the density of the stations will be naturally low compared to, for example many national monitoring station networks. Thus local level faults will be hard to detect, but detection large scale phenomena or system level faults will be faster and easier. In Finland, the GNSS-Finland service utilises CNR data produced by the national FinnRef-network [51] for GNSS interference detection. However, only a fraction of the available data is currently being included in the GNSS-Finland service. For example, historic information about disruptions in GNSS signal is available through FinnRef stations but this information is not logged by the service. Such information is valuable and GNSS market stakeholders have expressed interest in it. Other interesting information that could be derived from the GNSS-Finland data include the cause of interference, time information, and the possible inclusion of EGNOS (and PRS service in the future) monitoring information. This kind of signal quality control would require a large database and would improve the related services. This is the case especially for EGNOS, for which regional quality control would result in significant improvements in service quality, especially in the Northern regions, where the availability of the signal is already limited. The Galileo High Accuracy Service (HAS) is planned to become operational by 2024. Performance monitoring of Galileo HAS signals would be vital for knowing if the performance meets its expectation in the mid-to-high latitude region.

4.2 Future of Location and Time-Based Services

With the introduction of 5G-signal and Artificial Intelligence -based processing solutions, future systems such as IoT and autonomous transportation are likely to utilize cloud computing (or Big Data in general) to a greater extent than is currently being done. This will further emphasize the need for improved cybersecurity. However, these technologies require considerably more computational power and are not well suited for many consumer grade solutions, where low energy consumption is a critical requirement. For example adding modern navigation message authentication services to mobile phones would require considerable increase in required computational operations. Assisted GNSS technologies seem to be a promising solution, but will likely require more research before they can be adapted to consumer products. Furthermore, server-side solutions for navigation will likely be a good fit for several IoT applications, but the transfer of data between the servers and the various IoT devices will require further work to assure the speed and safety of the provided services.

Other significant future developments are quantum navigation and the use of Low-Earth-Orbit (LEO) satellites for positioning. These technologies are currently being studied to a large extent. The advantage of using LEO satellites is their closer proximity to Earth, so that the signal strength is higher. Because LEO satellites are smaller, they are cheaper to build allowing more extensive constellations to be deployed. However, dedicated LEO constellations for PNT do not currently exist, and there are several open research questions related to the LEO constellations. Should these be stand-alone systems, or assisting current GNSS systems? Should the signal be broadcast at the GNSS frequencies, or should these satellites use higher (or lower) frequency bands? There are several large research and development projects currently starting in Europe, thus the LEO concept and the capabilities of these constellations will become much clearer within the next 5 years. Quantum navigation is expected to provide high precision and secure navigation and timing solutions, but the problem with the current technology is the amount of needed supporting electronics, and thus the size of the systems.

The advancing receiver technology will increase the use of multi-constellation multi-frequency (MCMF) receivers. They will improve the stability of the services provided, especially in the timing domain, but the improved accuracy and availability will likely increase the use for location-based services. New services like Galileo OSNMA and PRS, particularly if combined with global monitoring effort, will offer increased resilience and security for both location and timing applications. However, even the most modern receivers are still not fully utilising the advantages provided by MCMF. For example, many receivers are still using GPS L1 channel as a primary, thus if this channel is not available due to signal jamming, the receiver stops providing a PNT solution. Although many receivers can detect and inform the user that they are detecting signal jamming (or spoofing), further research and development is required for receivers to be able to reliably identify jamming and spoofing and to stop using the affected frequency bands and only rely on the 'clean' frequency bands for PNT.

The accuracy needs of the GNSS end user summarised in Table 1, show a clear need for precises positioning and time synchronisation. There is also a clear need to increase the robustness and resilience of both location and time based services, as growing number safety critical services depend on GNSS-based systems. The future services offered by the Galileo constellation, PRS, OSNMA, and CAS, combined with the expected improvements provided by the emerging LEO-constellations (better signal strength, increased satellite coverage, and new services), will create a new type of markets, which will offer Secure and Precises Navigation as a Service (SaPNaaS). However, even these services cannot provide PNT under heavy jamming of spoofing attack. Combined with the increasing requirements on accurate positioning and time synchronisation needs, it is recommended that a system-of-systems approach is implemented, especially for safety critical system and national critical infrastructures. The quality-to-price ratio of inertial sensors, gyroscopes, and other MEMS (Micro-Electro-Mechanical Systems) based sensors has been steadily improving, thus adding additional sensor to support traditional GNSS based receivers will provide additional resilience, but will require more processing power from computers. Furthermore, fiber-optical systems or Chip-scale atomic clocks (CSAC), should be deployed to support GNSS based time synchronisation to systems that are critically dependant on precise time synchronisation. The individual components of this system-of-systems approach are well studied, but combining them together in a efficient manner and taking into account the increasing amount of data and security concerns can be challenging.

5 Conclusions

GNSS technologies have come a long way, and services based on GNSS solutions have become an everyday part of our lives. As the popularity of GNSS increases, so do the threats affecting GNSS-based services and the need for robust and resilient location and time information. The constant increase in demand in turn requires constant adaptation and development of new techniques and technology. This need for new technological solutions has become more apparent during the last decade, as our lives are more and more reliant on digital solutions.

The availability and safety of GNSS-based services is relatively good throughout Finland, although as we have discussed here, there are certain vulnerabilities and shortcomings that we have identified. We have attempted to offer guidelines and suggestions on how to further improve the situation. As discussed, the need for improved national level time synchronisation and a denser monitoring network for GNSS signals are two of the issues that should be focused on. Although the end user study was carried out in Finland, many of the findings can also be applied elsewhere too as many services run similarly in other countries as well.

The Finnish and international research will greatly improve the resilience and robustness of GNSS-based positioning and timing. International monitoring efforts will improve our understanding of the threats that these services face. GNSS constellations are expensive to create and maintain. Supporting technologies, such as cube satellites and hybrid or sensor-based navigation, will see an increase in interest in the future. The same goes for technologies based on quantum physics. In Finland, the GNSS markets, development, and research efforts will follow these trends, assuming that there will be enough experts to fill the required positions.

Acknowledgment. This work has been supported by Academy of Finland special funding for research into crisis preparedness and security of supply (project REASON - Resilience and Security of Geospatial Data for Critical Infrastructures, decision number:

338042) and National Emergency Supply Agency of Finland program Digital Security 2030.

References

1. 3GPP: Positioning for the internet of things: a 3GPP perspective (2016). https://arxiv.org/ftp/arxiv/papers/1705/1705.04269.pdf
2. Kurmanaev, A.: How fake GPS coordinates are leading to lawlessness on the high seas (2022). https://www.nytimes.com/2022/09/03/world/americas/ships-gps-international-law.html
3. Axell, E.: GNSS interference detection (2014). https://www.foi.se/rapportsammanfattning?reportNo=FOI-R--3839--SE
4. Bhuiyan, M.Z.H., et al.: H2020 STRIKE3: standardization of interference threat monitoring and receiver testing - significant achievements and impact. European Microwave Association (2019)
5. Bhuiyan, M.Z.H., Ferrara, N.G., Hashemi, A., Thombre, S., Pattinson, M., Dumville, M.: Impact analysis of standardized GNSS receiver testing against real-world interferences detected at live monitoring sites. Sensors 19(6), 1276 (2019). https://doi.org/10.3390/s19061276
6. Borio, D., Dovis, F., Kuusniemi, H., Lo Presti, L.: Impact and detection of GNSS jammers on consumer grade satellite navigation receivers. Proc. IEEE 104(6), 1233–1245 (2016). https://doi.org/10.1109/JPROC.2016.2543266
7. Cybernews: Hackers created an enormous traffic jam in Moscow (2022). https://cybernews.com/cyber-war/hackers-created-an-enormous-traffic-jam-in-moscow/
8. Czech Technical University: Fremen adviser, application to avoid crowds (2023). https://cs.fel.cvut.cz/en/news/detail/1572
9. Demyanov, V., Yasyukevich, Y.: Space weather: risk factors for global navigation satellite systems. Solar-Terr. Phys. 7(2), 28–47 (2021). https://doi.org/10.12737/stp-72202104
10. Dovis, F.: GNSS Interference Threats and Countermeasures. Artech House (2015)
11. Dumville, M., Pattinson, M., Manikundalam, V., Eliardsson, M., Payne, D., Towlson, O.: STRIKE3 D6.2: threat database analysis report (2019). http://gnss-strike3.eu/downloads/STRIKE3_D6.2_Threat_database_Analysis_Report_public_v1.0.pdf
12. EUROCONTROL: Does radio frequency interference to satellite navigation pose an increasing threat to network efficiency, cost-effectiveness and ultimately safety? (2021). https://www.eurocontrol.int/sites/default/files/2021-03/eurocontrol-think-paper-9-radio-frequency-intereference-satellite-navigation.pdf
13. Eurocontrol: Radio frequency interference to satellite navigation: an active threat for aviation? (2021). https://www.eurocontrol.int/sites/default/files/2021-03/eurocontrol-think-paper-9-radio-frequency-intereference-satellite-navigation.pdf
14. Euronews: Planes and smartwatches near Finland's russian border had GPS issues, and not for the first time (2022). https://www.euronews.com/next/2022/03/16/planes-and-smartwatches-near-finland-s-russian-border-had-gps-issues-and-not-for-the-first
15. EUSPA: Report on agriculture user needs and requirements (2021). https://www.gsc-europa.eu/sites/default/files/sites/all/files/Report_on_User_Needs_and_Requirements_Agriculture.pdf

16. EUSPA: Report on aviation user needs and requirements (2021). https://www.gsc-europa.eu/sites/default/files/sites/all/files/Report_on_User_Needs_and_Requirements_Aviation.pdf

17. EUSPA: Report on maritime and inland waterways user needs and requirements (2021). https://www.gsc-europa.eu/sites/default/files/sites/all/files/Report_on_User_Needs_and_Requirements_Maritime.pdf

18. EUSPA: Report on rail user needs and requirements (2021). https://www.gsc-europa.eu/sites/default/files/sites/all/files/Report_on_User_Needs_and_Requirements_Rail.pdf

19. EUSPA: Report on road user needs and requirements (2021). https://www.gsc-europa.eu/sites/default/files/sites/all/files/Report_on_User_Needs_and_Requirements_Road.pdf

20. EUSPA: Report on time and synchronisation user needs and requirements (2021). https://www.gsc-europa.eu/sites/default/files/sites/all/files/Report_on_User_Needs_and_Requirements_Timing_Synchronisation.pdf

21. EUSPA: EUSPA EO and GNSS market report 2022 (2022). https://www.euspa.europa.eu/sites/default/files/uploads/euspa_market_report_2022.pdf

22. EUSPA: Galileo services (EUSPA) (2022). https://www.gsc-europa.eu/galileo/services

23. EUSPA: EUSPA market report on EO and GNSS 2022 (2023). https://www.euspa.europa.eu/sites/default/files/uploads/euspa_market_report_2022.pdf

24. EUSPA/GSA: Power-efficient positioning for the internet of things (2020). https://www.euspa.europa.eu/sites/default/files/uploads/gsa_internet_of_things_white_paper.pdf

25. Ferrara, N.G., Bhuiyan, M.Z.H., Söderholm, S., Ruotsalainen, L., Kuusniemi, H.: A new implementation of narrowband interference detection, characterization, and mitigation technique for a software-defined multi-GNSS receiver. GPS Solut. **22**(4) (2018). https://doi.org/10.1007/s10291-018-0769-z

26. Glomsvoll, O., Bonenberg, L.K.: GNSS jamming resilience for close to shore navigation in the northern sea. J. Navig. **70**(1), 33–48 (2017). https://doi.org/10.1017/S0373463316000473

27. GOS: Satellite-derived time and position: a study of critical dependencies. Government Office for Science (2018)

28. GOV.UK: Government to explore new ways of delivering 'sat nav' for the UK (2020). https://www.gov.uk/government/news/government-to-explore-new-ways-of-delivering-sat-nav-for-the-uk

29. GPS-world: The system: GLONASS in April, what went wrong (2014). https://www.gpsworld.com/the-system-glonass-in-april-what-went-wrong/

30. GPS World: Spoofing in the black sea: what really happened? (2017). https://www.gpsworld.com/spoofing-in-the-black-sea-what-really-happened/

31. GPS World: ESA to use CORS networks for global error mapping (2019). https://www.gpsworld.com/esa-to-use-cors-networks-for-global-error-mapping/

32. GPS World: Finnish airline finds GPS interference near Russian border (2022). https://www.gpsworld.com/finnish-airline-finds-gps-interference-near-russian-border/

33. GSA: EGNOS safety of life service definition document issue 3.4 (2021). https://www.gsc-europa.eu/sites/default/files/sites/all/files/egnos_sol_sdd_in_force.pdf

34. Homeland Security: Report on Positioning, Navigation, and Timing (PNT) Backup and Complementary Capabilities to the Global Positioning System (GPS) (2020)

35. ICAO: An urgent need to address harmful interferences to GNSS (2019)

36. Inside GNSS: Sinister spoofing in shanghai (2019). https://insidegnss.com/sinister-spoofing-in-shanghai/
37. Islam, S., Bhuiyan, M.Z.H., Thombre, S., Kaasalainen, S.: Combating single-frequency jamming through a multi-frequency, multi-constellation software receiver: a case study for maritime navigation in the gulf of Finland. Sensors **22**, 2294 (2022). https://doi.org/10.3390/s22062294
38. Kaasalainen, S., et al.: Reason-resilience and security of geospatial data for critical infrastructures. In: CEUR Workshop Proceedings, vol. 2880 (2020)
39. Kankaanpaa, J.P.: GNSS related threats to power grid applications (2021). https://urn.fi/URN:NBN:fi-fe202103096912
40. Kazmierski, K., Sośnica, K., Hadas, T.: Quality assessment of multi-GNSS orbits and clocks for real-time precise point positioning. GPS Solut. **22**(1) (2017). https://doi.org/10.1007/s10291-017-0678-6
41. Khandker, S., Turtiainen, H., Costin, A., Hämäläinen, T.: Cybersecurity attacks on software logic and error handling within AIS implementations: a systematic testing of resilience. IEEE Access **10**, 29493–29505 (2022). https://doi.org/10.1109/ACCESS.2022.3158943
42. Khatun, A., Thombre, S., Bhuiyan, M.Z.H., Bilker-Koivula, M., Koivula, H.: Preliminary study on utilizing GNSS-based techniques for enhanced height estimation for vessels in Finnish waterways. FTIA Publ. **18** (2021). https://urn.fi/URN:ISBN:978-952-317-854-0
43. Kirkko-Jaakkola, M., et al.: Hybridization of GNSS and on-board sensors for validating the aurora ecosystem. In: Proceedings of the 32nd International Technical Meeting of the Satellite Division of The Institute of Navigation, pp. 2172–2185 (2019). https://doi.org/10.33012/2019.16916
44. Koivula, H.: Finnish permanent GNSS network FinnRef - evolution towards a versatile positioning service. Doctoral thesis, School of Engineering (2019). http://urn.fi/URN:ISBN:978-952-60-8630-9
45. Larsen, S.S., Jensen, A.B.O., Olesen, D.H.: Characterization of carrier phase-based positioning in real-world jamming conditions. Remote Sens. **13**(14), 2680 (2021)
46. Harris, M.: Ghost ships, crop circles, and soft gold: a GPS mystery in shanghai (2019). https://www.technologyreview.com/2019/11/15/131940/ghost-ships-crop-circles-and-soft-gold-a-gps-mystery-in-shanghai/
47. Miralles, D., Moghadam, M.S., Akos, D.M.: GNSS threat monitoring and reporting with the android raw GNSS measurements and STRIKE3. In: Proceedings of the 32nd International Technical Meeting of the Satellite Division of The Institute of Navigation (ION GNSS+ 2019), pp. 275–289 (2019). https://doi.org/10.33012/2019.16984
48. MIT Technology Review: Ghost ships, crop circles, and soft gold: a GPS mystery in Shanghai (2019). https://www.technologyreview.com/2019/11/15/131940/ghost-ships-crop-circles-and-soft-gold-a-gps-mystery-in-shanghai/
49. Murrian, M.J., Narula, L., Humphreys, T.E.: Characterizing terrestrial GNSS interference from low earth orbit. In: Proceedings of the 32nd International Technical Meeting of the Satellite Division of The Institute of Navigation (ION GNSS+ 2019), pp. 3239–3253 (2019). https://doi.org/10.33012/2019.17065
50. Nguyen, H.L., Troglia Gamba, M., Falletti, E., Ta, T.H.: Situational awareness: mapping interference sources in real-time using a smartphone app. Sensors **18**(12), 4130 (2018). https://doi.org/10.3390/s18124130
51. Nikolskiy, S., et al.: GNSS signal quality monitoring based on a reference station network. In: 2020 European Navigation Conference (ENC), pp. 1–10 (2020). https://doi.org/10.23919/ENC48637.2020.9317361

52. NLS: GNSS-Finland service (2021). https://gnss-finland.nls.fi
53. NPL: A complete guide to time stamping regulations in the financial sector (2019). https://www.npl.co.uk/products-services/time-frequency/npltime/guide
54. Offermans, G., Bartlett, S., Schue, C.: Providing a resilient timing and UTC service using eLoran in the United States. Navigation **64**(3), 339–349 (2017)
55. Pattinson, M., et al.: Standardisation of GNSS threat reporting and receiver testing through international knowledge exchange, experimentation and exploitation. In: European Navigation Conference 2016, p. 7 (2016)
56. Prol, F.S., et al.: Position, navigation, and timing (PNT) through low earth orbit (LEO) satellites: a survey on current status, challenges, and opportunities. IEEE Access **10**, 83971–84002 (2022). https://doi.org/10.1109/ACCESS.2022.3194050
57. Psiaki, M.L., Humphreys, T.E.: GNSS spoofing and detection. Proc. IEEE **104**(6), 1258–1270 (2016). https://doi.org/10.1109/JPROC.2016.2526658
58. Pullen, S., Gao, G.X.: GNSS jamming in the name of privacy potential threat to GPS aviation. Inside GNSS **35**, 34–43 (2012)
59. Pylvanainen, J., et al.: Towards digital and intelligent rail transport - final report of the Digi rail study, vol. 6. Publications of Ministry of Transport and Communications (2020). http://urn.fi/URN:ISBN:978-952-243-589-7
60. Rieck, C., Jaldehag, K., Ebenhag, S.C., Jarlemark, P., Hedekvist, P.O.: Time and frequency laboratory activities at rise. In: Proceedings of the 51st Annual Precise Time and Time Interval Systems and Applications Meeting, pp. 169–180 (2020). https://doi.org/10.33012/2020.17297
61. Rovira-Garcia, A., Ibáñez-Segura, D., Orús-Perez, R., Juan, J.M., Sanz, J., González-Casado, G.: Assessing the quality of ionospheric models through GNSS positioning error: methodology and results. GPS Solut. **24**(1) (2019). https://doi.org/10.1007/s10291-019-0918-z
62. Ruotsalainen, L., et al.: Toward autonomous driving in arctic areas. IEEE Intell. Transp. Syst. Mag. **12**(3), 10–24 (2020). https://doi.org/10.1109/MITS.2020.2994014
63. The Barents Observer: Pilots warned of jamming in finnmark (2018). https://thebarentsobserver.com/en/security/2018/11/pilots-warned-jamming-finnmark
64. The Guardian: Finland reports GPS disturbances in aircraft flying over Russia's Kaliningrad (2022). https://www.theguardian.com/world/2022/mar/09/finland-gps-disturbances-aircrafts-russia
65. Thombre, S., et al.: GNSS threat monitoring and reporting: past, present, and a proposed future. J. Navig. **71**(3), 513–529 (2018). https://doi.org/10.1017/S0373463317000911
66. Tiberius, C., Janssen, G., Koelemeij, J., Dierikx, E., Diouf, C., Dun, H.: Decimeter positioning in an urban environment through a scalable optical-wireless network. NAVIGATION: J. Inst. Navig. **70**(3) (2023). https://doi.org/10.33012/navi.589
67. USA-PNT-ABS: Protect, toughen, and augment: Global positioning system for users (2018)
68. Xue, D., Yang, J., Liu, Z.: Potential impact of GNSS positioning errors on the satellite-navigation-based air traffic management. Space Weather **20** (2022). https://doi.org/10.1029/2022SW003144
69. Zhang, H., Peng, S., Liu, L., Su, S., Cao, Y.: Review on GPS spoofing-based time synchronisation attack on power system. IET Gener. Transm. Distrib. **14**(20), 4301–4309 (2020)

Surveillance of Offshore Installations with Patrol Routine

Bartosz Skobiej[✉][iD], Frank Sill Torres[iD], and Finn-Matthis Minssen

German Aerospace Center, Institute for the Protection of Maritime Infrastructures, Fischkai 1, 27572 Bremerhaven, Germany
bartosz.skobiej@dlr.de

Abstract. This paper covers the problem of monitoring and surveillance of Offshore Wind Farms (OWFs) in the North Sea area of German Exclusive Economic Zone (GEEZ). The increase of risks connected to current geopolitical situation across Europe is clearly visible. Suspicious activity of Russian fleet in the North Sea, unidentified sources of underwater cables damage in Norway, or the sabotage of the Nord Stream pipelines near Bornholm could be recognized as Hybrid Threats (HTs). As a result, the current maritime risk landscape considers multi-factor hazards posed by variety of actors. Conducted analyses reveal that most of the German Federal Coast Guard activities take place within ca. 50 km limits offshore, in the areas of high-density traffic. This observation suggests a need for updated approach in case of surveillance of offshore installations located as far as 150 km from a shore, and even 300 km away in the future. The need is driven not only by distances exceeding typical operations or raised threat levels but also by new preventive function of German Federal Coast Guard aimed at protection of newly recognized offshore Critical Infrastructures (CIs). The article proposes two software solutions along with Multi Criteria Decision Analysis (MCDA) background for solving the patrol route execution problem for these offshore locations.

Keywords: Critical Infrastructure · Offshore Wind Farm · Coast Guard · Surveillance · Patrol Route

1 Introduction

The exploration of marine resources contributed greatly in the past to the prosperity of societies while the sea transport provided opportunities for trade and intercultural exchange. The current geopolitical situation however poses a threat both for economic prosperity of the European Union (EU) countries and for well-being of their societies.

The increase of risks connected to current geopolitical situation across Europe is clearly visible. Among many premises of elevated tension, one could name suspicious activity of Russian fleet in the North Sea [1–3] as well as in the Irish Sea [4], unidentified sources of underwater cables damage in Norway [5,6], or

S. Pickl et al. (Eds.): CRITIS 2023, LNCS 14599, pp. 208–223, 2024.
https://doi.org/10.1007/978-3-031-62139-0_12

destruction of the Nord Stream pipelines near Bornholm, Denmark [7]. Such events could be recognized as Hybrid Threats (HTs) [8]. It is worth mentioning that the HT activity "has been attributed to states like Russia, China, Iran and North Korea, to non-state actors like Hezbollah, Al-Qaeda, and ISIL, as well as to several proxy actors, transnational organized crime syndicates, ideological movements and profit-making "freelance" actors" [8]. As a result, the current maritime risk landscape considers multi-factor threats posed by a variety of actors, including espionage and sabotage threats, organized crime, social unrests and strikes of maritime workers [9–11]. Moreover, the ongoing war in Ukraine shows how important it is to protect waterways and govern coastlines in order to sustain logistic channels and support the flow of goods [12]. Unfortunately, the impact of any military conflict is not limited only to the countries at war but also inflicts third parties, in this case - the EU community.

Recognition of contemporary maritime risks and patterns leading to functional degradation or system collapse are the key factors to prevent, protect against, respond to, resist, mitigate, and absorb a disruptive event. To support the resilience of maritime infrastructures a number of initiatives are launched. Among them, the response of NATO forces is also considered necessary [13]. Since 2016, the Alliance has publicly stated that hybrid actions against one or more Allies could lead to a decision to invoke Article 5 of the North Atlantic Treaty. Following latest news, it is worth mentioning that NATO Allies have significantly increased their military presence around key infrastructure, including with ships and patrol aircraft. Additional arrangements by creation of the Critical Undersea Infrastructure Coordination Cell at NATO Headquarters response also against the current threats [14].

From the EU legislative perspective, the adaptive change could be observed in the update of the EU Maritime Security Strategy (EUMSS). As it is stated in the document "The overall strategic environment is experiencing drastic changes. Reshaped by the climate crisis and environmental degradation and aggravated by Russia's illegal and unjustified military aggression against Ukraine, it demands more action from the EU as an international security provider" [15]. This framework document identifies particular "threats and illicit activities" but also sets 6 strategic objectives for the EU. Among these objectives, the cooperation with partners, including NATO, plays significant role.

In order to protect the EU maritime domain, a number of organizations join the efforts, e.g. the European Centre of Excellence for Countering Hybrid Threats (Hybrid CoE), European Maritime Safety Agency (EMSA), Frontex - the European Border and Coast Guard Agency and European Fisheries Control Agency (EFCA). In the case of Germany as the EU member state, an important role in protecting offshore assets play German Federal Coast Guard - *Küstenwache*. As for the installations located in the German Exclusive Economic Zone (GEEZ) the article focuses on above-the-surface energy infrastructures - Offshore Wind Farms (OWFs). Since offshore energy assets have been named "Critical Infrastructure" (CI) and "Critical Entities" [16], the recognition of their importance predestines them to prioritized protection.

As a response to these issues the article develops a decision algorithm for patrol route execution. The proposed solution considers distances between off-shore CIs and risk levels provided by an external sub-system. The problem of risk assessment, encapsulated in the external sub-system, is not fully covered in this paper for two main reasons - its complexity predestine it to be discussed in a separate article, and in the case of German Coast Guard procedures it is the undisclosed issue. Nevertheless, selected references discussing the problem are introduced in the Sect. 2.3. The study starts with definition of area of interest, both geographical and infrastructural in Sect. 2.1. Then the legal and organizational aspects of German Federal Coast Guard is under review in Sect. 2.2. The Multi Criteria Decision Analysis (MCDA) approach is introduced in Sect. 2.3, and the following two sections - 2.4 and 2.5 describe implementation of the proposed solution. Finally, the article presents the results and conclusions in Sect. 3.

2 Materials and Methods

2.1 Areas of Interest

The area of geographical interest is the North Sea GEEZ as it is defined in GEEZ proclamation [17] and as it is shown in the Fig. 1 along with designated locations for offshore wind energy. From the Germany-Netherlands "overlapping" marine border in the west, reaching the Dogger Bank in the north-west (limited by the location: 55°55′09,4″ N; 3°21′00,0″ E), towards the Denmark coastline to the east.

The main concern is focused on OWFs as CIs. The attention is paid to above-the-surface installations which exclude Wind Turbine (WT) foundations and export cables, and in a case of floating WTs - mooring points and electrical reconnection points. This constraint is a result of limited capabilities to detect underwater anomalies by the German Federal Coast Guard. Another specific requirement connected to maritime patrol duty is distinction between prevention and intervention. The approach presented in the paper investigate patrol activities as a prevention against potential threats.

The list of recognized geographical locations used in the analysis is presented in the Table 1 and visually shown in the Fig. 2 along with simplified graph of estimated distances in kilometers and shortest path for visiting all the locations. The shortest path problem, known as the Travelling Salesman Problem (TSP), first formulated by Hamilton and Kirkman [18], is solved by spread-sheet solver. Separately from the offshore energy installations of GEEZ, the Table 1 contains two additional locations vital for patrolling operations - the Cuxhaven base of *Küstenwache* and Helgoland Island that will host future hydrogen installations [19]. The "Denotation" column in the Table 1 indexes locations for the analysis by letters - A to N and shown in Fig. 2, but also identifies relevant designations - EN1 to EN20, from the Spatial Planning Ordinance for the GEEZ [20]. Moreover, there are two OWFs in German territorial (coastal) waters: Riffgat and Nordergründe. The Riffgat OWF is included in the Table 1 since it is located near the disputed maritime border with the Netherlands but also it is close to

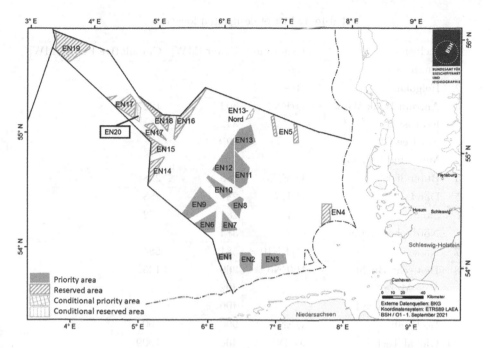

Fig. 1. Designations for offshore wind energy in the GEEZ North Sea [20].

the coastline which ease the access to the facility and thus is regarded as the location of raised concern.

Since the work is grounded on the graph based premise, it seems there is a niche for testing path searching algorithms. The issue we need to underline is that our approach is using dynamic values of weights in the context of a graph-based representation. It means that classical versions of Dijkstra or A* algorithms do not seem useful in changing environment, e.g. we cannot define the final location of the patrol route and the route itself would change every time we update risk levels in the system. Similar constraints affect possible implementation of e.g. Genetic Algorithm (GA), which would has to been re-run after each risk levels update.

2.2 German Federal Coast Guard - *Küstenwache*

Coast Guard is a maritime security organization covering wide spectrum of responsibilities. In case of EU countries, the list of these responsibilities can be found in "Practical Handbook" on European cooperation on coast guard functions [21]. One of the core functions, described in section 3.1.h. is "maritime monitoring and surveillance". Other functions, in random order of priority, are:

- Maritime Safety, Including Vessel Traffic Management;
- Ship Casualty and Maritime Assistance Service;
- Fisheries Inspection and Control;

Table 1. List of designated locations.

	Inclusion	Denotation	Power [MW]	Cumulative Power [MW]
1	Cuxhaven	A/–	–	–
2	Helgoland	B/–	–	–
3	Amrum Bank West	C/EN4	302	1227
	Kaskasi II		342	
	Nordsee Ost		295	
	Meerwind Süd/Ost		288	
4	Butendiek	D/EN5	288	288
5	DanTysk	E/EN5	288	288
6	Sandbank	F/EN13	288	672
	Nördlicher Grund		384	
7	Kaikas	G/EN10	581	581
8	Deutsche Bucht	H/EN6	260	1062
	Veja Mate		402	
	Bard Offshore I		400	
9	He Dreiht	I/EN7	900	900
10	Global Tech I	J/EN8	400	1009
	Albatros		112	
	Hohe See		497	
11	Borkum Riffgrund III	K/EN1	900	900
12	Trianel I+II+III	L/EN2	600	1816
	Merkur		396	
	Alpha Ventus		60	
	Borkum Riffgrund I+II		760	
13	Gode Wind I+II+III	M/EN3	900	2200
	Nordsee I+II+III		1300	
14	Riffgat	N/–	113	113

- Maritime Border Control;
- Maritime Environmental Protection and Response;
- Prevention and Suppression of Trafficking and Smuggling and Connected Maritime Law Enforcement;
- Maritime Search and Rescue;
- Maritime Customs Activities;
- Maritime Accident and Disaster Response;
- Maritime, Ship and Port Security.

Keeping in mind that EU is a political organization, above functions of Coast Guard are related mostly to a civil service. It is important to distinguish a Coast Guard as a military duty from Coast Guard as a civil service. Based on United

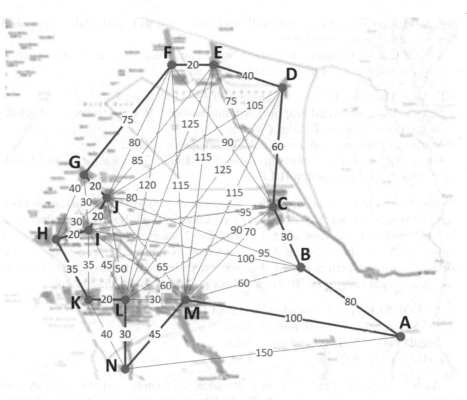

Fig. 2. Map of designated locations including estimated distances in km between them, with the identified shortest path of 595 km.

States Coast Guard (USCG) report on Coast Guard Concept of Operations for Offshore Assets [22], in case of military operations there are 8 identified missions for USCG:

- Drug Interdiction;
- Alien Migrant Interdiction Operations;
- Living Marine Resources;
- Other Law Enforcement;
- Search and Rescue;
- Defense Readiness;
- Ports, Waterways, and Coastal Security;
- Ice Operations.

Comparing both lists of Coast Guard functions and missions: [21] and [22], it is possible to identify similar items, e.g. Search and Rescue, Living Marine Resources, and Maritime Environmental Protection and Response. However, there are also missions dedicated solely for military vessels, e.g. Defence Readiness. Comparing military and non-military Coast Guard services, the differences between them in chain of command, available equipment and weapon systems, human resource limitations (e.g. civil workers are subject to the labor law), and rules of engagement, are visible.

Unlike USCG, Croatian, Italian or Norwegian counterparts, *Küstenwache* is a non-military service, which is divided into four segments:

- Federal Maritime Police - Bundespolizei See (BPOL SEE);
- Federal Waterways and Shipping Administration - Wasserstraßen- und Schiff-fahrtsverwaltung des Bundes (WSV);
- Maritime Customs Service - Kontrolleinheit See (ZOLL);
- Federal Agency for Agriculture and Nutrition - Bundesanstalt für Land-wirtschaft und Ernährung (BLE).

In order to understand operational aspects of *Küstenwache*, historical commercial AIS data from 2020 are used to visualize and analyze the movements of the vessels. Synthetic view of trajectories for 7 selected German Coast Guard ships in 2020 are shown in Fig. 3. The selection includes only long-range vessels operating in the North Sea area that are listed on official sites of the agencies. The figure comprises of ca. 10 million data points and contains info of:

- 2 BPOL SEE vessels: Potsdam and Bad Düben;
- 2 WSV vessels: Neuwerk and Mellum;
- 2 ZOLL vessels: Helgoland and Borkum;
- 1 BLE vessel: Seefalke.

As it is visible in Fig. 3, the majority of *Küstenwache* activity is focused on maritime transition routes - mainly Traffic Separation Scheme (TSS) Terschelling - German Bight (SN1) and TSS East Friesland - German Bight Western Approach (SN2) [20]. Since the TSSs are applied in areas of high-density marine traffic, it is understandable they are under distinct concern. Further analysis of Fig. 3 and Fig. 4 reveals that most of the activities take place within ca. 50 km limit offshore. This observation suggests a need for updated approach in case of surveillance of offshore installations. The need is driven not only by raised threat levels, distances exceeding typical operations, or introduction of Floating Offshore Wind (FOW) installations, but also by new preventive function of German Federal Coast Guard aimed at protection of newly recognized CIs - i.e. OWFs.

Analysis of movement trajectories for selected Coast Guard vessels shows that most of them operate 24 h per day at sea, i.e. the ratio of collected AIS data while roaming offshore, for daylight and night conditions, is equal. The only exception appears for WSV where the ratio is estimated as 3:2 in favor of daylight operations. The difference could be contributed to specific tasks realized by WSV, e.g. maintaining navigational markings, which often require daylight conditions to perform. It is noteworthy that AIS data shown in Fig. 3 and in Fig. 4 may comprise of interventions, patrolling activities, dedicated campaigns performed by selected agencies, or servicing and testing procedures including sea trials. It is also possible that specific *Küstenwache* tasks require switching the AIS transponders off. Moreover, since the data consist of combined satellite-

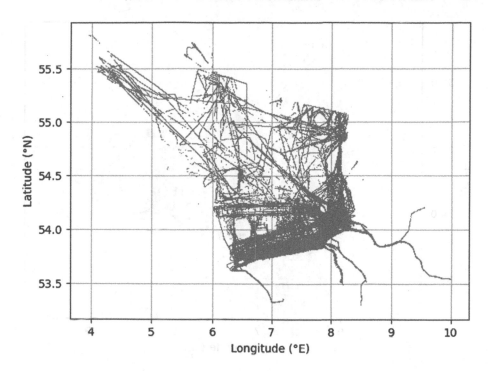

Fig. 3. AIS data of selected *Küstenwache* ships in 2020, in the North Sea area.

and terrestrial-based statistics, it is possible to detect occasional, local inconsistencies in the available information. However, it does not jeopardize the global understanding of the fleet behavior in this case.

In terms of maritime monitoring and surveillance the major responsibility belongs to the BPOL SEE. In order to fulfill the task, a new fleet of Offshore Patrol Vessels (OPVs) is introduced - the Potsdam class ships. As of beginning of 2023, there are three operational vessels of that type and one under construction. Two of them operate in the North Sea: BP81 Potsdam and BP83 Bad Düben, with the home port of Cuxhaven. These modern ships are well suited for long, offshore patrols contributing to the safety and security of the area. Equipped with helicopter landing deck, two interceptor boats, 5 × 20 ft mission container storage, and external firefighting system [23] - these vessels support BPOL SEE duties and counteract contemporary threats.

Based on the technical specification of the Potsdam class OPV [23] and press release info [24], following parameters are used for the study:

- Maximal speed 21 kts (ca. 39 km/h);
- Patrol speed/economical speed 11 kts (ca. 20 km/h);
- Cruising speed 3 kts (ca. 5 km/h);
- Ship autonomy > 7 days.

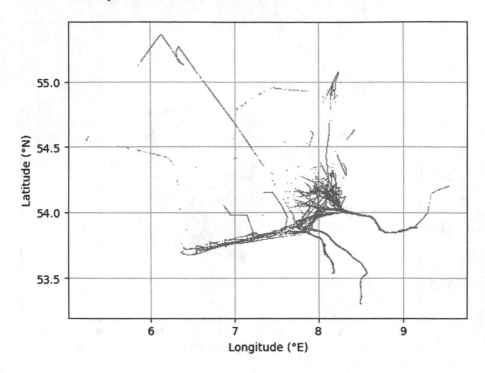

Fig. 4. AIS data of the Potsdam-class OPV BP83 Bad Düben in 2020.

2.3 Multi Criteria Decision Analysis (MCDA) for Destination Selection

Common prevention policies are based on recognition of threats and responding with patrolling activity in the geographical area of concern. As a result, it is expected that certain risk levels at a location would decrease. To effectively implement described mechanism, a proper Situational Awareness (SA) picture, including CI elements and threat recognition mechanisms, should be available for maritime security organizations. The problem of developing such solutions is a multi-factor challenge which is not considered in this paper. Nevertheless, the issue is addressed in a number of other publications [25–29].

For the sake of research, two simplified models of risk description are implemented. Keeping in mind that sequence of time-dependent risk levels at locations is not relevant to Markov chain, the first method used in a spreadsheet-based solution (described in Sect. 2.4) is founded on randomized values of risks. The presented solution however, also allows to input user-defined risk values for every location, at every step of decision making. The second method used in Python-based solution (described in Sect. 2.5) initiates with random values but each consecutive step of the algorithm increases the risk levels by user-defined value in all locations but the currently visited by the Coast Guard vessel. The risk level at the location currently being patrolled decreases by a user-defined value.

This newly established risk value is then used as a base for risk assessment when a *Küstenwache* vessel departs towards other locations. The second method does not regard external risk factors like extreme weather conditions or hostile ship maneuvers.

The risk level is one of the criteria for route selection decision making. Second selected criterion is distance to the location. The formula used for the multi criteria decision making is presented in Eq. (1) based on [30]:

$$R_{(S,L)} = \frac{(w_1 * risk_{(S,L)}) + (w_2 * dist_{(S,L)})}{w_1 + w_2} \tag{1}$$

where:

- $R_{(S,L)}$ is a ranking value at the algorithm step "S" for location "L";
- w_1 is a user-defined weight of risk, $w_1 \in (0,1)$;
- $risk_{(S,L)}$ is a normalized risk value;
- w_2 is a user-defined weight of distance, $w_2 \in (0,1)$;
- $dist_{(S,L)}$ is a normalized distance.

Estimation of travelling lengths is performed based on static distance table. Depending on the user-defined weights of the criteria presented in Eq. (1), it is possible to lean towards economic aspects of patrolling by minimizing the effects of risk levels and maximizing the weight of distance. As a result, shorter voyages would be favorable. On the other hand, focusing on risks would lead to more aggressive approach to patrolling and better counteracting current threads. Each decision on next destination, based on re-calculation of Eq. (1) for all relevant locations, is made after reaching target offshore installation. It means that in presented cases the decisions cannot be made while voyaging between locations. However, there is a possibility to implement time-based or other event-based triggers which would made the system more suitable for interventions.

The solution presented does not consider the usage of marine helicopters, Unmanned Surface Vehicles (USVs), or Unmanned Aerial Vehicles (UAVs) for supporting patrol duties. However, since a high seas bunkering is considered a viable option in this case, the assumed vessels' autonomy is not regarded as the constraint for the applied algorithm. In contrast to other solutions of maritime surveillance described in, e.g. [31–34] focused on USVs, dynamic risk counter-measures, and multi-agent systems, presented approach covers the contemporary, operational problem by introducing a tailored solution to specific needs of German Federal Coast Guard.

2.4 Spreadsheet-Based Solution

The first solution for patrol routing is based on spreadsheet editor software. The advantages of such solution are simplicity, robustness, low calculation cost, fast implementation and easy adaptation for operators. The required data inputs consist of:

- Distances matrix [km];

- User-defined weights for MCDA $w_1, w_2 \in (0, 1)$;
- Average patrol speed [km/h];
- Maximum time at location [h].

In the presented solution, maximum time at the location is a time period in hours that vessel spent patrolling a location with a risk level 1 (100%). For risk value 0.5 (50%) at a location and for maximum time at the location 3 h, the vessel will spend 1.5 h patrolling the local area with average patrol speed. The correlation could be denoted as:

$$patrolling\ time\ at\ location_L = \frac{maximum\ time\ at\ location}{risk\ value\ at\ location_L}. \tag{2}$$

The presented system is operating on event-based premises only, where decisions are made at the locations, after patrolling the area. Keeping in mind that risks for each step of the algorithm are randomly generated - the time spent at the locations will not influence the future decisions. Another assumption present in the spread-based system is that the risk level for current offshore location patrolled by Coast Guard drops to 0. This mechanism will prevent the vessel from staying at the same location for multiple steps of the algorithm and force the mobility of patrolling vessel.

The result spreadsheet seen in Fig. 5 gives answers to the following issues:

- Random number generations of risks for each location at each step of the algorithm with the *rand()* function;
- Min-max (0–1) normalization of distances to locations for each step of the algorithm;
- Calculation of MCDA values in order to determine the next travelling point;
- Estimation of planned and travelled distances, including:
  - Location-to-location distances;
  - Patrolling distances at the locations, based on time spent at the locations;
  - Total travelled distance, including return distance to location A (Cuxhaven).

2.5   Python-Based Solution

Alike the spreadsheet-based solution, the need of using distances matrix, weights for MCDA method, average patrol speed and maximum time at the location parameter is noticeable. In contrast to the previous solution, the user has a possibility to define the behavior of a patrol vessel at the location. The three new options for the decision-making process are introduced in this regard:

- vessel is moored;
- vessel cruise with a user-given low speed;
- vessel roaming with a patrol speed.

A significant change of risk development method is implemented in the python-based solution. Additional inputs consists of risk increment and risk reduction, both defined as percentages values. The risk increment describes the situation when a location is unsupervised and the risk value increases. The risk reduction is applied for a single location currently being patrolled by the Coast Guard. Still, the first step of algorithm is supported with random generation of risk levels.

3   Results

Exemplary spreadsheet-based solution is presented in Fig. 5. The figure shows 5 steps of the decision algorithm with a given assumptions:

- Risk MCDA weight $w_1 = 0.5$;
- Distance MCDA weight $w_2 = 0.5$;
- Average patrol speed = 10 kts (ca. 19 km/h);
- Maximum time at the location = 3 h.

The highest MCDA value at selected location drops to 0 after being patrolled and is highlighted in the Fig. 5. The final decision on returning to the point A (Cuxhaven marine base) is made by the operator. As it is seen in Fig. 5., the total patrol distance in the exemplary case is ca. 614 km, and the route consists locations: A, L, K, I, H, I, A. The specific locations are covered by the designations for offshore wind energy in the GEEZ North Sea [19] and presented in the Table 1. The 6 bottom rows in the Fig. 5 present the information for each route leg, from 1 to 5: "Maximum MCDA value" is the highest value reached for each of the algorithm steps, "patrol route" describes consecutive locations to visit, "point-to-point" indicates number of kilometers between two locations (current and future location), "distance at location" is a counter of kilometers travelled at the location while patrolling the local area of interest, "return to A" specifies the distance in kilometers to the starting location A, and "total distance" presents a calculation of total travelled distance for each step of the algorithm in case of user-driven termination of a mission.

The exemplary solution provided by the python-based system is shown in the Table 2. In contrary to the previous system, the random risk generation is performed only for the first step of the algorithm. The configuration of parameters used in this case are as follow:

- Risk MCDA weight $w_1 = 0.5$;
- Distance MCDA weight $w_2 = 0.5$;
- Average patrol speed = 10 kts (ca. 19 km/h);
- Cruising speed = 3 kts (ca. 6 km/h);
- Risk increase per step = 0.1 (10%);
- Risk reduction at current location = 0.9 (90%);
- On-site behaviour - cruising;
- Maximum time at the location = 3 h.

steps of the algorithm ->	1	2	3	4	5
A	0	0	0	0	0
B	0.648843	0.271307	0.237024	0.740792	0.352116
C	0.509737	0.192825	0.446318	0.687641	0.412974
D	0.509841	0.1124	0.247556	0.487094	0.611802
E	0.181093	0.320705	0.564985	0.51988	0.67892
F	0.428028	0.206562	0.572046	0.71374	0.706791
G	0.06763	0.36225	0.783765	0.829164	0.515379
H	0.479353	0.533884	0.608322	0.979505	0
I	0.294268	0.486132	0.922496	0	0.987239
J	0.479292	0.707629	0.600186	0.777903	0.729263
K	0.637103	0.958031	0	0.942902	0.917648
L	0.714111	0	0.919176	0.864798	0.66925
M	0.577177	0.853953	0.495293	0.383771	0.638059
N	0.611096	0.76817	0.699713	0.678485	0.734925
maximum MCDA value ->	0.714111	0.958031	0.922496	0.979505	0.987239
Patrol route ->	L	K	I	H	I
point-to-point [km] ->	130	20	35	20	20
distance at location [km] ->	17.61787	46.93921	40.69453	51.1686	52.78344
return to A [km] ->	130	150	180	200	180
total distance [km] ->	277.6179	364.5571	470.2516	561.4202	614.2037

Fig. 5. The spreadsheet-based solution example for patrol routine.

The exemplary patrol route performed by the vessel and shown in the Table 2. consists of locations: A, H, I, G, J, E, A. The total travelled distance equals 593 km, estimated patrol time is 38 h, travelled distance on-sites is 66 km, total time spent on-site is 11 h.

Table 2. List of events created by the python-based decision-making system.

Event number	Time [h]	Distance [km]	Event source	Event place	Notes
0	0	0	vessel	A	Starting patrol route
1	10	200	vessel	H	Arriving at the point
2	11.35765359	206.788268	vessel	H	Onsite patrol ended
3	12.35765359	226.788268	vessel	I	Arriving at the point
4	14.57020696	237.8510348	vessel	I	Onsite patrol ended
5	16.07020696	267.8510348	vessel	G	Arriving at the point
6	18.45529504	279.7764752	vessel	G	Onsite patrol ended
7	19.45529504	299.7764752	vessel	J	Arriving at the point
8	21.78110736	311.4055368	vessel	J	Onsite patrol ended
9	26.03110736	396.4055368	vessel	E	Arriving at the point
10	28.34191817	407.9595909	vessel	E	Onsite patrol ended
11	37.59191817	592.9595909	vessel	A	Ending patrol route

4   Conclusions

The solution presented in this article is just one of many possible options to support decision-making process of patrol route execution. The focus is paid to surveillance of offshore energy assets without covering the issue of dynamic interventions. The undisclosed maritime risk assessment system will provide dynamic risk levels that are implemented in the MCDA process. The local, specific constraints regarding German Federal Coast Guard are taken into consideration while performing the patrolling duty. This background studies respond to a novel challenge posed to the *Küstenwache* – protecting newly recognized offshore CIs. One of the shortcomings of the paper, that is briefly addressed in the Sect. 2.3, is a limited coverage of the risk assessment problem for security purposes. As the paper is focusing on the patrol execution, the risk assessment factor is regarded here as an external input signal that influences the decisions. Such approach allows to implement simplified risk generators based on randomization. The final foreseen solution is to be based on python software with external situational awareness system that will cover the aspects of weather conditions, real-time risk assessment and user-defined goals for effective surveillance of offshore installations.

References

1. Strauss, M.: Belgium investigates Russian 'spy ship' in North Sea. Reuters (2023). https://www.reuters.com/world/europe/belgium-investigates-russian-spy-ship-north-sea-2023-02-22/. Accessed 01 Feb 2024
2. Reuters. Russia targets Netherlands' North Sea infrastructure, says Dutch intelligence agency. Reuters (2023). https://www.reuters.com/world/europe/russia-targets-netherlands-north-sea-infrastructure-says-dutch-intelligence-2023-02-20/. Accessed 01 Feb 2024

3. Akerboom, E., Swillens, J.: De Russische aanval op Oekraïne een keerpunt in de geschiedenis. Ministerie van Binnenlandse Zaken en Koninkrijksrelaties; Ministerie van Defensie, The Hague (2023)
4. Gallagher, C.: Defence Forces monitoring Russian warships acting unusually off Irish south coast. (2022). https://www.irishtimes.com/ireland/2022/08/30/defence-forces-monitoring-russian-warships-acting-unusually-off-irish-south-coast/. Accessed 01 Feb 2024
5. Hommedal, S.: Ocean Observatory temporarily out of service. Institute of Marine Research (2021). https://www.hi.no/en/hi/news/2021/november/ocean-observatory-temporarily-out-of-service. Accessed 01 Feb 2024
6. Space Norway AS. Bortfall av reservekapasitet på Svalbardfiberen (2022). https://www.sysselmesteren.no/contentassets/8e497b11f18146029a022462c8dc09ca/pressemelding-fra-space-norway.pdf. Accessed 01 Feb 2024
7. Plucinska, J.: Nord Stream gas 'sabotage': who's being blamed and why?. Reuters (2022). https://www.reuters.com/world/europe/qa-nord-stream-gas-sabotage-whos-being-blamed-why-2022-09-30/. Accessed 01 Feb 2024
8. Giannopoulos, G., Smith, H., Theocharidou, M.: The landscape of hybrid threats: a conceptual model (public version). Publications Office of the European Union, Luxembourg (2021)
9. Savolainen, J., Gill, T., Schatz, V., Giannoulis, G.: Handbook on maritime hybrid threats: 15 scenarios and legal scans. The European Centre of Excellence for Countering Hybrid Threats, Helsinki (2023)
10. The Maritime Executive, LLC. Hamburg Port and Elbe Closed as Pilot Boats Join Public Sector Strike. The Maritime Executive, LLC (2023). https://www.maritime-executive.com/article/hamburg-port-and-elbe-closed-as-pilot-boats-join-public-sector-strike. Accessed 01 Feb 2024
11. Scislowska, M.: Poland reviews security after divers found near key port. Associated Press (2023). https://apnews.com/article/sports-poland-4b7ba09545adbab9f3a1c4c16da16458. Accessed 01 Feb 2024
12. Kuznietsov, S., Vladyshevska, V., Kuznetsov, S.: Coastal regions of Ukraine: governance transformation amid the Russian invasion. Lex Portus **9**(1), 37–49 (2023)
13. NATO. Countering hybrid threats (2024). https://www.nato.int/cps/en/natohq/topics.htm. Accessed 08 Mar 2024
14. European Commission. NATO stands up Undersea Infrastructure Coordination Cell (2023). https://ec.europa.eu/newsroom/cipr/items/786843/. Accessed 01 Feb 2024
15. European Commission: Joint communication to the European parliament and the council on the update of the EU maritime security strategy and its action plan "an enhanced EU maritime security strategy for evolving maritime threats". European Union, Brussels (2023)
16. Council, E.: Directive (EU) 2022/2557 of the European Parliament and of the Council of 14 December 2022 on the resilience of critical entities and repealing Council Directive 2008/114/EC. European Union, Brussels (2022)
17. Der Bundesministerium des Auswärtigen. Bekanntmachung der Proklamation der Bundesrepublik Deutschland über die Errichtung einer ausschließlichen Wirtschaftszone der Bundesrepublik Deutschland in der Nordsee und in der Ostsee. Bundesgesetzblatt, Bonn (1994)
18. Biggs, N.L., Lloyd, E.K., Wilson, R.J.: Graph Theory, 1736–1936. The Oxford University Press, Oxford (1998)
19. AquaVentus Förderverein e.V. (2023). https://aquaventus.org/en/. Accessed 01 Feb 2024

20. Gazette, T.F.L.: Annex to the spatial planning ordinance for the German exclusive economic zone in the North Sea and in the Baltic Sea dated 19 August 2021. Bundesanzeiger Verlag GmbH, Köln (2021)
21. EC Directorate-General for Maritime Affairs and Fisheries. Commission Recommendation of 20.7.2021 establishing a 'Practical Handbook' on European cooperation on coast guard functions. European Commission, Brussels (2021)
22. Zukunft, P.F.: Coast guard concept of operations for offshore assets, homeland security. United States Coast Guard, Washington D.C. (2017)
23. Fr. Fassmer GmbH & Co. KG. Fassmer 86 m Offshore Patrol Vessel. Fr. Fassmer GmbH & Co. KG, Berne (2020)
24. Pospiech, P.: Bundespolizei erhält neue Einsatzschiffe (2019). https://veus-shipping.com/2019/01/bundespolizei-erhaelt-neue-einsatzschiffe/. Accessed 01 Feb 2024
25. Swanson, C.: The Security Risk Handbook: Assess, Survey, Audit. Routledge, London (2023)
26. Baggett, R., Stout, A.: Critical infrastructure risk analysis and management. In: Masys, A.J. (ed.) Handbook of Security Science, pp. 1–21. Springer, Cham (2022). https://doi.org/10.1007/978-3-319-91875-4_1
27. Arvidsson, B., Johansson, J., Guldåker, N.: Critical infrastructure, geographical information science and risk governance: a systematic cross-field review. Reliab. Eng. Syst. Saf. **213**, 107741 (2021)
28. Rawson, A., Sabeur, Z., Brito, M.: Intelligent geospatial maritime risk analytics using the discrete global grid system. Big Earth Data **6**(3), 294–322 (2022)
29. Sill Torres, F. Kulev, N., Skobiej, B., Meyer, M., Eichhorn, O., Schäfer-Frey, J.: Indicator-based safety and security assessment of offshore wind farms. In: 2020 Resilience Week (RWS), Salt Lake City (2020)
30. Zionts, S.: MCDM-if not a roman numeral, then what? Interfaces **9**(4), 94–101 (1979)
31. Zhou, X., et al.: A comprehensive path planning framework for patrolling marine environment. Appl. Ocean Res. **100**, 102155 (2020)
32. Niu, Y., Zhang, J., Wang, Y., Yang, H., Mu, Y.: A review of path planning algorithms for USV. In: Wu, M., Niu, Y., Gu, M., Cheng, J. (eds.) ICAUS 2021. LNEE, vol. 861, pp. 263–273. Springer, Singapore (2022). https://doi.org/10.1007/978-981-16-9492-9_27
33. Ćosić, I., Komadina, P.: Croatian coast guard in the prevention of smuggling and trafficking in human beings from the aspect of state border and sea migration surveillance. Nase More **65**(2), 130–134 (2018)
34. Wang, J., Cui, L.: Patrolling games with coordination between monitoring devices and patrols. Reliab. Eng. Syst. Saf. **233**, 109109 (2023)

Relationships Between Security Management and Technical Security of Norwegian Energy Entities

Øyvind Toftegaard[1,2]([⊠]) [iD], Janne Hagen[3,4] [iD], and Bernhard Hämmerli[1,5] [iD]

[1] Norwegian University of Science and Technology, Gjøvik, Norway
oyvintof@stud.ntnu.no, bernhard.hammerli@ntnu.no
[2] Norwegian Energy Regulatory Authority, Oslo, Norway
oyat@nve.no
[3] Norwegian Water Resources and Energy Directorate, Oslo, Norway
janh@nve.no
[4] University of Oslo, Oslo, Norway
jannehag@ifi.uio.no
[5] Lucerne School of Computer Science and Information Technology,
Rotkreuz, Switzerland
bernhard.haemmerli@hslu.ch

Abstract. Security management standards such as ISO/IEC 27001 and NIST Cybersecurity Framework are common approaches to audit cybersecurity compliance and maturity. Little is known about how well such security management audits reflect an entity's technical security performance. Such relationships are, however, important to understand, as the performance of for example patch management and email security may be crucial to stop adversaries. This study is a correlation analysis applying Pearsons r and Spearmans ρ to test relationships between managerial and technical security. Our analysis was based on a scoring of 20 managerial and 22 technical security categories from 67 entities in the Norwegian energy sector. Our analysis did not show any clear correlation between the tested management scores and technical scores. Through factor analysis, we identified significant weak negative correlation between 8 security configuration categories and 3 security culture categories. Because the only identified correlation was negative, both security management and technical security should be assessed during audits.

Keywords: Security management · Compliance · Risk rating · Cybersecurity audit · Energy

1 Introduction

Cybersecurity audits are conducted to confirm or improve entities' security level. National authorities audit critical entities to check compliance with national security legislation. Audit frameworks designed to review auditee's management systems have been popular for the last decades [15, 16]. Today, the scope of cybersecurity audits conducted by Norwegian authorities is normally based on information security management standards. Prominent examples are ISO/IEC 27001

© The Author(s), under exclusive license to Springer Nature Switzerland AG 2024
S. Pickl et al. (Eds.): CRITIS 2023, LNCS 14599, pp. 224–241, 2024.
https://doi.org/10.1007/978-3-031-62139-0_13

and the baseline security principles for ICT-security provided by the Norwegian Security Authority [15]. The Norwegian baseline security principles build upon several standards, including ISO/IEC 27001 and NIST Cybersecurity Framework. Germany has practiced compulsory ISO/IEC 27001 certification since 2018 for their power grid operators [17]. Finland is another state with a public sector audit program built on ISO/IEC 27001 [7].

An important point with management system-based security audits is to increase trust among all stakeholders [7]. Such stakeholders include authorities, customers, partners, and society in general. The trust is based on an assumption that technical security performance is reflected in the security management maturity confirmed by the audit. However, little is known about the relationships between an entity's security management maturity and technical security performance. Without such knowledge, there is a risk that entities with low performance on technical security, but who scores high on security management maturity, are treated by the community as highly secure entities.

According to ISO 19011, an audit is a "systematic, independent, and documented process for obtaining objective evidence and evaluating it objectively to determine the extent to which the audit criteria are fulfilled" [18]. For cybersecurity, we can call this a systematic evaluation of the security of an entity's information system by measuring how well it complies with an established set of criteria. By security, we mean information security. We use the terms information security and cybersecurity interchangeably. ISO 19011 defines a management system as a "set of interrelated or interacting elements of an organization to establish policies and objectives, and processes to achieve those objectives" [18]. Normally, a management system contains systematic measures to ensure that an entity's activities are being planned, organized, executed, and maintained in compliance with the requirements set by authorities [16].

We know from past cyber events, that attacks do often have both social and technical components [19]. Table 1 shows methods applied in four advanced attacks. The table illustrates how methods with prominent social components are commonly applied in the early phases of the attacks. Examples of such methods are the utilization of social media, email, open-source intelligence, and messaging applications. Next, in the later phases, the adversaries seem to be moving to more technical elements, such as leveraging exploits, accessing interfaces, and installing backdoors.

Table 1. Methods applied in previous cyberattacks [19].

Phase	Desert Falcons	Deep Panda	Lotus Blossom	Snake
Reconnaissance	Facebook	Acunetix	Web research	Unknown
Delivery	Chat	Direct access	Email	Watering-hole
Installation	APK	Server-exploit	Office-exploit	Browser-exploit
Lateral movement	None	WMI	Unknown	Mimikatz, WMI
Exfiltration	Backdoor	Backdoor	Backdoor	Email
Erase evidence	Unknown	Unknown	Unknown	Unknown

Although a system is technically secure, it may be useless if the users misuse or bypass the security mechanisms or the secure system in itself [5]. Therefore, elements usually found in security management systems, such as educational programs, are essential. On the other hand, management systems may have a limited effect on the correct implementation of technical security measures. Consequently, it can be argued the technical security scope of audits is crucial as well.

We will explore whether there is any correlation between an entity's security management maturity and the same entity's performance on technical security. In Sect. 2, we present related work from academia and industry. In Sect. 3, we explain our applied methodology. In Sect. 4, we list our results including correlation values and other key outcomes. In Sect. 5, we discuss the meaning and quality of our results, before concluding in Sect. 6.

2   Previous Work

In 2022, Toftegaard analyzed the effect of ISO/IEC 27001 certification on the technical security of grid operators [8]. The author found a significant positive effect of certification on the technical security of small-sized grid operators, no particular effect for medium-sized grid operators, and indications of a negative effect for large-sized grid operators. On average, independent of the size of the operators, the author could not identify any positive or negative effect. As ISO/IEC 27001 is an information security management standard, the results indicate that an increased focus on security management does not have a corresponding effect on technical security performance. We utilized the same tools to score technical security performance in our study as the tools used in [8]. However, Toftegaard's study compared average scores for technical security performance between certified and non-certified operators only. By collecting additional scores on security management maturity, we were able to conduct a more in-depth analysis, looking for correlation between a variety of technical and managerial security indicators.

In 2011, Chang et al. explored relationships between IT capabilities and information security management [9]. IT capabilities was based on three non-security categories: strategic alignments, technical IT resources and IT operations. Information security management was based on information protection, restoration and accessibility. Together, these security elements should represent confidentiality, integrity and availability. Data was collected through questionnaire and analysed by the use of factor analyses and weighted regression models. The authors found that IT capabilities were significantly associated with the effectiveness of information security management. However, this only means that entities with larger IT resources have allocated more resources on information security, or that those entities who are confident of their IT capabilities are also confident of their information security. The authors do not enter into whether there is any relationships between security management maturity and technical security performance.

The security software vendor Tripwire published a white paper in 2022 arguing that compliance frameworks are not sufficient to be secure [3]. While compliance is about adhering to rules and regulations, security is about protecting cyber and physical assets. The white paper describes audits as having similar weaknesses to compliance frameworks. While the auditor focuses on compliance, there is a risk of overlooking what is really important for the security of the entity. Tripwire urges those working with security to regard compliance frameworks as helpful but not comprehensive, and pursue both compliance and security at the same time. As Tripwire is a commercial company, they may have an interest in separating compliance and security to sell more of their software products. However, Tripwire is not alone in arguing compliance and security is not the same thing.

In 2022, the defense and security news media Defence One described an experiment indicating security is not a compliance problem [4]. According to Defence One, the experiment was performed by staff at the US Navy and the Naval Postgraduate School and utilized a tool for automated red teaming. The Navy staff behind the experiment drew parallels with network security and getting soldiers combat-ready, which includes a lot of testing and exercising. In cyberspace, there is a continuous combat against adversaries, and based on their technical experiment, the Navy staff claim that compliance, and auditing compliance, is not an effective approach to security.

In 2020, the Norwegian Water Resources and Energy Directorate found that document-based controls, interviews, and physical meetings were the main audit methodologies of seven Norwegian authorities [15]. Only two of the authorities had experience with using technical tools as part of their audit methodology. The authors believe the application of digital tools during audits may become more relevant in the future.

The Security by Consensus (SBC) model (Table 2) was according to Kowalski [6] developed as a result of the discovery that a person's background was most important for how the person analyzed cybersecurity needs. An individual from a legal background would view needs from a legal perspective, and an individual from industrial/technical background would view cybersecurity needs from an industrial/technical perspective. The SBC model was proposed to create consensus among cybersecurity experts despite their different backgrounds [6]. Our slightly modified model shows a stacked version of the socio-technical system with managerial layers on top and technical layers at the bottom. Social requirements are part of the managerial framework and are used to guide the implementation of the managerial and technical layers.

Previous research in the field of comparing security management maturity and technical security performance is scarce. The projects described in this section have shown that actors from both industry and academia are criticizing the sole use of compliance-based audits. Such audits assess compliance with legal requirements or with information security management system standards. Despite these criticisms, and available opportunities to conduct technical tests, management system-based audit methodologies are commonly used alone. Any

Table 2. Security by Consensus (SBC) model [6].

	SBC model layers	Examples of social requirements
Managerial	Ethical Cultural	Codes of ethics and conduct
	Legal	Legislation and contracts
	Administrative Managerial	Risk assessments, Information security management system
	Operational	Configuration management
Technical	Application	Principles for secure applications, operating
	Operating system	systems, and hardware
	Hardware	

relationship between security management maturity and technical security performance remains to be proven. Therefore, it is important with a better understanding of whether the technical security performance is reflected in the security management maturity.

3 Methodology

We have applied a correlation analysis to explore relationships between security management maturity and technical security performance. Our main hypothesis (H_1) is that the state of security management maturity will correlate directly with the state of technical security performance. Our null hypothesis (H_0) is that there is no correlation between the state of security management maturity and the state of technical security performance. In the next section, we explain how we collected security scores to enable our analysis.

3.1 Data Collection

The security management scoring was based on the results of a survey performed in May 2021 by the Norwegian Water Resources and Energy Directorate (NVE) [13]. NVEs survey included 20 questions which we report as categories. In the survey, 121 entities in the Norwegian energy sector were questioned on security management and the implementation of security measures. The questions were designed in cooperation between the industry and relevant authorities, to be easy to understand and answer correctly, while also being relevant for measuring the state of security management. We got access to the raw data from the survey and utilized them to score the entities' security management maturity. Security management categories and related indicators are summarized in Table 3.

We utilized BlackKite's Technical Cyber Rating tool [11] and Security Scorecard's Security Rating tool [2] to collect technical security scores. This methodology is the same as the one Toftegaard used for analyzing the effect of ISO/IEC 27001 certification on grid operator's technical security [8]. During March 2022,

Table 3. Security management categories and indicators.

Nr	Security management categories	Indicators (Scoring) Entities = 67
1_M	ICT-strategy	Yes (10)/No (0)
2_M	ICT security strategy	Yes (10)/No (0)
3_M	ICT security in meetings	Never (0)/Seldom (5)/Often (10)
4_M	ICT contingency in management meetings last 12 months	Yes (10)/No (0)
5_M	Mgmt involved in ICT or SCADA security exercise last 3 years	Yes (10)/No (0)
6_M	ICT security audits in management meetings last 12 months	Yes (10)/No (0)
7_M	Incidents reported in management meeting last 12 months	Yes (10)/No (0)
8_M	ICT versions procured	Basic (0)/Advanced (10)
9_M	Home office risk discussed by management last 2 years	Yes (10)/No (0)
10_M	Digitalization risk discussed by management	Yes (10)/No (0)
11_M	Information security certification (e.g. ISO27001)	Yes (10)/No (0)
12_M	Hours a week per employee for cybersecurity education	None (0)/On-demand (5)/Regularly (10)
13_M	Security accounted for in pilot projects	Small (0)/Moderate (5)/Large (10)
14_M	Management's perception of security culture	Small (0)/Moderate (5)/Large (10)
15_M	Management's threat awareness	Small (0)/Moderate (5)/Large (10)
16_M	Cybersecurity education of managers (legal requirements)	Small (0)/Moderate (5)/Large (10)
17_M	Cybersecurity education of managers (risk management)	Small (0)/Moderate (5)/Large (10)
18_M	Management use of annual sectorial threat reports	Yes (10)/No (0)
10_M	Management knowledge of cybersecurity procurement rules	Yes (10)/No (0)
20_M	Fulfillment of cybersecurity procurement rules	Small (0)/Moderate (5)/Large (10)

BlackKite returned technical security scores from 67 of the 121 entities surveyed by NVE. Next, using Security Scorecard, we were able to get technical security scores from the same month for 44 of these 67 entities. With BlackKite's 19 categories and Security Scorecard's 10 categories, the two tools returned a total of 1.713 scores for the 67 entities. Adjusted for the 7 categories that overlapped between the two tools, we were left with 1.405 technical scores to use for the correlation analysis.

The two tools we used to collect technical scores were non-intrusive, meaning they only utilized passive methodologies. As a consequence, only indicators of technical security of the entities' IT systems observable from the outside were

Table 4. Technical security categories and indicators [8].

Nr	Technical security categories	Indicators BK Entities = 67	Indicators SS Entities = 44
1_T	DNS Health	Grade (F-A)	Numeric (0–100)
2_T	Email Security	Grade (F-A)	–
3_T	SSL/TLS Strength	Grade (F-A)	–
4_T	Application Security	Grade (F-A)	Numeric (0–100)
5_T	DDoS Resiliency	Grade (F-A)	–
6_T	Network Security	Grade (F-A)	Numeric (0–100)
7_T	Fraudulent Domains	Grade (F-A)	–
8_T	Fraudulent Apps	Grade (F-A)	–
9_T	Credential Management/Information Leak	Grade (F-A)	Numeric (0–100)
10_T	IP Reputation/Cubit Score	Grade (F-A)	Numeric (0–100)
11_T	Hacktivist Shares/Hacker Chatter	Grade (F-A)	Numeric (0–100)
12_T	Social Network	Grade (F-A)	–
13_T	Attack Surface	Grade (F-A)	–
14_T	Brand Monitoring	Grade (F-A)	–
15_T	Patch Management/Cadence	Grade (F-A)	Numeric (0–100)
16_T	Web Ranking	Grade (F-A)	–
17_T	Information Disclosure	Grade (F-A)	–
18_T	CDN Security	Grade (F-A)	–
19_T	Website Security	Grade (F-A)	–
20_T	IP Reputation	–	Numeric (0–100)
21_T	Endpoint Security	–	Numeric (0–100)
22_T	Social Engineering	–	Numeric (0–100)

analyzed. The processes applied by BlackKite and Security Scorecard to assess each category are summarized in [8]. Technical security categories and related indicators are summarized in Table 4.

To enable the classification of the 67 entities based on size, we utilized the Proff Forvalt business information tool [14]. Proff Forvalt returned revenue information, which we used to rank entities into annual turnover classes as defined by the European Commission [12]. The classes are shown in Table 5.

Of the 67 entities included in our assessment, 53 were grid operators, 11 were corporate groups and 3 were other types of entities. All the entities were related to the Norwegian power sector. Further, 9 of these entities were classified as micro, 30 as small, 15 as medium, and 13 as large size entities.

Table 5. Entity size classes [12].

Entity size	Micro	Small	Medium	Large
Revenue (turnover)	≤ € 2 M	≤ € 10 M	≤ € 50 M	> € 50 M

3.2 Data Analysis

After the data collection, we had 1.340 indicators of security management maturity and 1.713 indicators of technical security performance. The 1.273 technical
security indicators collected through BlackKite were ordinal data delivered as
letter grades from F to A. The 440 indicators collected through Security Scorecard were continuous variables from 0 to 100. The 1.340 security management
indicators were also provided as ordinal data with either Yes/No answers or levels of fulfillment of the various categories. To enable the correlation analysis, the
data from BlackKite and Security Scorecard had to be scored according to the
same scale. Therefore, to fit a scale from 0 to 100, the letters A-F were converted
to variable scores relative to 100%. Further, the security management indicators
were converted to variable scores as illustrated in Table 3.

To increase the comprehensiveness of our correlation analysis, we removed
categories from our dataset, where all entities had the same score. The reason
was that such categories could not be used to measure correlation and would
therefore only weaken the analysis. As a result, the number of technical security
categories used in the correlation analysis was reduced from a total of 22 to a
total of 18. The number of managerial security categories was reduced from 20
to 19. The following categories were removed from the analysis:

- 11_M Information security certification (e.g. ISO27001).
- 8_T Fraudulent Apps.
- 11_T Hacktivist Shares/Hacker Chatter.
- 12_T Social Network.
- 22_T Social Engineering.

The 18 technical security scores were compared individually against each
of the 19 managerial security scores. In addition, the average of the 18 technical scores were calculated before another comparison with average management
scores. For the technical security categories that overlapped between BlackKite
and Security Scorecard, the average of the scores within the category was also
calculated based on the overlapping scores. For the scores that were only available from either BlackKite or Security Scorecard, the individual score was used
instead of an average value. The equation used to calculate the average technical
security score per entity (s) is shown in (1).

$$\forall s \in Tech_{BK+SS}, \ s = \frac{1}{18} \sum_{i=1}^{18} (\frac{BK_i + SS_i}{2} |BK_i|SS_i) \tag{1}$$

$Tech_{BK+SS}$ is the dataset referred to in Table 7 and 8 and contains the
average technical security score of all entities. s is the average technical security
score of one entity. BK and SS refers to each category score from each of the
tools. The symbol | is used with the meaning "or" in this equation, and is used
because there were cases where scores were only available from BlackKite or
Security Scorecard.

We also applied a factor analysis to identify any invisible factors. The invisible factors consisted of groups of categories with high co-variance. Our factor

analysis returned one factor consisting of technical categories and two factors consisting of managerial categories (see Table 9). Last, we applied a correlation analysis between the technical and managerial factors to look for correlation between the hidden factors.

Our dataset contains both continuous variables and ordinal data. Therefore, we applied both Pearson's r and Spearman's ρ as correlation coefficients. The correlation values range from -1 to 1, where 0 represents no correlation and -1 or 1 represents perfect correlation. Whether the correlation value is positive or negative determines if the relationship is direct or inverse. We have labeled correlation strength based on [1], where

- weak correlation ≥ 0.3,
- moderate correlation ≥ 0.5, and
- strong correlation ≥ 0.8.

In the next section, we have visualized some characteristics of the security scores we collected, and we present the results of our correlation analysis.

4 Results

4.1 Descriptive Statistics

From BlackKite's 1.273 technical security indicators from 67 entities, 63% of the scores were the top grade A and 84% of the scores were grade A or B. This means 84% of the scores collected through BlackKite were within the upper 1/3. From the 440 scores for the 44 entities we collected through Security Scorecard, 85% was within the upper 1/6 and 94% was within the upper 1/3. This frequency distribution is visualized in the histogram in Fig. 1, which also illustrates how the data are skewed.

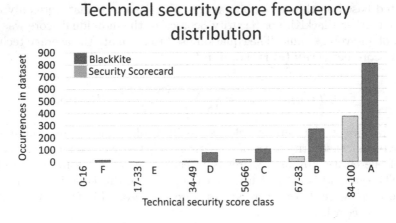

Fig. 1. Technical security score distribution.

Fig. 2. Security management score distribution.

Of the 1.340 scores we derived from the security management survey, 57% were within the upper 1/3. This frequency distribution is illustrated in the histogram in Fig. 2. The figures tell us our data sets have a distribution skewed towards the highest scores. Although the skewness is more prominent for the technical security scores than for the security management scores, it means that most entities assessed have implemented a high level of both security management and technical security.

We analyzed the correlation between BlackKite and Security Scorecard scores for the 7 overlapping technical security categories using Pearson's r. The results are provided in Table 6, where we see weak and moderate correlation values. Some of the security scores did not have any variation within their category, thereby making correlation analysis impossible. These cases are marked as NA in the table. The highest r-value of .73 is on IP Reputation from BlackKite which corresponds to Cubit Score from Security Scorecard. The correlation may be described as moderate

Table 6. Correlation between overlapping categories.

Nr	Technical security categories	Pearson's r
1_T	DNS Health	.033
4_T	Application Security	.21
6_T	Network Security	.409
9_T	Credential Management/Information Leak	NA
10_T	IP Reputation/Cubit Score	.73
11_T	Hacktivist Shares/Hacker Chatter	NA
15_T	Patch Management/Cadence	.578

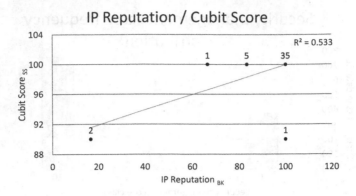

Fig. 3. Comparison of overlapping scores from BK and SS (N = 44).

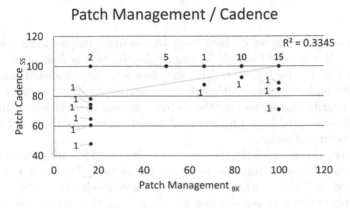

Fig. 4. Comparison of overlapping scores from BK and SS (N = 44).

In Fig. 3 and 4 we have plotted the IP Reputation/Cubit Scores and Patch Management/Cadence scores from BlackKite ($_{BK}$) and Security Scorecard ($_{SS}$) against each other. Because of BlackKite's use of letter grades, we have many co-incidents of points in the scattergrams. We have therefore labeled the points with the number of co-incidents to get an impression of how well the added trendline fits the data. In addition, by calculating the r squared, we see that 53.3% of the variation of IP Reputation and Cubit Scores are explained, and 33.5% of the variation of Patch Management and Cadence is explained by these variables. We emphasize the uncertainty in this analysis from having 44 observations only.

4.2 Correlation Analysis

In the main part of our analysis, we looked for correlation between the average of all the technical security scores and the average of all the security management scores with and without controlling for the size of the entities. As seen in Table 7 and 8, we found correlation values that can only be characterized as weak at best.

The highest direct correlation using Pearson's r can be found in Table 7 and is for micro-sized entities, where the technical scores are collected through Security Scorecard. This r-value of .39 can be described as weak correlation. Our plot of these data in a scattergram (Fig. 5), shows indications of a linear relationship. However, the result is very uncertain due to only 6 observations. The uncertainty is further reflected in the low r squared value in Fig. 5 and the P-value of .44 in Table 7. The scattergram in Fig. 6, shows how the correlation analysis becomes more complicated to conclude when adding the data of the other entity sizes.

The highest direct correlation using Spearman's ρ can be found in Table 8 and is for Medium-sized entities, where the technical scores are also collected through Security Scorecard. This ρ-value of .47 can also be described as weak correlaton. Again, the result has a high degree of uncertainty due to only 8 observations, and the uncertainty is further illustrated by the low r squared value in Fig. 7 and the P-value of .24 in Table 8.

The only result with a significant P-value is the Spearman's ρ of $-.25$ in Table 8 and is for all entity sizes, where the technical scores are collected through BlackKite. However, as the correlation value is too low to qualify for weak correlation according to our definition, we do not consider it as any identified relationship.

By combining all scores from BlackKite and Security Scorecard, from all categories and all entity sizes, we see no indication of correlation between technical security and security management scores (r-value at $-.11$ in Table 7 and ρ-value at $-.15$ in Table 8).

Table 7. Tech and Mgmt correlation by Pearson's r (and P-value).

Comparison	Micro	Small	Medium	Large	All Sizes
Tech$_{BK}$ vs Mgmt	$-.4$ (.29)	$-.08$ (.68)	$-.01$ (96)	$-.4$ (.18)	$-.19$ (.13)
Tech$_{SS}$ vs Mgmt	.39 (.44)	$-.14$ (.58)	.17 (.69)	.08 (.81)	$-.1$ (.52)
Tech$_{BK+SS}$ vs Mgmt	$-.31$ (.43)	$-.07$ (.72)	.01 (.97)	$-.22$ (.47)	$-.11$ (.37)

Table 8. Tech and Mgmt correlation by Spearman's ρ (and P-value).

Comparison	Micro	Small	Medium	Large	All Sizes
Tech$_{BK}$ vs Mgmt	$-.42$ (.26)	$-.06$ (.77)	.08 (.78)	$-.35$ (.24)	$-.25$ (.05)
Tech$_{SS}$ vs Mgmt	.2 (.7)	$-.28$ (.27)	.47 (.24)	$-.01$ (.97)	$-.21$ (.17)
Tech$_{BK+SS}$ vs Mgmt	$-.42$ (.26)	$-.04$ (.83)	.12 (.66)	$-.14$ (.66)	$-.15$ (.22)

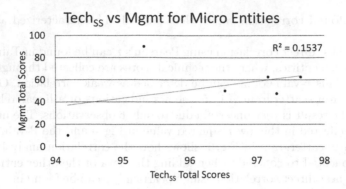

Fig. 5. Scattergram related to the highest r-value for direct correlation in Table 7.

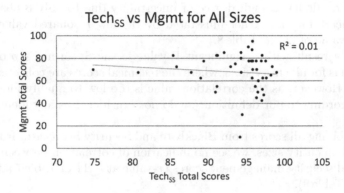

Fig. 6. Scattergram showing the lack of correlation when all Tech$_{SS}$ entity sizes is taken into account.

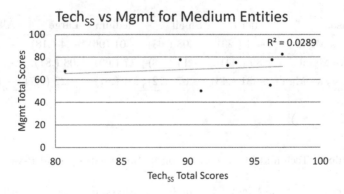

Fig. 7. Scattergram related to the highest ρ-value for direct correlation in Table 8.

We therefore applied a factor analysis using three factors. The first factor showed 8 categories with high factor loadings (>0.5). The second showed 3 categories with high factor loadings and the third showed 2. These results are provided in Table 9 where the most relevant variables (with the highest loading score) are reported first. The first factor contains technical security categories only, and due to the nature of the categories, we have named the factor "Security configuration". The second and third factors contain security management categories only, and due to the nature of the categories we have named the factors "Security culture" and "Security education".

Table 9. The 3 hidden factors and their categories with high factor loadings (>0.5).

Technical security		Security Management	
1	**Security configuration**	**2**	**Security culture**
13_T	Attack surface	15_M	Management's threat awareness
6_T	Network Security	10_M	Digitalization risk discussed by management
3_T	SSL/TLS Strength	15_M	Management's perception of security culture
10_T	IP Reputation / Cubit Score	**3**	**Security education**
15_T	Patch Management/Cadence	16_M	Cybersecurity education of managers (legal requirements)
5_T	DDoS Resiliency		
4_T	Application Security	17_M	Cybersecurity education of managers (risk management)
17_T	Information Disclosure		

Table 10 reports the results of the correlation analysis based on the three factors. The technical factor "Security configuration" is compared with the management factors "Security culture" and "Security education", first individually and then combined. The first comparison has a significant result both when using Pearson's ($r = -.36$ and P-value = .003) and Spearman's ($\rho = -.35$ and P-value = .003). The correlation value in both cases can be described as a significant weak inverse correlation. This relationship is illustrated in Fig. 8.

Table 10. Tech and Mgmt correlation using the 3 hidden factors.

Comparison	Pearson's r (P)	Spearman's ρ (P)
Security configuration vs Security culture	−.36 (.003)	−.35 (.003)
Security configuration vs Security education	.08 (.513)	.15 (.221)
Security configuration vs Culture and education	−.17 (.178)	−.07 (.562)

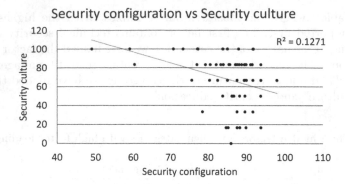

Fig. 8. The relationship between security configuration and security culture.

5 Discussion

Our analysis of security management maturity and technical security performance revealed very low correlation values in general. The lacking correlation may be caused by organizational barriers between staff working with security management and staff working with technical security. An example of such a barrier may be that security management personnel and technical security staff are located in different parts of the organization and rarely communicate. The overall correlation as shown in Table 7 and 8 is actually negative with r-value at $-.11$ and ρ-value at $-.15$. If the negative correlation is correct, it would mean that a large focus on security management tasks may negatively impact technical security tasks. For example, may tasks such as maintaining an information security management system and conducting risk assessments take time from conducting technical security tasks such as security configurations and security testing.

Toftegaard's effect analysis of ISO/IEC 27001 certification indicated a negative effect of such certification on large-sized entities' technical security performance [8]. According to the author, a negative effect may be a consequence of technical expert staff standpoints that conflicts with the standard, a compliance focus instead of a security focus, or organizational distance between management staff and technical staff. The distance refers to cases where focus is put on independent security management work, rather than on cooperation between technical and management staff. As a result, there may be a socio-technical gap where security management principles are not producing the intended improvement of technical security performance.

5.1 Security Culture and Configuration - A Socio-Technical Gap

Our correlation analysis based on the categories identified in the factor analysis, showed a significant weak inverse correlation between security configuration and security culture. In practice, this means that those entities who reported a high level of maturity on threat awareness, digitalization risk and security culture in general, were likely to score lower on security configuration performance.

What we have discovered in this study is that the top layer of the SBC model "Ethical/Cultural" (Table 2) is not linked to the lowest managerial layer "Operational". The management's perception of a mature security culture and code of conduct is not reflected in the operational configuration management. As technical security is directly affected by the configuration, we call this a socio-technical gap.

The gap we have discovered fits well with the socio-technical gap described in 2000 by Ackerman [20]. According to Ackerman, a socio-technical gap is "the divide between what we know we must support socially and what we can support technically". In his work, Ackerman identified a socio-technical gap where technological implementation did not provide the necessary feasibility to meet social requirements. In other words, the social-cultural expectations, similar to the managerial-cultural expectations in our case, did not match the actual implementation on the operative layer.

5.2   Validity Evaluation

There are weaknesses in our study that may have affected the outcome. 67 entities' is a low number of subjects for a correlation analysis. If we compare with the statistical analysis in [10], where correlation between technical security indicators and botnet infections was found using BitSight's security rating tool, the authors analyzed data from 37.000 entities. BitSight's security rating tool is similar to the tools from BlackKite and Security Scorecard.

We also have a weakness in that passive techniques were used for the collection of technical security scores. As a result, we only have a picture of the security state as seen from outside the entities' IT systems. We are unaware of what measures the entities may have implemented behind their firewalls or in their industrial control systems. Further, website security may for many of the assessed entities have been operated by a service provider. More intrusive tests such as traditional penetration tests and configuration analysis may have given other results.

The lack of strong correlation between overlapping categories as shown in Table 6, indicates that BlackKite and Security Scorecard are applying different techniques for security rating. For patching, for example, BlackKite seems to emphasize whether patches are installed or not, while Security Scorecard seems to focus on how fast patches are installed. This indicates that these vendors measure different things, which could be a challenge for reliability if using other cybersecurity rating vendors such as the previously mentioned BitSight.

The histograms in Fig. 1 and 2 show that the entities in our study had a common high level of cybersecurity. The little variation in the data used for our correlation analysis made our study extra challenging, especially when most of our data is based on ordinal data.

6   Conclusion

Our analysis did not show any clear correlation between the tested security management scores and technical security scores. The low correlation in general supports the H_0 hypothesis, that there is no correlation between the state of security management maturity and the state of technical security performance.

However, a factor analysis was used to identify three hidden factors, where a significant weak negative correlation was found between the factors "Security configuration" and "Security culture". The significant inverse relationship between these two subsets of technical and managerial security was surprising, as the main hypothesis (H_1) was that the state of security management maturity will correlate directly with the state of technical security performance. Therefore, we argue our data shows a socio-technical gap between the cultural layer and the operational layer with a negative effect on technical security. As the gap detaches the security management domain from the technical security domain, an entity's security management maturity cannot be used as an indicator of its technical security performance.

There were weaknesses in our study that may have impacted the results, such as few observations and a limited scope of our assessment. To address these weaknesses, a next step would be to score technical security based on an internal assessment of the entities' IT networks.

Disclosure of Interests. The authors have no competing interests to declare that are relevant to the content of this study.

References

1. Rumsey, D.: Statistics For Dummies, 2nd edn. Wiley, Hoboken (2016)
2. Security Scorecard: Consistent, data-driven ratings. https://securityscorecard.com/product/security-ratings. Accessed 24 Aug 2022
3. Tripwire: Mind the Cybersecurity Gap. https://www.tripwire.com/solutions/compliance-solutions/mind-the-cybersecurity-compliance-gap. Accessed 24 Aug 2022
4. Tucker, P.: An experiment showed that the military must change its cybersecurity approach. Defence One (2022)
5. Mujinga, M., Eloff, M., Kroeze, J.: A socio-technical approach to information security. In: 23rd Americas Conference on Information Systems, USA (2017)
6. Kowalski, S.: IT-insecurity: a multi-disciplinary inquiry. Doctoral thesis, Royal Institute of Technology, Stockholm, Sweden (1994)
7. Rajamäki, J.: Challenges to a smooth-running data security audits. In: Joint Intelligence and Security Informatics Conference, pp. 240–243 (2014)
8. Toftegaard, Ø.: An effect analysis of ISO/IEC 27001 certification on technical security of norwegian grid operators. In: 2022 IEEE International Conference on Big Data (Big Data), Osaka, Japan, pp. 2620–2629 (2022)
9. Chang, S.E., Chen, S.-Y., Chen, C.-Y.: Exploring the relationships between IT capabilities and information security management. Int. J. Technol. Manage. **54**, 147–166 (2011)

10. Edwards, B., Jacobs, J., Forrest, S.: Risky business: assessing security with external measurements (2019). http://arxiv.org/abs/1904.11052. Accessed 16 Aug 2022
11. BlackKite: Technical Cyber Rating. https://blackkite.com/technical-grade/. Accessed 15 Aug 2022
12. European Commission: SME definition. https://single-market-economy.ec.europa.eu/smes/sme-definition_en. Accessed 18 Aug 2022
13. Tøien, F., Fagermyr, J., Treider, G., Remvang, H.: IKT-sikkerhetstilstanden i kraftforsyningen. Norwegian Water Resources and Energy Directorate, Oslo (2021)
14. Proff: Kreditt- og Markedsverktøy. https://forvalt.no/. Accessed 18 Aug 2022
15. Svensen, T., Kallseter, K., Husabø, S.: Bruk av digitale verktøy i tilsyn med IKT-sikkerhet. Norwegian Water Resources and Energy Directorate, Oslo (2020)
16. Regjeringen: Statlig tilsyn med kommunesektoren. https://www.regjeringen.no/no/dokumenter/nou-2004-17/id386918/?ch=14. Accessed 22 Aug 2022
17. Bundesnetzagentur: Catalogue of IT security requirements. https://www.bundesnetzagentur.de/EN/Areas/Energy/Companies/SecurityOfSupply/ITSecurity/start.html. Accessed 22 Aug 2022
18. International Organization for Standardization: Guidelines for auditing management systems, ISO Standard No. 19011:2018. https://www.iso.org/standard/70017.html. Accessed 20 Aug 2022
19. Steffens, T.: Attribution of Advanced Persistent Threats, 1st edn. Springer, Heidelberg (2020). https://doi.org/10.1007/978-3-662-61313-9
20. Ackerman, M.S.: Intellectual challenge of CSCW: the gap between social requirements and technical feasibility. Hum.-Comput. Interact. **15**(2–3), 179–203 (2000)

Short Papers

Short Papers

Climate Change Risk Framework Using Complex Interdependent Critical Systems (Short Paper)

Andrea T. J. Martí[1]([✉])[iD] and José R. Martí[2][iD]

[1] Department of Civil Engineering, The University of British Columbia, Vancouver, B.C., Canada
andytjm@student.ubc.ca
[2] Department of Electrical and Computer Engineering, The University of British Columbia, Vancouver, B.C., Canada
jrms@ece.ubc.ca

Abstract. Canada encompasses a band of territory that extends from the glaciers in the Arctic to the agricultural areas on Parallel 49th at the border with the United States. As such, the territory is sensitive to various natural disasters, from floods to wildfires to windstorms and heat waves. The balance of the different regions in the territory is such that one or two degrees of change have large consequences, such as the increase in intense wildfires and droughts. These disasters greatly affect the livability of the communities settled in these landscapes, particularly the coastal and northern First Nations communities. This paper describes how to consider the interdependencies among infrastructures and the social cost of disasters for more detailed risk assessment indices under severe climatic events.

Keywords: Resilience metrics · Complex interdependent systems · Risk assessment tools

1 Context of the Work

1.1 The Relationship Between Climate Change and Natural Hazards

Climate change is the natural, long-term change in the Earth's atmospheric, land and water weather conditions. It is measured as the 30-year average global surface temperature (in degrees) relative to the baseline of pre-industrial levels (0° C from the years 1850–1900) [1]. However, with the increase in human industrial activities, the time window at which these changes occur has shown to be shortening, with a steady increase in surface temperature since 1960. In 2022, temperatures reached roughly 1.24°C above the 1850–1900 baseline [13]. This direct relationship between human activities is prominent when observing that the rise in global surface temperature change from the years 2000–2023 (20

S. Pickl et al. (Eds.): CRITIS 2023, LNCS 14599, pp. 245–255, 2024.
https://doi.org/10.1007/978-3-031-62139-0_14

years) was approximately the same as the rise in temperature in 40 years, from 1960 to 2000 (0.5°C and 0.6°C respectively [13]).

The relationship between the increase in global surface temperature and the increasing frequency and severity of natural hazards in Canada is also prominent. For example, the 40-year cycle from 1960 to 2000 corresponded to approximately 21,769 wildfires in Canada, while the 20-year cycle from 2000 to 2023 had roughly five times more wildfires in Canada (104,941 wildfires) and cost 22 times more (in $-million) [14]. This rise in temperature also causes the melting of glaciers and polar ice, increasing sea levels, which may result in floods and landslides impacting the same communities that had undergone a severe wildfire season [4]. In addition to short-term disasters, there are long-term ecological consequences from the sudden changes in weather patterns, such as altered animal and insect ecosystems that affect pollination, seed dispersal, and soil health and stability. These, in turn, increase the likelihood of future disasters [10].

1.2   Quantifying Risk in Interdependent Systems

In modern systems, all critical infrastructures are interconnected and something as pervasive as climate change affects all engineering and social structures with varying degrees of impact. Traditionally, risk indices are calculated by the planners of each infrastructure (e.g., the power grid) as cost on business that is not delivered by that infrastructure because of damage in the infrastructure.

Traditionally, risk calculations do not consider the business not delivered by other infrastructures due to problems in the first infrastructure and do not consider the cost of a lower wellbeing level in the affected communities. In terms of impact on the community, all lack of services, regardless of which infrastructure is directly responsible, affect the community's total wellbeing level, and the combined true risk for the society should include all infrastructures and social and personal costs. This paper presents a methodology to include these costs in calculating the risk index.

2   Climate Risk Assessment Frameworks

2.1   The Risk Equation

The concept of risk is widely used across disciplines to convey the idea of the cost of recovering from disasters. We adopt here the concept that is used in insurance industries to determine customer premiums [6]:

$$Risk\ for\ Given\ Event = Likehood\ of\ the\ Hazard \times Cost\ of\ Recovery \quad (1)$$

The period for the calculation is determined by the period of payment of the premiums. The recovery cost usually refers to the reimbursement cost of rebuilding the damaged asset. In the case of natural disasters, it can be directly seen that Eq. 1 does not consider the cost in terms of the wellbeing of the society or the individual.

2.2 The Traditional Framework

Climate risk frameworks are used to assess the effects of climate-induced impact on communities. International standards such as the ISO 14090:2019 [7] and the ISO 14090:2021 [8] are used as guidelines for institutions to develop adaptation plans in terms of vulnerability, impact and risk [3]. The results of such risk assessment studies are to identify and prioritize which areas of the community are most vulnerable to various climate change impacts [11].

Most climate risk assessment frameworks for communities define a value for risk (a risk index) as a function of how often the climate event happens, its severity, and its consequences [11]. Both quantitative and qualitative approaches can be used to assess risk, in which a qualitative assessment is usually made from quantitative information. An example of a qualitative approach is the risk matrix, which assigns likelihood and consequence values from 1 to 5 (very low to very high) in a matrix. Examples of the quantitative approach include using probability theory to calculate the probability of exceedance for each impact [2] or taking the geometric mean between the hazard, vulnerability, and lack of coping capacity, such as in the INFORM risk methodology [12], where risk is calculated as risk $=$ hazard/exposure$^{1/3}$ $\times$ vulnerability$^{1/3}$ $\times$ lack of coping capacity$^{1/3}$.

The main limitation of these traditional Risk evaluation methods is the lack of resolution of the Risk index with respect to the constituent factors. The method presented in this paper establishes relationships between the final Risk value and each one of the selected factors.

2.3 Proposed i2SIM Framework

The tool used to implement the relationships among the Risk factors is the Infrastructures Interdependencies Simulator i2SIM [5]. With i2SIM, we can integrate the causes of the damage and the effect of mitigating actions, and we can combine the consequences into a single global objective, which we can optimize to decrease the Risk.

In Eq. 1, the first term, *Probability of Occurrence* of the event (e.g., a Level 5 fire every two years), is a statistical variable determined by nature and the environment and is beyond the scope of this paper. The second term, the *Cost of Recovery*, depends on the damage caused by the event's magnitude and can be ameliorated by static and dynamic actions. Static actions include increasing the system's robustness by reinforcing the physical structures and planning the response of the population and first responders. Dynamic actions include early warning and quick optimized response.

In terms of costs, we consider not only the monetary cost of restoring the damaged structures (insurance companies) but also the cost of reduced quality of life in the affected communities.

3   Infrastructure Interdependencies Simulator (i2SIM)

i2SIM [5] provides a schematic building tool to connect the functional units of a system and optimize the value of a Global Objective Function. The basic functional units are called Cells (or "Production Cells") that describe the nonlinear relationships between inputs and outputs of a "factory." For example, a hospital Cell takes as inputs patients, electricity, water, doctors, nurses, medicines, instruments, etc., to produce treated patients.

In order to relate the inputs and output of a Cell, a table called the Human Readable Table (HRT) is defined. This table is then mapped into a Cell function with the form

$$y(\text{Cell}) = \min\{f_1(\text{input}_1), f_2(\text{input}_2), ..., f_n(\text{input}_n)\} \tag{2}$$

The functions f_1, f_2, ... are generally nonlinear and saturate at very low and very high values. The input variables input_1, input_2, ... are independent of each other. Equation 2 corresponds to Leontief production function [9] except that in Leontief's, the functions f_1, f_2, ... are linear and do not saturate. i2SIM's generality in the definition of the input and output functions allows it to represent a large number of physical and non-physical variables and behaviours.

The input or output variables in i2SIM can be physical variables, like the amount of CO_2 released to the atmosphere per day, or soft variables, like the wellbeing of a city. The data to populate the HRT tables can come from operational information data sheets (e.g., how much electricity is needed to operate the water station pumps), expert opinions (interviews and tabletop exercises) or historical data and literature reviews, and can also include human variables, such as the level of training and tiredness of the human operators. The variables in i2SIM are called Tokens and are visualized as flowing in the system. Tokens are generated in Sources that can be internal in the represented system or can come from the outside through Feeds.

The output of the Cells is connected to a Distributor that chooses how to split the output into the input flowing to other Cells. Distributors connect to other Cells through Channels that may have losses and time delays. The "distributor factors" control this allocation and are optimized by i2SIM to obtain the highest possible value of the Global Objective Function. The topological connections among Cells can be radial or can form forward or feedback loops.

The i2SIM Cells and other components represent a high-level equivalent of the actual system details, which is enough from an operational and management point of view to optimize the decisions that will result in the highest value of the Objective Function.

4   Case Study

4.1   Simulation Scenario with i2SIM

The case study presented is based on the Report "Preliminary Strategic Climate Risk Assessment for British Columbia" [11]. The study assesses climate-change consequences on Health, Social Functioning, Cultural Resources, Natural Resources, Economic Vitality, and direct Financial Costs to the B.C. Government. These consequences are assessed on a subjective scale from Insignificant (Value = 1) to Catastrophic (Value = 5). The analysis is repeated for several risk events.

The event "Severe Wildfire Season" (a season with a burn higher than one million hectares affecting nearby communities) is studied in this paper using the i2SIM methodology. In the traditional approach [11], a coarse view of the relationships among the physical and social infrastructures is made based on experiential evaluations. A final ranking of the consequences of the event (Level 5 wildfire) on a number of categories (Health, Social Functioning, Natural Resources, Economic Vitality, Cost to Provincial Government) is made based on the opinion of the experts. This results in a Ranking from 1–5 for each sector. These rankings are then normally averaged out arithmetically to get the Risk Index.

Where i2SIM is useful is that it provides a fine granularity in modelling the relationships and interdependencies among the infrastructures and the sectors. In addition, i2SIM can consider the Responders' actions to ameliorate the event's severity. For example, in the study, we consider how response actions can reduce the severity of a Level 5 to an equivalent Level 1 or Level 2 fire by preventing the fire from reaching homes and infrastructures.

4.2   Building the i2SIM Schematic

Figure 1 below shows the i2SIM case setup. On the left side, we consider how the responders' actions determine the direction of wildfire propagation. On the right side, we show the Critical Infrastructure Cells that affect the community's wellbeing. These Cells are physical infrastructure (i.e., water station, electric power supply, wastewater plant, transportation routes available) and socioeconomic infrastructures (i.e., economic loss, health, emergency responders, level of clean air and water). The Cells are chosen based on the Consequences Evaluation of [11] but are expanded into more detail for our study.

By detailing the interdependencies among infrastructures with i2SIM, we can, for example, determine which infrastructures need more reinforcement before the disaster happens and, after the disaster, determine the priority of restoration to bringing back the community's wellbeing as fast as possible.

4.3   Populating the HRTs

Tables 1, 2, 3, 4 and 5 show the HRTs for a sample of Cells in Fig. 1. Table 1 shows the Illness HRT. The inputs to this Cell are Clean Air, Clean Water, and Wildfire. In i2SIM, the input functions to the HRT need to be monotonically increasing since we want to improve the output ("production"). To comply with this requirement, we make the output of the Illness HRT to be "Non-Illness", and the inputs to be "Clean Air", "Clean Water", and "Non-Wildfire."

Table 1 shows, in bold, the reference scenario when the wildfire severity is at a level 5 (non-wildfire of 1), but the effect on clean air and clean water is not very

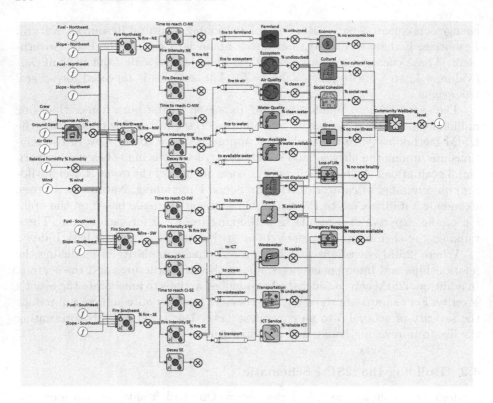

Fig. 1. Cost in terms of Community Wellbeing.

severe. For this scenario, 75% of the population does not incur new illnesses. The value in italics in Table 1 shows the scenario when an original wildfire of Severity 5 is dampened down to Severity 3 by the wildfire responder's actions. However, the smoke and air quality were not directly affected by the responder's actions, and the air quality was still reduced by 40% (clean air of 60%) because the fire was still burning at Severity 5 elsewhere even though the flames were prevented from reaching the communities and infrastructures. It is assumed that the water quality was only reduced by 10% (clean water of 95%).

Tables 2 and 3 show two examples of HRTs related to the environment. Suppose the amount of ecosystem non-degradation is 93% (row 4). In that case, the wildfire intensity is the limiting factor in Eq. 2, and both the Air Quality Cell and the Water Quality Cell are operating at row 5 with an output of 40% good air quality and 80% good water quality.

Table 4 shows the Economic Sector HRT as an example of a social infrastructure sector affected indirectly by the wildfire. The HRT was populated based on the traditional assessment of [11], where, for example, when economic losses surpassed $1 billion, the consequence was ranked at a Severity level of 5/5. For the HRT, this value was converted to 99.5% loss of economic productivity (0.5% no loss of economic productivity).

Table 1. Illness HRT.

Output Non-Illness (% of population)	Input Wildfire Non-Intensity (level)	Input Clean Air (%)	Input Good Water Quality (%)
100	5	100	100
99	4	90	95
95	3	80	90
85	2	60	85
7575	1	40	80

Table 2. Air Quality HRT.

Output Clean Air (%)	Input Wildfire Non-Intensity (level)	Input Ecosystem Non-Degradation (%)
100	5	100
90	4	99
80	3	95
60	2	93
40	1	90

Table 3. Water Quality HRT.

Output Good Water Quality (%)	Input Wildfire Non-Intensity (level)	Input Ecosystem Non-Degradation (%)
100	5	100
95	4	99
90	3	95
85	2	93
80	1	90

Table 4. Economic System HRT.

Output No Economic Loss (%)	Input Farmland Not Lost (%)	Input Non-displaced People (%)
100	100	100
10	99	99.8
5	95	92.3
1	93	77
0.5	90	67.2

4.4 Global Objective Cell

For the i2SIM Risk assessment method, the final Risk Index is the output of the Global Objective Cell. This Global Objective Cell needs to be defined according to the purpose of the assessment. For example, a purpose could be the monetary cost of restoring the damaged infrastructures in the system. This cost is of interest to the Insurance Companies. For this case, the i2SIM detailed participation of the constituent factors would show the responsibilities for this cost, for example, of the power utilities, water utilities, municipalities, etc. Responsibilities could include system reinforcement measures, such as building reinforcement, designing a more robust power grid, etc. Responsibilities are also the emergency response and recovery measures.

For our Wildfire Study, the Objective Function is Table 5. This table corresponds to the Risk Consequences table (Table 15 in [11]). The ranking in the traditional consequences table (1 - 5) is converted into columns in the HRT table. When filling in these columns, the values are skewed according to the weight of the rating in [11]. For example, a rating of 5 and 4 is given a positive skewing, while a rating of 2 and 1 is given a negative skewing. This skewing is somewhat arbitrary, and the mapping between these tables can be improved (for example, in [12], they propose geometric averaging rather than normal arithmetic averaging).

Table 5. Community Wellbeing HRT.

Output Community Wellbeing (level)	No deaths (%)	No illness (%)	Cultural and Psych. Health (%)	Homes available (%)	Power available (%)	Water available (%)	Sewage available (%)	Transportation available (%)	ICT available (%)	Economic health (%)	Social Cohesion (%)	Ecosystem Health (%)
5	100	100	100	100	100	100	100	100	100	100	100	100
4	90	95	95	90	90	90	90	90	90	95	95	90
3	75	85	85	75	75	75	75	75	75	85	85	75
2	60	70	70	60	60	60	60	60	60	70	70	60
1	40	60	60	40	40	40	40	40	40	60	60	40

4.5 Sensitivity to Response Actions

We calculated the sensitivity of the consequences when different response actions are taken to stop a severe wildfire from propagating toward homes and infrastructures. To compare with the traditional risk indices of [11], we mapped the i2SIM results to the normalized ranges used in [11], as follows: Score 0–5.9 = Low, Score 6–11.9 = Medium, Score 12–19.9 = High, Score 20–25 = Extreme.

The relationship between unnormalized and normalized is: Normalized = Percent × 25 /3, where 25 is for 5 discrete rankings assessments, and 3 is for a likelihood of the wildfire having a 50-year recurrence interval.

Table 6 shows the Risk Indices calculated with the i2SIM model of Fig. 1 for different Disaster Response Scenarios. The scenarios are described below and correspond to different actions of the wildfire responders to protect the infrastructures. The level of damage of the infrastructure is characterized as a weight, on a scale of 1–5, with 1 as the least damage and 5 as the most damage.

For each scenario, the input values for the considered variables are given by the sequence {Air Quality, Water Quality, Ecosystem, Farmland, Transportation, Homes, Power System, Water System, Wastewater System, ICT Service, Fatalities, Illness}. For example, the sequence {3, 3, 3, 4, 3, 1, 4, 3, 3, 4, 1, 1} in Scenario 2 means that the Air Quality level is 3, the Water Quality Level is 3, ..., the Power System Level is 4, ... in their corresponding HRTs.

In Table 6, Scenario 1 is the reference case in which no response action is taken, and the wildfire affects each infrastructure with the same severity of level 5. The Risk Index for this case was 59.7%.

In Scenario 2, response actions were taken to protect the transportation routes, homes, water supply, and wastewater system. As a result, the air quality and water quality were impacted less, resulting in fewer illnesses and deaths. As a result, the Risk Index decreased to 31.6%.

In Scenario 3, response actions were taken to protect, in addition to the infrastructures in Scenario 2, the power system and the communication towers. This led to a further reduction in the Risk Index to 23.9%.

Between Scenarios 2 and 3, a relatively large 8% reduction was achieved by protecting the power and ICT infrastructures. This shows the degree of interdependencies of these systems with other infrastructures (i.e., power is required for water and wastewater plants; ICT availability is required for the community to have a higher sense of social cohesion).

Table 6. The Three Scenarios and their Input Variables and Final Risk Indices.

Scenario	Damage Vector {$\bar{x}$}	I2SIM Risk Index (%)	Normalized Risk Index (level)
1	{5, 5, 5, 5, 5, 5, 5, 5, 5, 5, 5, 5}	59.7	(54%) High
2	{3, 3, 3, 4, 3, 1, 4, 3, 3, 4, 1, 1}	31.6	High
3	{3, 3, 3, 4, 3, 1, 1, 3, 3, 1, 1, 1}	23.9	Low-Medium

4.6   Risk Sensitivity to Increased Robustness Prior to the Event

Measures that increase the robustness of the system prior to the event can be expensive. However, similar to the response affecting the equivalent level of the event, increased robustness can make a Level 5 event have consequences of a Level 3 or 2 event. Given that the power infrastructure is critical for the operation of the other infrastructures, building an alternative supply line can reduce the Risk Index from that for a Level 5 fire to a Level 3 fire. For example, using Scenario 2 from Table 6, the Risk Index is reduced by 4% (from 31.6% to 27.5%), even when no response action is taken for its protection.

5   Conclusion

The Infrastructures Interdependencies Simulator i2SIM provides the tools to represent interdependencies among the sectors a natural disaster affects as they impact a community's wellbeing.

The HRT concept of saturation allows the inputs to maintain their physical (causal) nature. By formulating the consequences as a system of coupled non-linear equations, we can account for interdependencies in the consequence (cost) parameter of the Risk equation. i2SIM considers interdependencies and nonlinearities in the relationships among sectors, allowing for a higher resolution in focusing on the most sensitive parameters contributing to the Risk and taking reinforcement and response actions to protect these parameters.

For time-critical events, where response actions must match the dynamics of the hazard (e.g., changing wind speed within hours that changes the wildfire intensity in a particular direction), running i2SIM as a real-time simulator can inform of the level of consequences corresponding to different response actions and, therefore prioritize these actions.

This paper presented the methodology for a wildfire event, but can be applied equally to other natural disasters. For future work, we need a better assessment of the community wellbeing consequences of the degradation of the different sectors affected by a disaster. We also need to include the effect of specific climate change impacts, such as the CO_2 emissions from the economic sectors (transportation, construction, and manufacturing), that contribute to greenhouse gas emissions.

References

1. Allen, M., Dube, O., Solecki, W.: Global warming of 1.5°C. Technical report, The Intergovernmental Panel on Climate Change (2019)
2. Cox, L.A., Babayev, D., Huber, W.: Some limitations of qualitative risk rating systems. Risk Anal. **25**(3), 651–662 (2005)
3. Codes, standards and guidelines for climate resilience. Technical report, Government of Canada (2023)
4. Nesbit, Ben. Historically bad B.C.: wildfire season could be followed by floods, landslides in affected communities, expert says. CTV News, Vancouver, Canada. Accessed 2 Sep 2023 (2023)
5. i2SIM-RT Technologies: i2SIM Reference Manual. Vancouver, Canada (2023)
6. Insuranceopedia Staff: How do insurance companies calculate exposure?. Insuranceopedia. Accessed 13 June 2023 (2023)
7. Adaptation to climate change - Principles, requirements and guidelines. Technical report, International Organization for Standardization Standard No. 14090:2019 (2019)

8. Adaptation to climate change - Guidelines on vulnerability, impacts, and risk assessment. Technical report, International Organization for Standardization Standard No. 14090:2021 (2021)
9. Leontief, W.: Quantitative input and output relations in the economic system of the United States. Rev. Econ. Stat. **18**(3), 105–125 (1936)
10. Duffy, K., Gouhier, T.C., Ganguly, A.R.: Climate-mediated shifts in temperature fluctuations promote extinction risk. Nat. Clim. Chang. **12**, 1037–1044 (2022). https://doi.org/10.1038/s41558-022-01490-7
11. Preliminary strategic climate risk assessment for British Columbia. Report prepared for the Government of British Columbia, Victoria, BC. Technical report, ICF and the Ministry of Environment and Climate Change Stragety of British Columbia (2019)
12. Poljanšek, K., et al.: INFORM Climate Change Risk Index. Technical report, Joint Research Centre, European Commission (2022)
13. Rohde, R.: Global temperature report for 2022. Berkeley Earth (2024). Accessed 2023
14. The Canadian Disaster Database. Public Safety Canada, The Government of Canada. Accessed 2023

Emergency Resilience Closer to Citizens' Understanding (Short Paper)

Davide Prette[1][(✉)] , Matteo Maritano[1] , Jorge Joshua Campozano[1] ,
Filip Sever[2] , Jaakko Schroderus[3] , Fabio Perossini[4] , and Antonio Filograna[5]

[1] Volontariato Torino (Vol.To ETS), Via Giolitti 21, 10123 Torino, Italy
europa@volontariato.torino.it
[2] Kajaanin Ammattikorkeakoulu Oy (KAMK), Ketunpolku 3, 87100 Kajaani, Finland
filip.sever@kamk.fi
[3] Kainuun Pelastuslaitos (KAIPE), Opintie 1, 87100 Kajaani, Finland
jaakko.schroderus@kaipe.fi
[4] Kpeople Research Foundation (KPRF), Cornerstone Business Centre, Suite 1, Level 2, 16Th
September Square, Mosta Mst 1180, Malta
perossini@kpeople.com
[5] Engineering - Ingegneria Informatica Spa (ENG), Piazzale dell'Agricoltura 24, 00144 Roma,
Italy
antonio.filograna@eng.it

Abstract. In the last few years, the world population has been suffering from different forms of disasters such as natural, psychological and health (well-being), that are provoking a continuous status of (also emotional) emergency. The resilience of the population in history allowed the development of humanity up to the present day. In this paper, we present how the involvement of citizens in the policymaking process is an added value that helps to enhance emergency resilience during disaster risk management. This approach has been adopted in the DECIDO 101004605 project that aims to support the policy makers in the creation of data-driven policies along with the support of the citizens and the stakeholders, involved in the policy life cycle. The focus of this paper is the policy co-creation approach adopted in two of the cities involved in the project, the City of Turin (Italy) and the City of Kajaani (Finland). The concept of social hackathon was introduced, fostering innovation and inclusive policy solutions through interdisciplinary collaboration, and incorporating diverse viewpoints of various stakeholders.

Keywords: co-creation · policymaking · resilience

1 Introduction

Policies for prevention and preparedness are created in governmental organizations at the national and regional level. The government sets the agenda and guidelines, and regional organizations define and implement policies to fulfill the agenda. In addition to the work done by civil protection organizations, non-governmental and civil societies participate in activities for prevention, preparedness, and mitigation of disasters. Citizen engagement in the policy process is however limited and focuses on gathering feedback on draft policies. Existing literature shows that policy co-creation- is a viable approach in closing the knowledge gaps between disciplines and organizations [1].

2 Literature About Citizens' Resilience and Policy Development

In the context of disasters, resilience is defined as society's ability to mitigate disasters and their consequences, the ensuing loss of performance, and the time needed until full recovery [2]. Bergström [3] discussed how resilience has been established in the broader discourse on societal safety and security, proposing three conditions of possibility to establish resilience as an object of knowledge: *scientific availability, political needs and defining events*. Initially used in material physics to describe the material's ability to absorb energy [4], the term *resilience* has seen widespread adoption within science and beyond as it is intuitive and can be metaphorically understood. In psychology resilience describes the subjects' ability to thrive despite adversity, and as "a measure of persistence of systems and their ability to absorb change and disturbance and still maintain the same relationships between populations or state variables" [5]. For *political needs*, the aim is to incentivize citizens to organize their own safety and security. For *defining events*, providing validity and credibility of the real-life events through post-event discussions. To reduce the citizens' vulnerability and increase resilience, voluntary participation is required, through which learning can occur. A community-based approach empowers citizens in natural disaster management and decreases their vulnerability [6]. Therefore, policy development needs to look for the inclusion of civil society in the policy development process.

3 Method

3.1 Policy Co-creation

Policy co-creation is the process of involving citizens in the development of public services: it occurs when citizens participate actively in delivering and designing the services they receive [7]. For policy makers, citizens are seen as valuable contributors, possessing specific competencies and resources which are precious in developing public service delivery. However, the degree of implementation of co-creation in different countries depends on the influence of the state and the governance traditions. Examples from Estonia and the Netherlands show that where approaches and solutions to problems were identified, policy was changed in favor of co-creation. In Germany however, this occurred to a lesser extent, even though the type of governance in both Germany and the Netherlands is similar: formalized rules and procedures. The co-creation, learning and policy change processes occur to a higher degree if there is a tradition of working together with citizens, and society has a tradition of adherence to set processes and rules [8].

Citizens can contribute to policies through engagement in discussions, where policy makers should look to find reason and context to supplement further developments.

Information and data provide evidence which serves as the foundation to steer decision making and reasoning, whereas citizens can provide context and insights into where policies should aim to develop towards [9].

3.2 Hackathons and Policy Co-creation

The H2020 DECIDO 101004605 project utilizes a social hackathon approach to facilitate policy co-creation and citizen engagement. Social hackathons are events where public sector representatives, community members, end-users and other stakeholders are involved in co-creating solutions for challenges at the local level [10]. More specifically, in the H2020 DECIDO 101004605 project, the social hackathon serves as a key methodology to involve citizens, policymakers and practitioners in the development of policies related to prevention and preparedness.

Through the social hackathons in the DECIDO project, citizens are not only seen as passive recipients of policies but as active contributors and co-creators. Their perspectives, experiences, and local knowledge - seen as a form of non-academic new knowledge which is necessary in solving public problems [11] - are considered vital in shaping effective and context-specific policies. The hackathon process encourages open dialogue, interdisciplinary collaboration, and the integration of various stakeholders' viewpoints, fostering innovative and inclusive policy solutions. The hackathon participants, including citizens, policymakers, experts and practitioners, come together to brainstorm, ideate, and co-design policy interventions that enhance community resilience and disaster mitigation.

The outcomes of the social hackathons in the DECIDO project go beyond generating ideas. The collaborative efforts result in concrete policy recommendations, action plans, and prototypes that can be implemented and tested. The project ensures that the outcomes of the hackathons are translated into actionable policy interventions, thus making a tangible impact on disaster prevention and preparedness.

4 Results

4.1 Findings from the Italian Case

The Italian government has adopted a multifaceted approach to address emergencies, starting from the establishment of the Civil Protection Department as a key player in ensuring the safety and well-being of the population, providing support to regional and local authorities [12].

Each Italian region has its own Regional Civil Protection Agency, responsible for managing emergencies within its jurisdiction, working closely with the Civil Protection Department.

In November 2021, the Civil Protection Department and the Ministry of Education signed a memorandum of understanding to foster the dissemination of civil protection culture and good practices among the new generations [13]. This agreement reinforces good practices for raising awareness and training citizens that the Civil Protection Department has been carrying out for many years, such as the *"Io non rischio"* (I do not risk) communication campaign, which foresees many street events of awareness raising, with the contribution of voluntary associations at local level [14]. Furthermore, for fifteen years the Civil Protection Department has organised the *"Anch'io sono la protezione civile"* (I am the Civil Protection too) school camps, with the aim of enhancing the environmental protection skills of young people aged between 10 and 16 years old [15].

At the regional level, the Piedmont Civil Protection realizes yearly events linked to the *"Io non rischio"* campaign, as well as school camps for young people at the local level [16]. Also Volontariato Torino (Vol.To ETS), partner of the DECIDO project, is involved in the organisation of a yearly school camp for volunteers and students in collaboration with the Civil Protection of the Piedmont Region [17]. Moreover, the Civil Protection of the Piedmont Region organises two training courses for primary and secondary school classes, aimed at raising students' awareness about the risks of the area in which they live and the correct behaviour to adopt in the event of an emergency [18].

At local level, the Civil Protection Department has recognised the potential of the DECIDO project in improving emergency management in floods. It actively supported the implementation and adoption of the DECIDO project platform, which provides a centralised hub for data collection, analysis and visualisation, enabling local authorities to make informed choices based on real-time information. The DECIDO project foresees the active involvement of citizens who, through participation in co-creation sessions, contribute to the definition of new emergency intervention protocols. At the same time, a wider involvement of citizens leads to greater awareness of environmental protection and the dissemination of good practices to be adopted in the event of an emergency.

The request for opinions and views from citizens targeted by the mentioned campaigns - and concerning how to improve these campaigns themselves - still occurs on an occasional basis and tends not to involve the end-users: the hope is that the same methodology applied in the DECIDO project can soon be used for feedback concerning such important elements in building citizens' preparedness for emergencies.

4.2 Findings from the Finnish Case

The Kainuu case focuses on safety communication to citizens. Safety communication is one of the main tasks based on the Finnish Rescue Act. The Ministry of the Interior steers the rescue departments. The national agenda sets out the requirements that youth in Finland should be engaged four times in prevention and preparedness activities by the time they are 25 years old. To account for the needs and requirements of the various regions across Finland, citizens are closely engaged in co-creation towards the development of the national agenda on safety communication. Workshops are conducted with citizen groups representing non-government organizations such as village associations and other local groups [19]. This steering group consisting of government representatives and citizens proposes educational projects aimed at different age groups. Each regional rescue department chooses four of the activities to implement in their region. Once selected, a local fire officer contacts the municipal head for education and culture to begin preparations. The fire officer introduces the four-event concept which is to be carried out: the agreement for the activities is made on the municipal level, while practical arrangements are made separately with each kindergarten and school.

The first of the four safety communication activities are for kindergarten age children. An experiential learning method is used where children are introduced to firefighters' equipment, how to act in emergency, and that fire making equipment is for adults only. The teaching is carried out by the rescue departments. The next age group is second graders, approximately 8 years old. The learning program titled *"Palojärki"* includes an introductory session by the fire department, followed by 3 lessons given by their class teacher. The aim of the teaching is to communicate that electricity is the main reason for house fires, how to recognize broken devices, and act to reduce risks of accidents. The teaching materials are provided centrally by Finnish Rescue Association [20]. The third activity is around grade 8. It consists of a theoretical exam and practical competitions. The event is marketed age appropriately, with the support of social media influencers under the *"NouHätä!"* brand [21]. The project aims to teach young people what to do in case of an accident and reaches approximately 40,000 young people around Finland each year. The teaching materials are provided centrally by Finnish Rescue Association.The final activity, called *"Punainen Liitu"* takes place in upper secondary school, around the age of 16 to 19 [22]. The authorities tell of their experiences during traffic incidents. In addition, survivors who were severely injured in traffic accidents share personal experiences. After the guest session, students discuss what they heard with their class teachers. The sessions are organized by the Finnish Road Safety Council.

The feedback from the teachers and students participating is used to continuously improve the teaching contents and its delivery. If incidence rates of certain accidents change, the teaching contents are adjusted to address rising risks. The implementation of all four activities only started in 2022 in the Kainuu Region. The kindergarten activities and *"NouHätä!"* are organized across the Kainuu region for multiple years, while *"Palojärki"* and *"Punainen Liitu"* are in the process to cover the whole region. Based on co-creation sessions between the rescue department and faculty, the *"Palojärki"* and *"Punainen Liitu"* events have received constructive input for further improvements.

Reviews of the ongoing activities within the scope of the four events as well as other complimentary campaigns across Finland are evaluated annually. Stakeholder organizations consult incident data to measure the policy impacts within different cities, municipalities, and regions. Incident data and citizen feedback are used in parallel to measure policy impact and discover contextual information as to why incident rates may worsen or improve. Once examined, a policy update is drafted and published to citizens for consultation to collect public opinion on the proposed policy. Due to the sensitive nature of certain data, some information may be excluded from the draft. However, the decisions and reasoning for changes are included. Overall, the consultation process is well established, but does not prompt large numbers of citizens to engage in the process. At 64% of the population reporting trust in the government, Finland is above the 45% average of the OECD [23]. Much like in Germany and the Netherlands, the Finnish society has a high adherence to formalized rules and procedures.

5 Discussion and Conclusion

In line with Bergström's [3] reasoning, the four communication activities aim to: 1) build psychological resilience as part of societal growth through existing education channels, 2) which are planned and funded centrally, and implemented regionally by civil security bodies and education institutions, and 3) participation is legitimized through programs aimed at appropriate age groups and is supported through in-contact teaching organized by education institutions and regional rescue departments. The involvement of citizens is a key aspect to raise the awareness and resilience of population in emergency situations. Being a key actor, in the definition of a new policy or in the improvement of the existing one, feels the citizen at the core of the decision-making process. This leads to an easier acceptance of the new policy and the related rules to be followed. One of the most important aspects, emerged during the social hackathons, was the need for training to be prepared for an emergency. This is a key aspect in common in all the cities involved in the DECIDO project.

References

1. Liwång, H.: Defense development: the role of co-creation in filling the gap between policy-makers and technology development. Technol. Soc. **68** (2022).https://doi.org/10.1016/J.TEC HSOC.2022.101913
2. Giuliani, L., Revez, A., Sparf, J., Jayasena, S., Havbro Faber, M.: Social and technological aspects of disaster resilience. Int. J. Strateg. Prop. Manag. **20**(3), 277–290 (2016). https://doi.org/10.3846/1648715X.2016.1185477
3. Bergström, J.: An archaeology of societal resilience. Saf. Sci. **110**, 31–38 (2018). https://doi.org/10.1016/J.SSCI.2017.09.013
4. _University of Washington, http://depts.washington.edu/matseed/mse_resources/Webpage/definitions/def_resilience.htm
5. Holling, C.S.: Resilience and stability of ecological systems. Annu. Rev. Ecol. Syst. **4**, 1–23 (1973). https://doi.org/10.1146/annurev.es.04.110173.000245
6. Nodez, A.S., Yaghoubi, N.M., Keikha, A.: The effect of community-based crisis management on the resilience to disasters with the mediating role of social capital. Int. J. Hum. Capital Urban Manage 7(2), 205–216. https://doi.org/10.22034/IJHCUM.2022.02.05
7. Brandsen, T., Steen, T., Verschuere, B.: Co-production and Co-Creation. Engaging Citizens in Public Services. Routledge - Taylor & Francis, New York. p.1 (2018). https://doi.org/10.4324/9781315204956
8. Voorberg, W., Bekkers, V., Timeus, K., Tonurist, P., Tummers, L.: Changing public service delivery: learning in co-creation. Pol. Soc. **36**(2), 178–194 (2017). https://doi.org/10.1080/14494035.2017.1323711
9. Mattioni, D.: Constructing a food retail environment that encourages healthy diets in cities: the contribution of local-level policy makers and civil society. Int. J. Sociol. Agric. Food Paris France **27**(1), 87–101 (2021). https://doi.org/10.48416/ijsaf.v27i1.81
10. Kangro, K., Lepik, K.-L.: Co-creating public services in social hackathons: adapting the original hackathon concept. Public Money Manage. **42**(5), 341–348. Routledge - Taylor & Francis, New York (2022). https://doi.org/10.1080/09540962.2021.1940584
11. Sutley, E.J., Lyles L.W.: Theory of change: community engagement as an intervention to create disaster resilience. Front. Built Environ. Sec. Earthquake Eng. **9** (2023). https://doi.org/10.3389/fbuil.2023.1172659
12. Protezione Civile: https://www.protezionecivile.gov.it/it/
13. _Protocollo d'intesa: https://giovani.protezionecivile.gov.it/it/protocollo-dintesa-con-minist ero-dellistruzione/
14. Io non rischio: https://iononrischio.protezionecivile.it/it/
15. Campi scuola: https://www.protezionecivile.gov.it/it/approfondimento/anch-io-sono-la-pro tezione-civile--l-edizione-2019-dei-campi-scuola/

16. Campi scuola Piemonte: https://www.regione.piemonte.it/web/temi/protezione-civile-difesa-suolo-opere-pubbliche/protezione-civile/campi-scuola-anchio-sono-protezione-civile
17. Campo scuola Vol.To: https://www.volontariatotorino.it/presentata-la-xii-edizione-del-campo-scuola-di-protezione-civile/
18. Formazione Scuole: https://www.regione.piemonte.it/web/temi/protezione-civile-difesa-suolo-opere-pubbliche/
19. Safe and incident-free daily life 2025. Publications of the Ministry of the Interior 2019:36. https://julkaisut.valtioneuvosto.fi/bitstream/handle/10024/161958/SM_2019_36.pdf?sequence=1&isAllowed=y. Accessed 11 May 2023
20. _Palojärki: https://sites.google.com/view/palojarki/etusivu?authuser=0. Accessed 02 May 2023
21. NouHätä!: https://nouhata.fi/. Accessed 02 May 2023
22. Punainen Liitu: https://www.liikenneturva.fi/liikenteessa/nuorten-liikennekasvatus/
23. OECD, Drivers of Trust in Public Institutions in Finland, Building Trust in Public Institutions, OECD Publishing, Paris (2021).https://doi.org/10.1787/52600c9e-en

Development of Easy Risk Assessment Tool for Factory Cybersecurity: Short Paper

Hiroshi Sasaki[1,2]($\boxtimes$) (iD) and Kenji Watanabe[1]

[1] Nagoya Institute of Technology, Gokiso-cho, Showa, Nagoya, Japan
watanabe.kenji@nitech.ac.jp
[2] Manufacturing and Innovation DX Laboratory, Nagoya Institute of Technology, Gokiso-cho, Showa, Nagoya, Japan
h.sasaki.543@stn.nitech.ac.jp

Abstract. In the context of digital transformation (DX) worldwide, the digitization of factory systems is advancing and digital connections between supply chains are increasing. For example, sharing order and delivery information and sharing CO_2 emissions from factories as a decarbonization effort increases for achieving SDGs. With the increase in digital connections, the cybersecurity risks of factory systems are also increasing, and there have been many incidents of factories being shut down due to ransomware attacks. Large enterprises such as critical infrastructure (CI) can allocate budgets for cybersecurity and hire personnel, including outsourcing, but small and medium-sized enterprises(SMEs) making up the supply chain find it difficult to secure budgets and personnel. This paper presents a simplified and easy risk assessment method for factory systems using the checklist which has only 32 items from Japanese government. It provides support to SMES to improve their cybersecurity readiness of factory assets with lower cost. For the purpose, we newly developed the web based diagnostic tool of the checklist showing the risk score. We confirmed the tool provides the rough grasping of cybersecurity readiness from interviews. We also observed that 80% of the respondents indicate insufficient readiness. The easy risk visualization will help SMEs to allocate the appropriate budget and resources.

Keywords: Operational technology (OT) security · Risk management · impact and consequence analysis regarding C(I)I. · Risk assessment tool for factory system

1 Introduction

With the advancement of digitization of OT systems in factories, they have become more vulnerable to cyber attacks, leading to an increase in incidents that result in business interruptions and other consequences. Additionally, there is a growing demand for carbon-neutral businesses globally, and factories are

S. Pickl et al. (Eds.): CRITIS 2023, LNCS 14599, pp. 263–269, 2024.
https://doi.org/10.1007/978-3-031-62139-0_16

beginning to visualize and share their CO_2 emissions along the supply chain. As the data connections between factories increase, cybersecurity measures become a prerequisite for business participation since an unprotected player on the supply chain could cause harm to other businesses.

Despite the increasing importance of cybersecurity for factory systems, including CI, many enterprises are still not taking sufficient measures. This is due to the difficulty of assessing the level of risk associated with factory systems, making it hard to determine the appropriate level of investment required. This study aims to take the first step towards promoting cybersecurity measures for factory systems by visualizing the security risks associated with the current posture of factory systems and presenting an easy risk assessment method that can be used to obtain budget and personnel resources.

2   Prior Research

The following standard and framework are known as prior researches on cybersecurity risk assessment for factory systems. The most well-known international standards are ISA/IEC 62443 series, mainly focused on the security of industrial control systems. IEC 62443-3-3 which has 128 Items is often used by the requirement of OT system procurement along its security level in plant automation industry [5]. More details have been presented earlier [6,8].

The NIST Cybersecurity Framework (CSF) is also a very popular and voluntary framework to help organizations manage and reduce cybersecurity risk [9]. The framework provides a set of guidelines and best practices (108 items) that organizations can use to assess their current cybersecurity posture, identify gaps and weaknesses, and develop a plan for improving cybersecurity. More details on the NIST guidelines have been presented earlier [4,7].

The Cybersecurity Evaluation Tool (CSET)is a software tool to help organizations assess and improve their cybersecurity posture [2]. CSET is specifically designed for industrial control systems, used in CI sectors. It provides recommendations for improving the organization's cybersecurity program, based on industry best practices and standards such as NIST CSF and ISA/IEC 62443. CSET is designed to be flexible and customizable, and can be used by organizations of all sizes and types. The tool is free to download and use, and is regularly updated to reflect changes in cybersecurity threats and best practices. One challenge is CSET does not adhere to guidelines in Japan. More details have been presented earlier [1,11].

These previous studies are already very useful for companies and organizations that have established management system and secure budgets in factory systems. However, for SMEs with a few resources, it is a high hurdle because the number of requirements of the previous studies is over 100. It also needs a cybersecurity specialist for factory systems. In addition, it is difficult especially for the executives with low awareness, to understand the evaluation results, resulting security measures cannot be progressed.

Table 1. List of Items and Weight

Category	No	Item	Weight
People	1-1	The decision maker (factory manager, company manager, etc.) or management is aware of the need for security of factory systems, is in a position to obtain cooperation in terms of sufficient budget and personnel allocation.	4
	1-2	Cooperation and linkage arrangements are in place between the information system division, production related divisions, and other relevant divisions and departments to ensure the security of factory systems.	2
	1-3	The factory system security review organization and the person in charge are prepared, and the responsibilities and business contents are clarified.	4
	1-4	A person in charge in the event of a factory security accident* is prepared, and responsibilities and business contents are clarified, accident is prepared, and responsibilities and business contents are clarified.	3
	1-5	Provide on-site training such as receiving regular information and holding study sessions on trends in threats related to factory security.	1
Process	2-1	The risks to the business in the event of a system breach or outage are considered.	4
	2-2	Dedicated security policies in the factory system are specified and recognized.	3
	2-3	E-mail and Internet access** from the factory system is prohibited by the policy.	3
	2-4	Responsible person's response to the occurrence of security anomalies in the factory system is clarified.	2
	2-5	On-site workers understand and are trained on how to respond to security anomalies in factory systems.	2
	2-6	A ledger of devices (servers, client terminals, network equipment, facilities, etc.) connected to the factory network is created, including the use of information asset detection tools, and a system configuration diagram is created.	4
	2-7	A wireless LAN is installed in the factory, a system is in place to create a ledger of devices authorized to connect to the network and reject unauthorized devices.	3
	2-8	Periodic vulnerability assessments and penetration tests are conducted to identify attack methods and vulnerabilities that can be used to successfully infiltrate the system.	4
	2-9	Restrictions on the use and bringing of external storage media (USB memory sticks, flash cards) and portal media into the plant.	4
	2-10	There are password rules for systems in the factory, including password strength and expiration dates. (Excluding terminals such as display units that require emergency response related to safety).	3
	2-11	Old accounts (e.g., retirees, transferees, etc.) that are not in use with access rights to systems in the plant are deleted.	3
	2-12	For connected devices in the factory network, there is a procedure to verify in advance that they are not infected with viruses.	4
	2-13	Backups are made with the assumption of complete restoration of system functions, and tests of restoration from backup data are conducted periodically. In addition, the procedure is clarified.	2
Technology	3-1	Anti-virus software or application white lists are installed on terminals where anti-virus measures can be installed, and some alternative measures (e.g., USB-type anti-virus) are installed on terminals where installation is not possible.	4
	3-2	Security patches are applied to the application/operating system (OS). Or alternative measures are in place.	4
	3-3	Services and applications using the control terminal operating system are kept to the minimum necessary, and unused services and ports are stopped or disabled.	4
	3-4	Sufficient measures, such as level classification, are taken for physical access to important factory equipment. Or alternative operational measures are in place such as access control and escort of relevant personnel to outside visitors.	3
	3-5	Within the factory network, network segment management is conducted according to security level (e.g., VLANs).	3
	3-6	Protective measures such as authentication (e.g., two factor authentication) and network intrusion protection are taken when external internet access is possible for the purpose of remote maintenance of factory systems, etc	3
	3-7	A network detection/protection system is in place to identify suspicious communications on the factory network (including the boundary with the information system)	2
	3-8	Event logs of logins, operation histories, etc. of the factory's internal systems are being collected. Those logs are periodically analyzed or stored for the required number of days.	2
Supply chain risk management for factory asset	4-1	A liaison and coordination system has been established with control system vendors and construction companies to respond to security incidents in factory systems.	2
	4-2	Conducting security training for subcontractors involved in factory system maintenance, etc.	2
	4-3	A system for communication and coordination with control system vendors/builders is in place to ensure that information is shared promptly when security vulnerabilities related to delivered factory systems are discovered.	2
	4-4	Aware of threats to factory systems in the supply chain (subcontractors, production subsidiaries, etc.), the degree of impact, and the status of response (e.g., implementation of audits, etc.)	2
	4-5	Has a process to determine whether the factory system equipment to be delivered meets certain security standards, and an acceptance inspection.	2
	4-6	Security requirements are clarified in the design specification requirements for new system implementation.	4

Note: *accident = incident, **internet access means "web browsing by operators", does not include "internet connection of factory system"

Table 2. Selection Item and Score

Selection item	Risk Score
0.Not applicable	0.5
1. Not implemented	0.2
2. Partially implemented	0.4
3. Implemented	0.6
4. Implemented, control procedures are documented and automated, and measures are periodically reviewed	0.8
5. Implemented, control procedures are documented and automated, and reviewed as needed to check the current status	0.9

Table 3. Score and evaluation definition

Score	0-100	Individual items and answers (0-5) on the check sheet are weighted to score the status of security measures. When all items are selected as "implemented", Score(%) is equal to 60 and Evaluation is "B". It is easy for SMEs to understand Score and Evaluation look like a school examination.
Evaluation	Score(%)	Explanation
A	80-	Most necessary measures are in place and procedures are documented. Risks have been sufficiently reduced, and continuous improvements are being made.
B	60-79	Most necessary measures are in place, but procedures are not documented. Risks have been reduced, but there are issues with continuous improvement.
C	40-59	Inadequate implementation of most necessary measures. The risk has not been reduced, and it is assumed that the damage at the time of security breach will be large.
D	-39	Most necessary measures have not been implemented. The risk is not recognized, and it is assumed that the damage at the time of security breach is large.

3 Method

In this study, we utilized the checklist for posture assessment of the appendix E of the "The Cyber/Physical Security Framework for Factory Systems (draft) Version 1.0" as the basic tool (Table 1) [10]. The reason for this is that the burden is relatively low when implementing the only 32 items. In addition to the three basic classifications of "People", "Process", and "Technology" that can be understood by executives and factory people, the independent classification of "supply chain management for factory assets (FA SCM)", which has a recent issue, is also mentioned, making it easy to use for risk visualization. Based on this checklist, we developed a free web diagnostic tool whose source codes have been published on GitHub for the public use [3]. It is easier than downloading the assessment software such as CSET. Furthermore, we made an original effort to score the weight of risks for each item to understand the current risks along the amount of the effectiveness of risk reduction. In addition, there are six options for answering the items on the guideline checklist and we conducted score weight allocation as shown in Table 2. The one adjustment needs for the weight of "Not applicable" because we cannot judge whether the respondent grasps the question and current situation correctly or not. We need to assume a respondent from SMEs is not a specialist.

    In addition, by averaging the number of selected items for each of the four categories, adjustments were made to achieve a perfect score of 100%. The items leading to direct damage to business is positioned as more important ones if they are not sufficient. For example, if the network perimeter defense of the factory system is not in place, the risk of cybersecurity threats intruding into the factory network increases, but the factory system does not immediately suffer damage such as suspension or tampering. On the other hand, if a security threat penetrates the control terminal, it will lead to immediate damage, so it is positioned as a more important item and given higher weight. For the comprehensive evaluation, the weight of the item of FA SCM, which is external management, is 1/3 of the weight of the other three categories, and the average of the scores of the four categories is taken. Based on these scores, A to D risk assessment results were defined. For example, When the average score sums up to 60% but is below 80% the outcome is classified as B (Table 3). It looks like an examination result for SMEs to grasp the risk readiness intuitively. Based on the results of this evaluation, we aimed to help executives and factory people easily understand the risks and secure the budget and system for countermeasures.

4 Result

Figure 1 shows the input results of 225 factory sites using the web diagnosis tool of this research. As the research was still in its early stages, all input results were uniformly treated without particular consideration of industry or scale of companies. The tool inputs are mainly from factory automation industries such as assembly, machinery manufacturing factories, and automotive parts suppliers. However, we cannot find the significant difference with each industry so far. As a result, over 80% of the overall evaluations were "C" or "D", indicating that most companies are not progressing with security measures for their factory systems. FA SCM has the worse score distribution than the other three categories, but this is due to poor internal security controls that have been extended to external controls. It suggests that there is few resources for control of suppliers currently. In addition, as a result of conducting follow-up interviews with 30 sites that implemented the input, all people responded that the evaluation results in each category were appropriate (as expected). At present, the risk-weighted score is considered to be at a practical level.

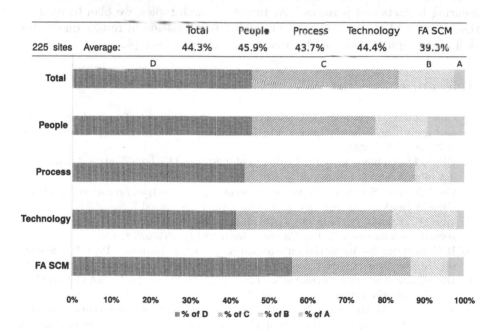

Fig. 1. Distribution of evaluation results of each category

5   Challenge and Discussion

During the follow-up interviews, we discovered that some of the respondents did not understand the scope of the factory system, and their answers were confused with the information system. In addition, although some respondents answered "0. Not applicable," but correct answer was "1. Not implemented" due to a lack of understanding of the items. That is why we reflected the ambiguity on the risk score of "0. Not applicable" in Table 2. We need to improve the web tool for the better understanding for users.

The beauty of tool we have found is the easiness. For example, the four category is more basic and much easier for the executives and factory people than the other guidelines. Only 32 items are also easy for them to grasp the security posture in shorter time.

6   Conclusions

In this study, as a tool for promoting security measures for factory systems, we presented a easy risk assessment method for factory systems that utilizes the checklist of Japanese government guidelines. The evaluation tool developed this time is effective for roughly grasping the current situation in order to promote security measures for factory systems. It helps executive and factory people to understand the rough cybersecurity risk easily, and it was found to be useful for securing budgets and personnel. As future research topics, we plan to improve the accuracy of the risk score by improving the variation in results due to the skill of the input person and increasing the number of samples.

References

1. Chaula, J.A., Luwemba, G.W.: Security control assessment of supervisory control and data acquisition for power utilities in Tanzania. Eur. J. Eng. Technol. Res. 5(7), 785–789 (2020)
2. CISA: The Cybersecurity Evaluation Tool (CSET) v11.5 (2023). https://www.cisa.gov/downloading-and-installing-cset. Accessed 7 Jan 2024
3. GitHub: OT Security Simple Assessment (2023). https://github.com/OTSec-Hiroshi-Sasaki/en-ot-security-simple-assessment. Accessed 7 Jan 2024
4. Goel, R., Kumar, A., Haddow, J.: Prism: a strategic decision framework for cybersecurity risk assessment. Inf. Comput. Secur 28(4), 591–625 (2020)
5. IEC: Security for industrial automation and control systems - Part 3-3, System security requirements and security levels. ISA global cybersecurity alliance (2013)
6. IEC: Quick start guide: an overview of ISA/IEC 62443 standards. ISA global cybersecurity alliance (2020)
7. Krumay, B., Bernroider, E.W.N., Walser, R.: Evaluation of cybersecurity management controls and metrics of critical infrastructures: a literature review considering the NIST cybersecurity framework. In: Gruschka, N. (ed.) NordSec 2018. LNCS, vol. 11252, pp. 369–384. Springer, Cham (2018). https://doi.org/10.1007/978-3-030-03638-6_23

8. Leander, B., Čaušević, A., Hansson, H.: Applicability of the IEC 62443 standard in industry 4.0/IIoT. In: Proceedings of the 14th International Conference on Availability, Reliability and Security, pp. 1–8 (2019)

9. Matthew, P.B., et al.: Framework for improving critical infrastructure cybersecurity ver1.1 (2018). https://nvlpubsnist.gov/nistpubs/CSWP/NIST. Accessed 7 Jan 2024

10. Study Group for Industrial Cybersecurity Working Group 1 Factory subworking group: The Cyber/Physical Security Framework for Factory Systems (draft) Version 1.0 (2022). https://public-comment.e-gov.go.jp/servlet/PcmFileDownload? seqNo=000023656. Accessed 7 Jan 2024

11. Terruggia, R., Dondossola, G., Todeschini, M.G.: Assessment of cyber security requirements for the future digital power system. CIRED Conference, Madrid (2019)

Work in Progress

Adoption of Explainable Artificial Intelligence, to Protect Key Decision Processes from Information Manipulations and Disorders (Work in Progress)

Fréderic Tatout[1](✉) and Christine Dugoin-Clément[2]

[1] ANATASE, Le Kremlin-Bicêtre, France
ftt@anatase.fr
[2] Chair "Risks" of IAE Paris Business School, Observatory of AI of University Paris1-Sorbonne, CREOGN, Paris, France

Abstract. Information security, applied to both systems and cognition, is a priority for states and private actors alike. Artificial Intelligence (AI) has the potential to be a game-changer in protecting autonomous critical information infrastructure, provided that AI systems are properly developed and adopted by users. This paper focuses on the early stages of developing a future AI system to prevent organizations from acute disinformation phenomena that could flaw or freeze critical decision-making processes of public authorities, with potentially catastrophic consequences. As such, it analyzes the state of the art of explainable AI (XAI) which can enhance users' trust in cybersecurity and the conditions necessary to ensure broad and long-term adoption of these systems by individuals and the society at large in the light of technology acceptability conceptual frameworks, especially UTAUT model. The central goal is to develop these systems in the light of the conceptual framework of technology acceptability and adoption, with a view to developing an acceptable and ethical XAI, people are willing to accept to interact with. This paper is the preliminary study to qualitative research using semi directed interview grid aiming at evaluating the technology's acceptability on a sample of future users.

Keywords: Explainable AI · cybersecurity · disinformation · acceptability of technology · adoption of technology · ethics

1 Introduction

Cybersecurity is a major issue for states and private companies. The increase in cyberattacks observed in 2019 and 2020, while the COVID-19 crisis has spiked both teleworking and the vulnerability surface [1], cast a harsh light on the need to further develop cybersecurity strategies, tools and practices. The sharp increase in cyberattacks attributed to Russia, following the invasion of Ukraine [2], confirms this observation. According to Cloudwards, a new organization is hit by ransomware every 14 s [3]. Governments' insistence that companies and institutions accelerate effective cybersecurity implementation

S. Pickl et al. (Eds.): CRITIS 2023, LNCS 14599, pp. 273–282, 2024.
https://doi.org/10.1007/978-3-031-62139-0_17

faces pitfalls related to the complexity of the topic, the investment required - cyber protection is an expensive, never ended task, that exhausts cybersecurity professionals – and the human dimension – everyone has to be concerned and act accordingly – [4].

Therefore, developing AI to detect and prevent cyberattacks seems particularly sensible. Nevertheless, the development of AI to improve cybersecurity is still recent, especially for explainable AI (XAI), which is specifically requested by many public authorities and institutions, from the European Union (EU) [5] to the US DARPA [6].

Infrastructure protection is a tricky issue for administrations, not least because they generally cannot match the salary levels offered by the private sector to recruit all the talented experts they need. This makes AI-based systems an even more relevant option, for them, to manage the protection of critical information infrastructures. Nevertheless, notwithstanding the cost of developing or purchasing such AI systems, their effectiveness depends on how well employees use them. Some research shows that trust in technology is linked to understanding it and how it works, and thus can be enhanced by explainable AI [7–12]. However, there is no universal definition of explainability, and in any case, the very characteristics of explainability must be aligned with legal norms and ethical principles. Will this be enough?

This work in progress will address the issue of the effectiveness of XAI dedicated to critical information infrastructures, including questions about the adoption and acceptability of cooperation with these systems by government officials. To do so, we first present a literature review on the characteristics of XAI, and a second one on adoption and cooperation with XAI in the security domain. Next, we will present the methodology that will be used in this work.

2   Literature Review

Due to the nature of the topic, the literature review will be divided into three parts. First, we will briefly present the state of art on the meaning of XAI, then elaborate on the close relationship between disinformation and cybersecurity, and finally, we will explore adoption of the technology and human-computer interface (HCI), as well as the human-computer cooperation (HCC).

2.1   XAI Characteristics

The concept of XAI should be understood as the techniques developed to improve human understanding of how AI works and "makes decisions" [13]. The terms have evolved in recent years, especially when explainability diverged from interpretability and focused on information extraction, while it was used indefinitely in the early days [14].

XAI can refer to different concepts, such as, namely, explainability, interpretability, intelligibility (or understandability), and transparency, to cite the most widespread. These concepts are the subject of comprehensive concept and taxonomy reviews [14, 15].

Specifically and from a more technical perspective, XAI can be divided into different categories, as explained by Zhang and al. [16]. Indeed, some models may focus on explainability from a post-hoc perspective, such as Local Interpretable Model-agnostic Explanations (LIME) [18] and Permutation Importance. In this case, explainability is the result of an analysis of how the model works after training; thus, it may be uncomplete or unstable. Therefore, embedded and intrinsic explainability achieved by developing explanation along with prediction, may be preferred, which can limit the complexity of AI models [17]. In addition, XAIs may be model-specific, e.g., where a graph neural network (GNN) explainer can provide justifications for the GNN-based predictive model on any graph-based Machine Learning (ML) problem [16, 19]; while they are model-agnostic, if the tools used for explanation (i.e. Shapley Additive Explanations (SHAP) [20], Saliency Map, Gradient-weighted Class Activation Mapping (Grad-CAM)) can be used for different types of ML models. On the other hand, XAI models can provide local explainability, i.e. throughout the description of a specific decision proposal – which is the main component of model transparency [17] – or provide global explainability, when or if they provide an explanation of the algorithm as a whole, encompassing the training data used, the applications of the algorithms, as well as any necessary caveats about limitations and warnings about inappropriate uses. Finally, the outcome of the explanation and the presentation of the results are also part of the XAI design itself, as both can have a non-trivial impact on the AI users' perception of the system's explainability.

This subject is far from trivial. Indeed, the stakes for AI use are very high, especially in some areas where decision wear tremendous weigh, such as finance and, considering the personal consequences, legal matters and medicine, which are two areas where regulation at least acts as a spur to research.

Researchers focusing on XAI and finance highlighted a strong increase in academic publications on that topic since 2013, including for AI implementation in this domain [21]. In that line, some studies dogged in the positive impact of XAI in technology adoption in medicine [22]. Other exploratory studies deal with some specific firms' motivation to adopt Ai in the light of Technology-Organization-Environment TOE framework, which is reframed in the UTAUT model this study will use [23, 24]. In the field of cybersecurity, a study showed that Important insights that affect the technology's usefulness and adoption, such as the importance of taking end users' work patterns, environments, and willingness to trust XAI outputs into account [25]. Those results motivate our study to dig in was can be the triggers of trust and adoption of a new XAI.

2.2 Adversarial Risk Analysis and Adversarial Machine Learning

Growing cybersecurity concerns have led to the exploration of adversarial ML applications in cybersecurity scenarios, particularly as the likelihood of AI being used in malware and cyberattacks increases [26, 27]. Thus, several studies have analyzed the use of adversarial ML concepts in intrusion and malware detection scenarios [28–35] and, more broadly, in adversarial attacks [26, 27, 36, 37]. Various studies point out that some systems are more resistant to cyberattacks, although performance and use in pure cyberdefense are still in progress, even though malware detection by defensive distillation and intrusion detection by denoising autoencoders (composed of adversarial networks) seem to be quite effective [28]. In addition, other defensive techniques based on image identification can be used for malware and intrusion detection, not to mention other anomaly detection methods based on deep learning which are still under development [28, 38].

2.3 Cybersecurity and Disinformation Adverse Effects on Public Authorities' Decision-Making

The general cybersecurity literature focuses on networks, devices, data and fundamental security objectives for data: confidentiality, integrity, and availability, which constitute a conceptual pillar, as explained by Samonas & Coss [39]. However, beyond the "Trusted Internet" model of the web, cyberspace can be seen, as by Libicki [40], as a space open to any types of organizations and subject, as such, to all types of confrontations, including attacks on networks, devices, and data security objectives, as well as attacks on psychological and cognitive dimensions.

Under this prism, it makes sense to develop an XAI aimed at protecting the information systems and processes that govern the decision-making of public authorities, against potential catastrophic consequences, in all their aspects, including the decryption of disinformation or the detection of weak signals that precede major hybrid attacks or information disorders that may distort or freeze decisions of public authorities.

Combating this threat is closely linked to cybersecurity, at least in terms of detection and characterization, as shown by a recent comprehensive study co-edited by the European Cybersecurity Agency (ENISA) presenting an integrated approach, based on a framework for analyzing and assessing disinformation, and another focusing on cyber-attacks [41]. In our work, we will follow this cross-fertilization approach.

2.4 Technology Adoption and Human-Machine Cooperation

Technology adoption is an important area of study because it is the cornerstone of a project's success as it is a key factor in its full potential use. Therefore, different models have aimed to find the main factors of adoption and acceptability of technology, including AI and XAI. As a result, many models have been built. These include the Technology Acceptance Model (TAM) developed by Davis in 1989; the Theory of Planned Behavior (TPB) proposed by Ajzen [8]; Roger's Innovation Diffusion Theory (IDT) [42]; Fishbein & Ajzen's Theory of Reasoned Action (TRA) [43]; the Technology-Organization-Environment (TOE) conceptual framework proposed by Tornatzky & Fleischer [10]. More recently, Venkatesh et al. [11] proposed a solution that combines eight theoretical models (TRA, TAM, Motivational Model (MM), TPB, a Combined Theory of Planned Behavior/Technology Acceptance Model (C-TPB-TAM), Model of PC Utilization (MPCU), IDT, and Social Cognitive Theory (SCT)) within the Unified Theory of Technology Acceptance and Use (UTAUT). In UTAUT, intention can be explained in the light of four independent constructs, namely: Performance Expectancy (PE), Effort Expectancy (EE), Social Influence (SI), and Facilitating Conditions (FC). These four moderating factors, shown in Fig. 1, are used to reduce the impact of independent variables on the dependent variables: gender, age, experience, and willingness to use [44].

Due to the nature of our topic, we propose to use an adapted UTAUT model to estimate the future adoption and use of the technology we wish to develop. UTAUT has been used in the cybersecurity domain, for example, to find ways to develop the implementation of Information Security Policies and Information Assurance Awareness within US federal entities [45]. Given the close links between operational procedures and

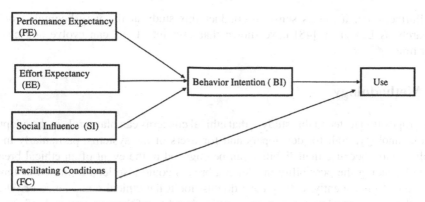

Fig. 1. UTAUT model adapted from Venkatesh et al. 2003.

ethical aspects, especially when disinformation leads to a crisis or a critical situation for the public decision-making process, we propose to add another independent construct, namely Ethical Concern. Ethics is paramount for public institutions, as highlighted in the Ethics guidelines for trustworthy AI edited by the European Commission [46]; with respect to disinformation, in crisis situations, public authorities may have to walk, literally speaking, on a tightrope to stay above the "fog" of disinformation, as J. Whyte [47] shown, for example. These situations can become problematic, especially when a crisis is triggered or maintained or even worsened by highly unethical disinformation or manipulation.

This is why we decided to test a model including this construct, especially when dealing with AI and XAI. This model is shown in Fig. 2.

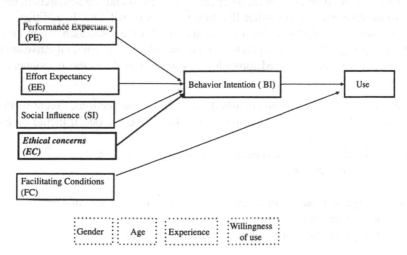

Fig. 2. UTAUT model adapted from Venkatesh et al. 2003 for the XAI project on disinformation detection. C. Dugoin-Clément & F. Tatout, 2023

Furthermore, it makes sense to conduct this study at the very beginning of the research, as Lee et al. [48] have shown that user intentions can evolve and change over time.

3 Methodology

The proposition tested in this study is that ethical concerns can play a role in the adoption of a technology, both for developers and for users of the systems, particularly in the public sector, because their liability can be engaged in the event of an ethical breach, notwithstanding the possibility that such a breach could also lead to biased or flawed decisions. Consequently, if they have doubts about the ethical compliance of AI and XAI, they may not adopt the system, resulting in a loss of time, money and efficiency.

With this in mind, to determine the potential for adoption and use of XAI systems in our field, we use the adapted model presented in the previous section. To clarify and detail the ethical aspects mentioned above, with a view to specifying the ethical concerns (EC) extension, we have capitalized on recognized practices and on the work of the EU-Hybnet European network.

In practical terms, we plan to submit to a panel of middle and senior managers from public institutions, a grid of questions for testing the variables set out by Venkatesh added to ethics, according to the adapted UTAUT model. Respondents will be chosen because of their position, which makes them responsible for deciding on the viability, use and deployment of a system incorporating XAI, and ultimately for choosing whether or not to follow the system's proposals.

This question grid includes the four dependent variables and a question to estimate the independent variable including a 7 degrees Likert scale. In order to respect respondents' anonymity, it was completed on an independent platform and the researchers have no access to the respondents' computer IP addresses or personal data. In addition, a short section explains the purpose of the survey and asked for the respondent's consent.

The question grid is in semi open format i.e. including room for qualitative analysis. The main items to be evaluated through this question grid are the respondent's *(cf.* Table 1*)*:

- technical literacy, risk aversion or affinity with AI (all the sections, except *section 1*);
- behavior and use position (in respect with the UTAUT model), including ethical concerns (e.g. *section 6*);
- trust in AI including ethical concerns (e.g. *sections 2 and 3*);
- ethical concerns perception:

  - knowledge and interest in ethics and development (e.g. *section 4*);
  - knowledge and interest in ethical use of AI (e.g. *section 3*);
  - knowledge and interest in regulatory drivers (e.g. *section 5*).

(*sections* refer to the fist column of Table 1).

Table 1. Question grid structuration. C. Dugoin-Clément & F. Tatout, 2023

Section	Questions' theme
1/Background	Gender, age, experience, willingness of use
2/Pillars of confidence	Performance expectance, effort expectancy, social influence, ethical concern, facilitating conditions
3/The functions of ethics	Ethical development of software or AI, vs. Ethics of software or AI [49]
4/Ethics in Tech Dev	HITL, SITL, algorithmic bias
5/Legal aspects	Impact analysis, accountability and responsibility associated with AI, personal data protection, freedom of expression
6/Behavior and use (UTAUT) and Ethics	Performance expectancy, effort expectancy, social influence, facilitating conditions (cf. Fig. 2), and weight of the ethical concerns

4 Expected Outcomes and Findings

The main purpose of this work in progress project is to evaluate the pertinence of the extended UTAUT model presented in part 2 above, as an exploratory study on ethical concern and its impact on adoption.

We also expect this work to provide useful information, some of which will complement the UTAUT model, for assessing relationship between respondents' regulatory knowledge, culture and ethical preferences on the one hand, the explanatory power of a given AI system on the other, and willingness to adopt it.

Beyond this, we hope that it will help developing fructuous links between developers, implementers and project sponsors wishing to use AI to anticipate critical effects of disinformation and manipulation, to conduct studies upstream of development and come up with a fair (if not optimal) long-term equilibrium between effectiveness, ethical concerns and adoption of AI.

5 Conclusion

The aim of this work is, prior to the development of an XAI, to evaluate its potential for adoption and use, but also to define the most important points in the behavioral intention as well as in the use that would be made of it. This study will also enable us to propose a modification of the UTAUT model by adding ethical concern to the initial model.

Indeed, while this subject has always interested institutions, interest has grown since 2003 to become central in 2019, as shown by the EU's edition of dedicated guidelines [46].

This exploratory work will provide insights that have not been fully considered in the acceptability and adoption of a technology in our field. Furthermore, we believe it is important to conduct this study upstream of development in order to integrate a real and solid "ethics by design" approach to this future project.

In further steps, this work may be adapted to applicable regulatory approach and shared fundamental values that contribute to strengthen ethical concerns; and may also take profit from current works to outline integrative and comprehensive frameworks for Responsible AI, such as [50].

Acknowledgements. Alexis Tsoukias, CNRS-LAMSADE, PSL, Université Paris Dauphine.

References

1. Lallie, H.S., et al.: Cyber security in the age of COVID-19: a timeline and analysis of cyber-crime and cyber-attacks during the pandemic. Comput. Secur. **105** (2021). https://doi.org/10.1016/j.cose.2021.102248
2. Willett, M.: The cyber dimension of the russia-ukraine war. Survival **64**(5), 7–26 (2022). https://doi.org/10.1080/00396338.2022.2126193
3. Kochovski, A.: Ransomware statistics, trends and facts for 2023 and beyond, cloudwards (2023)
4. Reeves, A., Delfabbro, P., Calic, D.: Encouraging employee engagement with cybersecurity: How to tackle cyber fatigue. SAGE Open **11**(1) (2021). https://doi.org/10.1177/21582440211000049
5. Ebers, M.: Regulating explainable AI in the European union. An overview of the current legal framework (s). An overview of the current legal framework. In: Liane Colonna/Stanley Greenstein (eds.) Nordic Yearbook of Law and Informatics (2020)
6. Gunning, D., Aha, D.: DARPA's explainable artificial intelligence (XAI) program. AI Mag. **40**(2), 44–58 (2019)
7. Atarodi, S., Berardi, A.M., Toniolo, A.-M.: Le modèle d'acceptation des technologies depuis 1986: 30 ans de développement. Psychologie du Travail et des Organisations **25**(3) (2019)
8. Ajzen, I.: The theory of planned behavior. Organ. Behav. Hum. Decis. Process. **50**(2), 179–211 (1991)
9. Rogers, E.M.: Diffusion of Innovation, Free Press, New York
10. Tornatzky, L.G., Fleischer, M.: The Processes of Technological Innovation. Lexington books, Lexington (1990)
11. Venkatesh, V., Morris, M.G., Davis, G.B., Davis, F.D.: User acceptance of information technology: toward a unified view. MIS Q. 425–478 (2003)
12. Dugoin-Clément, C.: Intelligence Artificielle dédiée à la gestion des ressources humaines: entre innovation, confiance biais humains et algorithmiques (2022)
13. Sahakyan, M., Aung, Z., Rahwan, T.: Explainable artificial intelligence for tabular data: a survey. IEEE Access **9**, 135392–135422 (2021)
14. Speith, T.: A review of taxonomies of XAI methods. In: ACM Conference Fairness, Accountability, Transparency, pp. 2239–2250 (2022). https://doi.org/10.1145/3531146.3534639
15. Schwalbe, G., Finzel, B.: A comprehensive taxonomy for explainable artificial intelligence: a systematic survey of surveys on methods and concepts. Data Min. Knowl. Discov. (2022). https://doi.org/10.1007/s10618-022-00867-8
16. Zhang, Z., Hamadi, H.M.N.A., Damiani, E., Yeun, C.Y., Taher, F.: Explainable artificial intelligence applications in cyber security: state-of-the-art in research. IEEE Access **10**, 93104–93139 (2022). https://doi.org/10.1109/access.2022.3204051
17. Arya, V., et al.: One explanation does not fit all: a toolkit and taxonomy of AI explainability techniques. arXiv:1909.03012 (2019)

18. Ribeiro, M. T., Singh, S., Guestrin, C.: "Why should I trust you?": explaining the predictions of any classifer. arXiv:1602.04938 (2016)
19. Ying, R., Bourgeois, D., You, J., Zitnik, M., Leskovec, J.: GNNExplainer: Generating explanations for graph neural networks. arXiv:1903.03894 (2019)
20. Lundberg, M., Lee, S.I.: A unified approach to interpreting model predictions. In: Proceedings of the Advance in Neural Information Processing Systems, vol. 30, pp. 1–10 (2017)
21. Chen, X.Q., Ma, C.Q., Ren, Y.S., Lei, Y.T., Huynh, N.Q.A., Narayan, S.: Explainable artificial intelligence in finance: A bibliometric review. Financ. Res. Lett. 104145 (2023)
22. Liu, C.F., Chen, Z.C., Kuo, S.C., Lin, T.C.: Does AI explainability affect physicians' intention to use AI? Int. J. Med. Inform. **168**, 104884 (2022)
23. Ridley, M.: Explainable artificial intelligence (XAI): adoption and advocacy. Inf. Technol. Libr. **41**(2) (2022)
24. Penu, O.K.A., Boateng, R., Owusu, A.: Towards explainable AI (xAI): determining the factors for firms' adoption and use of xAI in Sub-Saharan Africa (2021)
25. Nyre-Yu, M., Morris, E., Moss, B.C., Smutz, C., Smith, M.: Explainable AI in cybersecurity operations: lessons learned from xAI tool deployment. In: Proceedings of the Usable Security and Privacy (USEC) Symposium, San Diego, CA, USA, vol. 28 (2022). https://doi.org/10.14722/usec.2022.23014
26. Huang, L., Joseph, A.D., Nelson, B., Rubinstein, B.I.P., Tygar. J.D.: Adversarial machine learning. In: Proceedings of the 4th ACM Workshop on Security and Artificial Intelligence, NY, USA, pp. 43–58 (2011). https://doi.org/10.1145/2046684.2046692
27. Rosenberg, I., Shabtai, A., Elovici, Y., Rokach, L.: Adversarial machine learning attacks and defense methods in the cyber security domain. ACM Comput. Surv. (CSUR) **54**(5), 1–36 (2021)
28. Martins, N., Cruz, J.M., Cruz, T., Henriques Abreu, P.: Adversarial machine learning applied to intrusion and malware scenarios: a systematic review. IEEE Access **8**, 35403–35419 (2021). https://doi.org/10.1109/ACCESS.2020.2974752
29. Chen, L., Ye, Y., Bourlai, T.: Adversarial machine learning in malware detection: arms race between evasion attack and defense. In: 2017 European Intelligence and Security Informatics Conference (EISIC), Athens, Greece, pp. 99–106 (2017). https://doi.org/10.1109/EISIC.2017.21
30. Goodfellow, I.J., Shlens J., Szegedy, C.: Explaining and harnessing adversarial examples. arXiv:1412.6572 (2014)
31. Duddu, V.: A survey of adversarial machine learning in cyber warfare. Defence Sci. J. **68**(4), 356–366 (2018)
32. Papernot, N., McDaniel, P., Wu, X., Jha, S., Swami, A.: Distillation as a defense to adversarial perturbations against deep neural networks. arXiv:1511.04508 (2015)
33. Xu, W., Evans, D., Qi, Y.: Feature squeezing: Detecting adversarial examples in deep neural networks. arXiv:1704.01155 (2017)
34. Akhtar, N.: Defense against universal adversarial perturbations. arXiv:1711.05929 (2017)
35. Zhou, S., Liu, C., Ye, D., Zhu, T., Zhou, W., Yu, P.S.: Adversarial attacks and defenses in deep learning: from a perspective of cybersecurity. ACM Comput. Surv. **55**(8), 1–39 (2022)
36. Anthi, E., Williams, L., Rhode, M., Burnap, P., Wedgbury, A.: Adversarial attacks on machine learning cybersecurity defences in industrial control systems. J. Inf. Secur. Appl. **58**, 102717 (2021)
37. Apruzzese, G., Andreolini, M., Ferretti, L., Marchetti, M., Colajanni, M.: Modeling realistic adversarial attacks against network intrusion detection systems. Digit. Threats: Res. Pract. (DTRAP) **3**(3), 1–19 (2022)
38. Chandola, V., Banerjee, A., Kumar, V.: Anomaly detection: a survey. ACM Comput. Surv. **41**(3), 1–58 (2009)

39. Samonas, S., Coss, D.: The CIA strikes back: redefining confidentiality, integrity, and availability in security. J. Inf. Secur. **10**(3), 33 (2023). ISSN 1551-0123
40. Libicki, M.C.: Conquest in cyberspace, the RAND corporation (2007)
41. ENISA and EU External Action: Foreign Information Manipulation Interference (FIMI) and Cybersecurity – Threat Landscape (2022). https://www.enisa.europa.eu/publications/foreign-information-manipulation-interference-fimi-and-cybersecurity-threat-landscape
42. Roger, E.M.: Diffusion of Innovations, 4th edn. Free Press, New York (1995)
43. Ajzen, I., Fishbein, M.: Theory of reasoned action – theory of planned behavior, pp. 67–98. University of South Florida (2007)
44. Dwivedi, Y.K., Rana, N.P., Tamilmani, K., Raman, R.: A meta-analysis based modified unified theory of acceptance and use of technology (meta-UTAUT): a review of emerging literature. Curr. Opin. Psychol. **36**, 1318 (2020)
45. Raschid Muller, S.: A perspective on the intersection of information security policies and IA awareness. Factoring in End-User Behavior (2020)
46. European Commission: Shaping Europe's digital future - Ethics guidelines for trustworthy AI, Report (2019)
47. Whyte, J.: Cybersecurity, race, and the politics of truth. Secur. Dialogue **53**(4), 342–362 (2022). https://doi.org/10.1177/09670106221101725
48. Lee, Y., Kozar, K.A., Larsen, K.R.T.: The technology acceptance model: past, present, and future. Commun. Assoc. Inf. Syst. **12**, 752–780 (2003)
49. Siau, K., Wang, W.: Artificial intelligence (AI) ethics: ethics of AI and ethical AI. J. Database Manage. **31**(2) (2020)
50. Haidar, A.: An integrative theoretical framework for responsible artificial intelligence. Int. J. Digit. Strategy Govern. Bus. Transf. (IJDSGBT), **13**(1), 1–23 (2024)

Author Index

S. Pickl et al. (Eds.): CRITIS 2023, LNCS 14599, pp. 283–284, 2024.
https://doi.org/10.1007/978-3-031-62139-0

...ted in the United States
...ker & Taylor Publisher Services